Acting
NARRATIVE
SPEECHES

**The actor
as storyteller**

Tim McDonough

MERIWETHER PUBLISHING LTD.
Colorado Springs, Colorado

Meriwether Publishing Ltd., Publisher
PO Box 7710
Colorado Springs, CO 80933-7710

Executive editor: Arthur L. Zapel
Project editor: Renée Congdon
Cover design: Jan Melvin

© Copyright MMII Meriwether Publishing Ltd.
Printed in the United States of America
First Edition

Library of Congress Cataloging-in-Publication Data

McDonough, Timothy Kerrill, 1942-
    Acting narrative speeches : the actor as storyteller / by Timothy
Kerrill McDonough.
        p. cm.
Includes bibliographical references and index.
    ISBN 1-56608-076-2
1. Acting. 2. Dramatic monologues—History and criticism—Theory,
etc. I. Title.
    PN2061 .M33 2002
    792'.028—dc21
                                    2002008204

1   2   3   4   02   03   04

Dedication

To Thomas Harold Akers, author.

To my wife, Janice Akers, partner in everything.

To my students over the past twenty-five years, for teaching me.

To my theatrical colleagues, especially Vincent Murphy,
who has given me direction and opportunity in and out
of the theaters; and Jon Lipsky, who years ago taught
me a great deal about telling stories.

To my academic colleagues, especially Michael Evenden, who
as the Chair of Theater Studies at Emory University
encouraged me to write this book; and Alice Benston,
whose generous leap of faith brought me to Emory.

To the Tanne Foundation and to the University Research Committee
of Emory University, for their support of my research.

Acknowledgments

Aeschylus, *Agamemnon,* from *The Oresteia,* translated by Robert Fagles, © 1966, 1967, 1975 by Robert Fagles. Used by permission of Viking Penguin, a division of Penguin Putnam Inc.

Jean Anouilh, *The Lark,* translated by Christopher Fry, Oxford University Press, Inc.

Bertolt Brecht, *Mr. Puntila and His Man Matti,* © 1951 by Suhrkamp Verlag, Berlin, under the title *Herr Puntila und sein Knecht Matti.* Translation © 1987 by Stefan S. Brecht, published by Arcade Publishing, New York.

Anton Chekhov, *The Seagull,* translated by Stark Young. Used by permission of Flora Roberts, Inc.

E.E. Cummings, "anyone lived in a pretty how town." © 1940, 1968, 1991 by the Trustees for the E.E. Cummings Trust, from *Complete Poems: 1904-1962* by E.E. Cummings, edited by George J. Firmage, used by permission of Liveright Publishing Corporation.

Robert Frost, "The Span of Life," from *The Poetry of Robert Frost,* edited by Edward Connery Lathem. © 1936 by Robert Frost, © 1964 by Lesley Frost Ballantine, © 1969 by Henry Holt and Co. Reprinted by permission of Henry Holt and Company, LLC.

Athol Fugard, *Hello and Goodbye,* in *Blood Knot and Other Plays,* Theatre Communications Group, 1991.

Herb Gardner, *I'm Not Rappaport,* in *The Collected Plays of Herb Gardner,* Applause Theatre and Cinema Books, 2000.

Isabella Gardner, "Summer Remembered," from *The Looking Glass.* By permission of The University of Chicago Press.

John Guare, *Landscape of the Body.* Reprinted by permission of International Creative Management, Inc. © 1978 by St. Jude Productions, Inc.

William Hanley, *Slow Dance on the Killing Ground.* © Renewed 1992, 1993, William Hanley. © 1964, 1965, William Hanley. © 1964, William Hanley as an unpublished dramatic composition. CAUTION: The excerpt from *Slow Dance on the Killing Ground* included in this volume is reprinted by permission of Dramatists Play Service, Inc. Nonprofessional stage performance rights for this play are controlled exclusively by Dramatists Play Service, Inc., 440 Park Avenue South, New York, NY 10016. No professional performance of the play may be given without obtaining, in advance, the written permission of Dramatists Play Service, Inc., and paying the requisite fee. Inquiries concerning all other rights should be addressed to Dramatists Play Service.

Ralph Hodgson, "Eve". Used by permission of Canaday Library, Bryn Mawr College.

Hugo von Hofmannsthall, *Elektra*. © 1963 by the Bollingen Foundation. Reprinted by permission of Princeton University Press.

Langston Hughes, "Dream Deferred" from *The Collected Poems of Langston Hughes*, © 1994 by The Estate of Langston Hughes. Used By permission of Alfred A. Knopf, a division of Random House, Inc.

Eugéne Ionesco, *Exit the King*, by permission of Grove/Atlantic, Inc.

Jon Lipsky, *Living in Exile*. By permission of the author.

Archibald MacLeish, "Ars Poetica," from *Collected Poems, 1917-1982*. © 1985 by The Estate of Archibald MacLeish. Reprinted by permission of Houghton Mifflin Company. All rights reserved.

Eve Merriam, Paula Wagner and Jack Hoffsiss, *Out of Our Fathers' House*, by permission of Marian Reiner, Literary Agent, on behalf of Eve Merriam.

Alfred Noyes, "The Barrel Organ" by permission of The Society of Authors as the Literary Representative of the Estate of Alfred Noyes.

Michael Ondaatje, "After Shooting Gregory", *The Collected Works of Billy the Kid*. © 1970 by Michael Ondaatje. Used by permission of W. W. Norton & Company, Inc.

Laurence Perrine, *Sound and Sense: An Introduction to Poetry*, Third Edition. Harcourt Brace & Co., 1969.

David Richards, "Opposites Attract When One Actor Shows Two Sides," *The New York Times*, February 28, 1993.

Juan Rulfo, *Pedro Páramo*, by permission of Grove/Atlantic, Inc. Translation by permission of Sidney Goldfarb and Paul Zimet of the Talking Band.

Peter Shaffer, *Equus*. Reprinted by permission of Scribner, a division of Simon & Schuster. © 1973 Peter Shaffer.

Sam Shepard, *Cowboy Mouth*, © 1976 by Sam Shepard and Patti Smith, and Suicide in B^b, © 1978, 1979 by Sam Shepard, from *Fool for Love and Other Plays* by Sam Shepard. Used by permission of Bantam Books, a division of Random House, Inc.

Sam Shepard, *Curse of the Starving Class*, © 1976 by Sam Shepard; Buried Child, © 1979 by Sam Shepard; and Tongues, © 1981 by Sam Shepard and Joseph Chaikin, from *Seven Plays* by Sam Shepard. Used by permission of Bantam Books, a division of Random House, Inc.

Tennessee Williams, *Orpheus Descending*, from *The Theater of Tennessee Williams*, Vol. VIII, © 1977, 1979 by University of the South. Reprinted by permission of New Directions Publishing Corp.

Contents

Preface 1

Section One
Story Sense 5

Chapter 1
The Other Time and Place 7

Chapter 2
Choosing a Speech 30

Chapter 3
Setting the Scene... 37

Chapter 4
Implicit Scenes... 61

Chapter 5
Playing All the Parts: Characterization and Indirect Quotes 79

Chapter 6
Gesture 100

Chapter 7
Movement..116

Chapter 8
Space...126

Section Two
Sound Sense 143

Chapter 9
Onomatopoeia..145

Chapter 10
Rhythm 170

Section Three
Shape Sense..201

Chapter 11
Fades and Builds 203

Chapter 12
From/To 231

Chapter 13
Putting Together the First Draft 256

Chapter 14
Architecture...269

Section Four
Opposites and Layering 275

Chapter 15
Opposites 277

Chapter 16
Single Images 324

Chapter 17
Layering...332

Epilogue
A Narrative Approach to Acting 361

Appendices...369

Appendix A
Excerpts..371

Appendix B
Speeches 377

Appendix C
If You Are Working on a Speech by Shakespeare ... .393

Appendix D
Shopping for Speeches 416

Appendix E
A Sample Syllabus for a Course on Acting Narrative Speeches 425

Index 441

About the Author 445

Preface

This book is a manual of the ancient, primal art of the actor as storyteller. I offer it for five reasons.

1. The skills required for performing speeches that tell a story — which occur in virtually every theatrical period and genre — are essential for the complete actor.

From the very beginning, narrative speeches have played an important role in theater. Clytemnestra's murder of Agamemnon, Oedipus blinding himself, the poisoning of Hamlet's father, the reunions which occur toward the end of *The Winter's Tale*, Richard III's miserable youth, the death of Falstaff, Tartuffe's conning of his benefactor Orgon, the suicide of Blanche Dubois' husband, the angel appearing to young St. Joan, Jerry's attempt to kill a dog in Edward Albee's *The Zoo Story* — all these events are central to their respective dramas, and all of them happen off-stage. They are brought on-stage by stories in which the events are relived. In contrast to film, which uses flashbacks and fantasy sequences to dramatize the past and the future, theater uses narrative speeches to transport audiences to other times and places.

2. Narrative speeches are an excellent training ground for both the experienced and the novice actor.

A good narrative speech is actor-centered, elemental, everything-is-possible theater, and it exercises all of an actor's skills, including some usually associated with interactive scene work. Working on narrative speeches teaches an actor that the story itself — what happens moment to moment — is more important than any other consideration, and that the choices which enable an audience to experience the events of a story also allow a character to relive them.

3. The approach to narrative speeches developed in this book has implications for re-understanding all of acting.

The epilogue suggests how the skills learned from acting narrative speeches may be applied in all areas of acting work. Suffice it to say here that a narrative approach to acting is an alternative to systems that see the essence of acting as playing emotions, pursuing objectives, responding impulsively, or behaving "realistically."

1

4. Actors need principles and methods for shaping speeches of every sort.

There is a good deal in print about interactive scene work, character development, voice and body, the actor's emotional life and many other performance issues. There is relatively little systematic advice about developing and structuring speeches. If what is in print is a trustworthy index to what is emphasized in teaching, then it is not surprising that speeches in performance are so often disjointed and shapeless.

Whatever else they do, artists create and perform shapes. Powerful performers know how to build to a climax and to give heightened emphasis to central moments. They use fades and other modes of transition to live from moment to moment, so that each event is tied to what precedes and follows. The skills essential to shaping speeches can be applied to scene work and to the development of a role.

5. Actors need a systematic approach to creating conflict within characters.

Central characters, whether comic or tragic, are conflicted souls. It is the divided self that we find fascinating and relevant to our own experience. Conflict between characters is certainly important in drama, but it is the conflict within that gives a performance complexity and depth.

In order to create a character who is not one-note, says Stanislavski, an actor must search for qualities which counterbalance what the author has emphasized.

> Life is never like bad plays on the stage where some people are all black and others are all white. So when you play a hypochondriac, seek where he is happy, virile and full of hope... .When you play a good man look for the places where he is evil. And in an evil man look for the places where he is good... . When you play an old man, look to see where he is young. When you play a young man, look to see where he is old, etc.[1]

---

[1]Konstantin Stanislavski, *My Life in Art*, Theater Arts Books, 1948.

Stanislavski claimed to have made this discovery early in his career, but his notes suggest that "he only arrived at this principle of opposites many years later..."[2] In any case, the issue did not come to the forefront of the Stanislavski system.

It should have. Inner conflict is a central issue in acting, of much wider application than narrative speeches. The subject deserves a book in itself; or rather it deserves to be included in every acting book. Yet there is little in print about what I call "opposites work" apart from a couple of pages in Michael Shurtleff's *Audition*, in which opposites are one of his "guideposts." Chapters 15-17 outline a series of steps for conceiving and exploring opposites, then shaping them as the layers of a conflicted speech.

Acting Narrative Speeches is based on a semester-long university course that evolved from a professional workshop developed twenty years ago. Putting a series of classes into book form presents many challenges, particularly with respect to the fact that much of the learning in an acting class is occasioned by the work of fellow students, both more and less experienced than oneself, some with kindred sensibilities, others who make choices very different from one's own.

I imagine that the present book may serve actors in several contexts. One is the classroom, where teachers can discover their own way to guide their particular students through the exercises, exploring many of them in class and assigning others for performance in subsequent sessions. A sample syllabus is outlined in Appendix E. Acting studios and informal groups who join together to explore narrative speeches may also use the book to structure their work.

Many actors may wish to explore narrative speeches on their own, and I have written the book for them as well. New topics are introduced by multiple examples that a group should explore on its feet; if an individual is working alone, it is important to try different choices for each exercise, so as to grasp the open-ended possibilities. I have suggested variations and contrasting choices that will introduce every reader of this book to the range of what I have learned from students, from fellow actors, and from my own performance experience.

---

[2]Jean Benedetti, *Stanislavski*, Routledge, 1988.

3

Section One
Story Sense

Chapter 1
The Other Time and Place

Theater brings us events from another time and place: a castle in Denmark haunted by a murdered king, a wealthy Parisian household invaded by a seventeenth-century con man, a working-class apartment in New Orleans just after the Second World War, or an imaginary world such as the fairy kingdom of Titania and Oberon. If a production is successful, another place comes *here* and another time happens *now*; lively theater is always *present* in both those senses. What theater creates is not illusion if the work is authentic. Actors, with the help of their many collaborators, can actually enter the world imagined by a playwright and make it real. The characters who inhabit a script come here, take on life now, when actors are possessed by them: what happened in another time and place happens all over again.[1]

But a play is not confined to its setting. Playwrights commonly dramatize events that occur outside the time frame of the play or in a locale that does not come on stage. Their means for doing this, of course, is the narrative speech, which tells a story about off-stage events so as to make them just as present as what the audience sees enacted. In this way Greek messengers make us experience quite graphically the horrific events they have witnessed. It is by way of narrative speeches that characters intensely relive past events. By telling a "story" of what they imagine will happen, dreamers give their fantasies a virtual reality, visionaries conjure transformed worlds, villains hatch their plots and heroes their counterplots. In a narrative speech an actor single-handedly, playing all the parts, using all the tools available to a performer, does precisely, quintessentially, what theater does: make another time and place present to the audience.

The Narrative Speech as Theatrical Flashback

Herb Gardner's *I'm Not Rappaport* takes place in 1982 in Manhattan's Central Park, where two old men share a bench. They argue, they joke, they sing, and for a very considerable part of the show they tell stories: about childhood, falling in love, losing a job, having a heart attack — even

---

[1] This concept is brilliantly developed in David Cole's *The Theatrical Event*, Wesleyan University Press, 1975.

some stories which never happened except in the telling, because they are fantasies or outright lies. Their stories happened at some other time, many years past or last year or yesterday, and in some other place — the basement of an apartment building, for example, or a library reading room. These stories (one hopes) are told so vividly, brought to life with such sensuous detail, that the play is for the moment no longer happening in Central Park in 1982. Both character and audience are transported by these stories to some other time and place.

Let's look at one of the stories, in which Nat relives what happened at a union meeting over 70 years ago. This was a formative experience, and it accounts for many of Nat's choices in the rest of the play. I have suggested in italics what an actor might do in order to make the remembered events happen in the theatrical present, so that the audience does not simply hear about them, but experiences them firsthand.

Cooper Union; November, Nineteen-Nine ... [...] I'm only eight, the Shirtwaist Makers are there, thousands of them ... [...] I'm standing in the back with my father, he holds me up so I can see.

On the actor's face we begin to see — faintly at first, growing very gradually — the wonder and excitement of a young boy at this massive, tense, colorful gathering. This energy creeps into his voice.

A meeting has been called to protest conditions. Gompers speaks, and Mary Drier, Panken and Myer London.

Here the actor may use subtle vocal changes to individualize these speakers, so that instead of simply reciting their names, Nat echoes their voices.

All speak well and with passion, but none with the courage to call a general strike. All speak of the Bosses who value property above life and profits above people, but all speak with caution ...

There are opportunities here for Nat's audience, onstage and off, to hear clips from these speeches. Certainly "Bosses" and the rhetoric about valuing "property above life and profits above people" should be voiced as the actor imagines they were spoken to the disgruntled crowd in 1909. The actor can also give us a glimpse of the speakers' faces. Might we see, for example, a touch of their caution in Nat's eyes, a moment in which one of them is nervously holding back?

[…] Until suddenly from the back of the hall, just near us, rises a skinny girl, a teenager; she races up onto the platform, this little girl, she races up unafraid among the great ones; she shouts in Yiddish to the thousands, this girl, with the power of inspiration … this girl is Clara Lemlich. "I am a working girl, one of those striking against intolerable conditions. I am *tired* of listening to speakers. I offer a resolution that a general strike be called — now!"

It is perfectly clear that by the time Clara Lemlich speaks, the actor playing Nat is also playing Clara, and Clara in high passion. We hear her words as she spoke them; we see something of her gestures, her face. The line about her racing up "unafraid among the great ones" should establish Clara's point of view: we might even hear this bit of narrative as if from her mouth.

(softly) A moment of shock …

Here we have a sudden change in point of view, to that of the crowd. The playwright's stage direction instructs the actor to play the moment of shock with the very hush that happened just before the crowd erupted.

and then the crowd screams, feet pound the floor!

The actor must give us an echo of the thousands, and his feet may get involved, or perhaps a hand pounds a thigh.

The Chairman, Feigenbaum, calls for a second; the thousands cry "second!" in one voice.

The solo actor here plays dialog: Feigenbaum and the crowd.

Feigenbaum trembles. He shouts to the hall, "Do you mean this in good faith? Will you take the Jewish oath?" Three thousand hands are raised — my father is holding me up, his hands are not free. "Raise your hand, boy, raise your hand for us and I will say the oath" — my hand goes up, I feel his heart beating at my back as my father with the thousands chants the solemn oath: "If I turn traitor to the Cause I pledge now, may this hand wither from the arm I raise!"

Does it not seem a natural impulse for the actor to raise his arm as the boy did? Whether the arm goes up suddenly or slowly is a matter of interpretation and aesthetic shaping.

Again there is silence in the hall … […] and Feigenbaum shouts — *(He raises his fist in the air.)* "A general strike has been called!"

9

> *Or the boy's raised hand becomes a fist, an economical and satisfying gestural development.*

Where is the character at the height of this speech? It is truer to say that he's at a union meeting in 1909 than to say he's in Central Park in 1982. The story transports both character and audience to another time and place, to a scene in which Nat plays Clara, Feigenbaum, the speakers, his father, his young self and a crowd of thousands.

A film, one suspects, would recreate this scene, with hundreds of extras and a boy playing young Nat. And that is just what the screenplay of *I'm Not Rappaport* does: the union meeting in fact opens the movie. Theater does something more actor-centered. It is Nat who creates the flashback: he must set the scene, play all the parts, and bring the story to life so that an audience is given not a speech but the events themselves.

We don't go to the theater to be told about significant events that have happened off-stage or in the past. We expect to witness them; we expect to live through them along with the actors. If a narrative speech is done well, we sometimes remember its events as having taken place on stage. In fact they have, though not in a scene. A narrative speech is another way to dramatize. As Nat tells the story of the union meeting, he "gets into it," as we say: he enters the story. He *relives* it; which is to say, the events happen all over again, here and now, in the theatrical present.

This is not simply artifice. It happens just this way in everyday life. If you tell a friend the story of something that mortified you yesterday, you may well get embarrassed all over again as you walk yourself through the sequence of events. Some stories remain embarrassing forever. The stories central to our lives live on in us, ready to be called up by circumstances that remind us of them.

Remembrance of Things Past
When to the sessions of sweet silent thought
I summon up remembrance of things past,
I sigh the lack of many a thing I sought,
And with old woes new wail my dear time's waste. [...]
Then can I grieve at grievances foregone,
And heavily from woe to woe tell o'er
The sad account of fore-bemoanèd moan,
Which I new pay as if not paid before. (Sonnet XXX)

When we remember past sorrows, Shakespeare reminds us, we grieve all over again. Storytelling, of course, is just such an act of remembrance, and we pay our dues every time we tell an important story. Even a bystander — a Greek messenger, for example — relives the events which he reports. And insofar as a messenger vicariously identifies with the characters in his story, to that extent he will experience again *their* conflicts and decisions.

It may be truest to think of stories as alive. They are liable to revisit us when they are relevant. They can grow, change shape, even change their meaning. At times of epiphany, a story that has haunted us may reveal its mysterious hold. Why do stories have such power, both in life and in theater?

> So much of living is made up of storytelling that one might conclude that it is what we were meant to do — to tell one another stories, fact or fiction, as a way of keeping afloat. [...] [W]e cannot help ourselves. We have the story of others to tell, or of ourselves, or of the species — some monumentally elusive tale we are always trying to get right. Sometimes it seems that we are telling each other parts of the same immense story.[2]

It may be that stories — of what happened, of what will happen — are all we care about. They fill our days; they are our conversation, our entertainment, our news, our therapy. Ads are stories, legal arguments and diagnoses are stories, memories and fantasies and proposals are stories. Freudian theory is a story about the psyche, astronomy and biology and theology are stories of their respective universes. This is, I suppose, a corollary of the play theory of culture: we are all at play — actors and scholars, engineers and salesmen, chefs and surgeons. A good part of our play involves telling each other — and ourselves — stories. Mankind is the species which tells stories, in search of whatever wisdom it can extract from them. And stories are where we live:

The universe is made of stories,
not atoms.[3]

Juliet Conjures the Tomb

We will look next at a soliloquy from *Romeo and Juliet* in which Juliet's imagination of what *might* happen transports her (and the audience) to

[2]Roger Rosenblatt, "Dreaming the News," an essay in *Time*, April 14, 1997.
[3]Muriel Rukeyser, in the title poem of *The Speed of Darkness*, Random House, 1968

another time and place so horrid it drives her almost to distraction. The situation is this: Juliet, secretly married to Romeo who is now banished from Verona because he killed Juliet's cousin Tybalt, is in a dilemma because of her parents' insistence that she marry Paris. Friar Laurence's solution is to give her a potion that will make her appear dead for forty-some hours: she will be laid to rest in her family's tomb, and when she wakes up, the friar promises, she will find Romeo there to spirit her off.

Juliet is alone in her bedroom — alone, that is, on the bare platform of Shakespeare's Globe Theatre. The Nurse has just exited, and Juliet takes out the potion. Just as she is about to drink it from the vial, she begins to have doubts. She thinks: What if this concoction doesn't work? What if it's poison? No, Friar Laurence wouldn't do that, he's a good man. But what if I wake up in the tomb, the vault where all the Capulets are buried, before Romeo gets there to rescue me? I'll be alone with all those dead bodies!

> **Acting and gender**
>
> Juliet's terror is unisex. In this speech and in most of the other materials used for exercises, it is possible to play the story, and to explore the performance issue at hand, as if the character were of your own gender.
>
> In some cases you may decide that it is interesting to step into the shoes of a character of the opposite sex. There is a long established tradition, for example, of actresses playing Hamlet (as a male). The role of Juliet, let us remember, was originally played by a boy actor. In Sam Shepard's *Tongues/Savage Love*, one male actor speaks for a wide range of characters, including a woman who is holding her newborn infant for the first time (see Excerpt 22 in Appendix A).
>
> Just as acting allows us to enter and explore lives very different from our own in terms of class, race, age and historical period, so exercises like these are an opportunity — *if and when you choose to be conscious of gender* — to explore a character whose gender is not your own.

Let me talk you through some moments an actor might discover as she explores this story of waking up alone in the tomb. Though I will give you specific actions to explore, an actor in rehearsal — in dialog with her director, in response to possibilities inherent in the set, and mindful of the thrust of the emerging production — would have to make her own choices about how to play each image and event in the text. But everything that Juliet imagines must happen, one way or another, in the present: *here* and *now*. If the tomb does not become desperately real to Juliet, she will never drink the potion: she takes it, it seems to me, to escape the horror of what she has imagined.

Read Speech 15 in Appendix B.

How if, when I am laid into the tomb,
I wake before the time that Romeo
Come to redeem me? There's a fearful point!
Shall I not then be stifled in the vault,
To whose foul mouth no healthsome air breathes in,
And there die strangled ere my Romeo comes?

1.1   *Read this section of text while focusing on what happens to Juliet's breathing. Begin with an almost imperceptible quickening of breath, and let this develop by degrees into a quite pronounced shortness of breath. Try to do this without fracturing the verse.*

Why is Juliet breathing like this? For two reasons. She imagines that she will have trouble breathing in the other time and place — the tomb — because there is no wholesome air to breathe. The very thought so frightens her that in her bedroom, about to drink the vial, her breath becomes short. The change in breath therefore has significance in both worlds — the imagined and the actual. Juliet has a foot in each of these realities. Her shortness of breath signifies *fear* in the here-and-now of her bedchamber, *suffocation* in the there-and-then of the imagined tomb. An audience readily grasps the double meaning.

Discovering what is going on for your character *now* by exploring what is happening in the story *then* is typical of what I call narrative acting. In this case, the Juliet actor learns how Shakespeare wants her to play this phase of Juliet's panic. It is not any old expression of fear that grips Juliet at this moment, but a change in her breathing — precisely what is happening in the story.

So what is Juliet "feeling" as she speaks these lines? "Fear" is really too simple and too generic an answer — which is why emotional labels are useful only as shorthand in talking about acting. What Juliet is "feeling" in response to her imagined circumstances is a physical reaction, which is precisely what an emotion is: she feels *stifled, strangled.* There is no need here for psychological analysis or an emotional substitution based on a personal experience of fear.

Nor is the question of motivation helpful here. While it is true that Juliet is trying to decide whether to take the potion, she does not bring up being stifled *in order* to make up her mind. Her involuntary, instinctive responses are not intentional or deliberate. Juliet is simply living through the story she is telling herself about what might happen in the tomb, and when she imagines the foul air, she reacts much as she would in the real event. In this soliloquy a consideration of Juliet's motivation will not help the actor to define and play specific actions, whereas a narrative approach can stimulate impulses which bring the events of the text to life.

Let's look at a series of smaller moments. Try these on your feet; explore each moment several times. All you need is a bit of bare wall and some open space in which to take a few steps. You will be dealing with very short texts — a sentence, a phrase — so that you can work without text in hand and focus on what you are doing.

Shall I not then be stifled in the vault

1.2   Against the wall, which is both a wall in Juliet's bedchamber and a wall of the tomb, speak this line as you struggle to breathe, given the lack of air. Try this several times.

1.3   Try a different choice: speak the line as if you were refusing to breathe the stench from the vault's "foul mouth."

As in a vault, an ancient receptacle

1.4   Let Juliet venture out from the wall. Walk as narrowly as you can: on either side of you, Capulet skulls stare and grin. Try not to look — but you can't help yourself.

Where bloody Tybalt, yet but green in earth,
Lies festering in his shroud

1.5   For a production in which we imagine that Juliet's bed is already on stage, grab a stand-in for her bedsheet — it could be a towel, or your sweater, even a piece of paper. Walk with this "sheet" dangling from one hand, perhaps dragging on the ground. Don't look at it, but let your hand decide at some point that it is holding not a clean sheet but a bloody shroud, damp with Tybalt's festering. How does your hand react?

where, as they say,
At some hours in the night spirits resort

1.6 Start several steps away from the wall. Back up toward it as you sense the presence of spirits in the tomb. Be specific about where your eyes look — into which dark corners are you straining to see? Listen intently — do you hear anything? Where? When you reach the wall, put your head back against it and close your eyes to shut the spirits out.

Alack, alack, is it not like that I,
So early waking

1.7 "Like" here means "likely." By "early," Juliet means before Romeo arrives. As you speak the words "So early waking," explore opening your eyes as if you were actually waking up in the tomb. In the absence of other information, you might play this as if you were coming out of a coma, or recovering consciousness after a heavy dose of anesthetics. Try this.

1.8 But Friar Laurence has promised that you will "awake as from a pleasant sleep" (IV.i). So play this, which strikes a wonderfully unexpected, blissful note.

1.9 That Juliet opens her eyes at this point has another sense. While she imagines waking up in the tomb, in her bedroom she is at the point of realizing that being there alone is likely to drive her mad, and surely her eyes open wide as she grasps this. Perhaps "Alack, alack!" starts with her eyes shut tight; at some point they pop open. Try doing the text with this sense of fearful realization.

Once again what Juliet is doing in the here-and-now of her chamber corresponds with what she imagines doing in the tomb scene. If an actor opens her eyes at this point, that action is doubly significant.

1.10 Explore playing the two meanings at once: as you open your eyes you are both waking up in the tomb and realizing the terror of your predicament. A complex, rich little moment! Try this several times.

1.11 Another way to play both these energies would be to let Juliet wake "as from a pleasant sleep," then have her realize that she is not in her bedroom but in the tomb. Explore this for a bit.

what with loathsome smells

1.12 Imagine along with Juliet that the stench of the tomb is filling your nose and throat. What happens in your head, face, hands? Seek truthful physical behaviors, favoring fresh, idiosyncratic impulses over responses that are all too probable.

And shrieks like mandrakes torn out of the earth

1.13 The root of the mandrake plant is forked and suggests a human figure; folklore held that the mandrake root shrieked when it was pulled up and that a person hearing this would go insane. What your voice does with "shrieks" can let the audience hear what Juliet imagines hearing. What is Juliet's physical response to this sound from the waist up? Explore.

Images are miniature scenes. They not only reveal in a fresh, evocative way precisely what a character is experiencing but suggest what the actor is doing. The rest of this mandrake image not only expresses how distraught Juliet is but tells you how she is behaving: when people hear a mandrake, they "run mad." From the waist down, it seems, Juliet is moving quickly. She imagines herself driven mad in the tomb, and she is losing it in her bedroom. All of Juliet's next images, in fact, describe the actions of a deranged person.

That living mortals, hearing them, run mad

1.14 Explore "running mad" three different ways:
- She doesn't know where to go and moves in several different directions.
- She runs upstage to the door by which she entered the scene, as if to leave her bedroom, then realizes that this is not really an option.
- She runs down to the edge of the stage and madly scans the audience.

And madly play with my forefathers' joints

1.15 *What is wonderfully loony here is the notion of Juliet playing with her ancestor's bones. Sit on the floor against the wall and play Juliet's mad game. Use the fingers of one hand as your "forefathers' joints." Make your play specific enough so that it seems a real game, however ghastly.*

1.16 *Create another version of this event by using space so that one of your hands seems separate from the rest of you. It might, for example, stick out from under a blanket, or be on the other side of a post, or be perched on top of a table as if severed from you. Reach over to manipulate the fingers of this hand as if they were inanimate bones.*

1.17 *Now create your own image of Juliet's mad play. What would be an interesting way to focus the audience's eyes on the action itself rather than on your face?*

Juliet is by this point speeding toward the climax of her speech, and you would not dally with this moment of madness in performance. But in rehearsal you must take time to explore each image so that you know what you are talking about and why it is important to the story. You can always simplify and edit as you put the pieces together.

Where is Juliet during this soliloquy? In her imagination she has entered the tomb, 42 hours later; it is more true to say she is *there* than in her bedchamber. It becomes so true that she freaks herself out.

And the actor playing Juliet — where is she? The commonplace answer would be that she is on stage or in the rehearsal hall (or wherever you have been working on these moments), and that she is pretending to be in the bedroom and then the tomb. I hope this book convinces you that someone who is acting Juliet's soliloquy and acting well, who enters the other time and place so that impulses and organic responses take over, is really in the tomb — waking, smelling, hearing, seeing, running mad. Humans can transport themselves to other times and places, just as Juliet can. You are wired with the ability to imagine a story and to act as if you were inside it. Once inside, instinct prompts choices that you can shape into a performance. *Acting Narrative Speeches* is about techniques of positioning yourself inside a story and shaping the resultant impulses.

Shamans

The peoples of northeast Asia and of some Native American tribes looked to priestly figures called shamans (sometimes referred to as "medicine men" or "witch doctors") to act as intermediaries with the spirit world. Shamanic rituals were performed in order to make the coming hunt successful, to call down rain on the crops, to heal the sick.

For certain ritual events, the shaman depended on rhythmic music, atmospheric lighting, and on the assistance of what we would call stage managers — who might, for example, be outside the hut ready to shake it on cue. But the shaman's main tools were those of a performer: voice, text, gesture, movement and lots of skills now associated with circus and street performers. It was the shaman, apparently, who invented sword swallowing, juggling, and acrobatics. A somersault made visible the presence of spirits with whom the shaman was wrestling. In this way the other time and place of the spirit world was made present for the community.

That the shaman was a performer did not make him a con artist or rob his performance of its spiritual and healing powers, any more than an actor's rehearsal preparations make the events of a play unreal. What happens in *Romeo and Juliet* really happens, just as surely as what is reported in the news, but it happens in another dimension of reality. Try stopping Romeo from killing himself in the tomb; you may disrupt the performance, but Romeo *will* kill himself.[4]

If an actor uses all the tools at her command — voice, rhythm, gesture, movement, space — to create what Juliet imagines happening in the tomb, the audience is transported along with her into the spirit world of the story, sees what is invisible, experiences each event. The audience is *right there* with the actor, in the other time and place.

This is possible because an actor's choices can conjure — bring to sensuous life — the sights and sounds which are the tomb, can make the audience smell the stench, feel the festering on its skin. The word "conjure" is used advisedly: the actor conjures as a shaman does, making the spirit world (in Juliet's case, the tomb and all the fearful energies with which it surrounds her) appear out of thin air, so that the audience of an

[4]Cf. Michael Goldman's *The Actor's Freedom*, The Viking Press, 1975, p. 121.

inspired performance feels a spell has been cast on it. It is this phenomenon which is the true "magic" of theater. On a bare stage the Juliet actor conjures bones, bloody shrouds, shrieks, ghosts, madness; the Rappaport actor, without a set change or lighting cue, without other actors or any costumes or props, must call up the spirits of his father, the heroic young girl and thousands of union members. The actor's primal magic is to conjure another time and place.

Acting a Montage

The skills involved in performing narrative speeches give actors and audiences such pleasure that they constitute one of the central joys of theater. Sometimes an actor is given a speech which exhibits these skills in virtuoso fashion, in a rapid series of miniature scenes, each one creating another time and place. In *Romeo and Juliet*, for example, Mercutio's famous fantasy about the Celtic fairy queen quickly sketches an entire gallery of characters over whose sleeping bodies tiny Queen Mab travels at night, causing them to dream. Mercutio begins by conjuring Mab's hazelnut chariot, drawn by gnats. Then he takes us for a wild ride.

Read Speech 16 in Appendix B.

Mercutio is a flashy character, as mercurial as his name suggests, and you should imagine him taking stage, moving all over the set as he conjures one character and scene after another. On your feet, explore how a visit from Queen Mab affects the dreams of a lover, a lawyer and a soldier.

and then they dream of love

1.18 *Against a bit of wall, put yourself asleep as one such lover. What sleep movement might reveal the specific romantic moment the lover is dreaming? Remember that Mercutio is a jokester, so have fun with this. Try two or three different possibilities. Speak the line from within each imagined event, as if you were the lover.*

O'er lawyers' fingers, who straight dream on fees

1.19 *Still against the wall, stretch out one arm in a manner which will ensure that the audience is seeing your "lawyer's fingers." One way* to do this is to obscure your face — for example, by placing the other arm across your eyes; another is to place the hand you want the audience to focus on quite close to your face. What motion in your fingers might be appropriate for this fee-hungry lawyer? What does the lawyer sound like?

And then dreams he of cutting foreign throats

1.20 If the soldier is cutting a foreign throat in his dream, and if he speaks this bit of narrative as he does the deed, how should the line sound? Try it a couple of times, imagining different scenes, each with a specific action.

Of breaches, ambuscadoes, Spanish blades

1.21 In rapid succession, the soldier dreams of breaking through ("breaching") the enemy line, of an ambush ("ambuscado"), of swordplay. This is a sketchy scenario, open to different interpretations. Work on a version in which Mercutio's soldier dashes forward, ambushes the enemy, slashes his way to victory. Choreograph these scenes in bravura fashion, with each action flowing into the next. Use as much space as is available to you. Here is an opportunity to hurdle chairs, leap atop a platform or fight off a whole army. (Be careful.)

1.22 Work on an alternative version, in which it is the enemy who is on the offensive: they back you up, attack from another direction, surround you with drawn swords.

Of healths five fathoms deep

1.23 Suddenly you are catapulted into a tavern, offering a toast — that's what a "health" is. Imagine that you have been drinking a while and are in very good spirits. You climb atop a table and your regiment gathers boisterously. You raise a glass. Use this line to offer a "health" to your fellow soldiers and their hard-earned victory.

and then anon
Drums in his ear, at which he starts and wakes,
And being thus frighted, swears a prayer or two

1.24 Shakespeare has shaped these lines so that Mercutio will land heavily *on "Drums" in his lower register. It is this word which wakes the soldier from his dream of being in a tavern; it might so startle him that he drops prayerfully to his knees. Try this.*

1.25 *"Swears a prayer or two" can be spoken so that we hear the voice of the soldier praying. What sort of prayer? Until you get specific and decide exactly what promises or pleas are being made, how can you know how the soldier's prayer should sound? Try improvising the soldier's terrified prayer in your own words, then explore making some of Shakespeare's text sound like that.*

Every actor who does this speech will play it differently, and there are other considerations besides the montage of little scenes that Mercutio fantasizes: his temperament and world view, his relationship to Romeo, what sort of Verona a given production attempts to realize. But for each Mercutio, the cast of characters and the sequence of events in the Queen Mab speech remain the same. They are the raw material for whatever the actor sets out to realize.

How Not To Act a Speech That Tells a Story

By way of clarifying how a narrative approach to acting stories differs from other methods, let us consider a speech from Sam Shepard's *Curse of the Starving Class*. At the beginning of Act Three, Weston — the drunken, razor-tongued father who passes out on top of the kitchen table in Act Two — has undergone a total transformation. Sober and cleaned up, he is speaking gently to a sick lamb penned up in the kitchen and folding the family laundry. When his son Wesley arrives and asks his father what has caused this change, Weston explains that he had gotten up early and taken a walk around the farm, "and a funny thing started happening to me."

Read Speech 8 in Appendix B. Pay special attention to the part about the bath.

What is an actor to do with such a speech? What does this material ask us to do? How should we approach it? Where do we start?

Being "really real"

Some actors seem to believe that the actor's task is to be as "realistic" as possible. They proceed to develop blocking and stage business that

21

looks like everyday life. Lines are spoken with the energy of the invented actions, which become more important than what the text is talking about.

Then I walked straight in and made myself a hot bath. Hot as I could stand it.

1.26 Try saying this while exploring these activities with lots of realistic detail:

- sweeping;
- making a peanut butter and jelly sandwich;
- sensing, locating, and fixing a nail that is poking up inside your shoe;
- smoking a cigarette and drinking a cup of coffee.

What is wrong here? All of these "really real" activities, no matter how well executed, are irrelevant to the text. They have nothing to do with the story.

Acting from impulse

An actor's training should certainly include exercises that free up impulses. Intuitive choices are essential to any rehearsal process, and a sense of spontaneity is important in performance. But acting is not pure instinct; an actor's impulses need to be informed by the material and its interpretation. Some performers seem to approach acting as pure improvisation; at the furthest extreme, they act as if they were in flight from any action suited to the text and in search only of the unexpected.

Freshness, novelty, and surprise are virtues in acting, but they are no substitute for sense. If impulses do not help to tell the story, they are irrelevant.

Just sank down into it and let it sink deep into the skin.

1.27 What might you do physically as you tell this part of the story? Explore quite freely and impulsively, but stay focused on the events of the text: sinking into the hot tub, the water soaking into you. Try the line many different ways: slow, fast; big, small; in many different spaces; with radically different energies; experimenting with different images (for example, you are drowning); etc. Focus on the interplay of impulse and meaning.

22

Let it fog up all the windows and the glass on the medicine cabinet.

1.28 Now explore a wide range of impulses, but reject those that have anything to do with what the text is about. You might, for example, kick a table leg, try to land a hat on a hat rack across the room, tap dance, build a little structure with dishes and cups, do an imitation of a cartoon character, spar with your son, etc. Walk about the room and give over to random impulses which are not connected to what happens in the text.

Impulses of this sort seem to come out of nowhere — and tend to go nowhere. Once you have imaginatively situated yourself inside a narrative speech, you may have all sorts of unexpected impulses, but they will be part of the story.

Emoting

Acting choices in the mainstream of contemporary media suggest that a majority of actors believe that acting is about figuring out what emotional state a character is in at a given moment. Some actors simply play a repertoire of readily accessible emotions on cue — as if acting were like painting by number: color this bit of text blue, that one fiery red, etc.

1.29 Try reading the bath speech as if you were:
- *in a giggly mood, laughing and having the best time as you tell this funny story;*
- *in a rage, fire coming out through clenched teeth;*
- *on the verge of tears, in a soap opera or a cry-of-the-week TV movie.*

What is going on here? Color me sad, color me mad, color me jolly: all of these choices are about what you are feeling in the here-and-now, as you tell the story. Even if you worked on these emotional choices until they were quite genuinely felt, they would tell precious little about what Weston experienced *inside* the story, scalding and freezing himself in a ritual of transformation — unless you really think he was raging or laughing or weeping in the tub.

Focusing on what the storyteller is feeling while telling the story may actually distance the audience from the story itself, because what is communicated is that the character is, for example, angry — not what he is angry *about*. Playing the emotion of the here-and-now draws a veil over the story and makes it harder to see what is happening; this sort of emoting is in fact just as irrelevant as a "really real" choice like sweeping the floor.

In a monolog by Gus Edwards,[5] Dwayne reflects on how the media respond to events like the assassination of President Kennedy by focusing on photogenic displays of grief: "The spectacle of viewing someone in tears to me calls attention to the crier, and not the event they're supposedly crying about. When I think about it, it's more than offensive, it's obscene." When an actor calls attention to his or her own emotion rather than to the events of the story being told, the distortion is much the same.

What a character telling a story is feeling *now* may or may not be what was felt *then*, as the events occurred. It is possible, for example, for a character to repress the pain of a story; and how s/he feels about what happened in the past may have changed. To the extent that emotions are relevant to the story — and they are only part of the picture — it is what the character felt *in the other time and place* that matters. That is what the audience should vicariously experience.

Emotional substitution

Some "Method" actors, concerned with playing emotions as honestly as possible, use a technique called "emotional substitution." Imagine that in order to play what your character feels at a certain moment, you:

- think about a personal experience in which you felt roughly the same sort of emotion;
- put yourself in touch with that emotion by recalling details of the circumstances in which you felt it;
- play these emotions from your own life as if they belonged to your character.

In this way your emotions are "substituted" for the character's.

---

[5]Gus Edwards, "Where I Was, Where I Am," *Monologues on Black Life*, Heinemann, 1997.

> This process amounts to telling yourself the story of a personal experience in order to stir up feelings. Might you not tell yourself your character's story, with the same attention to narrative detail, and thereby elicit fresh emotions which are both yours and the character's?
>
> Making connections between your own life experience and that of a character is, of course, a natural and desirable development. But a habit of substituting your own experiences for those of your character condemns you to playing your own life over and over again — whereas acting ought to expand your horizons and your experience of human diversity. Reliance on emotional substitution indicates a lack of faith in the ability of actors to identify with their characters — and to feel what they feel. It is sympathy that makes acting possible.

Stories and objectives

Since Konstantin Stanislavski published his acting theories, we have had acting systems which structure performances on the basis of how "objectives," what characters want,motivate actions and put characters into conflict. Certainly this issue is of relevance to every play, but how objectives relate to acting narrative speeches needs clarification — and can teach us something about the nature of stories.

Within a story, in the other time and place, motivation plays a role just as it does in life and in drama. Why a character behaves as he does — whether in a scene or in a story — is always a sensible question. So one may work on the motivations of various characters *within* a narrative speech. But what about a character's motive in telling a story? That is the interesting question.

It is certainly true that a story may be told with a specific goal in mind. In Shakespeare's *Julius Caesar* (I.ii), Cassius tells Brutus a story about a time when he rescued Caesar from drowning, and Cassius has a motive: he wants to enlist Brutus' support in denying Caesar a crown. No doubt Cassius, who greatly resents standing in Caesar's shadow, is himself comforted by retelling a story in which he is a hero and Caesar appears weak. But Cassius' motives will not conjure the events, will not lead to acting choices which bring them alive so that they seem to happen all over again. Asking "what's my objective?" about *why* a story is told, while it

25

may clarify its relevance and tone, will not help an actor to create or relive the events.

An actor seriously committed to the objectives approach might decide that Weston's objective in the bath speech is to convince his son that he is no longer the same person, that he is a new man. True enough, but this observation will not generate moment-to-moment choices about how Weston might make his son vicariously experience what happened in the bath.

The whole point of formulating an objective is to put a character into action. If the intent of telling a story is to shed light on the issue at hand, then the story itself is the action to be played. One must play the story in order to play the motive.

In everyday life, stories seem quite often to emerge of their own will, perhaps by way of association, without discernible motive. In a well-crafted play, of course, a story will be relevant to what the play is about, but it may not advance the action. In such a case, it seems truest to say that the "motivation" to tell a story is the story itself. Stories exist to be told, whether or not they accomplish anything.

What is remarkable about Weston's bath story, moreover, is that he is reliving the events as he tells them, and what is the motivation for that? Re-experiencing what happened in a story as you tell it is not a purposeful act. It is as natural as breathing, and just as involuntary.

A narrative approach

"Then I walked straight in and made myself a hot bath." Half of the speech is about a bath. What does this material ask of the actor? Not moment-to-moment impulses or realistic activities in the here and now, not an objective the character may have with respect to his son, not Weston's feelings after the fact. What must be acted is the story itself. The actor needs to conjure the other time and place in which Weston scalded himself and then endured ice cold water.

There are of course different ways to realize this. Let's imagine one possible approach. The whole play takes place in a kitchen; picture Weston standing at the kitchen table in front of his chair. As he speaks, his eyes disengage from his son's, as one does when remembering precisely what happened. Weston is no longer really in the kitchen; he is in the bathroom earlier that morning.

Then I walked straight in and made myself a hot bath. Hot as I could stand it.

1.30 Imagine Weston sitting very slowly into the chair, as if he were gingerly lowering himself into a hot tub. He is not consciously doing this — he is not demonstrating, as people sometimes do. Weston is still digesting the very fresh details of his transformation; he is playing catch-up to his just-a-while-ago experience. It is his body — from the neck down — which recalls and relives the sensations of heat and cold. In the here-and-now, absorbed in memory, talking to his son, Weston slowly, distractedly sits in a chair; in the other time and place, his body lowers itself into the steaming tub. Try this several times, paying attention both to the here-and-now and to the other time and place.

Just sank down into it and let it sink deep into the skin.

1.31 Let your bottom slide down the seat of the chair. Impulsively connect to any space available to you: your head may rest against the chair back or a bit of wall; a foot might very naturally go up onto another chair. Weston is reliving what he experienced then. Was he ecstatic? grinning? excited? fearful? bewildered? numb? wincing in pain? hungry for change? some combination of these? Explore.

Let it fog up all the windows and the glass on the medicine cabinet.

1.32 Consider how people sometimes gesture vaguely about the location of what they are talking about — up by the oak tree, at the other end of the pond, etc. Let Weston gesture in this way about the steam rising from the tub, how it swirled above him as he soaked. As your hand rises, let your wrist turn and your fingers move independently of each other — all in slow motion. The motion of your hand is the steam. Weston may or may not be aware of the imagistic nature of his gesture, but his hand is re-experiencing something he'd raptly watched while in the bath.

Then I let all the water drain out

1.33 The event here is the tub water going down the drain. Let your voice mimic this by arcing from a higher to a lower pitch: from a highish

"Then" to a lowish "out." This should sound like very natural storytelling, which it is; actors can shape texts like this because people do it instinctively in everyday life. Try it once with an everyday storytelling gesture that also goes from high to low: the hand that was conjuring the steam is still up above your head and available to do this.

Just sat there and let it creep up on me till I was in up to my neck.
1.34 Now the water is ice cold. What does this do to your body as the tub fills? Imagine the water coming up your chest; what happens in your neck, your face, your voice? Try this once with a vocal arc that starts low on "just sat there" and rises to its highest note on "neck."
1.35 Now speak the text with a voice which is "frozen" on one pitch as Weston endures the cold: that is another option.

In both cases, the text is spoken from inside the other time and place of the story.

This is not the only way to act the bath speech from a narrative point of view, but focusing on what happened in the tub is the actor's work here. *Acting Narrative Speeches* will outline and exercise the skills needed to recreate and relive the events of a story while making sure that your character's behavior in the here-and-now is fully justified, natural, even necessary. Being in two places at once is remarkable, magical and at times very powerful, but it is not so difficult to achieve as you might think. Storytelling plays such a large part in our everyday lives that we have all experienced the state of being simultaneously here and somewhere else: inside a story, in another time and place.

Living a story from the inside

Most actors have at some time or other been cautioned by teachers — and directors — not to *indicate* what is happening to a character but simply to experience it, not to *show* but to *be*. At this early stage of learning about narrative acting, it may worry some that what you have been doing on your feet "illustrates" the text in a manner akin to the dreaded sin of indicating.

An actor who is indicating is not living what his character is experiencing but using a kind of sign language — a cliché gesture, a tell-tale conventional behavior, or an unfelt symptom of emotion — that tells the audience what to think about the moment. The problem is not that the actor performs a meaningful action which is read by the audience. That is of course precisely what actors do: create moments that are significant, actions which "sign" meaningfully. What is problematic about indicating is that it comes from *outside* the dramatic moment — as if the actor were standing next to the character and acting out a more or less subtle charade of what is going on *inside* the character. But if an actor inhabits the character, then there is no question of indicating, because actions come from within.

It is certainly possible to stand outside a story and indicate what is going on inside of it with actions that illustrate the story. This is not narrative acting, any more than indicating is acting. Narrative acting requires that the actor be positioned *inside the story*, living through each event.

If you get at least one foot inside the story you're working on, you will be positioned to make other discoveries that take you farther inside. Once you get inside a narrative speech, you will find a scene, and inside that scene are actions waiting for you to discover them. Playing those actions puts you into something very like the play state that children so easily enter. Inside that play state, you are free to follow impulses and respond organically to imagined events as if they were really happening.

Your best shot at convincing your audience is to convince yourself. What works for one actor may not, of course, work for another. So a teacher or coach has to suggest this and that, just as a director does, hoping to press a button or two that works for you. You need to develop a wide-open rehearsal process that enables you to find your own buttons.

Chapter 2
Choosing a Speech

As the first topics are introduced, your acting work will focus on the *excerpts* from narrative speeches in Appendix A and on the *speeches* in Appendix B. It is possible, of course, to continue work on these materials for as long as you wish, by way of exercise; they provide you with a spectrum of possibilities with respect to each issue.

After Chapter 4, however, you will need a speech of your own as the central context for explorations. Using the approaches formulated chapter by chapter, you will fully develop this speech. Later on in this process you should begin work on a second speech; working on two in tandem can provoke discoveries in both.

What Sort of Speech Are You Looking For?

You are looking for a narrative speech, material in which your character relives events so vividly that an audience vicariously experiences them. You want a speech that asks you to travel to another time and place, or — what is to say the same thing — to make the other time and place present here and now.

There are, of course, other kinds of speeches — which vent emotions, for example, or which try to persuade by way of argument and rhetoric, without recourse to anecdote. You can use narrative skills to situate yourself for the acting of such speeches, and you can certainly apply the shaping skills and the opposites approach to inner conflict developed in later chapters to every sort of speech. But for the reasons outlined in the preface, this book will focus only on speeches that tell a story.

A narrative speech may involve one extended scene, as in the speech from *I'm Not Rappaport* about the union meeting; several different scenes which might, for example, tell about a romantic attraction, then about the events of a first date, then about a break-up; or even many mini-scenes as in the Mercutio speech about Queen Mab. If you are interested in a speech of this last sort, it would be better to work on it after you have worked on one or two narrative speeches with longer scenes.

Varieties of Narrative

Most commonly, narrative speeches remember *past* events, whether they happened long ago or just before the storyteller came on stage. As a character tells a story, he or she typically relives its events. All over again the character falls in love or commits a great sin or loses a friend. What gave pleasure or pain before is enjoyed or suffered again. Such a speech might begin:

- When I was ten years old, my mother ...
- Something very odd happened to me this morning ...
- Last night I had the most amazing dream ...
- Here's how it happened ...
- Your majesty, the battle was certainly lost until the young prince arrived, and ...

And what? What happened? The actor's job in shaping such a speech is to make the events present in the here and now. If that doesn't happen, then one might as well read the play and save oneself a trip to the theater. If the actor merely speaks the words, however feelingly, nothing really happens.

Other speeches may envision or imagine another time and place, as Juliet does when she conjures the tomb. Such speeches may be fantasies or daydreams, speculations or proposals, plots or prophecies; they are narratives about what will or might or ought to happen. These are the stories of our hopes and fears, our dreams and anxieties:

- Here's what we should do...
- You know where I want to live?
- Someday it will be different. Someday...
- It will turn out awful. Don't you know what will happen?

What? What might happen? The actor's job here is to conjure the possibilities so vividly that they actually do happen in our imaginations.

By way of review: the speech should be essentially narrative; the events of the story you tell may be past or future, real or imagined; the story may involve one or more scenes.

Narrative Speeches in Dramatic Literature

Speeches that tell a story have been part of western drama since the outset. Your search for material can therefore begin with Greek drama. In the plays of Aeschylus, Sophocles, and Euripides, deaths always happen off-stage. But they are vividly reported by messengers, who conjure every sort of carnage imaginable: battle scenes, ambushes, horrific murders, fatal chariot races, double suicides, ritual sacrifices, bodies torn limb from limb. In Euripides' *The Phoenician Woman*, one such messenger takes center stage for several pages and gives us, blow by blow, the sword fight of two brothers: they mortally wound each other and speak their last words to their grief-stricken mother, who then kills herself on the spot. That scene is meant to happen right in front of us. We should note that in the original productions of Greek tragedies, two or three actors changed masks and played all the roles, including the messengers, whose speeches required powerfully skilled performers.

Since the narrative speech has ever since been a means whereby plays travel in time and space beyond their settings, your search can continue on through the ages. Perhaps you are interested in a period, a country, a style, or a particular author. You might look to the Roman comedies or the tragedies of Seneca; to Shakespeare and his contemporaries in the Elizabethan and Jacobean ages; to the Spanish Golden Age of Lope de Vega and Calderon; to Corneille, Racine, Moliere; to the Restoration comedies; and on to Ibsen, Strindberg, Chekhov, Shaw, Pirandello, Lorca, Brecht, O'Neill, Williams, Beckett, now — including the work of contemporary monologists.

Where to Look: Some Resources

The speeches in Appendix B give you some idea of the range of narrative speeches you might consider. Several of the excerpts in Appendix A are taken from excellent speeches.

Browse in the library, in bookstores which have reasonably extensive theater collections, and on your own and your friends' bookshelves. In addition to dramatic sources, you may consider other sources in literature and nonfiction. I have had students work successfully on narratives excerpted from novels and short stories; first-person fiction is often indistinguishable from dramatic material when stories are told, but third-person narratives can also be performed. Rhymed poetry won't work, generally speaking — though I have had a student perform Lewis Carroll's "Jabberwocky." I have seen good work done on prose poems by E.E. Cummings and on the blank verse monologs of Robert Browning ("My Last Duchess," for example). As for nonfiction, one might consider excerpts from slave narratives, oral histories, memoirs, magazine articles, etc. I have transcribed good speeches from the subtitles of foreign films — and later improved on the translation. Some actors write or adapt materials for themselves.

A good many anthologies have been published for actors looking for audition materials. A list of companies which publish speech and monolog collections appears in Appendix D, along with a selective list of anthologies. If your local bookstore does not carry titles you are interested in, you can order them from the publishers or from a store that specializes in theater (several are listed in Appendix D). In order to satisfy actors' demands for fresh materials — auditioners seem to tire of seeing the same speeches — publishers have offered collections of monologs from last year's plays, from Canadian and British playwrights, from film scripts, from lesser-known classical plays and playwrights, from neglected periods, from non-dramatic fiction. There are even books of speeches written just for auditions. You can search in any of these directions for narrative speeches that interest you.

Needless to say, the pressure to fill the covers of new collections has resulted in uneven quality: you'll no doubt come across some second- and third-rate writing in your search. Exercise taste. Quality is a lot more important than novelty. If you are going to do quality work, you need to choose quality material.

Some Criteria for Selecting Speeches

The story which your speech tells should be richly diverse. A good narrative speech offers you a *variety* of moods, energies, circumstances, events, perhaps characters. You want a speech with *contrasts* in it; a speech which is all one note will not provide you with opportunities to explore in various directions nor will it give you a workout in terms of doing the exercises which teach narrative skills. What you want is a speech that asks you to use the full range of your voice, to move, to create high contrast changes in energy, and to live through a sequence of complex and intriguing events.

The other time and place of the story should ask you to conjure events quite *sensuously.* Look for expressive and intriguing circumstances, evocative details, sensory specifics. These will afford you the opportunity to create a vividly particular world.

The speech should involve a *journey,* in which a character travels through a series of events and ends up in a different place than where he or she started. It may be that the character grows up a bit, comes to a realization, makes a decision, arrives at a turning point. The catalyst may be victory or loss, crisis or ecstasy, betrayal or temptation, confusion or discovery. Some journeys are more or less straight lines; others are roller coaster rides full of surprises and turnabouts.

At least one of the speeches you choose to work on should be a *stretch* for you: something different that is challenging and unlike you, not at all close to home.

In order to explore the many faces of the narrative speech in various periods and styles and to diversify your portfolio of audition speeches, one of the speeches you work on should be something other than contemporary American realism: a classic or something from another century, another culture, another genre. If you choose something by Shakespeare or one of his contemporaries, see Appendix C for some preliminary work you should do on the text as part of your rehearsal process.

For purposes of learning the approaches of this book, you need not consider whether a speech is frequently done. Even if you are presently developing a portfolio of audition speeches, you should not reject a speech in which you are strongly interested just because it is well known or has been done quite a bit. If you make a familiar speech fresh again, that is to your advantage.

Each speech you choose should genuinely *interest* you. In one sense or another it should speak to you, whether because it resonates with your experience or seems wholly removed from it. It may intrigue you, disturb you, scare you, seem terribly important, strike you as outrageously funny. But it must matter to you somehow, so that it calls forth committed work. This doesn't mean that you need to know at the outset how you will interpret events and act critical moments. On the contrary, one reason to choose a speech is that you don't understand it and need to, because you care about its puzzles and ambiguities. The best speeches hide some mysteries, ask tough questions, have lots of possibilities and dimensions to explore; they spark you into investigation on your feet. Search for material that isn't going to bore you after a few weeks — a story which challenges and which has depths to explore, no matter if it is comic or serious or both.

Don't waste your time on a speech unworthy of your time and effort. Comedy is *really* funny when it reveals us to ourselves; serious comedy is more substantive than easy sitcom jokes or one-liners. Material that *really* moves us is not soap-opera emoting over trivial events or cliché relationships; genuine emotions must be earned — they are *about* something. Beware of hip posturing that doesn't go anywhere, of shock for its own sake, of issues which aren't really explored. Reject the white bread of inferior, derivative, superficial writing in favor of material that will nourish your acting. Be hungry for *substance*. Exercise taste. You will be as good as your material.

Editing

If you intend to use a speech later for audition purposes, it should generally be $1^1/_2$ to 2 minutes in length.

You can edit a longer speech by stopping short of the end, by starting midway, by cutting out a middle section, by making judicious small edits throughout.

It is possible to piece together several smaller speeches, provided that the result makes sense and flows. Cutting and pasting a speech may require your inserting transitional language.

Sometimes it is necessary to add a word or two or to rewrite a line so that a speech is clear out of context. If a speech begins with a pronoun which has no antecedent, for example, you will need to change it to the noun to which it refers. An important circumstance may need to be spelled out. Perhaps a reference to events elsewhere in the play is unclear and should be cut. Perhaps an obscure word can be changed without violating the tone of the text.

An awkward bit of translation may need to be changed so that it falls more easily out of your mouth. You may wish to consult a variety of translations in search of a more contemporary, less British, more actable version. You might even put together your own composite translation.

For Your Own Speech

1. Begin your search for a narrative speech. You may discover more than one you want to work on, but select one which is solidly, richly narrative for the first round of exploratory exercises.

2. If you choose a speech from Shakespeare or one of his contemporaries, see Appendix C for an outline of the work you should do on the text before getting on your feet.

3. Before you read the next chapter, familiarize yourself with the narrative speeches in Appendix B. Note how each asks the actor to bring to life specific events and circumstances in another time and place.

Chapter 3
Setting the Scene

Narrative speeches ask the actor to conjure another time and place, to make present the events of a story. The first section of this book is focused on story sense — what an actor does to make sense of a story.

In the next while, it will be instructive to watch people telling stories: what they do in order to convey to others exactly what happened. Acting builds on these everyday impulses. Note the changes that someone telling a story goes through in the act of narrating. If he or she is really inside the story, you will see signs of the events being relived.

Until you begin shaping sections of your speech, you will work as you did in the exercises in Chapter 1, with brief texts from an excerpt in Appendix A or from a speech in Appendix B.

We begin our consideration of story sense with what I call *setting the scene* — that is, recreating the circumstances and events of the story: where it happens, when it happens, and what happens.

In *The Collected Works of Billy the Kid*, Michael Ondaatje creates in prose and poetry a voice for the infamous desperado. The book, which Ondaatje adapted for the stage, has several powerful prose narratives which might be performed as speeches.

In Appendix B, read Speech 5.

Imagine that you are telling this story not on stage but in real life — before storytelling jumps to its feet and begins to dramatize what happened. Imagine too that you are very committed to communicating every detail as truthfully as possible. You should always assume that the stakes are high when your character tells a story.

Say each bit of text with any physical impulses you have to *make visible* what you're talking about. Try to make each event vividly present: make the story happen here and now. The more detail there is in each of your physical choices, the better: be very specific about precisely what happened at each moment in the story, though there is considerable room for interpretation, as you shall see.

Stay seated for this first series of exercises.

when this chicken paddles out to him

3.1 Each time you speak this line, work on making the chicken's movement visible. First put it into your hands: how they move should embody just how a chicken moves. Then transfer the impulse into your feet. Work next with your arms (which become wings), then your neck (so that the motion of your head is like a chicken's). If some of this strikes you as funny, that's fine; Billy the Kid thinks it's funny too, and absurdity is one component of the grotesque. But strive for honest-to-goodness chicken-ness each time. If you have other physical impulses, play them out — but stay in your chair.

3.2 Use one or more of these ways of becoming the chicken to play the following scene while remaining in your chair. A really famished chicken staggers into the street. It spots Gregory and is suddenly alert. There is a marked change of energy as the chicken heads for him. Play those three events: moving as if faint with hunger; seeing Gregory; making a beeline for him.

3.3 Why does the poet say that the chicken "paddles" out to Gregory's body? One meaning of this verb is to walk like a small child. Explore in your chair how this chicken might move like a toddler.

and as he was falling hops on his neck

This line tells of two events: Gregory falling and the chicken hopping on his neck. It also suggests two different points of view: Gregory's and the chicken's.

Work first on *how* Gregory fell. On the page, five little words tell you nothing specific, but if you simply play "falling," the resulting action will be generic. Generic actions are like clichés: they say very little and they fail to capture attention or to stir the imagination. The actor must, in collaboration with the playwright, play concrete particulars — even if they are not spelled out in the text. Getting specific is "setting the scene" work.

3.4 Start standing and collapse into your chair each time you "fall." Work in slow motion, so that you can explore specifics.
  - *First fall so as to let the audience see where the bullet hits Gregory.*
  - *What's the really violent version of this?*
  - *Is Gregory in pain, in shock, surprised, afraid, angry? Answer this in the manner of your fall.*

3.5   The chicken should have a very different energy. How might you get the "hop" into your body while remaining seated?

3.6   When one of the characters in your story is an animal, you are likely to find yourself projecting human qualities into the creature. Consider, for example, the expression on this chicken's face. You might discover that the chicken's mouth is watering or that it has its eye fixed greedily on a throbbing vein. Play with fleshing out the chicken's point of view as it hops on Gregory's neck.

digs the beak into his throat

How, specifically, does the chicken do this? Experiment with trying to capture this event quite graphically.

3.7   Imagine that your mouth is the beak. How do your neck and upper body come into play? How does this affect how you speak the text?

3.8   Play with your hand as the beak. Try to conjure the beak's shape and motion. If you contact anything, what might you do to make visible precisely how the beak "digs" into Gregory's throat?

3.9   What about Gregory's point of view? What is the expression on his face? How does he physically react to the chicken's attack? What might he do to defend himself? Explore several possibilities.

3.10   It is possible to play both points of view consecutively. How might you make the transition from playing the chicken to playing Gregory?

3.11   It is also possible to play the two points of view simultaneously: your hand, for example, might play the chicken, while your face and neck (and perhaps your other hand) are Gregory's. Try this.

Each of this story's events might be played in various ways. There is no single "right" way to act any of these moments. Some choices may bear a family resemblance to each other, since they are versions of the same event; but other choices may envision what happened quite differently.

straightens legs and heaves
a red and blue vein out

3.12   Experiment with rising out of your chair to play this moment. Try a slow, steady pull on the vein. Try a fast move as if the vein came out suddenly with one jerk.

3.13 What might you do to convey the length of the vein?

3.14 If you imagine that the vein is in your mouth, how does this affect how you say the line?

The first step in working on a narrative speech is to explore how its events might be made visible. Your focus should be on what happened, and in what circumstances. You must set the scene. What did the chicken do, what did Gregory do? To tell us precisely how, you may need to collaborate with the author by providing details that are not spelled out in the text. And you must interpret what is there on the page. It may well be that Gregory's last words are outraged, but there are other interesting possibilities: he may die in a state of disbelief, fear, queasiness, even laughter.

You don't have to do something for every event and circumstance in a story. In most cases that would make your speech too busy, too cluttered. You need to be selective about which particulars are most important and evocative, which are of interest to you and your production. But for learning purposes I will encourage you to notice and explore every detail. That is good rehearsal training, because it keeps you open to possibilities. You can always edit, but you want to edit from a wealth of actions that you have considered on your feet.

Getting inside

Setting the scene requires that you position yourself inside the story. So how do you get yourself inside? Largely by setting the scene! *It is what you do to set the scene that takes you inside the story.*

The great Russian acting teacher Konstantin Stanislavski called this process "the magic if": if thus and such were happening, what would I do, how would I behave? You convince your imagination that you are in the other time and place by acting as if you were. That's how acting works: behaving as *if* thus and such were true makes thus and such real to us. As you explore the story's circumstances and events, you discover actions that place you imaginatively — and physically — inside it. And the deeper you get inside a narrative speech, the better positioned you are to discover actions not spelled out in the text.

> Getting inside means that you enter an imaginative play state in which you react to events as if they were really happening *now*, in the theatrical present — which is the whole point of acting. Inside the story is where those organic reactions called emotions well up spontaneously. Try to get yourself *inside* each of the moments you work on.
>
> Telling a story as if you were the detached narrator of a documentary does not help to make the events happen here and now. Nor does it help you get into the story. Speak narrative text from *inside* the moment you are playing. Speak as a participant, with a specific point of view.

Brecht borrowed the basic premise of *Mr. Puntila and His Man Matti* from the Chaplin movie *City Lights*. Puntila is a wealthy landowner in Tavastland (Finland). When he is drunk, which he is quite often, he is a friendly, generous, charming soul who treats his chauffeur Matti as a buddy. But when he sobers up, he is a cold, status-conscious, capitalist villain.

Read Excerpt 2 in Appendix A.

Why has this text been included with the narrative excerpts? Puntila appears to be standing atop a high point and looking at the Finnish landscape. Where's the story? Where's the other time and place? The circumstances are in fact unusual. At the end of the play, Puntila, drunk once again, announces in his office that he wants to climb Mount Hatelma to have a look at his property, and with Matti's help he builds a "mountain" by stacking furniture atop his desk. He climbs to the top of this pile and imagines seeing the land he owns and the cut timber which makes him wealthy. To play this scene you must call on the same skills required for acting any narrative speech: like Puntila, you must conjure the view from the peak of an imaginary mountain.

For this sequence of exercises, stand on a chair to get the feel of Puntila's perch.

Do you see that little one?

3.15 Finland has tens of thousands of lakes. Imagine that Puntila pretends to pick out a small one and corrects where Matti is looking, with a physicality that says "No, no, that one." How does this affect how you say the line?

and the tugboat with a chest like a bulldog

3.16 *Put this image into Puntila's body, as if he instinctively identifies with the tugboat. Let what your body is doing inform the words.*

This physical impulse is also expressive of Puntila's pride as the owner of all this land: his swelled chest is doubly significant.

The way they float in the cool, clear water

3.17 *Suppose that Puntila's arm is still pointing toward the timber floating on the lake. Let your hand conjure the movement of the logs as they gently bob. Try to be exquisitely accurate: moving too much or too fast will not help the audience see what Puntila sees. The word "float" should be light, buoyant.*

3.18 *Now try the same motion with your whole body. For the moment you are a floating log. Remember that Puntila is drunk. But he does not stagger; Brecht says in his notes that Puntila is a "balletic" drunk. His subtle sway here is doubly expressive — of the floating tree trunks and of his drunken state.*

Ah, the smells we have here in Tavastland

3.19 *Set the scene: Puntila imagines he is on a mountaintop and the air is exhilarating. As you play with this line, fill your lungs. Your nostrils are flooded with sweet scents. Ask your imagination to be specific about what you are smelling.*

and you've had yourself whipped with a big bundle of them

After a sauna, what could be more invigorating than to have an attendant "whip" you from head to foot with a bundle of birch leaves — ohhhh yes!

3.20 *Imagine that as you say this line you are whacked once on the back with the birch leaves. How would your body register the pleasurable sting? Where in the line might you place this event? Speak the line from inside the scene.*

3.21 *Try it again, adding a second blow somewhere else in the line.*

or in the morning as you lie in bed

Here is another scene to set. How might Puntila's body make the new circumstances visible? Your imagination may need to be more specific than the text to inspire truthful actions. What day of the week is it? What's the temperature out? What do you need to say to yourself to make this moment intensely pleasurable in an organic way?

3.22 *Speak the line as if you were luxuriating in bed. Let the energy of this scene come into your voice. Ahhhh, you don't have to get up. What impulses come into your body? Choreograph these with how you speak the line. Keep in mind that Puntila is still drunk, still proudly in love with his land. These circumstances should also find expression in the image of lying abed.*

Setting the scene is very sensuous work. To experience empathetically the successive images that Puntila envisions, the audience must float in the lake, feel the sting of the birch leaves, breathe the mountain air, nestle into the warm bedcovers. It is the specificity and sensory richness of your acting choices that take the audience to these other times and places. Generic, cliché choices are not sensuously specific and do little to set the scene.

Proteus

Proteus was a Greek divinity who could assume different shapes at will. If you wrestled with Proteus, you might find yourself holding the tail of a monkey at one moment, the neck of a bird at the next, and then have water trickling through your fingers. The Elizabethans thought of actors as protean, since they transformed themselves from show to show and even played multiple roles in one performance. Puntila's quick succession of images asks the actor to transform from tugboat to floating log, and to skip from mountaintop to sauna to bed. Learning how to act speeches that tell a story will equip you with the skills to be as protean as the material demands.

Out of Our Fathers' House is a performance piece drawn from the memoirs of historical women, one of whom is the founder of the women's suffrage movement, Elizabeth Cady Stanton, who tells us about the death of her only brother. Because her father was so grieved at the loss of his son, and because as a girl she seemed to be invisible, Elizabeth set out to compensate by studying subjects normally undertaken only by boys — and by winning an academic prize.

Read Excerpts 8 and 9 in Appendix A.

"I recall going into the large darkened parlor." A writer can simply state that she entered a room, but it is impossible for an actor to play such an unspecified action without seeming to be sleepwalking. Given the situation, Elizabeth must have entered the parlor with quite specific energy, but the text does not say *how*. What is the actor to do? She cannot enter neutrally, without making a choice. Once a character is in front of an audience, they will read her face, her body language, and her actions for information about what she is experiencing. The performer must of necessity be more specific than the writer and must make choices that amplify what is on the page. Playwrights depend on this collaboration.

In the following sequence I ask you to enter the room in a variety of ways. One or another of these choices may strike you as more probable than others, but the range of possibilities makes clear the actor's need to interpret and to be specific. You must tell yourself a good story about what you are doing, in precisely what circumstances. Here I will provide the gist of several different stories, on which you may elaborate so as to spur yourself into action.

Give yourself a space to work in. If a door or doorway is available, use it. But coming around a corner or a pillar or a chair can serve as your entrance.

I recall going into the large darkened parlor

3.23 *Imagine that you have been forbidden to go into the room: you are not to disturb your father. You sneak in. You discover the sheets on the mirrors and pictures, the casket, then your father. Your eyes are wide. You barely breathe. Speak the line from inside this particular setting of the scene.*

3.24 *Imagine now that you hate the idea of going into that spooky room, where your brother's body is lying in a coffin, but you have been told you must spend some time with your father. Against your will you* enter. What is different about how you come through the door, about your eyes, about how you react to the changes in the room, about how you say the line?

3.25 Suppose this time that you have had no experience of death and no preconceptions; you have only curiosity. In fact you can't wait to get in there and see for yourself all the odd things you've heard about, and to see how your brother looks — they bought him a new suit! What is the energy of this entrance? How do you move about the room?

3.26 Come in with something for your brother, something you leave with him. Imagine the details of this story for yourself. What's different about your entrance? Say the line not as you enter but as you play out the transaction with your brother.

3.27 Finally, imagine that you have been playing and have broken something that you want your father to fix. You have entirely forgotten about the room and about your father's grief. Rush into the room and let the circumstances change your energy — as you speak the line.

he took no notice of me

3.28 Use a chair as a surrogate for Elizabeth's father. Come up next to it as you imagine young Elizabeth might have. What sort of contact might she have with her father — the chair — as she makes a subdued, subtle effort to get his attention? Try different tactics, different physical contacts.

I climbed upon his knee

3.29 How should you insert yourself in the chair so as to suggest that you are sitting in your father's lap? The adult Elizabeth is not play-acting what happened full out, but her body is remembering the action even as her mind pictures it, and there is something young in how she sits into the chair.

3.30 Precisely how Elizabeth climbs onto her father's knee depends, of course, on how she came into the room in the first place. Go back to two or three of the choices you made about coming into "the large darkened parlor" and follow through on each energy to see how it changes how you get into your father's lap.

my head resting against his beating breast

3.31 *Compose several different "snapshots" for this moment, and speak the line from inside the feel of each. Although playing what happened in the parlor years ago is your focus, your physicality should in each case be quite natural behavior for the older Elizabeth, who is absorbed in memory as she tells her story.*

- *Sit sideways in the chair and put your head against the back of it.*
- *Rest your head on your arms on a table surface.*
- *Put the back of your chair against a wall so that your head can lean back against the wall.*
- *Create a snapshot of your own.*

3.32 *Choose one of the snapshots that you find particularly evocative and do the line one more time. Focus this time on listening to your father's heartbeat, as if it could somehow tell you what is going on inside him.*

Searching for choices that are all your own

An *idiosyncrasy* is a characteristic habit or mannerism that is peculiar to an individual: *idios* is Greek for "one's own" and *syncrasis* means "mixing together"; so an idiosyncrasy is a mix that's all your own (and your character's). Idiosyncratic choices — highly individualized ways of doing things — are one way to grab an audience's attention and convince it that your character is indeed a particular human being.

In William Hanley's *Slow Dance on the Killing Ground*, a young woman, pregnant and unmarried, tells the story of losing her virginity to a boy she didn't really like in a dusty attic — and her grandmother walks in right in the middle of it! Rosie's account is both funny and awful. It is introduced by a wistful vision of a different version of her life.

Read Excerpt 5 in Appendix A.

the sounds coming through the window

The setting for this play is a little corner store in New York City. This moment might be played at the store's window, but we will explore a different approach to setting this scene.

3.33 Using a chair, compose several different snapshots of Rosie looking out the window of her imagined apartment in Bohemian, very un-middle-class Greenwich Village. In how many different ways can you use the chair (and how you relate to it) to create an illusion that you are looking out a window? Your physical choices should not be blandly generic but very specific, idiosyncratic ways of picturing this character at the window. Speak the line on impulse with the particular energy of each snapshot.

Acting is reacting

"Acting is reacting," an old saw among acting teachers, means that everything you do on stage should be in response to something. Acting is less about what you *do* than about reacting to what is *done* to you.

If acting is reacting, then what about acting a speech that tells a story? Aren't you doing the speech all by yourself — creating all the events and playing all the parts? What can you react to?

Acting a narrative speech requires that you make the story's events happen, so that you can react to them just as you would in a scene with other characters. What spurs you to action inside the story? That is what you must create by setting the scene: what your character reacts to.

Reacting presupposes that what happens matters to your character. It takes weeks of rehearsal to make yourself vulnerable to the events of a play, and the same is true of a narrative speech. You must figure out why the story is important to your character — what is at stake — and position yourself so that what others say and do really matters.

Latin verbs are either active or passive: an action is either performed or received. The Latin verb from which the word "passion" is derived means to "undergo," "experience," "suffer," and it is, as you might expect, a passive verb. A passion is a reaction; so is every emotion. Emotion is another mode of reacting to events.

3.34 Focus on Rosie listening to the sounds coming through the window. What sounds? Make them real, consider what they might mean to Rosie and let her quietly react to them.

the breeze blowing through the curtains over the bed

Is it possible to make the imagined breeze visible? What the audience can see is Rosie's physical response to it. You are looking for idiosyncratic ways of reacting. A shaman uses back flips to make the spirits with whom he is wrestling visible; what you do to make the breeze visible is the same sort of magic, if less acrobatic.

It will help you make specific choices if you set the scene for yourself so as to inspire your imagination and generate impulses. It might be a sweltering August day, for example, or it might be the first day when the air feels like spring and the window has been shut all winter.

Another approach would be to tell yourself the story of why this breeze is so important to Rosie. Of all the details that she might have imagined, why this? Perhaps this breeze is the antithesis of all the dust in that attic in suburban New Rochelle, all the suffocating stuffiness of her old life. Here in this fantasy apartment she can finally breathe. This endows the breeze with significance and raises the stakes; it also makes it easier for you to react to the breeze in a specific way.

3.35 Set the scene for yourself. What time of year is it, what time of day? What are the prior circumstances — that is, what happened before this moment and how does that affect how you play it? What do you imagine the breeze means to you? How do you physically react to it? Explore taking that breeze into your body. Try several different choices.

3.36 Rosie imagines this Greenwich Village apartment as an alternative to the dusty attic in which she lost her virginity, and the breeze is blowing through the curtains "over the bed" — which perhaps implies that this fantasy is subliminally a love scene. Even if you do nothing that would explicitly tell an audience you are with a lover, speak the line from inside the romantic scene you imagine. This is another approach to making the scene sensuously specific.

Exploring Many Different Ways to Play a Moment

In Chapter 1 we looked at several moments in the Juliet soliloquy which culminates in her taking the potion. We were already working on what we now call setting the scene.

Alack, alack, is it not like that I, so early waking

We imagined then that as Juliet spoke this line she opened her eyes, and we noted that in this context such an action would have a double significance. In the other time and place, Juliet wakes in the tomb; in her bedchamber, here and now, her eyes open in terrified realization.

There are, of course, other ways to act the waking up. Let us look at a few of them. As you explore each of these choices, keep in mind the secondary meaning of the action: Juliet is realizing that she might wake up alone in the tomb.

3.37 *Lean your body against a wall, which will serve for the moment as a bed. As Juliet wakes, let your head come away from the wall. Investigate different rhythms for both the line and the action.*

3.38 *Still against the wall, place one arm across your eyes, as people sometimes do while sleeping. As you speak the line, uncover your eyes. Choreograph this action with the line.*

3.39 *Lie on the floor. Cover yourself with a blanket or a substitute. As you speak the line, pull the blanket off you as if you were about to get out of bed. What's the quick version of this — as if she suddenly woke up? What's the rhythm if it is slowly dawning on her that she will wake up in the tomb?*

3.40 *This time, pull the cover over you as if to hide or protect yourself.*

3.41 *Imagine that Juliet sits straight up in bed. Then try sitting up slowly.*

3.42 *Explore one new way to play this moment. Play your action so that it is both a waking up and a panicky realization.*

Conscious and "Unconscious" Storytelling

A character may or may not be aware that he or she is physically re-experiencing events while telling a story. Sometimes we quite deliberately demonstrate or play-act what happened. At other times, our bodies remember and relive events without our being aware of it.

Imagine, for example, that Billy the Kid is eating a spaghetti dinner while telling the story of Gregory and the chicken. This admittedly absurd context gives the actor a new vocabulary of possible actions.

digs the beak into his throat, straightens legs and heaves a red and blue vein out

3.43 In a conscious version, Billy sticks his fork into the spaghetti and lifts a few strands with a deliberateness that clearly means "It happened like this." He might even tug at the spaghetti a couple of times to convey that the chicken had a hard time pulling it out. Try this, focusing on the intention of showing your audience what happened. Both audience and performer pretend, of course, that the spaghetti is a fortuitous circumstance: we imagine that Billy is improvising and that this action is a spontaneous impulse.

If Billy is, on the other hand, totally oblivious of the grotesque coincidence, the action will likely strike people as funny — especially if he does not seem seriously affected by what happened. Lack of consciousness (and consequently of control over events) is one ingredient of farcical comedy.

But there is another possibility, one in which some part of the storyteller knows, below the level of awareness, that there is a relationship between the spaghetti and the vein, between the tomato sauce and the blood.

A metaphor for what is conscious and "unconscious"

The very word "unconscious" implies a clearly defined boundary between what is and what is not conscious. Actors would do better to think of consciousness as a pool of softly focused theatrical light on an otherwise dark stage. What we call awareness is centered at the "hot spot," where the light is most intense. Actions which are premeditated or deliberate are brightly lit. Each step away from the center makes awareness dimmer. On the very edge of what we call consciousness, motives and feelings lurk in shadowy half-light. Energies farthest from the light are barely discerned, but we sense their presence.

> This metaphor is actually closer to the reality of consciousness than the notion that the unconscious mind is like a locked cellar. The French philosopher John-Paul Sartre criticized Freud's theory of repression with a very logical question. If I am really keeping a certain thought shut out of my consciousness, how can I know what to repress unless I am conscious of it? Sartre concluded that the "unconscious" does not exist.
>
> This means that *nothing we do is really unconscious*. There is no place on stage which is not to some degree illuminated by that pool of light called consciousness. There are only degrees of awareness.

3.44 Billy is deep inside the story of Gregory's death, reliving it. As he tells about the chicken pulling out the vein, he lifts a forkful of spaghetti to his mouth. This action is no coincidence. Without his being aware of it, Billy's hand is making the connection between the spaghetti and the vein — "unconsciously," as we say. Try this: your action is perfectly in synch with the text.

If you intend to make your hands (or any other part of your body) do something that your character is unaware of, don't look at the action. The clearest indication that a character is aware of something is that he or she looks at it.

Suppose you interrupt Billy as he lifts the spaghetti to his mouth and ask, "Do you see what you're doing?" He might quite honestly reply, "What I'm *doing*? What are you talking about?" But if he looks down at his fork, a light bulb will go off and he will become aware of the significance of his action. The next exercise focuses on this transition from "unconscious" to "conscious": Billy's action moves from the shadowy edge of consciousness into the hot spot of conscious awareness.

3.45 As he digs into the spaghetti and lifts it to his mouth, Billy is engrossed in his story. His hand is playing the scene, but at first he is not aware of this. At some point he realizes what he is doing. How does he react once he makes this discovery?

There is another way to think about this moment. At first Billy's mind is preoccupied with what is happening in the other time and place, which is why he is so oblivious of what is going on here and now with the spaghetti. When his mind is brought back to what he is eating, he becomes aware of a connection between the two worlds, one which his body had already made.

A Preview: Putting the Story Together

So far we have focused only on moments. Eventually, of course, moments need to be connected and shaped so the story flows. We will focus on this process in Chapters 11-14. By way of preview, let's look quickly at a short sequence of moments to suggest how an actor might put them together.

In Appendix B, read Speech 13.

When Oberon and Titania, the Fairy King and Queen, first encounter each other in *A Midsummer Night's Dream,* they resume an argument which has resulted not only in their separation but in bad weather and failed crops. Their disagreement is about a young boy in Titania's entourage; Oberon wants him as his own squire. In this speech, by way of explaining her refusal, Titania tells a story which explains why she won't part with the boy.

I have seen a number of productions which left audiences in the dark about why that little boy is so important to Titania. How could that happen? Because many actors make the mistake of playing what they perceive to be Titania's emotion instead of the story. Since she is having an argument with her husband, they play her angry.

3.46 Do a bit of the speech as if you were in the middle of a rip-roaring argument. Then try some more of it as if Titania were keeping a lid on her anger: her quiet fury is icy.

What does this give the audience? That Titania is angry, but not why. It is true that she is engaged in a dispute, but her answer to Oberon takes the form of a story, and that is what must be acted. Emoting on one note misses the other colors that a straightforward exploration of the story would bring to life. The boy's mother, Titania explains, was "a vot'ress of my order" — that is, she had taken a religious vow and attended on Titania. "And in the spicèd Indian air by night / Full often hath she gossiped by my side ..."

gossiped

3.47 Play with "gossiped" as if the word itself were a juicy bit of gossip. Make specific choices: gossip about what? Are you talking about family secrets, romance, an embezzlement, something funny or shocking or infuriatingly typical?

And sat with me on Neptune's yellow sands

3.48 They used to sit together on the beach. Imagine that right now Titania is sitting on the ground. Her hands or feet remember the sand; her face feels the sun, the ocean breeze. Set the scene, and speak the text from inside it.

Marking th'embarkèd traders on the flood

3.49 They sat there observing ("marking") the ships ("traders") which have taken on cargo and passengers (and are therefore "embarkèd") in preparation for their voyage across the sea ("the flood"). What are Titania and her votress so busy watching, do you suppose? Remember that they like to gossip, so you might provide them with an intriguing cast of captains and merchants and strangers to tattle about. Be specific so that your interest is not generic. Who is exceedingly handsome or scandalously crooked or fabulously rich, and how might these different choices affect how you say the line? Explore gestures and movements that make visible how they used to point out ships to one another. Such gestures might be fully played as if happening now, or they might be more tentative, as if they were echoes of the original actions.

When we have laughed to see ...

3.50 If you played a wash of anger, you would miss here the good times which bonded Titania with the boy's mother. At least an echo of laughter ought to color this line; it is even possible that what Titania remembers makes her laugh aloud. Play with several degrees of laughter in Titania's voice.

So what were they laughing about, there on Neptune's yellow sands?

When we have laughed to see the sails conceive
And grow big-bellied with the wanton wind

As the sails catch the wind, they grow as big-bellied as pregnant women. Someone (who?) has wittily remarked that the wind is pretty promiscuous ("wanton") to have made so many sails "conceive." And since Titania's votress is pregnant with the boy in question, we may assume that the joking compares her big belly with the sails.

3.51 Play with this scene. The laughter now should have a very specific tone. What sorts of gestures might have accompanied this bawdy joking? What can you do to make the joke visible to your audience?

Which she with pretty and with swimming gait
Following, her womb then rich with my young squire

3.52 What does the votress look like as she sails upon the land? Remember that she is pregnant; if they are joking about her belly looking like a ship's sail, she must be quite far along and moving low in the water, weighed down by the "cargo" in her womb. There may in fact be a witty tension between the brisk lightness of "Which she with pretty and with swimming gait" and the heaviness of the mother-to-be's movement, but the joke is lost if the audience cannot see and hear the contrast. Explore how Titania might playfully accentuate it.

Fading into and out of the story

In many narrative speeches, a character gradually journeys into the story. As Titania begins this speech, she is in the same time and place as Oberon and the rest of her audience. She may have a toe or a foot or a leg in the other time and place — to the degree that she is already in touch with what happened to the boy's mother. But the first moments in her story are not likely to be relived as vividly as later ones, because she is still much more *here* with us than she is *there*, inside the story. Let's say that Titania is 90% here, 10% there as she begins her narrative. At this point, her actions faintly echo what happened. As she gets more "into it," more inside the story, the percentages change to 70/30, 50/50, 40/60, and so on. Each successive moment seems more present than the previous; what was past becomes more and more *now*.

At the climax of her story, Titania approaches being 100% in the other time and place: she is wholly absorbed in reliving what happened. The Titania actor will play this moment with the same immediacy as she would act any critical event in the play. As she finishes, Titania returns to the here and now, though a percentage of her may linger a while in the events of the story.

In this way, a character may fade into and out of a story. Imagine, for example, that Titania weaves her way through her fairy retinue toward Oberon as she begins to speak about the boy's mother. Her mouth happens to pass quite near Mustardseed's ear just as she says "gossiped": this bit of blocking, in combination with how she speaks the word, might delicately suggest a moment of gossip. Then, quite spontaneously and with no apparent intention to play-act, Titania might sit next to Peaseblossom in a position that supports her line about being on the beach; now she is a bit farther into reliving her relationship with the boy's mother. Her next action, which gestures out toward the ships, takes her still more deeply into the other time and place, and the laugh — which she might share with her attendants — is yet another step inside the story. By the time she jumps to her feet to do the "swimming gait" she is quite far in. "But she, being mortal, of that boy did die" is the quiet climax: here Titania is fully in the other time and place, perhaps watching her votary die just after giving birth, perhaps remembering how she held the baby in her arms as his mother was buried. The next two lines would slowly bring her back to the here and now of her encounter with Oberon.

That is one among many possible versions of the story. Another actor might start the speech with her arms around the boy, and play it with him as a surrogate partner — as if she were telling him once again the story that brings his mother to life.

Guidelines for Work on Setting the Scene

A narrative approach to speeches that tell a story is quite objective and craft-centered. Your task in rehearsal is to explore how you might make the events of the story visible. As you explore a moment like "the breeze blowing through the curtains over the bed" in Rosie's Greenwich Village fantasy, you can ask yourself: if I were in the audience and saw the action that I'm playing now, would it make me feel the breeze? The goal is quite concrete.

Work at getting yourself *inside* each moment. For now, you should assume that a character is reliving events in the other time and place quite fully.

Speak the text from inside the moment you are playing. What you say should not be a voiceover spoken by a neutral narrator; everything you say should be spoken from the point of view of one of the characters in the story.

Consider the advantages of each possible point of view.

Explore freely, in all directions.

Search for *actions*. Explore physical choices that make visible and audible and palpable the circumstances and events of each moment. Conjure the where, the when, precisely what happened. Your actions should be so sensuously expressive of events that your audience vicariously experiences them.

Work at *specificity*. The more specific you make each action, the more vividly you set the scene and the more deeply you place yourself inside the story. Choices which are generic, cliché, or superficial will not stir your imagination — or that of your audience. God, as they say, is in the details.

An *idiosyncratic* choice helps to make a moment your own.

Remember that acting is reacting. Everything you do in performance should be a response to circumstances and events. You must make them so real that they get to you.

Rehearse until you can play a moment full out. Terrific performances are built of terrific moments. Memorizing the brief text for each exercise will free you to act.

Where in your body might you make visible each particular event? Explore several different physical choices for each moment. Get your whole body involved.

Everything you do in terms of reliving the story should be believable behavior in the here and now of telling the story. At the same time you should be bold in your choices: theatrical storytelling extends the borders of realism, and characters reliving stories enter an altered state of existence.

Be on the lookout for choices which are doubly significant — that is, moments which have meaning in the here and now as well as in the other time and place — such as the moment when Juliet's breath quickens as she imagines being stifled in the tomb and grows panicky in her bedroom (see 1.3).

For each moment you work on, consider to what degree the character is aware of reliving events. Are some actions deliberately demonstrated? Is the character not conscious of an action which his or her body remembers?

As you play with moments, explore and exploit the possibilities of the space you are working in: the corners and levels, the windows and doorways, the furniture, etc. You shouldn't confine your work to the empty space in the middle of a room. Work in a variety of locations, and let the architecture and furnishings of each environment supply you with impulses.

Practice in Setting the Scene

Very early in *Curse of the Starving Class*, after a couple of pages of dialog, Wesley tells us how his father came home drunk last night and kicked in the kitchen door trying to get in the house: that accounts for the wood Wesley is throwing into the wheelbarrow as this speech begins.

Read Speech 7 in Appendix B.

Swaying very quietly like they were being blown by someone's breath.

3.53 *Work on two contrasting versions of this moment. Explore several locations and a variety of physical positions. Put the motion of the model planes in different parts of your body.*

• *What other point of view besides Wesley's might you explore?*

• *Precisely how do the planes move? Try to conjure the quality of their movement. It should not be too fast or too much. Explore how the swaying might vary in direction and rhythm.*

• *Presumably the planes are set in motion by drafts in the room. But might it be "someone's breath" which move the planes? Whose? This is a direction you might explore in one version of this moment.*

• *How might your voice and the way in which you speak the words help you to conjure this image? Pay particular attention to "quietly," "blown," and "breath."*

I listened like an animal. My listening was afraid. Afraid of sound. Tense.

3.54 What is animal-like about Wesley's listening? The text gives no details about what kind of animal, in what circumstances. Set the scene for yourself by playing specific choices that make visible how Wesley's description of the moment is truthful.

In the novel *Pedro Páramo*, everyone in the village knows that Dorothea is barren and cannot accept the fact. She carries around a stick wrapped up in cloth; this is her son. One day Dorothea loses her child and is distraught. That night she has a dream in which she goes up to heaven to look for her son. An angel reaches inside her and pulls out her shriveled womb.

Read Excerpt 10 in Appendix A.

[He] sank his fist deep into my stomach.

3.55 Is this a kindly angel engaged in an act of mercy? Or a hellfire-and-brimstone accusatory angel? Or is the angel's energy as blank as his face? Explore.

3.56 When the fist goes into Dorothea, does it go in easily, or does it have to force its way in? Is the action gentle or violent? Once in, does the hand go right to her womb or does it search about? Does it pluck the womb like a grape or tear it out? Explore.

3.57 What is Dorothea's reaction? Does this hurt? Or is the contact with a supernatural being somehow ecstatic? Does she know what the angel is doing or not? If she does know what he is doing and why, is she ashamed? embarrassed? angry? in grief? Explore.

3.58 Work on three versions of this moment:
* *from the point of view of Dorothea;*
* *from the point of view of the angel;*
* *from both points of view — either simultaneously or in sequence.*

Explore several different ways of combining the two points of view.

For Your Own Speech

Explore three moments of setting the scene with texts chosen from the excerpts in Appendix A. So that you can explore without text in hand, work with no more than a sentence or two.

Guidelines

Aim for *sensuous specificity*. The more specificity you give each moment — the more detail you create to make visible what happened — the more vividly you conjure the event for us. Sensuous acting choices have a sensory effect on audiences — and on you.

The most important task is to get inside the story. Inside the story you are free to play. In rehearsal, being inside the story positions you to discover details and actions not spelled out in the text. In performance, being inside makes it possible for you to play the events as if they were really happening. To make the events happen now, in the theatrical present, is the whole point of telling the story. Your goal is to give us the events themselves.

You should strive to develop an outside eye for your acting choices, so that you can step back from your work and assess it, just as a writer or visual artist must. If you saw what you just did from the audience, would it make you see and vicariously experience what happened at that moment in the story?

Needless to say, the room for interpretation is considerable. If a group of actors were to work on the same moment, you would see a range of choices, some quite different from your own version, and there might be a couple that you feel you *never* would have thought of. This is a cause not for dismay or self-doubt but for celebration of the diversity of actors and acting possibilities: acting (like life) would be a dull business if everyone thought like you. Each choice, hopefully, has its own merits.

Continue your search for possible speeches

If you have been looking only at contemporary U.S. materials, consider looking at an anthology of selections from the classics, a collection of British or Canadian speeches, or plays by a European author. There are anthologies of speeches from Shakespeare, Molière, Shaw, Wilde, Chekhov. See Appendix D.

If you choose a speech from Shakespeare or one of his contemporaries, see Appendix C for an outline of the work you should do on the text before getting on your feet.

Don't neglect the Greeks, especially the messenger speeches, in which you get to play all the parts, stage battles, witness miracles, and perhaps die a couple of horrible deaths.

There are books of Neo-Classical speeches, 19th-century speeches, speeches adapted from literature, speeches from plays written by women, speeches from African-American plays.

Think about nondramatic fiction that you really like. You may decide to work on a speech drawn from literature.

There are short prose pieces by Sam Shepard in *Hawk Moon*, and contemporary monologs by Eric Bogosian, David Cale, Spaulding Gray, Gus Edwards (*Monologues on Black Life* and a sequel), and others. There are four strong monologs for women by Nobel Prize winner Dario Fo and his wife Franca Rame in *Female Parts*.

Think about nonfiction narratives, such as the monologs shaped by Anna Devere Smith from her interviews: *Fires in the Mirror* (about the conflict between African-Americans and Hassidic Jews in a Brooklyn neighborhood) and *Twilight: Los Angeles, 1992* (about the L. A. riots and their aftermath).

One year, two of my students worked on slave narratives, which proved to be terrific material.

There are a lot of directions to go in. Stay open. Ask around.

Remember that you will be as good as your material.

Chapter 4
Implicit Scenes

Up to this point we have been exploring texts which are explicit about events: a chicken paddles out to a dying cowboy, hops on his neck, pulls a vein out — all that is terribly explicit. A story is being told, and the gist of what happened is clearly stated.

Here's a text from Athol Fugard's *Hello and Goodbye*, in which Johnny is telling his sister Hester — who's been out of touch for a long time — about his efforts to get their invalid father to eat:

"He's thin. Skin and bone. He won't eat. I try all sorts of delicacies. Sardines on toast. Warm buttered toast with the silver little fishes ... "

Johnny does not appear to be telling a story; no events are explicitly described.

But a scene is *implied*, complete with objective and action. At least once Johnny tried to coax his father to eat by bringing him sardines on toast.

Sardines on toast. Warm buttered toast with the silver little fishes ...

4.1　*Suppose that Johnny is remembering a particular occasion when he entered his father's room with a plate of sardines on toast. Is this an old favorite of his father's, or is it something entirely new? It will make a difference in how you say the line. How might the first sentence be different in tone from the second? Imagine that Johnny comes through the door with a tray and grandly announces the menu: "Sardines on toast!" Then, as he sets the plate in front of his father, he tries to tempt him, making the food sound as mouth-wateringly delicious as possible. Play this scene full out as you think it might have happened.*

4.2　*Now imagine that you are sitting at a kitchen table across from your sister as you remember this occasion. Your voice echoes how you said the line in the real event. Perhaps your hand extends as if you were offering him the plate. (Since you are sitting at a kitchen table, you could easily manage to have a plate available to you as a prop for this little scene.) This gesture might be unconscious or it might be a deliberate effort to show your sister the kinds of efforts you've* made. *Explore these possibilities for reliving the implicit scene as you talk to your sister.*

He's thin. Skin and bone. He won't eat.

4.3 *Johnny is fretting about his father. That is happening now, as he speaks, but it has been going on for a long time — he is trying to make that clear to his sister, and he is reliving what he has been through since she last visited home. In what circumstances in the past might Johnny have worried about his father like this? Where might he have been? At what time of day? What might he have been doing? Because Johnny is not at all explicit about the events implied by what he says, you have considerable latitude in imagining how to set the scene.*

- *Play this line sitting on the edge of the kitchen table late one night. Your father has eaten nothing today. Pound your head as you try to figure out what to cook tomorrow.*
- *Root around in the kitchen cupboards and the fridge, looking for something he might like for lunch.*
- *Sit quietly, pushing around the food on your own plate. You have no appetite yourself, and you're at a dead end.*
- *Go down the aisle in a supermarket. Perhaps you are piling one item after another into your cart. Perhaps you are unable to find anything you haven't tried.*

How might each of these implicit scenes translate into how Johnny behaves now, with his sister? Each of the energies you have improvised can be played, as can many of the actions. He might sit there and fret or play with his food just as he has on many a night, or pace around the kitchen as if he were prowling through a supermarket. He might throw open a cupboard to show his sister all the delicacies he's tried and even start to pull things out, as he has in the past. The possibilities for setting the scene are essentially the same as for texts which are explicit about what happened. If you play the scene implied by Johnny's words, you position him — and yourself — to relive the events that make what he says concrete and specific.

I try all sorts of delicacies. Sardines on toast.

4.4   You might decide that yet a third scene is implied here, as a transition from the fretting scene to the coaxing scene. Let's call this the "getting-the-idea scene." On "I try all sorts of delicacies," work at trying to think of something your father might find appetizing. And then let the new idea well up: how about sardines? On toast, maybe! Note how this turns this statement into an event and makes the moment feel very present.

In a text that did not at first seem narrative, in which no events are explicitly described, we have found that a sequence of scenes is implied. These implicit scenes can be explored in search of actions, which can be played in much the same way as moments that are expressly mentioned in a story. In this way the skills learned from acting stories can be applied to texts that are not essentially narrative. A keen nose for the scenes implied by texts is invaluable to an actor.

Let's look at a spectrum of texts which might not seem at first glance to suggest scenes to play. If one or another of these *does* strike you as being explicit about playable actions, then you are ahead of the game. One actor's implicit is another actor's explicit: the border between the two is not a thin, hard line but a zone which different actors will perceive differently. But the sum of these examples will clarify what is meant by "implicit" scenes.

When Rosie talks about the Greenwich Village apartment of her dreams, she imagines the sounds "of traffic and people" coming through the window (Excerpt 5 in Appendix A). This little detail implies a wide range of possible scenes.

and people

4.5   Use a chair to situate yourself as if you were looking out a window (as you did in 3.33). Alternatively, since a storefront window might be part of the set, you might use a real window. Let's imagine a parade of different kinds of "people" on the street below. How Rosie relates to each type might be made visible in her face, her voice, in gesture and movement, even in fantasized interactions. Each time you say "and people," explore how Rosie — who has grown up in stifling New Rochelle and dreams of the bohemian Village — might react to:

- *hippies with outrageous hair dancing in the streets;*
- *actresses who do Off-Broadway plays and might even be in the movies some day;*
- *fascinating, romantic men — so different from the guy who fathered her child;*
- *rebels who openly defy everything Rosie herself hates;*
- *a cop who might be looking for her as a missing person;*
- *and other characters who boggle her mind, scare her, etc.*

Some of these implicit scenes might help you to discover an action: a dance step, a shy little wave, a political gesture such as a fist in the air; others might lead you to specific moods. If you chose to develop this moment, you would have a great deal of latitude in exploring it, because there are no specifics in the text. What would recommend one choice over another is that it fleshes out your particular Rosie and seems truthful for your interpretation of this speech.

Out of the blue, Betty, the central character in John Guare's *Landscape of the Body*, receives a proposal of marriage from Durwood, an ice-cream vendor whom she barely knows. With a spontaneity characteristic of this play, she accepts, and he takes her to South Carolina, where his family has a big farm. Betty's description of what happened as they arrived there is quite explicit. But one phrase about their trip implies a scene and invites exploration.

Read Excerpt 3 in Appendix A.

after what a night at the Olde Dixie Hotel

What a night they had! The question is, what *kind* of a night did they have? The text doesn't say, but an actor, unless she decides that Betty is being deliberately mysterious, must make a choice. It is quite probable that a sexy or romantic tone here would not be far off the mark, but there are many ways to be more concrete in that vein, and there are in fact several other directions that might be explored. The exercise of exploring in all directions also demonstrates how malleable a text becomes in a performer's hands, especially when it is not explicit about details.

4.6   This is a series of fast improvisations about possible implicit scenes. For each of the following, imagine enough specifics to get you on your feet. Speak the line from within each of these scenes, as you play a specific physical action.

- *They danced till the wee hours.*
- *They had no idea what to say to each other.*
- *He kissed her neck over and over.*
- *She couldn't sleep a wink thinking how crazy she'd been to say yes.*
- *They got really drunk.*
- *They got into a huge argument.*
- *They laughed themselves silly.*
- *He said so many sweet things to her.*

Exploring every corner

Not every detail of a story needs to be acted; you must be selective about which details you use in setting the scene. But rehearsal should be an inclusive, wide-open process that investigates all the corners of your speech — including implicit scenes — so that it comes together from a wealth of possibilities. Even details which you choose not to make visible will help you to play a story if you have explored them.

Read Excerpt 18 in Appendix A.

Weston thinks his wife has run off with the lawyer who's been skulking around the property. In a moment he will start ranting about what he's going to do about it, but first he speaks with ominous restraint about how this lawyer fellow will make the mistake of trying to talk things out.

To go out and have a business lunch and talk things over.

In the rush of Weston's rhetoric, one might slide by this text and not catch the scene it implies. It is not that one *must* play out the fantasized business lunch, but one might find in it a nice counterpoint to Weston's simmering rage — and interesting actions.

4.7   Imagine that Weston sits at his kitchen table and starts play-acting the business lunch. He has a good bit of liquor in him, so he will not

> be inhibited. *How might he set the scene for himself? There will only be time for one or two actions: what might they be?*

4.8 *How might the phrase "talk things over" be spoken from within the implicit scene? From whose point of view?*

Weston's drunken threats against his wife and the lawyer are quite explicit. But there is one intriguing detail that suggests several different possibilities.

Read Excerpt 19 in Appendix A.

I'll splatter their brains all over the vibrating bed.

Why a "vibrating" bed? What makes that word pop out of Weston's mouth? It is true that some motels in that period had coin-operated vibrating machines hooked up to the bed, but it is unsatisfying to think that Weston flashes on that for no reason.

4.9 *Each time you speak this line, explore on your feet a different circumstance or action that might trigger "vibrating":*
  - *Weston is shaking with rage;*
  - *he is shivering from grief/loss/hurt;*
  - *as he takes a gun from a drawer, he is so nervous that his hand shakes;*
  - *as he mimes shots which make his hand recoil in quick succession, the overall effect is a kind of spastic vibration;*
  - *he grabs the kitchen table as if it were a bed and he shakes it;*
  - *he grabs his son and shakes him;*
  - *he is thinking of the two of them making love, and he bitterly vibrates his lower body as he says the second half of this line;*
  - *against a wall, he imagines how they will be riddled by his bullets;*
  - *he is filled with such glee at the idea of what he is going to do to them that his celebratory gesture has his whole body vibrating.*

"Vibrating" suggests that something about this moment — something physical and visible — has triggered this word. The different choices you have explored all read back from that word to an action or condition that prompted it. Anticipating what your character is about to say in this manner makes for an organic connection between action and text: what comes out of your character's mouth is a consequence of what s/he is already doing.

Read Excerpt 15 in Appendix A.

Cavale is a tough-talking young woman who grew up with a terrible self-image and has tried to make a virtue of being bad. She has kidnapped Slim with the intention of making him into a rock 'n' roll star. The events of this story are for the most part explicit, but the implications of certain details might be overlooked if one has not developed a finely tuned sense of how narrative may be translated into action.

and get shit flung at me
Many actors might settle for playing how Cavale feels about this incident and fail to investigate the event. Cavale's expletive doesn't really tell us *what* got thrown at her. Nor are the circumstances spelled out. What might you discover by exploring what it is not spelled out here? Sensitivity to what might be implied makes you alert to a world of possibilities and enables you to dig deeper, in search of what really happened.

4.10 *You are young Cavale playing the ugly duckling, and the other kids start throwing things at you — perhaps crumpled up newspaper, with a few other objects maliciously included by some of your classmates. Say the line as you imagine that:*
   • *this is the first rehearsal of this scene and you are shocked;*
   • *this is opening night and the audience starts to laugh;*
   • *you start ducking and dodging;*
   • *you stand there frozen and wads of newspaper bounce off you;*
   • *you pick up a couple of paper "rocks" and fling them back;*
   • *someone hits you with a handful of something gross and you wipe it off;*
   • *you cannot look anyone in the eye and hang your head in shame;*
   • *you look them all defiantly in the eye so they won't suspect you're hurt;*
   • *you tear off part of your costume as if to quit;*
   • *you react in other active ways that occur to you.*

Read Excerpt 9 in Appendix A.

Whenever an event is described in general terms, you must collaborate with the writer by investigating the circumstances and events that the text implies. You must often be more specific than the text. In order to act statements like "I didn't feel good" or "We fell in love," you must make the generality specific by exploring the scene that it implies.

When Elizabeth Stanton tells us that "I strove for one and took the second," we know what happened, but none of the particulars. How did she strive? What did she do? In what circumstances did she win the prize? What really happened? Surely something more particular than Elizabeth earnestly plucking an imaginary prize out of the air — an action just as unspecific as the line. You cannot *act* generalities. You need to set the scene, and since the text gives you no details, you have lots of room to explore.

I strove for one

4.11 How might you play this "striving" if you set the scene in a classroom? In this implicit scene, you might explore:
- *raising your hand with the eager energy of one who knows the answer;*
- *speaking the line as if you were very carefully conjugating a Greek verb for the teacher.*

4.12 If you set the scene late at night in your room, you might explore:
- *bleary-eyed exhaustion as you memorize;*
- *confusion as you flip back and forth between a difficult Greek sentence and your dictionary;*
- *frustration and despair about an upcoming exam that leads you to fling your book across the room.*

4.13 Suppose that the mention of academic prizes had led you to set the scene at a graduation ceremony. You are sitting with your classmates on the auditorium stage in cap and gown, and they are just now announcing the winners of the two prizes in Greek. Play Elizabeth as she listens to the principal describe the prize on which she set her sights. "The award for General Excellence in Hellenic Studies is given to that student who ... blah blah blah. And the winner this year is ... "
In this suspended moment how do you say, "I strove for one"? How

do you sit in your chair? Suppose that your body starts to rise of its own accord.

and took the second
4.14 "And the winner of the award this year is ..." — not you. Set the scene: get inside the precise moment of hearing this. How might "and took the second" be spoken? What happens in your body?

I strove for one and took the second. One thought alone filled my mind. "Now," said I, "my father will be satisfied with me."
The bad news is that you didn't get the prize you had aimed at. The good news is that you won not second prize but a different one — let's say it's an equally prestigious award for the best translation of a Greek poem, which will be published in the school magazine, etc. Perhaps it had not occurred to you that you could win this. In a moment you will be racing to show the prize to your father. The story ends happily.

4.15 At the graduation ceremony, play three moments: the expectation, the disappointment mixed with surprise, and then the welling up of joy that your father will now be satisfied with you. I have used words that refer to emotional states, but your job as an actor is to translate these into actions. Speak the text as if you were 100% within the other time and place; let every event be played out in your body.

In order to speak this line truthfully, you have to do some exploration of the scene (or scenes) which it implies. To what extent should you play actions from the implicit scene when you perform this moment? That is an aesthetic judgment call. At one end of the spectrum you might choose to internalize the implicit scene — that is, play its events and actions inwardly, speaking the text as if you were in the circumstances you imagine, although they remain wholly invisible. In such a case the audience perceives your energy, even if it is unaware of the implicit scene which is generating it.

The bolder, more theatrical choice is to play what is implicit as if it were explicitly described in the text. Sometimes an implicit scene can be played quite fully. It is also possible to play one significant moment from an implicit scene — the scene in a nutshell — without acting out all of its circumstances. The audience need not know that you are at a graduation ceremony in order for you to rise slowly from your chair as you relive the moment when you won a prize.

Similarly, you might play the exhaustion and self-doubt of late-night study for "I strove for one" without any physical choices that make the implicit scene explicit. The audience doesn't have to see pages turned or exercises written out. On the other hand, you might effectively play actions discovered in improvising the implicit scene — for example, clenching your teeth, rubbing your temples, wringing your hair, agitatedly tapping on a table top, or flinging down a book. Whether played full out or more faintly, as echoes of what happened, choices such as these can stand on their own.

Actors must learn how to sniff out implicit scenes, because inside them are actions. Hunting for details that inspire action should become a habit. When you are working on a speech that tells a story, search for everything that happened. Thinking about your material in terms of implicit scenes will lead you to moments that are not spelled out in the text.

Jon Lipsky's *Living in Exile* imagines the nine years which lead up to the events of the *Iliad*. A narrative speech tells the audience what it was like for the Greeks to be living in exile as they laid siege to Troy. It was quite a roller coaster ride.

Read Speech 3 in Appendix B.

By the sixth year, the Greeks had become forgetful.

The face of that old friend ... That well-known maneuver ...
This is wonderfully elliptical storytelling. Lipsky, whose plays are full of stories, knows that an actor can get inside the two scenes implied here and play specific circumstances which make sense of the lines.

4.16 Where are you when you forget the face of that old friend? What is the occasion for talking about him? Who is he? What happens to you when you realize you cannot picture his face? Your reaction might go in quite a number of different directions, perhaps several at once. Speak the first half of this text as if you were in the very instant of not being able to remember.

4.17 Set the scene for the second half of the line: where are you and when? What are you doing as you realize you have forgotten? How do you react? Your response here should be distinct from the previous moment. It should also build on it, so that the audience has a sense of Patroklos living through a series of forgetful moments as the sixth year progresses.

Read Speech 8 in Appendix B.

Weston tells his son quite explicitly what he experienced when he went for a walk on the farm. Both the real and the imagined events are clearly stated. Then he talks about the land. It's not fancy, he says, but it's peaceful.

It's real peaceful up here.
This line seems merely descriptive. But the actor, ever in search of actions and moments to play, will see that it implies a scene, and that it is part of the story of what happened that morning.

4.18 *Where is Weston as he takes in the peacefulness of his land? We know that it is early morning, so you can imagine the air, the light, the birdsong, etc. Place him somewhere very specific — on the fence out front, under the willow tree, on a boulder out in the brook — and let this location shape your body. Now translate this same image into the kitchen where he is talking to his son: he might be up on a counter, in a window, against the fridge, etc. But at this moment it is truer to say that Weston is somewhere outside rather than in the kitchen. He might even be 100% in the other time and place of the implicit scene. Your physical position should embody peacefulness, so that when you come to this point in your performance, it is perfectly truthful to say the line.*

Metaphors as Implicit Scenes

A metaphor is an implied comparison: something is spoken of as if it were another, different thing because the two share certain qualities or properties.

All the world's a stage,
And all the men and women merely players.
They have their exits and their entrances,
And each man in his time plays many parts,
His acts being seven ages. (Speech 11, Appendix B)

When Romeo first sees Juliet in the balcony scene (II.ii), only metaphor can express how dazzled he is: "What light through yonder window breaks? It is the east, and Juliet is the sun." What a metaphor says is that this moment — what I'm seeing, what I'm feeling, how I'm behaving right now — is like another moment, another time and place, another kind of person. Particularly when an experience is so new or unique or intense that ordinary words fail us, characters resort to metaphor.

Metaphor is not simply poetic language for heightened occasions; it is, quite fundamentally, how we think. It is the essential act of art — plays and novels, for example, are metaphors of experience — and science imagines metaphors for the structure of the universe, the atom, the psyche, etc. Creativity of every sort is generated by metaphorical insights. Suzanne Langer's *Philosophy in a New Key* proposes that metaphor is the basis of all knowing.

Humans are wired to think metaphorically, and growing up gives us lots of practice. In everyday life we often use metaphor or simile (a metaphor made explicit by the use of words such as *like* or *as*) to compare an experience of something new with another experience more familiar. Perhaps we have met a person unlike anyone we've ever known: "She's so different," we say, "she's like ... " And we search for something to liken her to. Metaphor is how we attempt to articulate what we can't quite capture with conventional categories and everyday labels. When we are at a loss to explain how we reacted to an event, we grope for words: "It was as *if* ..." "I felt as *though* ..." Maybe a childhood memory comes to mind, or a photograph, or the lyric of a song. Or we may fantasize a set of circumstances and in this way create an original metaphor.

Metaphor happens not only when we are confronted by the new, but when we try to express old truths in fresh ways. And metaphors can talk about the mysteries when ordinary words fail us.

In all these cases we resort to metaphor of necessity. Metaphor is no artsy frill, without which we would be forced to speak the plain truth. It captures what cannot otherwise be said. Inspired metaphors are not so much fanciful as true. If X is really like Y, there is an *actual resemblance*, which the metaphor helps us to see. When Phil goes home to visit his parents, let's say, he sits there as if he were doing calculus problems in his head. If this metaphor has validity, then Phil's behavior really is like that, and to act Phil in these circumstances, one might truthfully play this metaphor. Imagine a girl en route to her first prom who comes out in her finery to say goodbye to Dad. He is surprised and oddly embarrassed; she feels shy but is pleased by his stammered compliments. Two actors might play this scene as if it were the first date of two young people attracted to each other, without implying an Electra complex (itself a Freudian metaphor for what daughters feel for their fathers).

Metaphor is a habit of mind essential for actors and can be applied to all areas of acting work. Ask yourself, with respect to anything you are working on: what is this *like*? What is this situation like? What is this movement like?

My character is like …

Our relationship is like …

This scene is like …

This moment is like …

This touch, this turn, this look is like …

Metaphors give actors much more than insight. Actors are looking for *actions* to play. Metaphors can be *acted*; exploring them can discover specific, playable choices that embody the metaphor you have proposed. The prom-bound daughter and embarrassed father, for example, could develop actions for their scene by improvising the nervous behavior at the beginning of a first date. Discovering actions is the bottom line for actors in rehearsal. Any metaphor worth investigating should put you into action. If it doesn't, you must search for one that does.

At the end of his rhapsody about what he imagines seeing from a mountaintop, Puntila exclaims: "Where else do you get such smells? Or a view like this? I like it best when it's hazy," he says; "it's like sometimes when you're making love, you half close your eyes, everything's blurred" (Excerpt 2, Appendix A).

This metaphor sums up Puntila's sensual relationship to his timber-rich land: he not only loves it, his feeling for it is erotic. In a speech which has in quick succession conjured floating logs, the smell of berries, a vigorous massage, and lazing in bed, the scene implied by "it's like sometimes when you're making love" may strike you as yet another time and place to enter and make visible. That is in fact the case, but the metaphorical nature of the scene may blind some actors to the possibility of playing it for real. If Puntila's comparison of looking at his land and making love is true, then playing the metaphor should bring the similarity to life.

73

it's like sometimes when you're making love, you half close your eyes, everything's blurred

4.19 For old time's sake, stand on a chair: you're back on the top of Mount Hatelma. Half close your eyes until the vista is blurry. You are making love; I leave it to your imagination to set the scene. Let the events that you imagine subtly inform your body and voice: we should hear Puntila's erotic pleasure, and we should see it in his drunken sway.

Knowing how to act metaphors is an important skill. Once you have absorbed the narrative perspective of this book, metaphors should seem to suggest actions quite explicitly.

Unpacking a metaphor

Exploring a metaphor requires that we search beyond the resemblance that is immediately apparent, because this is just the tip of the iceberg. A good metaphor has much more to reveal, below the surface, and we need to dive into improvisation to search for all the actions that the comparison implies. I sometimes call this process — here we switch metaphors — "unpacking" the metaphor, as if it were a treasure chest full of potential actions. A *really* good metaphor seems bottomless.

For this reason an actor should acquire the habit of exploring everything that a metaphor might mean. A metaphor is a tool for discovery if you take careful inventory of its specifics. In how many ways might it correspond to what you are working on? If you decide that the relationship of two sisters is like that of a suffering wife and her husband's mistress, for example, how many different transactions, situations, and events might you list for possible exploration in rehearsal? It is useful to investigate as many different ways of playing the metaphor as you can imagine.

---

the breeze blowing through the curtains over the bed, like in them movies (Excerpt 5, Appendix A)

Rosie wishes she had lost her virginity in a nice Greenwich Village apartment with billowing curtains, "like in them movies." In context, it is clear that she is fantasizing about a Hollywood love scene. Rosie's imagination has entered that metaphorical time and place: she is, for the moment, in the movies.

Why would her mind make this leap from "the breeze blowing through the curtains" to the movies? Something has triggered a synaptic connection. One might say that Rosie had seen such an image on the silver screen, but this answer is not satisfying to an actor because it refers to something the audience cannot see, whereas we are in the business of creating actions that make what is happening to a character visible. One might as well say that Rosie mentions the movies because it's the next line. What could an actor *do* to make the reason why movies pop into her head visible? If the metaphor has any truth in it, as we have said, then there must be something really movie-like about the Greenwich Village scene that Rosie has imagined herself in, and we should be able to see it. Rosie may, for example, have settled unconsciously into a pose that feels glamorous or romantic.

4.20 *You have already explored the possibility that Rosie's fantasy of a Greenwich Village apartment is subliminally a love scene (see 3.36). That breeze blowing through the curtains is caressing you and your Hollywood lover. Experiment with physical choices that make this feel like a romantic moment in a movie — that is the other time and place, and it should trigger "like in them movies."*

The romantic moment leads right into the movie moment in a way that makes visible to the audience how and why the character made the transition. Playing what is implied helps to tell the story.

Implicit Versus Explicit

Whether a moment is implicit or explicit is sometimes a troublesome distinction. There is no hard and fast border between the two, only a sliding scale of what is more or less expressly stated. Everyone's threshold for perceiving what is implied is different, moreover, and one person's implicit is another's explicit. There is no sense in splitting hairs. As long as you get inside the moment in question, deciding whether it is explicit or not doesn't really matter. But knowing that a narrative speech almost always contains implicit scenes should encourage you to dig more deeply in search of playable, evocative actions.

An implicit murder

Macbeth is thinking about killing King Duncan in order to take the throne himself. Struggling with his conscience and with his fears, he comes on stage alone.

If it were done, when 'tis done, then 'twere well
It were done quickly." (I.vii)

"It" is the murder, and Macbeth says that if he could get away with it, he would not worry about punishment in "the life to come." But his soliloquy proceeds to spell out the reasons for *not* doing it.

- Imagine an actor who pulls out his dagger at the beginning of this speech and moves downstage as if he were sneaking up on the sleeping king.
- As he finishes the opening section about his willingness to commit the murder, he raises his arm.
- As he starts to talk about how good a ruler Duncan has been, perhaps he kneels reverently, as if brought to his knees by the sight of the venerable old king.
- When he imagines how Duncan's virtues "Will plead like angels, trumpet-tongued" against the murder, perhaps he jumps to his feet as if startled and looks up to the heavens as if the metaphorical angels were becoming real to him.
- Pity for the king, says Macbeth, will "blow the horrid deed in every eye." Perhaps he looks about at the audience as if they were all lords whose eyes accuse him of murder.

None of this is really happening; but the images imply these or similar events, and they might be played so as to make the moral struggle and its specifics more concrete in a dramatic way.

For Your Own Speech

If you are working on a speech by Shakespeare, your initial work on the text should consider the issues outlined in Appendix C. A number of these apply to other sorts of dramatic verse and to "heightened" texts in general. A strong case can be made for applying the skills associated with "classical" texts to all periods: expressive rhythms are embodied in contemporary language in many of the same ways as in verse, for example, and the language of every period needs clear and varied emphasis.

1. Develop five setting-the-scene moments for your speech using short texts, as in your work with the excerpts.

- Investigate precisely *what* happened and *where* and *when.*
- Search for *actions.* Explore physical choices that make visible the circumstances and events of each moment. Your actions should be so *sensuously* expressive of events that your audience vicariously experiences them as if it were right there.
- Work at *specificity.* The more sensuous detail you create, the more vividly you will set the scene and make visible (and audible, palpable, etc.) what is happening. The more specific you are in playing a moment, the more you will be able to imagine yourself inside the story. Choices which are generic, cliché, or superficial will not stir your imagination.
- Work at getting yourself *inside* each moment. For now, you should assume that your character is reliving the events quite fully — that he or she is nearly 100% in the other time and place.
- Speak your text from inside the moment that your character is reliving. What you say should not be a neutral voiceover but something spoken from the point of view of a participant.

2. In addition to the events and actions explicitly mentioned in your speech, there are probably other moments for you to explore inside scenes implied by the text. Develop one or two such moments with a short bit of text.

- Does the text refer to any scenes that are not explicitly described?
- Are there any details — circumstances, actions, events — not mentioned in the text which might help you to conjure what happened in the other time and place?
- Are there any abstractions or generalities that could be made concrete by your playing a more specific scene?
- Do any metaphors imply another time and place?

Guidelines
Memorize each text, so that you are free to act.
Explore freely, in all directions.
Consider the advantages of alternative points of view.
Where in your body might you make visible each particular event?

77

Explore several different physical choices for each moment. Get your whole body involved.

You shouldn't confine your work to the empty space in the middle of a room. Work in a variety of locations, and let the architecture and furnishings of each environment supply you with impulses.

Everything you do in terms of reliving the story should be believable behavior in the here and now of telling the story. At the same time you should be bold in your choices: theatrical storytelling extends the borders of realism, and characters reliving stories enter an altered state of existence.

The most important task is to get inside the story. Inside the story you are positioned to live through the events of another time and place. To make those events happen *here* and *now*, in the theatrical present, is the whole point of telling the story.

To what degree is your character aware of reliving these events? Are some actions deliberately demonstrated? Which details are remembered in the body without conscious awareness?

Be on the lookout for choices which are doubly significant — that is, moments which have meaning in the here and now as well as in the other time and place.

Rehearse so that you can play the moment full out. Terrific performances are built of terrific moments.

Hanging loose

None of the choices made for your speech are written in stone. As is the case in any rehearsal process, initial choices may gradually evolve or change radically; some may endure throughout the process, or return after you have explored other possibilities. Since you are encouraged to investigate how *every* event and detail might be acted, even though some need not be played, it is certain that some choices will be edited out when you are putting your speech together.

Chapter 5
Playing All the Parts: Characterization and Indirect Quotes

Telling a story often means playing multiple roles, and more than one character may speak in a story. Storytellers have exploited both of these possibilities through the ages. They have also developed conventions that permit performers to shift quite easily from one persona and voice to another.

When a story is told in the third person (she said this, he did that) by a narrator, it is possible to speak part of the narrative as if it came from the mouth of one of the characters. A passage that seems on paper to describe an event objectively may in this way be given a particular point of view. This is another route inside a story. The audience, instead of being told what happened by an observer, witnesses the event itself, from the specific perspective of a participant. Narrative becomes event.

We need a vocabulary so that we can talk about what actors do when they play all the parts in a story. In the first place, we must distinguish between being your own character and playing *other* characters.

Characterization

By *characterization* I mean what your character is doing when s/he plays other characters — and what you are doing when you play someone other than your own character. You characterize other people by taking on their physical life, playing out their actions, and reacting to events from their perspective.

Shortly after Hamlet's encounter with his father's ghost, Ophelia comes to her father Polonius in a state: "O my lord, my lord, I have been so affrighted." A disheveled Hamlet, looking quite mad, pale as his shirt and with a piteous expression on his face, had entered her chamber "As if he had been loosèd out of hell/To speak of horrors." In fact he said nothing, but Ophelia tells us exactly what he did.

Read Excerpt 13 in Appendix A.

In a movie, of course, we would expect a flashback to the events in Ophelia's bedroom. Olivier's film does this, with Ophelia's speech as a voiceover; in the Zefferelli version with Mel Gibson, the scene is played silently, without any text. Only in the Branagh film does Ophelia play this speech as Shakespeare intended.

Shakespeare would have had no difficulty in showing us what happened between Hamlet and Ophelia on his bare stage, where the locale changed from scene to scene. He decided instead to give us both Hamlet's behavior and Ophelia's response by way of a narrative speech. This makes the event evern more ambiguous, since we are forced to experience it from Phelia's perspective. To what extent is Hamlet play-acting madness, and to what extent is he genuinely distraught? He has, after all, just learned of his father's murder, but he has also decided that he will protect himself from suspicion by acting mad — and perhaps he is planning to get word of his madness to the king by way of Ophelia and her father.

When Ophelia plays Hamlet in this speech, she gives the audience its first glimpse of his feigned madness. She is also grappling with a very complex moment.

Hamlet grabs Ophelia by the wrist, then backs off to stare at her.

And with his other hand thus o'er his brow

Notice the word "thus," which tells the actor that Ophelia is now playing Hamlet; she is *characterizing* Hamlet, playing out his action.

5.1 *As you speak this line, raise your hand to your brow. Let your facial expression also change to that of Hamlet: piteous, pale, mad — and what else? Try a second version of this gesture, and a third.*

And thrice his head thus waving up and down

Once again the word "thus" assures us that Ophelia is doing what Hamlet did. She is not only showing her father, but she is reliving the event, still processing what happened.

5.2 *Put your hand to your brow and nod your head up and down three times. Do this action as if Ophelia has imagined herself inside Hamlet's skin; she is replaying exactly what he did in an effort to grasp what it meant. Do the action with these very different meanings:*

  • *I think I'm beginning to understand you, Ophelia.*

80

- *Yeah, I'm crazy.*
- *Yes, yes, yes, you are beautiful.*
- *You know why my heart is broken — you refused to see me.*
- *It's the end, it's all over.*
- *I know your kind, you dishonest little liar.*
- *But the nodding is ambiguous. It is not clear to Ophelia what Hamlet means, which is in good part what frightens her. Try combining several of the messages that you've just played: play them simultaneously so that Hamlet is sending mixed signals.*

This characterization is as subtle and as multi-layered as many of the moments that the actor playing Hamlet will play.

Characterization is an integral and natural part of storytelling. It is also something that actors are good at, so it should not surprise us that characterizing is a major tool for actors telling stories. You have in fact been doing a good bit of it already. When you played the chicken and dying Gregory in Billy the Kid's story, you were characterizing them (see 3.1-14). When you explored how Titania's pregnant votary walked "with pretty and with swimming gait," you were characterizing her (see 3.52). Now we can say that the actor playing Nat in *I'm Not Rappaport* is called on in the speech about the strike meeting to characterize young Clara and the head of the union and his father (see Chapter 1). Mercutio characterizes a whole gallery of sleeping characters in the Queen Mab speech (see 1.18-25).

Deciding on a point of view

Sometimes it is obvious that you ought to play a point of view other than your own character's — because that other perspective is more important to the story you are telling. When Billy the Kid talks about the chicken paddling out to Gregory, for example, it would be foolish to play Billy watching; *what* he is watching is much more interesting. Similarly, when Dorothea goes to heaven in her dream, we want to see the angels. But playing Dorothea's point of view might be a useful way to set up your characterization of the angels.

But all the angels' faces were the same blank faces, no expression at all. (Excerpt 10, Appendix A)

5.3   *Start the line as Dorothea and let what she sees drain all expression from her face, so that the line ends in a characterization of an angel's blankness.*

and this real pretty blond-haired girl dressed in a white ballet dress rose up behind me as the swan (Excerpt 15, Appendix A)

Here again it is clear that you should choose one point of view over the other. You *could* play Cavale's reaction as the blond-haired girl rises up behind her. But the alternative — having Cavale characterize the pretty swan — is an important opportunity to glimpse the romantic yearning beneath her bad-girl, rock 'n' roll swagger. Letting Cavale play the swan *now* will let us see how badly she wanted to back *then* — and that she might have done it beautifully. If the audience does not see Cavale as the swan, it will not see why the whole experience was "really shitty," although the way in which the swan appeared was quite the opposite of "shitty."

5.4 *Play Cavale playing the pretty girl as the swan. Let her do it well: we should see that she had it in her then and still does. The text should be as radiant as the image.*

Notice what would be lost if the actor playing Cavale allowed her to be sarcastic here, as if she were looking down on the pretty blond-haired girl and her swan. Quite the opposite is true: Cavale sees herself as the ugly duckling and looks up to the rising swan in awe. What must be exposed is Cavale's vulnerability about her self-image, which sarcasm's pretense to superiority will only mask.

Is it characterization if grown-up Cavale plays herself as a child? The term is best reserved for playing characters other than your own, but in a case such as this the distinction hardly matters.

The choice about point of view is not always so obvious as it is with Cavale and Dorothea. Deciding between playing one's own character or characterizing another is in many cases an aesthetic judgment call. The actor needs to explore the alternative points of view and weigh what is gained and lost with each.

In Wesley's speech about the argument between his parents, he hears his father drive up to the house and turn off the car. "My heart was pounding," says Wesley. "Just from my Dad coming back." There is a long silence. Wesley wonders why his father is just sitting in the car. Then he figures it out.

Why's he waiting to get out? He's plastered and can't move.
(Speech 7, Appendix B)

One choice for the actor playing Wesley would be to stick with his own character's point of view.

5.5 *Imagine Wesley by a kitchen window as he relives this moment. He is careful not to let his father see him. What's going on out there? Speak the second sentence just as the truth dawns on him. Wesley's heart pounds faster.*

If we stay focused on Wesley, we will see that realizing his father is drunk ratchets up his fear and anxiety another notch. Alternatively, Wesley might characterize his father.

5.6 *Wesley has been sitting in a chair trying to figure out what's going on. Sit him forward with his elbows on his knees. As he says the first sentence, he leans back in the chair. Suddenly he gets in, and the answer is in his body, his slack face: he is the image of his father's drunken stupor. Speak the second sentence from his father's point of view. Is Wesley's characterization sympathetic or a mockery of his father? Try it both ways.*

This is a different kind of opportunity to investigate Wesley's relationship with his father. Each of these choices about point of view has its merits.

In a performance piece called *Tongues*, developed by Sam Shepard with Joseph Chaikin, a solo actor speaks on behalf of people in a wide spectrum of circumstances: he gives each of them a tongue. In one speech he imagines that he has just given birth.

Read Excerpt 22, Appendix A.

The first part of this text implies a scene in which expectant mothers are being prepared for childbirth. Should you focus only on the mother-to-be's point of view or might there be something in playing the instructor? One would need to explore both possibilities to see what is gained and lost with each of the choices.

They told me how to breathe. How to relax. How to think about something else.

5.7 *Get on your back and play the mother-to-be in class, trying to do the*

> *exercises. Are you frightened or confident? Do the exercises come easily or not?*
>
> *5.8 Get on your feet now as the instructor. Since the instructor is only implied, you have considerable latitude in characterizing her. Is she an enthusiastic newcomer teaching her first class, a bored old-timer who gets impatient with those who seem unable to relax, a hands-on spirit who whispers reassuringly? Try a couple of different characterizations.*

The actor playing Elizabeth Cady Stanton as she encounters her father grieving over his dead son must also make a choice about point of view.

and my father seated, pale and immovable (Excerpt 9, Appendix A)

> *5.9 Set up a chair as a stand-in for young Elizabeth's father. Imagine that she walks up behind it, taking in her father's energy. Some part of her touches the chair as if she were making contact with her father.*
>
> *5.10 Seat yourself as you speak the line. Begin to sit as Elizabeth but finish as her father.*

Notice how seamlessly Elizabeth can slip into her father's point of view, without calling any attention to the transition.

> *5.11 Sit pale and immovable. This time you are both Elizabeth and her father. In the here and now, Elizabeth is remembering her father; in the other time and place, her father is grieving. How you sit there should embody both points of view at once.*

When you are characterizing, it is often the case that you are playing two points of view — and two personas — at once.

Juliet sends her old Nurse to find out from Romeo when and where they will be married. For three excruciatingly long hours she awaits her Nurse's return.

Read Speech 14, Appendix B.

The couplet that concludes this soliloquy bemoans how long it takes old folks to do anything. The lines themselves move slowly.

But old folks, many feign as they were dead,
Unwieldy, slow, heavy and pale as lead.

5.12 Imagine that impatient young Juliet acts out an extremely old person who crosses to a chair and slowly sits. Be specific about how she moves, about what hurts, etc. Choreograph your movement so that it is in sync with the rhythm of the lines. The language should flow continuously; elongate the words rather than put pauses between them. You should not be fully settled in the chair until the very last word.

Slow movement is also expressive of Juliet's exasperated despair.

5.13 Juliet mopes across the stage and sinks down heavily into a chair. She has been waiting, waiting, waiting. Let her end up "dead" in a manner expressive of her mood in the here and now.

5.14 Play both at once: the character and the characterization.

Sometimes a characterization is a quick sketch. In *Curse of the Starving Class*, Taylor is a lawyer who has been snooping around the farm. Apparently he represents clients interested in the land for a housing development. Wesley spells out for his kid sister what he thinks will happen.

Read Excerpt 16, Appendix A.

There'll be foremen with their sleeves rolled up and blueprints under their arms.

5.15 This is the foremen's only appearance in the play. You might or might not stick something or other under your arm; you might or might not play with your sleeves. It might be more effective to play a moment in the scene implied here. For example:

- *Speak some of the text as if the foreman were yelling orders to workers.*
- *Walk about and clap your hands as if to get your crew back to work.*
- *Pull up your pants as you survey the site and nod appreciatively at the progress.*

This is a cameo appearance, but it needs specificity. A thumbnail sketch doesn't have to be a cliché or a cartoon.

They'll be filing through the doors pretty soon.

The extended metaphor of a zombie invasion is something to have fun with. How often do you get to play a zombie?

5.16 *Play with several versions of a zombie. Experiment at least once with coming through a door.*

But this is a specific breed of zombie: lawyers and developers.

5.17 *If the zombie is a lawyer, how might you make that visible in your characterization?*

5.18 *Return to your characterization of the foreman. In context, he is probably a zombie. Play your score for him in this light.*

Two characterizations in *Romeo and Juliet*, both *metaphorical* in nature, are important clues about how to play the moments in which they are spoken.

In the balcony scene, Juliet says goodnight and goes into her bedchamber. Romeo thinks the encounter is over.

Read Excerpt 12, Appendix A.

Love goes toward love as schoolboys from their books.

5.19 *How does a schoolboy go from his books? The implicit scene is something like the end of the school day: doors fly open and boys run from their books. If Romeo is not just standing there reciting poetry — if this metaphor is truthful — then he must be moving quickly. In what direction? Remember that Juliet has just exited. Let the energy of your movement inform how you say the line.*

But love from love, toward school with heavy looks.

5.20 *In which direction is he moving now? At what pace? In As You Like It, Jacques speaks of a schoolboy "creeping like snail / Unwillingly to school." Here we have the same image. For the moment Romeo moves just that slowly and reluctantly. Let this inform the rhythm of the line.*

5.21 *Now put the two directions and rhythms together in a sequence. This metaphor is charming when enacted; it can even get a laugh.*

Now it is Juliet's turn. She has secretly married Romeo; this very night he will visit her to consummate the marriage. At the end of a soliloquy that urges night to come faster (III.ii), Juliet searches for metaphors that can do justice to her heartfelt impatience.

Read Excerpt 11, Appendix A.

So tedious is this day
As is the night before some festival
To an impatient child that hath new robes
And may not wear them.

This metaphor of an impatient child invites the actor to read backwards from the line to the behavior that must have prompted it. It is because she has been acting like just such a child that Juliet's imagery is truthful.

5.22 Establish the impatient child as specifically as you can. When you are ready, speak this text from inside the scene you are playing.

Read Speech 17, Appendix B, with special attention to the final image.

Macbeth's famous "Tomorrow and tomorrow" soliloquy, spoken in response to the news that his wife is dead, ends with a metaphorical characterization which is so famous and so gorgeously written that we may miss what it really says. We are at risk of hearing it as an abstraction about our fear that life means nothing.

Years ago I saw Sir Ian McKellan doing a one-man show about his experiences acting Shakespeare. At a certain point in the evening, he sat on the edge of the stage and invited the audience to open their programs, where this speech was printed, and to consider with him what each of the images contributed to the speech. He would jump to his feet, for example, to act out the poor player strutting and fretting his hour on the stage. When he came to the last sentence he did an extraordinary thing: he acted full out a village idiot who is in high passion about something or other but who speaks only gibberish. Lots of sound and fury, but it doesn't mean a thing. That is what life is like, the metaphor says; this image wells up in Macbeth because it expresses precisely what he feels as he realizes that the end is near and all is naught. At this moment Macbeth *is* an idiot and anything he says — including this speech — is meaningless.

It is a tale
Told by an idiot, full of sound and fury,
Signifying nothing.

5.23 First play out your version of this image. Be bold in portraying an idiot who is in a dither, practically frothing at the mouth. What comes out of him are meaningless sounds and fragments of language.

5.24 Now speak the text as if Macbeth had been reduced to idiocy by the course of events. He feels considerable passion but he can find no words to express it, only a statement that what he is saying doesn't mean anything. Perhaps he has some trouble forming the words. His face may be absurdly animated, as if he were at a loss for words and could hardly speak. Take this as far as you can.

Years later I saw a video clip of McKellan doing this speech in a different context. He was shot in extreme close-up, and I am sure he had scaled down how he played the image to suit the medium. But the idiot was quietly there: as he came to this line, it was as if Macbeth's I.Q. plummeted. In his slack face you could see that he had no answers about anything.

5.25 Play the line again in a subdued manner, but be just as specific about playing the characterization.

The difference between the two versions you have explored is simply a matter of scale.

Indirect quotes

In *Mr. Puntila* and *His Man Matti*, the character of Bootleg Emma has a charming little scene with Puntila and appears briefly a couple of other times. The real meat of the role consists in telling the story of a political prisoner named Athi and his mother. These two characterizations are more complex and memorable than Bootleg Emma herself.

Athi has been sent to a prison that sounds much like a concentration camp; there is not a blade of grass or a leaf in sight because the inmates have eaten everything green. Athi's mother makes a long journey to visit him; she brings with her a fish and some butter, both given to her by the landlord's wife. Athi will not accept these gifts because of his political convictions: he will take nothing from "them."

Read Excerpt 1, Appendix A.

In this excerpt there are two direct quotations — that is, statements inside quotation marks that give the exact words of the speaker. But storytelling provides the actor with other opportunities to "quote" characters by treating narrative as if it were dialog.

It is no great leap, of course, to treat a report of what was said as if it were the actual dialog. If you imagine quotation marks around a statement summarizing dialog and then speak it from the point of view of the character, you create the illusion that we are hearing the character's voice.

Athi said hello

Athi may have used the word "hello," but we cannot be sure. He might have said, "Hi, Mom" or "How are you, Mother." But it is certainly truthful to put the word "hello" in quotation marks and speak it as you imagine Athi might have in the circumstances.

5.26 Set the scene for yourself and speak the word "hello" as if it were dialog. Some possibilities to explore:

- *Athi is shocked to see her; he can hardly believe his eyes.*
- *A surge of joy wells up in him.*
- *He is so weak that he can hardly speak, so numb that he feels nothing.*
- *His eyes are fixed hungrily on her package.*
- *He is angry that she has taken this gift from his political enemies.*

and asked about her rheumatism and some of the neighbors

We don't know exactly what was said, but you can put these words in quotation marks. That the verb is past tense does not matter, just as in everyday storytelling, if you speak as if Athi were saying this *now*.

5.27 Athi is saying these words to his mother. Explore these possibilities as you converse with her:

- *Athi talks a mile a minute, breathlessly, because he is so hungry for news.*
- *His weakness makes it difficult for him to think; his mind goes blank on him.*
- *He is grinning and holding her hand.*
- *Athi knows he will have to refuse his mother's gift. He feels sorry for her. What can he say to her?*
- *He is wondering if he can possibly accept the food on behalf of his comrades.*

I call this device of putting quotation marks around a bit of narrative and treating it as dialog "indirect quotes," in contrast to direct quotations. The opportunity to play reported dialog as real dialog occurs frequently.

but nothing could make him take the fish or the butter

We know nothing about what Athi said, only that he refused. But this narrative description can serve as dialog, a choice that makes what happened much more immediate and present — as if we were witnessing the event itself instead of hearing about it.

5.28 *In your script you might pencil in quotation marks around this text to remind yourself that your voice should put quotation marks around it. Some possibilities to explore:*

- *Athi says this calmly, evenly, as if spelling it out to his mother one more time that he can't.*
- *He loses it and screams this at her.*
- *He presses the heels of his palms against his forehead. His eyes are closed. He whispers this.*
- *Prison has made him stronger in his convictions: he says this with a fiery look in his eye and a proud grin on his face.*
- *Imagine that his mother had said to him, "Well at least take the butter." How might this change how words are emphasized in your line? Note that this change, which seems quite natural, is possible only because you are treating this text as dialog.*

I kept begging them to tell me where my son was. (Excerpt 10, Appendix A)

5.29 *Speak this line without any sense of it being dialog — as if you were simply telling someone the gist of what happened.*

All sense of immediacy and high stakes disappears. As soon as an actor approaches Dorothea's frantic state, this line inevitably becomes dialog — which is to say that the event of what she said becomes present, and that Dorothea is reliving the moment.

5.30 *Play the line as if you were begging a group of angels right now. Put the quotation marks around "tell me where my son was" and note the change in your voice as you come to this phrase.*

I tried to tell him it was just my stomach

At such a climactic point it would be foolish to come out of the story to talk about what was said inside it. The audience deserves to witness the moment itself. You must set the scene and let us hear what Dorothea said in the other time and place.

5.31 *Explore what Dorothea might be experiencing as you put quotation marks around "it was just my stomach." Some possibilities:*

  • *You are greatly embarrassed: look about furtively at all the angels staring at you.*

  • *Back off from the sight of the evidence in shock: you are seeing the truth for the first time.*

  • *Deny the truth: shake your head vehemently, turn away, etc.*

  • *It makes you very angry that the angel has done this to you — and that fate has denied you a child. Spit the line at the angel as you move aggressively forward.*

  • *What other versions occur to you? Make sure that each has an action.*

He's counting on me to use my reason. To talk things out. (Excerpt 18, Appendix A)

Here Weston takes on the point of view of Taylor, the lawyer who he thinks is having an affair with his wife: he imagines Taylor trying to talk his way out of trouble. Approaching these lines in terms of indirect quote seems true to the spirit of the text. How much of the text you choose to make into dialog is up to you. You might put quotation marks around the second sentence, or you might begin to play Taylor as you say "use my reason."

5.32 *Imagine that Taylor is a chuckling, extroverted good ole boy who winks at Weston and speaks these lines as if to say "What's the problem?! Heyyyy, we can have a beer and ... "*

5.33 *In a different version, the lawyer is a stuffed shirt who smiles nervously as he tries to calm Weston.*

Speaking the unspoken

This technique is not limited to texts in which dialog is reported or paraphrased. Lines that tell us what a character is thinking, feeling, or intending may also be treated as indirect quotes. Even an action may be made to speak, if its meaning is spelled out in words that can be spoken by the character.

he thinking of the wreck of all his hopes in the loss of a dear son
(Excerpt 9, Appendix A)
Elizabeth tells us that she and her father sat in silence. But making this line an indirect quote lets us hear what her father is saying in his head.
5.34 Explore this line as a mix of several different emotions, but approach each of them in terms of action. Speak the line as the father:
- *burns several snapshots of his son;*
- *crumples his will and flings it across the room;*
- *strokes his dead son's forehead;*
- *stares numbly at his daughter as if he felt nothing for her.*

In Sam Shepard's *Suicide in B*♭, Laureen fantasizes about looking out a window and seeing herself — a male version of herself — down on the street.

Read Speech 10 in Appendix B.

He starts to nod his head and smile as though you've finally got the message.
5.35 Laureen's alter ego nods and smiles as if to say "You've finally got the message." Put these words into his mouth as he points to his own head and then up to Laureen. Experiment with different tones.

He's plastered and he doesn't want to move. (Speech 7, Appendix B)
Wesley has just realized that his father hasn't gotten out of the car because he's drunk (see 5.5-6).
5.36 Suppose Wesley goes out to help his father out of the car, but Weston resists. As Wesley takes his arm, Weston pulls it away. Where might you put quotation marks here? What word would the father emphasize in these circumstances? How might he sound?
This puts words into Weston's mouth, but the result is true to the material and to the moment. More of the speech becomes an event.

Using characterization and indirect quote in tandem
Characterization and indirect quote give an audience people, actions, and dialog instead of narrative description. Characterization is the physical work you do to play characters other than your own: gestures and

movements, behaviors and actions. Indirect quote means speaking narrative text so that it seems to come out of another character's mouth. What Wesley does physically to picture his father sitting out in the car is characterization; if Wesley says something as if it were spoken by his father, that is indirect quote.

Each of these devices can be used on its own, but characterization and indirect quote often work hand in hand. It is natural enough that people you characterize should say something when they come to life.

In half an hour she promised to return. (Speech 14, Appendix B)
When Juliet sent her to meet Romeo, the Nurse promised to return in thirty minutes. That was three hours ago.

5.37 *Imagine that Juliet's face takes on an expression that says "What are you worried about?" She gestures as if to say "Calm down." Her stance becomes more like old Nurse's. All that is characterization.*

5.38 *If Juliet puts quotation marks around "In half an hour" and speaks this phrase as if the Nurse had said it just that way, this is indirect quote.*

Practice in Characterization and Indirect Quote

Read Speech 11 in Appendix B.

This speech is so famous that many actors simply plant themselves and recite it as so many generations of schoolchildren have. But an Elizabethan actor might well have seen it as an opportunity for a virtuosic display of characterizing. The soldier, the judge and the pantaloon are stock characters from commedia dell'arte, and there were physical conventions for playing each of these types. Jaques may only be warming up when he begins with the infant, but by the time the schoolboy is creeping like a snail, he is almost certainly in motion.

This speech is no paean to man, nor is it bemused or whimsical: it chronicles how absurd and unhappy we are at each stage of life. Jaques is by temperament a melancholic, which in Elizabethan times meant a hypersensitive, high-strung, sharp-tongued personality, with a black view of the human condition and little tolerance for folly. Melancholics are at times depressed, but they can also be manic and flamboyant.

Jaques' characterizations invite you to set the scene: where and when does each vignette take place? Shakespeare tells you the schoolboy's circumstances, and the justice is likely in court (after a lunch of capon given to him as a bribe?), but where is the lover with his woeful ballad, and where is the soldier?

It is certainly possible to stand outside these characters, merely indicating a detail or two about each of them. But the following exercises ask you to explore how Jaques might characterize the seven ages of man by becoming each person and playing a little scene. Don't talk and gesture *about* the schoolboy, the lover, the soldier, etc. Get inside them.

5.39 *When you mention the schoolboy's shining morning face — think about his mood as he creeps toward school — your facial expression should get a laugh. Impulses of your own may serve to flesh out Shakespeare's portrait: perhaps the schoolboy kicks a rock as he trudges along, then turns toward home with folded arms when he says "unwillingly." Try this scenario, then one of your own.*

5.40 *Work on the physical life of:*
- *the lover,*
- *the soldier,*
- *the justice,*
- *the pantaloon.*

For each of these, create a scene with specific circumstances. Where are they, and when? What are they doing? What happens? With whom do they interact? Keep in mind that from Jaques' melancholy perspective this is a gallery of fools, each in his own way miserable.

5.41 *Where does the "last scene of all" take place? What happens?*

5.42 *There are numerous opportunities to use indirect quote. For example:*
- *The schoolboy's "unwillingly" might well be put in quotes and spoken (with a whine) as if to say "I don't want to go." The word "school" might also be heard as if from the boy's mouth.*
- *The justice's "wise saws and modern instances" — his proverbs and his rather trite examples — might be heard as if he were delivering a verbose verdict.*
- *Perhaps it is the miserly pantaloon himself who refers to his hose as "well saved": he's proud that he's saved some money by holding onto them even though they no longer fit his skinny legs.*

5.43 *Note in Jaques' speech how the sound of the following words and phrases contributes to the characterizations:*

> *mewling (crying or whimpering)*   *sighing*
> *whining*   *quick in quarrel*
> *creeping*   *pipes and whistles*

Chapters 9 and 10 will focus on sound sense: how the sound of words and the rhythm of texts contribute to the telling of stories.

Harry Percy, called Hotspur, is a spirited warrior, as hot-blooded as his nickname suggests. He has been called on the carpet by King Henry IV because he did not hand over prisoners of war when requested to do so. Hotspur defends himself by explaining exactly what happened. At the center of his story is the King's emissary, characterized as a fop whose asinine, insensitive behavior so infuriated Hotspur that he flew into a rage and — well, he doesn't even remember what he said, but the prisoners didn't get handed over.

Read Speech 12 in Appendix B.

Came there a certain lord, neat and trimly dressed,
Fresh as a bridegroom
5.44 *Compose a snapshot for yourself of a perfumèd, beribboned, lace-at-the-wrists, self-consciously clever fop. The fop's body should match his clothes: fresh, neat, lace at the cuffs, very fashionable, carefully posed. Repeat the phrase at will as you explore this character's physical life.*

which ever and anon / He gave his nose, and took't away again
5.45 *He raises a little perfume box to his nose whenever he detects an unpleasant odor, and the battlefield is full of them.*

and still he smiled and talked;
And as the soldiers bore dead bodies by
5.46 *The first line lends itself to characterization and to indirect quote. The next line, in stark contrast, is from Hotspur's point of view, and here you must carefully set the scene so as to play Hotspur's grief. Dead bodies, some horribly wounded, are carried by men under his command; among the casualties, perhaps, is someone close to him,*

who he didn't know had been killed until this moment. Explore how Hotspur switches from characterizing the lightweight lord to watching with heavy heart these fallen comrades.

The next lines are certainly indirect quote. It is critical to Hotspur's defense that we hear not Hotspur's point of view but the fop himself.

He called them untaught knaves, unmannerly,
To bring a slovenly unhandsome corpse
Betwixt the wind and his nobility.
5.47 *Act these lines full out as the fop. Explore his voice. Does he keep his cool and underplay this, smiling still, or does he have a little hissy fit, and overdramatize how offended he is? What gestures might be played with this text? Note that the fop is offended by how the bodies smell.*

With many <u>holiday and lady</u> terms   *affected and effeminate*
He questioned me, amongst the rest demanded
My prisoners in your Majesty's behalf.
5.48 *He smiles a lot and talks incessantly in a carefully calculated way. His vocabulary is full of words that are all the rage among the ladies at court — and the sort of men who dally all day with them. All three lines might be spoken by the fop, but you should also experiment with going in and out of his voice. Where do you want to place the quotation marks?*

What Hotspur does by way of playing himself in the other time and place is not characterization, but when Hotspur talks about what he himself said in these circumstances, he is in effect indirectly quoting himself.

Answered neglectingly, I know not what,
He should, or he should not
5.49 *Hotspur's answer to the king stands or falls at this moment: his excuse is that he was so outraged and flustered that he could barely speak and that he doesn't even know what came out of his mouth. Play the moment as if you were 100% in the other time and place, which is to say that the story is happening now. In the present, of*

course, recounting these events has made Hotspur lose his temper all over again. He is on the verge of being incoherent — both then and now, both there on the battlefield and here in the court.

And talk so like a <u>waiting gentlewoman</u>   *lady-in-waiting*
Of guns and drums and wounds

5.50 *Shakespeare invites a baritone actor to mimic a woman's higher register: the first line becomes an indirect quote. This sets the stage for a dramatic contrast. The next line's back vowels (o and u are formed in the back of the mouth) quite naturally engage the lower register, the more so in this emphatic context. So Hotspur's voice might drop a couple of octaves from the falsetto of a gentlewoman's voice to the bottom of his own. Explore this vocal effect by coming down in pitch in steps, on "guns" and "drums" and "wounds."*

And telling me the sovereignest thing on earth

5.51 *The eight-line passage that begins with this line amounts to a speech by the fop. Try it two ways:*
  • *as one long indirect quote;*
  • *as a series of words and phrases quoted by Hotspur as he summarizes the speech.*

In both cases the quotes should give us the fop, not Hotspur's scorn, which can be expressed elsewhere in the speech.

You should not leave this speech without noting how the vocal texture of words helps to conjure the other time and place — for you and for your audience.

5.52 *Look at the following words and phrases in context and experiment with speaking them so that their sound expresses what you are talking about. Note how doing this helps you to get inside the moment, and how it helps to make the moment sensuously real for the audience.*

rage (a residual, after-the-fight rage)	slovenly
breathless	smarting
faint	pestered with a popinjay
neat and trimly dressed	impatience
fresh	made me mad

ıèd   shine so brisk

                                       smell so sweet

Note how emotions and moods can be built into language. When Hotspur complains of being "pestered with a popinjay," those *p's* tell us exactly how he feels, and the very act of forming those explosive sounds makes the actor as irked as he needs to be. Consider also the muscularity of pressing your lips together forcefully on "made me mad." An actor does not need to get himself angry to say these words; it is the words — committing to those three *m's* — that get the actor to anger. Even the facial expression produced by speaking this phrase is angry. The Hotspur actor has lots of other words to feed his character's fiery temper: rage, smarting, impatience, etc.

The poet Shakespeare builds feelings into his text brilliantly, but he is able to do this only because all of us do it in everyday life. By attending to the expressive possibilities in the sound of a text, actors can shape a performance with such sound sense that to speak the words is to feel the feelings.

For Your Own Speech

1. Prepare two characterizations, using brief texts for each. You may work on two moments for one persona or on two different characterizations.
   - Consider what is gained and lost by playing the other character's point of view as opposed to that of your own character.
   - Are there any generalized references to categories of people that might be personified? Groups can be characterized as if they were an individual.

2. Prepare two moments in which you indirect quote a word, a phrase, or a sentence.
   - Are you indirect quoting reported dialog?
   - Are you putting words in a character's mouth? How is this truthful?
   - Are there opportunities in your speech to speak neutral narrative from a particular character's point of view?

• Experiment with precisely where you place the quotation marks. Do you fade into the quotation or pop into it?

Guidelines

Set the scene so that your characterizations and indirect quotes are grounded in specific circumstances.

Chapter 6
Gesture

By gesture I mean what is referred to as "body English." Gesture is by no means confined to the hands: you can gesture with any part of your body, even with your whole body.

Narrative Gesture

Some gestures serve as sign language: we give approval with a "thumbs up" gesture or an "OK" sign, we nod or shake our heads, we shrug our shoulders to indicate ignorance or indifference. Other gestures make visible the structure of what we say: we indicate that two ideas are opposed by gesturing "on the one hand ... on the other hand ... ," and a hand ascending in steps marks the stages in some progression. We pulse or jab or wave to punctuate what we say or to emphasize words. Such conventional and rhetorical gestures may come into play in the course of storytelling, but what the actor of a speech that tells a story needs to explore are what might be called *narrative* gestures, which are improvised to make visible what is happening in a story. Narrative gestures always embody events in the other time and place. Gestures that refer only to the here and now are not narrative.

Although Betty talks about her friend Mavis throughout *Landscape of the Body*, Mavis never appears — except, of course, in narrative speeches. At one point the audience hears, quite out of the blue, that Mavis has become gravely ill.

Read Excerpt 4, Appendix A.

They had cut off her breasts and she had lots of radiation treatment and her hair had gone.

6.1   *As Betty talks about Mavis' condition, imagine the sorts of gestures she might use in connection with each of these three details. What gestures might she consciously use? What sorts of physical responses might be less conscious?*

This is interesting, complex, delicate acting work, but Betty's gestures here are not narrative. They are not really about events happening in

100

another time and place, but about her reaction here and now to Mavis' condition. In the next section of the text, as Betty relives an exchange with Mavis in the hospital, any gestures that Betty recreates — her own or Mavis' — would be narrative because they are happening within the story.

And I said, "Mavis, is there anything I can do for you?" And she said, "Yes, there is this new book: <u>The Sensuous Woman.</u> Bring it. Read it to me."

6.2   *Imagine that Betty reaches forward and puts her hand on Mavis' arm. Use a piece of furniture (in the play you might use another character) to land this gesture, so that you are not miming the contact. As Mavis makes her request, she fiddles with a wisp of what little hair she has left*

These are narrative gestures.

Gesturing from Inside the Story

In general, storytelling gesture is more evocative when it is played not by a narrator standing outside the story but by a character that is inside it, reliving events.

Read Speech 9 in Appendix B.

Real low down like he's coming in for a landing or something, then changing his mind and pulling straight back up again and sailing out away from me.

6.3   *If Weston simply talks about what happened without reliving it, he is outside the story. His voice might sound something like the narrator of a documentary: he is an observer, not a participant. One hand calmly traces the path of the eagle's flight.*

This positions Weston a step or two outside the moment, gesturing about what happened in the other time and place. His gesture is not happening inside the story.

6.4   *Now make the path of the eagle's "downright suicidal antics" as dynamic and exciting as this former pilot finds it. Your hand is the eagle. Your gesture finishes by "sailing out away" from you.*

This gesture is narrative: it is an action inside the story.

6.5   *Now place your whole body inside the story and play Weston's point of view. The eagle swoops down from high above. You instinctively duck — perhaps your hands fly up protectively; then you slowly rise, pivoting in place, as it flies off.*

This "body English" is a different way of reliving the moment.

He's down on that shed roof with his talons taking half the tar paper with him

If Weston remains himself and shapes his hands merely to indicate open talons, he stands outside the event as a narrator who gestures *about* what happened. But it is possible to commit to such a gesture so wholeheartedly that Weston's hands *become* the talons.

6.6   *Your talons swoop down and the eagle seizes its prey. Ground your gesture in space; your hands might dig into the pile of laundry on the table or land on the kitchen counter.*

6.7   *Now commit your whole body to playing the eagle. How might you stage this event in the kitchen?*

Weston may use his hands or his whole body to play the eagle: his gesture may be the whole event or part of the event. In either case, what makes the gesture narrative is that it is happening in the other time and place.

Gestures Which Recreate Gestures Inside the Story

Many narrative gestures, of course, relive gestures that happened inside the story. Nat speaks in the present tense about raising his hand at the union meeting: "my hand goes up" (see Chapter 1); his gesture now simply makes visible exactly what he did (or remembers doing) seventy years ago. When Ophelia tells her father about the strange events in her bedchamber, her head gesture reenacts Hamlet's: "And thrice his head thus waving up and down." (Excerpt 13, Appendix A)

When Laureen sees her alter ego down on the street, he is gesturing.

Read Speech 10 in Appendix B.

He's pointing to his head, to his own head, then pointing back to you. He keeps repeating this over and over, as though it's very important. As though it's something you should have understood a long, long time ago but never did

6.8 *You might start this gesture tentatively, as if Laureen were exploring what it might mean, then fade into an emphatic reenactment of what she saw him doing.*

After Laureen picks up the gesture, he indicates his approval.

He starts to nod his head and smiles as though you've finally got the message. But you're still not clear what he means.

6.9 *The nod and smile are in the first place his, but since Laureen has been doing the pointing gesture along with him, it will also seem that she is nodding and smiling. What is the quality of the nodding and smiling from Laureen's point of view?*

Storytellers instinctively imagine the gestures happening inside their stories, even if the text is not explicit about them. Puntila's drunken rhapsody about his land includes a reference to "the morning as you lie in bed" (see 3.22); as his body imagines this scene, Puntila might spontaneously gesture as if he were luxuriating in bed. When Titania speaks of "marking th'embarkèd traders on the flood" (see 3.49), it is quite natural for her to gesture as if toward the sea.

Did you beg them from the landlord's wife? (Excerpt 1, Appendix A)
6.10 *Imagine that Athi's angry question is accompanied by a begging gesture.*

Answered neglectingly, I know not what,
He should, or he should not (Speech 12, Appendix B)
6.11 *Imagine that Hotspur's arms are flailing, partly in angry exasperation, partly in inability to remember what he said — a doubly expressive bit of body English, since it takes place both in the court and on the battlefield.*

And being thus frighted, swears a prayer or two (Speech 16, Appendix B)

After Queen Mab drums in the ear of a sleeping soldier, he wakes in a great fright.

6.12 Whether or not he has dropped to his knees, Mercutio and the soldier might well fold their hands in prayer.

"What you see here is the proof" (Excerpt 10, Appendix A)

An angel has just pulled from Dorothea "something that looked like a walnut all blackened and cracked."

6.13 Is this a private moment between the angel and Dorothea, or a public moment in which the "proof" is exhibited for all to see? Try the moment both ways. Make a specific choice about how the angel holds and presents Dorothea's shriveled womb in each case.

Read Excerpt 7, Appendix A.

Eugène Ionesco's *Exit the King* is an absurdist *King Lear*. It centers on an old king who must come to terms with the inevitability of exiting for good.

On top of everything else, I've got a headache.

The King might well touch his head at this point, but this would not be a narrative gesture, because there is no other time and place: the king's headache is very much in the here and now, and this is a literal, not a metaphorical statement.

I thought I'd banished the clouds.

6.14 Imagine that the King marches to a window and gestures imperiously for the clouds to depart. This is still an event in the here and now, though it might be done with overtones of repeating a gesture he's done earlier.

There's an idiotic cloud that can't restrain itself, like an old man, weak in the bladder. What are you staring at me for? You look very red today.

6.15 When he sees the rain, the King reacts as a child does to running water: he needs to pee. This might be made visible in his stance. When he notices the maid staring at him, he is embarrassed — which he projects on her. Play this sequence of moments.

Now we come to the interesting part.

You look very red today. My bedroom's full of cobwebs. Go and brush them away.

Where does the line about "cobwebs" come from? It is too easy to say that it just pops into his head, or that this is an absurdist play and anything goes. An exploration of gestures implicit in the text reveals the sense here.

6.16 When the King tells the maid that she looks "very red today," he wants her to leave. Suppose that he starts flapping the back of both his hands at her, as if to say, "Get out of here." Now imagine that this gesture happens to be identical to the action of someone who has walked into a big spider web. Explore the physicality of trying to get cobwebs away from your face and chest. If the king's gesture of dismissal is cobwebby, it triggers "My bedroom is full of cobwebs" — and gives him a reason to send her away.

Gestures about Actions Involving the Hands and Arms

Actions that involve a character's hands and arms readily lend themselves to gestural expression. When the angel sinks his fist into Dorothea's stomach, when Puntila talks of having himself whipped with a bundle of birch leaves, when the fop who outraged Hotspur puts a pouncet box up to his nose, the actor quite naturally gestures.

When Clytemnestra addresses the elders of Argos after killing her husband Agamemnon, she gives them a blow-by-blow account of the murder.

Read Speech 1 in Appendix B.

and then I strike him/once, twice

6.17 The weapon she used was a double-headed ax with a short handle. Imagine how she might gesture to recreate the two blows. How might the two be different?

105

And in this rage, with some great kinsman's bone
As with a club, dash out my desperate brains (Speech 15, Appendix B)

6.18 At the climax of her panic about what she might encounter after waking up in the tomb, Juliet imagines that she will do violence to herself. How might you gesture toward your head at this moment?

6.19 There are, of course, other possibilities. Imagine, for example, that Juliet smashes her head against a pillow on her bed. Or she might tap the back of her head against one of the pillars on the Globe stage.

he mechanically put his arm about me (Excerpt 9, Appendix A)

6.20 Play this action as if you were the distracted father. Such a gesture will seem unnatural if played in empty air — try this and see how oddly like mime it looks. Using the back of a chair or a post to receive the action will ground the move in space. The same effect might be accomplished by a slow, mechanical reaching that concludes when your hand arrives somewhere — perhaps on the surface of a table. Try these alternatives.

6.21 On the other hand, you might well decide that it is Elizabeth's point of view that should be played. Sit. You have just climbed in your father's lap. Perhaps when you sense that he is about to put his arm about you, you lean into the contact. But it feels "mechanical." How does your body respond? The body English that makes visible how you receive your father's gesture, while subtle, should be perceptible to everyone but your distraught father.

And then dreams he of cutting foreign throats (Speech 16, Appendix B)

6.22 What the sleeping soldier is dreaming might be gestured by Mercutio. But he might also grab Romeo from behind and pull out a dagger as if to do him in — dangerous play! Try both versions; in each case, choreograph the physical move with the line.

I had to kneel on the stage and cover my head with a black shawl (Excerpt 15, Appendix A)

6.23 Should you consider giving Cavale a substitute for the shawl? Perhaps — as long as the prop does not call attention to itself or to *your acting work. But Cavale might simply gesture without anything in hand. Try a version of this which starts and ends with the line, as if Cavale, deep in memory, were reliving in slow motion what happened in the other time and place.*

Gestures As Body English About Almost Anything

Up to this point we have focused on gestures which are either about gestures or about the motion of limbs doing something in a story. But gestures can be used to conjure anything. When Puntila proudly pointed out a "tugboat with a chest like a bulldog," his chest gestured as if it had become the boat's prow (see 3.16). When you used your hand and, alternatively, your whole body to image the logs floating on a lake, you were using gesture to make visible their motion (3.17-18). In a similar vein, the model planes that Wesley remembers "swaying very quietly" might be two hands held as if they were suspended (3.53). You have gestured with hands and feet and other parts of your body to mimic a chicken paddling out to a dying gunslinger — and then hopping onto his neck, pulling a vein out, etc. (3.1-14) We use gestures to talk — in body English — about all manner of events. Remember, for example, the suggestion that Weston's memory of the steam rising off the bathtub in which he scalded himself might prompt his hand to rise, slowly twisting and swirling as the steam did (1.32).

There'll be giant steel balls crashing through the walls. (Excerpt 16, Appendix A)

6.24 What size and force of gesture could conjure this image? Choreograph what you do physically so that it supports and drives how you speak the line.

He's not counting on what's in my blood. He doesn't realize the explosiveness. (Excerpt 18, Appendix A)

6.25 Explore a variety of explosive gestures in search of an impulse that seems freshly expressive rather than emphatic in a commonplace way.

It was like peeling off a whole person. A whole stranger. (Speech 8, Appendix B)

6.26 *This is what Weston says about taking all his clothes off when he came in from the walk that triggered his transformation. In telling this story to his son, he has journeyed back to this moment, before the bath, before he even knows he will take a bath. The quality of Weston's gesture should be expressive of his hunger not to be his old self anymore. A glancing reference to his clothes will not do: he peels off a stranger. The urge to scald himself should be implicit in this gesture.*

Like I could almost feel his feathers on my back. (Speech 9, Appendix B)

6.27 *Here is a chance to act with your back. Imagine that Weston had been bent over his work. Create a slow gesture with your back as if to make visible the sensation of feathers brushing it — a first installment of the "icy feeling up my backbone" when Weston rises to cheer for the eagle. This is one way that an actor might play Weston's mix of fear and excitement.*

His wings made a kind of cracking noise.

6.28 Coordinate your gesture with what you do with the sound of "cracking."

A man in a white robe, with two white wings reaching from the sky to the ground. (Speech 2, Appendix B)

6.29 *Joan is a girl again as she relives this moment: her youthfully expansive gesture should remember the wings as huge.*

When the angel first appears to her, Joan's sheepdog is lying with his head in her lap, and she feels the dog's reaction first.

suddenly I feel his body ripple and tremble, and a hand seems to have touched my shoulder, though I know no one has touched me

6.30 *How might Joan's body register the trembling in her lap? Let a slow shoulder gesture respond to the sensation of the angel's touch. Joan may not be startled or frightened so much as awestruck, perhaps even thrilled.*

Objects and Gesture

Objects can trigger gestural impulses, and once in hand, objects can specify and extend gestures, or develop them into full-blown actions in the other time and place.

I try all sorts of delicacies. Sardines on toast. Warm buttered toast with the silver little fishes.

6.31 At the beginning of Chapter 4 it was suggested that for this moment, which takes place in a kitchen, you could easily manage to have a plate at hand as a prop for the scene implicit in this text. Explore how the presence of a plate might prompt Johnny to pick it up quite spontaneously and gesture with it as if offering it to his father.

digs the beak into his throat
straightens legs and heaves a red and blue vein out (Speech 5, Appendix B)

You have played with the fanciful notion of Billy the Kid eating a plate of spaghetti as he tells this story (see 3.43-45). The fork digs in, twists, and pulls a long piece of pasta up to his mouth.

6.32 Imagine, alternatively, that Billy has the impulse to use something located on or near his neck as the vein — in the spirit of an actor spontaneously using a found object as a substitute prop in rehearsal. What sorts of objects might come into play? For the moment, don't worry about what is appropriate in terms of the period. What matters for now is how the object might in a sensory way conjure something about the event. What physical qualities might be useful?

Self-mutilation became a source of glory. Suicide, though despised, was commonplace. (Speech 4, Appendix B)

6.33 What form might the self-mutilation take? Imagine that a knife is available to you. Notice how gestures with the knife are much more graphic. Is the suicide impulse a new one, or a development of the mutilation gesture?

A drunken Puntila had invited Bootleg Emma and three other women to eat and drink at his daughter's wedding. Now sober, he has refused to admit them, and the women head home. It is in this context, while the women rest and refresh themselves by the side of the road, that Bootleg Emma tells the story of Athi and his mother.

Read Excerpt 1, Appendix A.

Look, here is a fish and some butter

6.34 *Perhaps one of the other women has just passed a loaf of bread to Bootleg Emma, who quite naturally gestures with it as if she were Athi's mother offering him the food she has brought. Do this without even thinking about it.*

You can take it back with you, I don't want it.

6.35 *Suppose that Bootleg Emma has a piece of bread in her hand as she comes to this point in the story. Impulsively she flings the bread away, as if Athi had done this with his mother's gift. Note that this action would also be expressive of Bootleg Emma's present feelings, which are the reason she has told the story: she is angry, and her disgust with Puntila has taken away her appetite.*

To go out and have a business lunch and talk things over. (Excerpt 18, Appendix A)

Objects at hand in the kitchen might trigger specific impulses for the implicit business lunch.

6.36 *Imagine using one of the laundry items on the table as if it were a napkin. What article of clothing might be expressive of Weston's feelings about Taylor having an affair with his wife?*

6.37 *Pick up a coffee cup and treat it as if it were a fancy cocktail.*

6.38 *Suppose that one of the notions of fancy restaurants in Weston's mind is that they offer finger bowls. Imagine pouring some beer into a cereal bowl, dipping your fingers into it, and then drying them daintily with something from the pile of laundry.*

And every time I cut a lamb I'd throw those balls up on top a' the shed roof. (Speech 9, Appendix B)

6.39 *As Weston begins this story, he is folding laundry. Imagine that he has returned to this activity after the climax of the speech. He might pause at this point to gesture empty-handedly about the action in*

110

the other time and place. But he might also finish folding a pair of socks into a neat little ball and toss it into a laundry basket. What is the difference between gesturing and creating such an action?

In auditions, actors do not use props, unless they can be worn or easily pocketed. But even if you are working on a speech with auditioning in mind, you may wish to explore it as if preparing for a full production, with a rehearsal set and substitute props. Production values can later be subtracted, and moments can be adapted for an audition performance.

Practice in Narrative Gesture

In *As You Like It,* Rosalind, in disguise as a male, declares to Orlando that love is "merely a madness." Then she tells him how she once cured a man of love by play-acting the object of his affection in such a fickle manner as to drive the fellow crazy — and straight into a monastery.

Read Excerpt 14, Appendix A.

would now like him, now loathe him; then entertain him, then forswear him; now weep for him, then spit at him
6.40 *It was switches like these that drove Rosalind's patient to renounce ("forswear") love. Find a gesture and stance for each moment. An abrupt change might be effective at one or another point, but most of your physical choices should evolve quite naturally into what follows. Your gestures should seem to flow.*

Sometimes a single object or space can unify a passage like this and facilitate the fast changes.
6.41 *Explore this sequence in terms of the various ways that you might use a scarf.*

I drave my suitor from his mad humour of love to a living humour of madness, which was to forswear the full stream of the world and to live in a nook merely monastic.
In Renaissance psychology, the relative proportions of four fluids called humors determined a person's temperament and emotional state.
6.42 *On the Elizabethan stage, clutching one's hair as if to tear it out was*

a conventional sign of madness. We still have this impulse when we
are distressed. Try it for "living humour of madness."
6.43 Explore how Rosalind might gesture as she leaves the world and
becomes a monk.

**Then I could picture my Dad driving it. Shifting unconsciously.
Downshifting into second for the last pull up the hill.** (Speech 7,
Appendix B)
6.44 Cars, which take on mythic dimensions in Shepard's plays, are
perhaps a strong connection between this father and son. Wesley
characterizing his father is also Wesley fantasizing about driving
Dad's great old Packard.

Read Excerpt 24, Appendix A.

**and they just spread their wings and go to sleep on the wind like
other birds fold their wings and go to sleep on a tree. They sleep
on the wind.**
6.45 Imagine that Val, who obviously identifies with these birds, slowly
spreads his arms and that the gesture is not complete until the last
word of this segment.
6.46 Explore playing this image in a doorway or window frame with arms
extended and braced on either side. Here the "gesture" is
established at the outset and appears to be less conscious.

Her whip, of cricket's bone; the lash, of film (Speech 16, Appendix B)
6.47 Mercutio might well use gesture to conjure the whip. On what word
would you choose to flick it?

O'er ladies' lips, who straight on kisses dream
6.48 Imagine Mercutio having fun with what happens to these ladies' lips
after Queen Mab has driven across them.

**My words would bandy her to my sweet love,
And his to me.** (Speech 14, Appendix B)
Juliet thinks that her instructions should have sent the Nurse speeding
toward Romeo like a tennis ball, and that *his* words (about where and

when they will be married) should have sent her quickly back again. The original meaning of "bandy" was to strike a ball to and fro, as in tennis.

The monosyllables of "And his to me" should be spoken slowly, as if Juliet were doting on Romeo, her "sweet love." In Shakespeare's verse a short line such as this indicates a pause: Juliet is lost in her feelings about Romeo and the marriage plans en route to her.

6.49 *Suppose that Juliet gestures as if a forehand stroke were sending a ball to Romeo. Doing this on "bandy" defines its meaning. If Juliet leaves her arm extended toward Romeo on "sweet love," she can bring her hand back on "As his to me." Or her hand can slowly retreat after she has spoken, so that this action fills the pause. Try it both ways.*

Finding your own way

There is an old theater story about a director who demonstrated to an actor in considerable detail how a moment should be played. In the next day's rehearsal, the actor duplicated exactly what the director had shown him. The director was horrified: "You must find your own way to do this!"

Years ago the director Mike Nichols knew from the first day of a particular rehearsal process precisely what he wanted an actor to do at a climactic moment — which was to cover his nakedness with an American flag, part of the set. For weeks he refrained from saying anything about this; when the time was ripe, the actor discovered the action on his own. Why such restraint? So that the actor could feel the moment was his and could own it in performance. When you play a moment that has been given to you, you are a spokesperson for someone else's product.

I must also say that I have been given wonderful moments to play by directors without feeling imposed on. Part of an actor's work, after all, is to make the actions of others their own — whether those others are characters or directors. But the principle of leaving an actor room to find his or her own way is a good one. It is your imagination that must be engaged, and you must eventually play *your* acting moment.

The exercises in this book are meant to clarify issues and to provide you with practice. I often ask you to play a particular version of a moment. You should always feel invited to explore a different approach than the one I have given you. But try mine first!

O look! Methinks I see my cousin's ghost
Seeking out Romeo, that did spit his body
Upon a rapier's point. Stay, Tybalt, stay! (Speech 15, Appendix B)

6.50 *Suppose that Juliet points toward her cousin's ghost. Her next gesture — on "Stay, Tybalt, stay!" — should ask the apparition to stop. Rather than thinking of these as two separate gestures, let the first flow into the second.*

Seeking the bubble reputation (Speech 11, Appendix B)

6.51 *Reputation is a bubble because it is so short-lived. Imagine that Jaques' soldier, hungry for fame, reaches to grasp it; he suddenly clasps his hand right after the word "bubble" and "reputation" sounds disappointed. The bubble has burst and thereby escaped him.*

His youthful hose, well saved, a world too wide
For his shrunk shank

6.52 *Imagine that Jaques' pantaloon — a skinny, miserly old man in commedia dell'arte scenarios — reaches down to adjust his hose, but interrupts this action to rub his thumb and first two fingers together in a money gesture as he says "well saved."*

He called them untaught knaves, unmannerly,
To bring a slovenly unhandsome corpse
Betwixt the wind and his nobility. (Speech 12, Appendix B)

6.53 *Besides holding his pouncet box up to his nose, what gestures do you imagine the fop might use as he berates the soldiers carrying dead bodies upwind of him?*

For Your Own Speech

Prepare three moments in which you use gesture to help tell the story of your speech.

- Is your gesture recreating a gesture inside the story, or reliving an action done with the hands and arms, or is it body English about something else entirely?
- Explore body English in all parts of your body. Be inventive.

Guidelines

These gestures should not be rhetorical or conventional, nor should they simply punctuate the text; they should be gestures that your character invents to tell the story — impulses that are quite specific to the text.

Whenever possible, gesture inside the story, rather than from outside it.

Gestures should be phrased so as to coincide with a piece of text. What you do physically should be choreographed to begin and end at a definite point. At the same time, of course, your body English should seem perfectly natural and spontaneous.

Objects may trigger and extend gestural impulses.

Chapter 7
Movement

By movement I mean the body moving through space. The border between gesture and movement is not always clear, and the two sometimes overlap, but gesture is generally stationary.

Characters telling a story can use movement to make visible all manner of motion in the other time and place, but narrative movement, like narrative gesture, can be used to conjure anything. Movement can say things that have nothing to do with movement.

In the last chapter you worked on quite a variety of excerpts in order to survey the range of narrative gesture. Here you will explore different ways to use movement expressively for a single text, one that does not mention motion.

Dress to move.

I could feel myself in my bed in my room in this house in this town in this state in this country. (Speech 7 in Appendix B)

Shortly before his father arrived the night before, Wesley had been lying in bed, looking up at his model planes swaying quietly, smelling the avocado blossoms, listening to the coyotes and the stock cars squealing down the street. And then this line, unpunctuated as if to suggest a continuous whole. Except for the battle royal, we know little about the family at this point, so there is not much context to tell us what Wesley means: the sentence seems very open to interpretation. Is this sentence about claustrophobia or expansive celebration? Is life in this house, this town, etc. energizing or depressing? Or both? For the moment we will search in all directions.

Movement is not the most obvious way to approach this text. Your first impulse might be to explore it in terms of voice or gesture or space. But the very fact that the line is not about moving in any literal sense will make it easier to see how a variety of movement choices can contribute to the meaning of the line.

Movement Pure and Simple

7.1 Crouch. As you speak, slowly rise, so that you are erect only at the end of the line. Do not play any other values.

Even this simple movement is expressive: what it attaches to the text is a sense of ascending, expanding. The direction is up.

7.2 Stand against a wall that you can slide down. Slowly descend as you speak, so that you reach bottom only on the last word. Do not play any emotion.

This more or less abstract movement — you have not played anything so concrete or specific as depression or defeat or exhaustion — is nevertheless expressive: it would seem that the line is about sinking, going down, getting smaller.

Resisting familiar labels

Suppose that you try to get more specific about what these simple movements mean by asking yourself what the character is *feeling* as s/he rises or sinks. Such a question points you toward a relatively limited number of categories: happy, sad, angry, afraid, etc. Even if you come up with more interesting ideas — the rising is expectant or ambitious, the sinking is enervated or intimidated — you are still dealing with concepts that you already know. If you translate everything you encounter into tried and true formulas, you narrow your horizons. What should be unique is reduced to the familiar; remarkable events become unremarkable. Neither the actor nor the audience learns anything new.

Acting is not about pigeonholing characters, nor is it clinical psychology. As artists, actors are licensed not to practice psychology but to *invent* psychologies. Out of the themes and images that constitute the universe of the play, an actor must construct a novel psychology for each of the roles that he or she undertakes.

Theatrical practice, unfortunately, is not always so innovative. Emotional and psychological terms are too often used like Post-its, as if attaching a label to a human experience could actually explain or comprehend it. Language about feelings can be useful as shorthand to point actors in the right direction. But such a limited and conventional vocabulary cannot suffice for artists who are trying to say what has not quite been said before and to re-state old truths in fresh and arresting ways.

Metaphorical Movement

A habit of mind that is much more discovery-oriented than using emotional and psychological labels is to think in terms of metaphor. In the case at hand, what is this rising *like*? This sinking is like *what*? Such questions both deepen and broaden your search, and they greatly increase the likelihood of your getting at answers you really didn't know before. If you learn how to act the metaphors that surface in response to your questions, your work will not only be more original, but you will have freed yourself from the trap of playing generic emotional labels.

> ### Listening for metaphors
>
> Metaphorical thinking is a sensibility which performers, like all creative people, should cultivate. A key skill is learning how to *listen* for responses to metaphorical questions. "What is this event *like?*" you might ask yourself. The left hemisphere of your brain, of course, will want to rush in with an answer — most likely something you already know. Turn down the volume on your left hemisphere, play dumb and *listen*. The silence of *not knowing the answer* makes it possible to hear imagination and memory suggest comparisons.
>
> There are other ways to spur the mind to metaphorical inspiration. One may deliberately set out to make connections, for example, between a character and various categories of fanciful comparison: If my character were a bird ... an athlete ... a household appliance ... a flavor of ice cream ... Any approach that sparks the intuitive leap to a truthful and playable metaphor will do.
>
> Metaphors may also be suggested by research, or by directors and fellow actors. The most apt metaphors are likely to come from the playwright, whether they are in the speech you're working on or elsewhere in the script.

Let's look at some metaphorical possibilities for Wesley's line. In rehearsal, of course, you would be searching for metaphors that rise from and speak to your own imagination, but you should also develop a facility for exploring metaphors proposed by a playwright or a director.

7.3   *Speak the line as you slowly rise from a crouch like:*
  • *a seed sprouting;*
  • *a nearly dead ember becoming hotter, then bursting into flame;*

· *a Macy's Day Parade balloon being filled with helium until it is three stories high.*

A quirky, highly physical character like Wesley might well play such metaphors full out, whether or not the audience is aware that it is seeing a seed germinate or an ember flame up. But metaphors like these can be acted even in plays that are much more realistic than *Curse of the Starving Class.*

7.4   *Sit in a chair with your feet up, your arms around your legs, your chin on top of your knees. You are secretly a seed, though the audience sees Wesley curled up in a position that looks contemplative, perhaps self-protecting. As you speak the line, slowly unpack your body so that you end up standing on the roots you have sent down to the floor. Find a way to let your arms rise so that the gesture seems perfectly natural.*

An audience might not think "seed" in such a case but it will see a very specific quality of movement expressive of life stirring. Metaphors are often perceived subliminally.

7.5   *Slide down the wall:*
· *like a wilting plant left in a car on a hot day (first the leaves, then the stem, then the roots dry out);*
· *like a party balloon with a slow leak;*
· *as if a giant hand placed on your head were pushing you down.*

In telling a story, then, movement can be used metaphorically as well as literally. The images you have been exploring speak to the audience along with the text. What Wesley felt, these metaphors say, is like *this*: that is, like the qualities of movement you are seeing now.

Actors should note with interest that metaphors are very playable.

Metaphorical Scenes

The metaphors you have played thus far consist of single events. Metaphorical scenes involve a sequence of different actions.

7.6   *Imagine that you are having a nightmare. Wesley's line is what you are saying in your sleep. What is happening in the dream that causes you to be anxious or fearful? Maybe you are living through events and images that will occur later in the play. Let your nightmare develop in stages. At what point in the line do you wake up? In what condition? You may play this metaphorical scene lying down or leaning against a wall.*

The audience will be conscious of this metaphor if it is acted quite explicitly. But the nightmare scenario might be played so that it seems to be an anxiety attack or an explosive restlessness in the here and now, in which case the metaphor remains buried beneath the surface. In either case, playing this image writes between the lines of the text: living here is like being in a nightmare. The audience reads your metaphorical movement just as it reads everything else in the production.

7.7 *Imagine that this is your first night in a new apartment. You have awakened to go to the bathroom, have not been able to locate a light switch, and are groping your way blindly through a minefield of boxes and helter-skelter furniture. At some point, realize that you are lost and don't know which way to go.*

In a case such as this, the metaphorical circumstances (new apartment, bathroom, boxes, etc.) are important only to you — as a means of being specific about playing the action that you want the audience to read. Living here is like this groping in the dark, you are saying; it is like being lost in the place you live.

7.8 *You are home alone and have heard several noises that convince you that someone has broken into the house. You move cautiously, all senses alert, to investigate. Play this scene full out, using the resources of the space you are working in.*

7.9 *Translate the same metaphorical scenario into how you move as you cross the stage, let's say, from the fridge to the sink. It is your energy and the quality of your movement that the audience will read into the words you speak.*

Metaphorical Actions in the Here and Now

Perfectly ordinary activities and behaviors — actions grounded in your character's present circumstances — can also stand in metaphorical relationship to events in your story.

7.10 *Improvise a scene in which Wesley is bored out of his skull: there is absolutely nothing interesting to do. Pick up magazines: boring. TV:*

boring. *The mail, the view out the window, the stack of CDs: all boring. Let the physical life of the scene be variations on this one theme. Repeat the text as needed.*

7.11 Imagine that you are looking for something — say, the keys to the car — and can't find them anywhere. Keep looking. This activity might be frustrating, mystifying, upsetting — depending on which version of the activity seems the truest metaphor.

In each of these examples, what your character is doing in the here and now is not just any old realistic activity, but one which has metaphorical significance: living in this house, in this town, in this state, in this country is like this …

7.12 What other activities — games, chores, modes of self-expression, acts of destruction, etc. — occur to you as possible metaphors for what is under the surface of this text? Play one or two of them.

Scale

By scale I mean the relative size of an action. Circumstances such as the space available to you may determine the size of a movement. The style of a script and of its production will certainly influence the physical and vocal fullness of acting choices. But scaling down a moment does not mean that you give up on playing it.

And shrieks like mandrakes torn out of the earth,
That living mortals, hearing them, run mad (Speech 15, Appendix B)
Mandrake roots are forked like the legs of a man. In folklore, mandrakes were believed to emit a sharp, shrill cry when uprooted; hearing this sound would drive a person mad. Juliet imagines that she will hear such shrieks in the tomb and that she will go crazy.

7.13 If Juliet were hearing horrific shrieks, how might her upper body react to the sound as she starts to run? Use this physicality in the following sequence.

- *Imagine that you are on the Globe stage and that you make a diagonal cross of 50 feet as you run mad. (Movement on this scale might well incorporate more of Shakespeare's text: the cross could start two lines earlier.)*
- *Now suppose that you are on a much smaller set. Play the running mad with the same intensity, but you can move only 8-10 feet.*

• *In this version, you are standing next to an armless chair. The "running" consists of sitting suddenly. You are still playing Shakespeare's image full out.*
• *Sit in the chair with your legs to one side. On the line, spin so that your legs end up facing in the opposite direction. Remain specific about the scene you are playing.*
• *Scale down your action even more. Look to your left, then whip your head to the right.*
• *Finally, imagine that you are being filmed in extreme close-up. Only your eyes move, from one side to the other. But you run mad with just as much commitment as in larger-scale versions of this action.*

Scale is a consideration in every area of acting, whether the variable is physical or vocal or psychological.

And then the lover,
Sighing like furnace, with a woeful ballad
Made to his mistress' eyebrow. (Speech 11, Appendix B)

7.14 Suppose that this unhappy lover, his passion hot as a furnace, is singing his sad song in the wee hours after too many glasses of wine, and that he moves with abandon through a large, deserted square.

7.15 This time the lover, just as unhappy, his romantic temperature just as hot, slides desolately down a wall.

Scale is influenced by where you are in the story. How presently and fully you play a moment depends on how far your character has journeyed inside the other time and place. The earliest moments in a narrative speech are often scaled down as echoes of what happened, because the character is still more here than there. Near the climax, actions are relived on a much more heightened scale.

Practice In Narrative Movement

7.16 Explore movement possibilities for the following texts.

and then all of a sudden one of those angels walked right up to me (Excerpt 10, Appendix A)

Life's but a walking shadow, a poor player
That struts and frets his hour upon the stage
And then is heard no more. (Speech 17, Appendix B)

I started feeling like I should be running or hiding or something.
Like I shouldn't be there in this kind of a neighborhood. (Speech
8, Appendix B)

Re-read Speech 7, Appendix B.

Feet coming. Feet walking toward the door. Feet stopping. Heart
pounding. Sound of door not opening. Foot kicking door.

7.17 *Set the scene for yourself. It is late and Weston is drunk. He may*
already be in a belligerent mood, but the script does not tell us this.
He might be looking forward to coming home and feeling
desperately that he has to see his family — a more complex choice
that explains why he will be so upset when he discovers he's locked
out. Explore this interpretation in terms of the quality of Weston's
movement as he walks from the car to the house.

7.18 *Wesley tells us that his heart is pounding as his father approaches,*
but we know nothing about what he is doing, so you have a great
deal of room to imagine the scene from his point of view. Is Wesley
frozen in the middle of his room? Is he cringing in a corner, hiding
under the bedcovers? Is he pacing like a caged animal? Experiment
with these alternatives.

7.19 *One movement possibility, which reflects both points of view, is for*
Wesley to back up as his father approaches, step by step. How might
Wesley react when his father first kicks the door?

Foot kicking. Foot kicking harder. Wood splitting. Man's voice. In
the night. Foot kicking hard through door. One foot right through
door.

7.20 *Explore this text from the son's point of view. Each time the father*
kicks, let Wesley scoot backward as if he were dodging it. This
movement should escalate. How does Wesley react when his father's
foot comes through the door?

You will next explore movement versions of two earlier moments in this speech, neither of which seems at first to be about movement.

My P-39. My Messerschmitt. My Jap Zero.

7.21 This is an opportunity to play each of the planes. Stage this as a dogfight between ace pilots. Your characterizations should be distinct not only in terms of nationality but in terms of how each aircraft moves.

I could feel the headlights closing in. Cutting through the orchard. I could see the trees being lit one after the other by the lights, then going back to black. My heart was pounding. Just from my Dad coming back.

7.22 Imagine that Wesley is trying to escape these headlights, as if he were in one of those old movies about a prison break and trying not to get caught by the searchlights. After the first three sentences, Wesley freezes: the only thing moving is his heart.

At the beginning of the *Iliad*, Agamemnon takes for himself a Trojan woman originally given to Achilles as a prize: Briseis. In *Living in Exile*, she gives us a very different perspective on the Trojan War: the story of the women taken captive in the nine years before the *Iliad*.

Read Speech 4, Appendix B.

The seventh year we were lunatics. Sleeping by day, roaming at night. We went with animals, ate in rituals the wounded's severed limbs. Our wombs became breeders of jealousy and envy, torturers of desire.

7.23 You need not make visible every detail of a text. Eating imaginary limbs, for example, is not an appetizing task for an actor. It is sometimes helpful to focus on one element. A movement version of this text might take its inspiration from "roaming at night" and "we went with animals." Play this for the entire text.

Moving in space
You will limit the range of your movement if you always work in empty space. Walls, corners, pillars, levels, and furniture can help you shape and support movements that are impossible in open space. Against a wall, for example, you can lean at extreme angles, slide slowly to the ground, or pull yourself up from the ground hand over hand; out in the middle of the room these choices are impossible or look like mime rather than acting. As you explore movement, stay alert to the possibilities afforded you by space.

Even when movement takes place in the open, spatial issues like direction and distance are important. If movement is to help you tell your story, it must be sensitive to space.

For Your Own Speech

Prepare three moments in which movement helps to tell the story of your speech.
- How might you recreate movements in the other time and place?
- Might you use movement as a metaphor for any moment in your speech?
- Do any implicit scenes suggest possible movements?
- Explore the question of scale with at least one of your movements.

Guidelines

Make sure your movements are grounded in specific circumstances: set the scene.

Get your whole body involved.

Movements should be choreographed to begin and end at a definite point in the text.

Let your body speak: how you say the text should be in synch with how you move.

Your movement should seem natural and spontaneous.

Consider using space to help you shape and support some of your movements.

Chapter 8
Space

Space is neglected by many actors, who seem content to let directors and designers locate what they do.[1] Yet space is a powerfully expressive tool. When you are acting a speech that tells a story, moreover, it is critical to orient the audience spatially. Since there is no set for the other time and place and since the other characters are all played by you, the whereabouts of characters and events depends entirely on the spatial clues you give the audience. Narrative speeches require a performer to use space as one of the means to make visible what happened.

Everything that happens on stage happens in space, which is defined not only by the architecture and furniture of the set, but by every element of a production. If you hold something up in front of your face or hide it behind your back, if you go in and out of light, if you move from the periphery to center stage, if you take a circuitous rather than a direct path, those are spatial events. Your proximity to and orientation toward the audience are questions of space. If you stand behind or in front of or above or below or next to or far from another character, these choices create potentially significant spatial relationships.

Space is also defined by how you insert your body into it. Imagine challenging a dozen people to take turns inhabiting a chair without repeating anything done before. The number of possible rounds is greatly increased if the chair can be manipulated however an individual chooses.

In *Curse of the Starving Class*, the refrigerator is a hub of the action; the fact that it is usually empty is a central image in the play. The ensemble of a production directed by Vincent Murphy[2] were invited to make a strong spatial choice about relating to the fridge in one of their scenes. So the sister of the family used the refrigerator door to shield herself from the lawyer when he startled her: she acted their exchange with her face and her feet. The father leaned his back against the front of the refrigerator and slid down it as he talked about sinking into debt. When a bar owner to

---

[1] The problem is compounded by the conditions in which we rehearse. When there are no walls to lean against, and when levels are indicated by different colors of tape on the floor, there is a tendency to stand in front of the scenery as if it were a painted backdrop even when the set materializes. Unless real efforts are made in the rehearsal hall to supply surrogate spaces, and unless actors are encouraged to install their performances in the nooks and crannies of the set once they hit the stage, a production's acting will not mesh with its design.

[2] Reality Theater, Boston, 1979.

whom the father had signed over his farm came to check the place out, he stuck a six-pack in the freezer and vaulted himself into a sitting position atop the fridge, the better to survey his new property. When the son discovered that its shelves were miraculously full and proceeded to gorge himself, as the script directs, he sat down in the bottom of the fridge and reached around and above to grab more food. All of these choices were provoked by treating the refrigerator more as space than as an appliance.

Using Real Space to Create Imagined Space

The first use of space in narrative speeches is to conjure locations within the story. It is often possible to use a space at hand as a stand-in for one in the other time and place. When drunken Weston rages about his wife's affair with the lawyer, he may suddenly see the kitchen table as the hotel bed on which he splatters their brains. When he tells his son about the bath, he may slide down in his chair and put his feet up on another as he relives sinking into the hot tub. When he remembers how very peaceful his farm seemed earlier that morning, he will use some space in the kitchen to situate himself once again out in the fields. It is as if characters telling stories were improvising spaces in the rehearsal hall. A window might become a painting on the wall of a museum; the back of a chair might become a window sill. Need a coffin? Try the couch.

Simple adjustments in space can be very significant in storytelling. Suppose that a character is telling a story about giving testimony in court. She crosses to sit at a table where her scene partner is already seated. If we are to see her in the witness stand, she should not sit facing into the table, because that is not a witness's spatial relationship to the judge's bench in a jury trial. If her partner is sitting behind the table and if she sits to one side of it facing in the same direction, this will help us to visualize her in the courtroom. This spatial choice also casts the other character as the judge, so that she can play snippets of her testimony to him.

Keep in mind that spaces can become associated with characters and events. When Elizabeth Stanton approaches her "father seated pale and immovable" (Excerpt 8, Appendix A), we have seen how an empty chair might serve as a surrogate for him, and that she might use its seat as his lap, its back as his chest, etc. In a similar way, a place on stage can become associated with a specific event or impulse, so that crossing there means you are revisiting what happened at that location.

In a speech about exterminators torturing a rat (in Kay Adshead's *Thatcher's Women*), a character has a conversation with the unfortunate rodent. An actor working on this speech shoved his foot against a black cube as he recreated how his co-workers trapped the rat, thereby placing it; then sat down rather suddenly in the same spot as he became the rat; later answered the rat by addressing himself to that same space.

> **Geography**
>
> Every story has a geography. In short order you can orient your audience as to the location of places and characters: the beach is that way, the garden is over here. If you move in one of those established directions, we know where you are going. In this way an actor can map the terrain of a story.
>
> Suppose, for example, that the actor playing Joan of Arc (Speech 2, Appendix B) places the angel in the audience to her right and the safe haven of her home behind her to her left. This gives the audience reference points for her dialog with the angel and for her running away. When she later returns to the place of the apparition, it is clear in what direction she should move. These two locations — home and the field — might become the poles whereby the audience gauges Joan's inner progress: moving toward the angel brings her closer to accepting her vocation; backing off toward her home puts her in retreat.
>
> Paying attention to the geography of your speech locates your character in space and in the journey of the story. In both these senses, geography makes visible where your character is at.
>
> Once spatial reference points have been defined, an actor must be careful not to confuse the audience by violating established conventions. If the devil is to your left and the angel is on your right, they must generally stay put. If exiting stage right means you're going into battle and exiting left means you're deserting, those directions must stay fixed, however much your character vacillates.

I showed I was sensible by running away to safety. That was all that happened the first time. And I didn't say anything about it when I got home: but after supper I went back. (Speech 2, Appendix B)

8.1 *Play the geography of these events. Locate the field where Joan sees the angel. In what direction does St. Michael appear? One generally places unseen characters and events in or above the audience. Now map the direction in which you run away. What are the stages of your flight from the angel? How do you situate yourself in space when you arrive "home"? Be careful about how you use space as you begin heading back toward the field. Set the scene carefully; the playwright leaves much to your imagination here. Are you sneaking back? Are you irresistibly drawn? Are you afraid or aglow?*

At the beginning of his speech about the eagle, Weston is folding laundry at the kitchen table. He is speaking to a sick lamb (it has maggots), which is penned up by the stove.

I'd set myself up right beside the lean-to out there. Just a little roof-shelter thing out there (Speech 9, Appendix B)

The narrative task at this point is establishing one important detail about the geography of the other time and place: the location of the lean-to. This is a reference point to which the speech returns near the climax: Weston throws the lamb testicles onto the lean-to's roof, and this is where the eagle makes its spectacular landing.

8.2 *So that you have a physical context in which to work, rough out a kitchen set for yourself: table, chair, stove, lamb-in-pen, refrigerator, sink.*

You will experiment with two different approaches to locating the lean-to.

8.3 *One approach is to work in open space on the kitchen set and simply indicate the direction in which the lean-to is located, without reference to anything in the room. Do that as you speak the text. Later in the speech you will throw a handful of testes "on top a' the shed roof." Gesture as if you doing that now; be specific about direction, distance, and height.*

8.4 *Now experiment with tying the geography of the story into your set. Where in the room might you find a space that becomes the shed roof? Explore different possibilities: as you speak the text, point out to the lamb just where in the kitchen the lean-to is located. Once you have located a "real" shed roof, you can consider actually throwing something onto it later in the speech.*

The lean-to is probably not a very high structure, but the references to "roof" do suggest some elevation — relative to where Weston is in space. If he is crouching as he works, the top of the kitchen counter might serve as a roof; if he is standing, some higher spot is called for.

What will happen when the eagle lands on the shed roof? If you have been working with an imaginary location "over there," it is quite possible for space to collapse, so that wherever you are when you characterize the eagle becomes the roof. But if you have located the lean-to in a particular spot in the kitchen — on the table, let's say — you can land the eagle there.

Textual References to Space, Explicit and Implicit

Whenever a text refers to space, however fleetingly, an actor should consider whether it would be worthwhile to make the spatial allusion visible.

I started wondering if the real owner was gonna' pop up out of nowhere and blast my brains out for trespassing. (Speech 8, Appendix B)

8.5 *Here is an opportunity to characterize a phantom "owner" and to put some of the text into his mouth as an indirect quote. Explore using space as part of how you play this moment. What opportunities for "popping up out of nowhere" does the room you are working in provide? (You needn't fully disappear before you pop out.) What spaces in the kitchen might you use to create the illusion of appearing suddenly — and to show us Weston's playful impulse as he relives his walk?*

Environèd with all these hideous fears (Speech 15, Appendix B)

What Juliet conjures in her soliloquy is the tomb: what was her bedroom has become another space entirely. The frightful details that have accumulated in her imagination now surround her: "environèd" means encircled, hemmed in.

Shakespeare's stage, except for the two massive pillars supporting the canopy, was a bare platform. Where might the original Juliet have situated herself at this moment of feeling environèd? She might have turned in place at center stage. She might have fled to a downstage corner, as if to escape the stage. Perhaps she peeked out from behind one of the pillars or tried to hide downstage of one.

8.6 *Explore on impulse the room you are working in: to what spaces might Juliet retreat in this environment? Be specific about how you play each space.*

Exhausted after a long drunken tirade, Weston passes out on top of the kitchen table. As he slips into unconsciousness, he vividly remembers piloting a bomber in World War II.

I flew giant machines in the air. Giants! Bombers. What a sight. Over Italy, The Pacific. Islands. Giants. Oceans. Blue oceans.
(Excerpt 17, Appendix A)

8.7 *How might you use the table to help the audience see what Weston is visualizing? The panorama below you is vast. At the same time, explore how Weston gets bedded down. Suppose that he starts these lines sitting on the edge of the table; how does he get prone?*

Read Excerpt 20, Appendix A.

I just went off for a little while. Now and then. I couldn't stand it here. I couldn't stand the idea that everything would stay the same. That every morning it would be the same. I kept looking for it out there somewhere.

Weston has repeatedly gone AWOL on his family. The "here" he couldn't stand is painfully clear. Where should you locate "out there somewhere"? You might leave it as vague as it seems to be in Weston's mind, or you might put him at a window, looking out. But there is a way to play the opposition of "here" and "out there" that is more specific to the play, and more telling. Weston's central conflict is whether he should leave or stay. On the set, we know, is a kitchen door — the one Weston destroyed the night before the play begins, which his son has replaced. Imagine that the doorway is where Weston gravitates: it is where his spirit vacillates. He lives with one foot on either side of the threshold.

8.8 *The text looks outward, then into the house, then outward again. Plant yourself in an open doorway and change the direction in which you look along with the text.*

8.9 *Explore moving in and out of the house as if you cannot decide where to be.*

I kept looking for it out there somewhere. And all the time it was right inside this house.

8.10 *If Weston has played this speech betwixt and between the two directions just explored, how might you bring these last lines to a spatial conclusion?*

Space As an Expressive Tool

As with gesture and movement, space can be used in expressive ways that go beyond locating events in physical space.

Swaying very quietly like they were being blown by someone's breath. (Speech 7, Appendix B)

8.11 *Position yourself on a table or another elevated surface. Place the motion of the model planes below you. Blow on them to change their movement.*

What are the implications of placing Wesley in this spatial relationship to the swaying planes? Whether you see him as a god, a puppeteer, or simply a child at play, he seems more powerful, more in control: he is in fact on top of the action, above it, which is quite different from being below the planes, looking up. You might play the same values as you did before, but this spatial change has altered what the image says quite substantially.

The next two texts do *not* refer to space. But even when it is not the issue, space can help you tell a story.

The ninth year we went numb, We tasted war. But felt nothing. We smelled death. But felt nothing. We ate, drank, slept ... Nothing. The sand burned with more desire than we, the sundried meat. (Speech 3, Appendix B)

8.12 *How might space help you to get inside the physical life of this year — and to create a landscape into which an audience can project itself?*

Grounding yourself in space should position your body to speak truthfully.

At which time would I, being but a moonish youth, grieve, be effeminate, changeable, longing and liking, proud, fantastical, apish, shallow, inconstant, full of tears, full of smiles; for every passion something (Excerpt 14, Appendix A)

8.13 Rosalind is engaged in a demonstration of how she once cured a lover by subjecting him to maddening changes of mood. How might space help Rosalind improvise "for every passion something"? Explore a single space as the hub for a series of simple physical adjustments that create an easy flow of characterizations.

• You might, for example, use a chair to shape a flow of images that quite specifically capture the essence of each little scene.

• Then play with spatial variations on a pillar or post or tree.

• Choose one other space into which you might insert yourself in a variety of expressive ways.

As you investigate how to use these spaces, you will need to take your time. Eventually, the physical score you put together should help the text to move along; blocking should never impede a text's forward motion. Body and voice should share the same rhythmic pulse.

The Actor As Visual Artist

Read Excerpt 21, Appendix A.

This is the end of a wild ride and a terrific speech. Carol is a patient in a clinic, which is simply furnished: a hospital bed, a chair, perhaps a side table. Carol has awful migraines, and in this speech she fantasizes how one day her "head will blow up. The top will come right off." This will happen, she imagines, while she is skiing, and she begins with a sensuous and highly physical account of speeding down hill. When the migraine hits, she collapses and starts rolling at great velocity, snapping bones; she imagines that her head will "roll down the hill and become a huge snowball and roll into the city and kill a million people." And then she conjures this very still scene.

My body will stop at the bottom of the hill with just a bloody stump for a neck and both arms broken and both legs.

8.14 Use space to create several different "snapshots" of a headless torso

133

and four thoroughly broken limbs. (Bonus points for using space to suggest that you are at the bottom of a hill.) How can the architecture and the furnishings of the space you are working in help you to sculpt this image? Use space to shape your body. Don't worry about being literal; work at capturing the essence of the moment. Your head may or may not be visible, for example; what is important is the visual, and visceral, effect. Note how space can visually sever one part of your body from the rest. It can also help you to focus the audience's eye on physical details: a broken wrist placed on the seat of a chair sits on a kind of stage, and a broken leg projecting up above a window sill has a frame around it. After completing each snapshot, take a moment to see with your mind's eye the image you have created. Then say the text from inside it; let the physicality of the picture speak.

Theater is a hybrid art form that combines text and voice, gesture and movement, scenic design and technical machinery, sound effects and music. If the actor playing Carol wants to have at her command all the elements of the medium, she must develop sensibilities that include — in the case of this last exercise — those of a visual artist.

Before we leave Carol, let's imagine how space might help you play her long descent down the hill. The text tells us that her skis lock, her knees buckle, she rolls downhill, her arms thrash about until they are so broken they simply drag, her whole face peels away, her head snaps off. This is obviously too much to work on all at once. What you want is not the sort of realism that a stuntwoman might bring to the film version, but selected details that embody the essence of the event.

8.15 How can the room and its furnishings help you stage her descent? Move about and let the possibilities of different spaces provoke you into slow-motion snippets of Carol's fall. Explore distinctly different versions of the event. You might focus on your arms for a while, then on rolling and tumbling, then on your face and head. What can you do with the help of space that you couldn't do otherwise?

There are versions of Carol's fall that are fun, balletic, slippery smooth; others that are terrifying, seemingly out of control, bumpy and jagged. Space greatly increases the spectrum of possibilities. I once saw an actress place one side of her face against an exposed brick wall and then slide to her knees; what I imagined happening to her face could be felt vicariously on my own skin. Space is what made that choice possible.

Practice in Space

8.16 Each of the following texts has a spatial dimension that might be made visible. Focus on using space to set the scene and tell the story.

I recall going into the large darkened parlor and finding the casket, mirrors and pictures all draped in white (Excerpt 8, Appendix A)

We came down this alley of trees (Excerpt 3, Appendix A)

He had this farm with white fences. I never saw so many white fences. (Excerpt 3, Appendix A)

They sleep on the wind — never light on this earth but one time when they die. (Excerpt 24, Appendix A)

I could feel the space around me like a big, black world. (Speech 7, Appendix B)

In the third year, we guarded jealously the nests we clawed out in the wounded landscape. (Speech 4, Appendix B)

There'll be giant steel girders spanning acres of land. (Excerpt 16, Appendix A)

Cowardly. Sniveling. Sneaking around. (Excerpt 18, Appendix A)

I'll track her down and shoot them in their bed. In their hotel bed. (Excerpt 19, Appendix A)

Her chariot is an empty hazel-nut (Speech 16, Appendix B)

As in a vault, an ancient receptacle
Where for this many hundreds of years the bones

Of all my buried ancestors are packed (Speech 15, Appendix B)

The whole of my thoughts. Vanished. The whole of my feelings. Vanished. The whole of my self. Vanished. The whole of what I call myself. Vanished. The whole of my body was left. (Excerpt 23, Appendix A)

still tugging at the vein
till it was twelve yards long
as if it held that body like a kite (Speech 5, Appendix B)

8.17 *After the horizontal tugging of the first two lines, the kite image, so much lighter than its context, seems to float up. We think of kites high above us, weightless on the wind. How might your body reflect this shift without suggesting that the dying cowboy is literally flying?*

Practice In Gesture, Movement and Space

In performance as in life, gesture, movement, and space are organically linked. Some of the following exercises ask you to consider alternative physical approaches to texts; others provide you with opportunities to integrate these different aspects of your physical work.

I coil him round and round
in the wealth, the robes of doom (Speech 1, Appendix B)

When Agamemnon came out of the bath, Clytemnestra wrapped him in robes that incapacitated him. Then she struck.

8.18 *What gestures might Clytemnestra use as she speaks these lines?*

8.19 *What is the movement version of this moment? Remember that Agamemnon's body is lying there on stage.*

I kept trying to piece it together. The jumps, I couldn't figure out the jumps. From being born, to growing up, to droppin' bombs, to having kids, to this. (Excerpt 21, Appendix A)

8.20 *There are two related images here. Weston's life feels like a jigsaw puzzle that he cannot assemble. It also seems like a series of "jumps" — abrupt discontinuities that have kept him off balance. Both metaphors imply actions. Explore gestures with which Weston might try to capture these qualities of his life.*

8.21 Explore movement versions of these same images. Instead of gesturing about the pieces, for example, move about inside the puzzle. How might space help you to physicalize the "jumps"?

You struggle to the window. You hold yourself up by both elbows and stare down at the street, looking for your life. But all you see down there is yourself looking back up at you. You jump back from the window. You fall. You lay there gaping at the ceiling. You're pounding all over. You crawl back for another look. You can't resist. You pull yourself back up to the window sill and peer down again. (Speech 10, Appendix B)

8.22 The geography of this scene needs to be carefully mapped. Your movement should be scored so that Laureen arrives at the window and peers out at precisely the right moment. How are the two arrivals different from each other? You can work with a real window or with a substitute space.

Then you make a clean jump all the way to the bottom. And your life goes dancing out the window.

8.23 Explore a gestural version of this fantasized event. What might a movement version look like? How might you use space?

I started wondering who this was walking around in the orchard at six-thirty in the morning. It didn't feel like me. It was some character in a dark overcoat and tennis shoes and stickers comin' out of his face. (Speech 8, Appendix B)

8.24 How might gesture and movement combine as Weston relives this walk?

Last night, Wesley fantasized about the model planes suspended above his bed.

I could feel myself lying far below them on my bed like I was on the ocean and overhead they were on reconnaissance. Scouting me. Floating. Taking pictures of the enemy. Me, the enemy. (Speech 7, Appendix B)

8.25 Earlier Wesley had described his planes as floating in the air; now he imagines himself floating on the ocean. Explore moving back and forth between these two points of view in terms of gesture, movement and space.

Read Excerpt 6, Appendix A.

In 1903 the Austrian playwright Hugo von Hofmannsthal re-imagined the story of Electra, the daughter of Agamemnon and Clytemnestra. As in Sophocles' play, Electra has long dreamed of avenging her father's murder by killing Clytemnestra and her lover. But Electra has been living under house arrest, and years of despair have taken a toll on her health. Her present state is revealed in this diatribe against her mother, the "you" on whom Electra wishes the worst fates she can imagine. The images that surface are a window into the nature of her own suffering. Electra is the shipwreck survivor, the prisoner, the child trapped at the bottom of a well, and this speech is her "vain cry" of despair. Each image is another time and place that you can explore — in terms of gesture, movement, and space — as a way inside the character.

Let us suppose that the set has a Greek column and a small stone bench.

What agony is that of shipwrecked men
When their vain cry devours the night of clouds
And death

8.26 *Imagine that Electra — who complains of being too weak to do the murder herself — is sitting on the ground next to the bench, holding onto it as if she were clinging to a floating timber, adrift at sea. She can't last much longer. Given Electra's feverish condition, her voice is not terribly strong, but it should have in it the echo of a drowning man's cry. Her behavior should seem quite natural in the here and now of this confrontation with her mother.*

All that are chained to prison walls

8.27 *Imagine Electra against a column. Her arms are above her head in a restless, weary gesture that subliminally suggests she is chained to a wall. She is in fact a prisoner in her mother's house, helpless to escape. Her physical position should seem perfectly in tune with what she is feeling.*

And cry in darkness from the bottom of a well

8.28 Sit on the floor, your back against the wall. Reach up toward the circle of light far above. You are calling for help from deep in a well.

Triggering a text

Why does Electra threaten her mother with these particular images of suffering? Quite possibly because they are implicit in her own weakened condition: in how she moves, how she collapses, how she inhabits space. Her physical life may subconsciously prompt what she says.

Sometimes a character's body language speaks before the text. When a verbal image arises from what is happening in a character's body, the words seem like an organic expression of what the audience can see is plainly true. You can create this effect by playing a textual image before it is spoken.

A gesture, movement, or location can also trigger a memory or a train of thought. What your character says can be sparked by what is in your body — if your body anticipates what is said.

Now tie the three images together. Work without text. Your movement should embody Electra's enervated state.

8.29 Your starting point is the shipwreck image. Crawl a few steps as if landing at last on shore, pull yourself up on the column, and turn to your mother in the image of a chained prisoner before sliding down into the well. This sequence of moves — each with its own rhythm and texture — should flow without seeming choreographed.

Thinking Space

Consider the question of space for your speech as a whole.

Where in your rehearsal space do you want to place your speech so as to take advantage of the room's architecture? How might you use this space to help you tell the story? What furniture do you want? These are empirical questions: experiment.

For now, as you develop your speech, you can use as much set as you wish, as if you were in rehearsal for a full production. If you plan on performing your speech in auditions, you can later work on a version that needs no set or props. In auditions, of course, where you have so little to work with, space is a vital issue.

Playing space in auditions

Most audition spaces are rather blank, with a chair or two available. There may or may not be a window or door or wall within playable reach; it is best not to count on any architecture. On the other hand, it is often stimulating to incorporate found space spontaneously — leaning on a proscenium wall, using a platform level or a corner, playing around a column, etc. Interesting spaces invite improvisation.

What is always available to you is your spatial relationship to the auditioner(s), and how you use the open area. Some speeches can be done very simply in terms of movement and space. But you should consider where you start and end up, and explore a variety of expressive spatial choices in between.

The audition chair is a very flexible spatial tool. You can sit on it in any number of expressive ways, stand or kneel on it, lean on it, crouch behind it, sit on the floor next to it, prop your elbows on the seat, etc. Two chairs allow you to recline.

Spatial choices that energize the audition room and endow it with a sense of locale can make a big impression.

For Your Own Speech

1. Prepare three moments in which you use space to tell the story.
- What geography does your speech need? Map the story's terrain: where are the various people and places to which you refer? How might you make visible the spatial relationships inside the story?
- Would there be value in associating a particular space with an event? Defining a space in this way allows you to use it as a reference point and to return to it whenever you wish. Might any space be used as a surrogate for another character?
- Can you use space expressively for moments which are not explicitly about space?
- How might space help you to shape movements otherwise impossible?

Guidelines

How your body inserts itself in space and how your body relates to the physical world should be specific and sensual. Ground yourself in space so that it helps you to get inside the story.

2. Explore one moment in which your physical life — a gesture, a movement, where you are in space — precedes and triggers what your character says. The idea or memory or image in your text should be prompted by what is already visible in your body.

Section Two
Sound Sense

Chapter 9
Onomatopoeia

Sound Sense

True ease in writing comes from art, not chance,
As those move easiest who have learned to dance.
'Tis not enough no harshness gives offense,
The sound must seem an echo to the sense [...]

The sound of words, says Alexander Pope in *An Essay on Criticism*, should echo what they mean. He proceeds to give us a series of examples in rhymed couplets. The first demonstrates how a poet should write about a gentle stream or the light western breeze that the ancient Greeks personified as Zephyr. In order to make sound echo sense, Pope has carefully constructed the lines with consonants that flow as softly and smoothly as Zephyr itself.

Soft is the strain when Zephyr gently blows,
And the smooth stream in smoother <u>numbers</u> flows *metrical feet*
A consonant that can be prolonged as long as the breath lasts, without a change of quality in the sound, is called a *continuant*. Of the forty-four consonants in these two lines, thirty-five are continuants.
9.1 *Read the couplet aloud several times, focusing on how smoothly the sounds flow. These lines are the gentle movement of the west wind and the stream.*

Pope's next couplet, by contrast, sounds as violent as the seascape it describes. The "r"s (nine of them) are not gentle as in the previous couplet but muscular and rough like the roar of the surf.

But when loud surges lash the sounding shore,
The hoarse, rough verse should like the torrent roar
9.2 *Read the couplet aloud, and try to create with sound a picture of the scene described. Note how "surges" actually seems to swell like a wave, and how that wave seems to hit the shore on "lash" — how wet the "sh" sounds, as if it were ocean spray! "Hoarse" and "rough"*

145

> should both sound like what they mean, and in this context "verse"
> is robust and athletic. The double "r" of "torrent" is part of the final
> "roar."

A very substantial part of what these lines mean is conveyed by how they sound. Pope's words do more than echo sense; they embody what he means. *Embody:* in poetry, as in all expressive language, sound is the flesh of sense.

A speech that tells a story — whether the text is richly poetic or quite commonplace language — should not just tell us what happened; it should embody what happened in how the words are spoken. Sound sense conjures the events of a story because it makes them happen *now* — sensuously — in the ears of the audience. Actors who are sensitive to the ways in which sound is sense do not talk about events but give us the sound of the events themselves, so that we hear the story.

Sensuousness

Sound speaks to the senses, and it has an effect on them. Audiences do not hear sensuously spoken language so much as they experience it.

Robert Browning's "Meeting at Night" is remarkable for how vividly it appeals to the senses with visual, aural and tactile images — and thereby conjures a lovers' tryst.

Meeting at Night
The gray sea and the long black land;
And the yellow half-moon large and low;
And the startled little waves that leap
In fiery ringlets from their sleep,
As I gain the cove with pushing prow,
And quench its speed i' the slushy sand.

Then a mile of warm sea-scented beach;
Three fields to cross till a farm appears;
A tap at the pane, the quick sharp scratch
And blue spurt of a lighted match,
And a voice less loud, though its joys and fears,
Than the two hearts beating each to each!
The slow monosyllables of the first line let us hear the distance that

must be traveled. In the second line, the vowel of "low" is formed in the back of your mouth and is naturally voiced in your lower register: Browning's moon sits low because it sounds low. We can hear movement in the rhythmic pulse of "startled little waves that leap/In fiery ringlets from their sleep": the little leaps are right there in the sound of the text.

And quench its speed i' the slushy sand

9.3   Why "slushy" sand? Why not "wet" or "soft"? The sound sense of "slushy" so perfectly conjures what Browning is talking about that you can almost feel the texture of the sand on your feet. How does the "ch" of "quench" relate to "slushy"? What happens to the other "s"s in this aural context? Alexander Pope might say that this line echoes the sound of the boat pushing into the beach. Explore how the words embody this event.

A tap at the pane

9.4   Any native speaker of English senses that "tap" ought to sound like what it means. The "a" of "at" so quickly echoes the previous vowel that it makes us hear another little tap. Why "pane" and not, for example, "window" or "glass"? The "p" of "pane" repeats the earlier "p" and gives us yet another tap. Explore speaking this phrase so that you recreate the sound of the event.

the quick sharp scratch

9.5   Say "scratch" so as to create the sound of a match scraping against a surface. How does "sharp" contribute to the effect? "Quick" should sound quick and start the scratching sound. Play with the phrase as a unit rather than as three separate words.

spurt

9.6   Conjure the event of the match bursting into flame with the sound sense of this word.

If a poem is about something, it is not because the poem *talks* about what it means but because it *is* what it means: its meaning is embodied in its text. That is the gist of a poem by Archibald MacLeish, the Latin title of which announces that it will be a statement about the art of poetry.

147

Ars Poetica
A poem should be palpable and mute
As a globed fruit,

Dumb
As old medallions to the thumb,

Silent as the sleeve-worn stone
Of casement edges where the moss has grown –

A poem should be wordless
As the flight of birds. [...]

MacLeish concludes that "A poem should not mean/But be."

A narrative speech should not talk about events but give us the events themselves. Our acting should not mean, but be. Our text should not be words so much as the incarnation in sound of what we are talking about.

A poem should be palpable and mute
As a globed fruit
9.7 *Start with the word "globed." Take your time forming the word in your mouth; make the sound of it as round as possible. Now extend that sound sense to "fruit," so that the phrase is as spherical and three-dimensional as an apple. Now go back to the word "palpable" and feel in your mouth how its "l"s and "b" and "p" make its sound kin to "globed." Speak the two lines and note how "poem" and "mute" contribute to the sound sense.*

Dumb
as old medallions to the thumb
9.8 *The "m"s here pick up on those in "mute" and "poem." When the sound "m" is held a while — as the isolation of "dumb" on its own line suggests — it forms the mouth into the same expression that we use when we silently suggest that our lips are sealed. Mum's the word, the poet is saying.*

9.9 Read these first two stanzas of William Blake's "The Tiger" aloud. What consonant dominates these lines? The fifteen recurrences of this consonant create an undercurrent of sound.

The Tiger
Tiger! Tiger! burning bright
In the forests of the night,
What immortal hand or eye
Could frame thy fearful symmetry.

In what distant deeps or skies
Burnt the fire of thine eyes?
On what wings dare he aspire?
What the hand dare seize the fire?

9.10 Read these lines again and lean into the "r"s, holding them a fraction longer than you would in another context. It is as if a tiger were quietly growling throughout.

There are sixteen more "r"s in the next eight lines. These wonderfully muscular verses, which imagine God as a blacksmith shaping the tiger in his smithy, are the equivalent in sound of Blake's drawings of God the Father, which picture Him with a brawny physique such as Michelangelo might have drawn.

And what shoulder, and what art,
Could twist the sinews of thy heart?
And when thy heart began to beat,
What dread hand forged thy dread feet?

What the hammer? what the chain?
In what furnace was thy brain?
What the anvil? what dread grasp
Dare its deadly terrors clasp?

twist the sinews
9.11 This phrase is as tough and fibrous as a sinew, and your mouth

should mold the sound of it in muscular fashion. Let each consonant build up pressure behind your teeth and lips before you release it. It should feel as though your mouth were doing the twisting and that it required the strength of a blacksmith to forge these words.

And when thy heart began to beat...
9.12 Can you hear the heartbeat in this line? Get it into your voice.

What the hammer? What the chain?
9.13 More sound effects: the blacksmith begins to pound his hammer on the anvil. Experiment with continuing this rhythmic pulse into the two lines that follow.

The word "soundscape," modeled on "landscape," describes a sustained aural effect, a picture in sound. Blake has in these four stanzas created a very particular soundscape, which, in the next verse, changes dramatically. Listen for the point at which something new emerges.

When the stars threw down their spears,
And watered heaven with their tears,
Did he smile his work to see?
Did he who made the Lamb make thee?

The first two lines have seven "r"s, even as the tone softens. But "smile" arrives like a quiet revolution; it is as if such a gentle word had never been spoken before. The fearsome muscularity of the poem up to this point relaxes. The tiger's growl is quieted by the very sound of "smile" — and of the word in the next line that echoes it.

Did he smile his work to see?
Did he who made the Lamb make thee?
In Christian symbolism, Christ is the Lamb of God, sacrificed like the paschal lamb of Judaic tradition. Here the word "lamb" (reinforced by the two "m"s surrounding it) combines with "smile" to create a new soundscape.
9.14 Read these lines as if the world were transformed. Take your time forming the word "smile": notice how the sequence of "m" — long

"i" — "I" actually seems to start a smile at the corners of your mouth.
Blake's central question — whether the God who forged the fearful
tiger is the same God who created the Lamb — is posed not only in words
but in the sound sense of his poem. This issue is embodied especially in
the "r"s, "m"s and "l"s.

Informing yourself about sound sense

In the famous storm scene in *King Lear*, the old king
commands the heavens to destroy mankind and the world it so
ungratefully inhabits. "Spit, fire! Spout, rain!" he cries. An actor
whose spittle is flying over the footlights intuitively grasps the sense
in a forceful attack on the initial sound of "spit" and "spout." That
actor may not know that a family of words share the same sound
sense *(spurt, spew, spray, spatter, splatter, sputter, splutter, spume,
spark, splotch, spill, etc.)*; that what these words have in common
is some kind of explosion or ejection, usually moist, which is best
defined by the event of your lips producing the sound sp-; or that
some linguists term particles like sp- "phonetic intensives." What
matters is that the Lear actor spit out these sp- words as
Shakespeare surely intended.

Similarly, you can grasp the sound sense of
Soft is the strain when Zephyr gently blows,
And the smooth stream in smoother numbers flows
without knowing that its thirty-five continuant consonants consist of
ten nasals *(m, n, ng)*, eight liquids *(l, r)*, and seventeen fricatives *(s,
z, f, v, th)*, with an especially high proportion (ten) of sibilants *(s, z)*.

If you feel intimidated or a bit overwhelmed by references to
such technical terms, you can take comfort in the fact that actors
may be sensitive to the expressive possibilities of language without
acquiring linguistic terminology. What the actor needs is practical
know-how and an informed sensibility. As long as you sense that
Browning's use of "slushy" is aurally expressive, you can get by
without knowing that sl- is a phonetic intensive.

Knowledge, of course, is a handy way to inform yourself, and the
sort of information that actors acquire in voice and speech classes can
be put to immediate use. Terminology can raise your consciousness
and help you to discover more of the sound sense in a text. People
who know the names of things tend to notice them more.

> What is absolutely essential to the actor is a passion for the expressiveness of spoken language. If you do not take as much delight in playing with sounds as you did in the crib, your technique will remain technical. A fascination with sound sense translates into a relish for the athletic activity of producing it.

Onomatopoeia

A word that imitates the sound of what it names has been formed by a process called onomatopoeia [oh-no-mah-toe-PEE-ah]. The root meaning of onomatopoeia is "to make a name."

9.15 The sound of each of the following onomatopoetic words mimics its meaning. Go as far as you can in making the words sound like what they name.

gag	*hum*	*tinkle*	*blare*
buzz	*snap*	*gurgle*	*bark*
hiss	*crackle*	*murmur*	*chickadee*
bang	*pop*	*boom*	*cuckoo*

Alexander Pope would be pleased to know that linguists refer to the "echoic" origin of onomatopoetic words: their sound is indeed an echo to their sense.

The number of such words is relatively small. It is increased somewhat by adding certain families of words that take their meaning from a shared phonetic element that is aurally expressive. Laurence Perrine's *Sound and Sense: An Introduction to Poetry* analyzes several examples:

An initial *fl-* sound [...] is often associated with the idea of moving light, as in *flame, flare, flash, flicker, flimmer.* An initial *gl-* also frequently accompanies the idea of light, usually unmoving, as in *glare, gleam, glint, glow, glisten.* An initial *sl-* often introduces words meaning "smoothly wet," as in *slippery, slick, slide, slime, slop, slosh, slobber, slushy.* Short *-i-* often goes with the idea of smallness, as in *inch, imp, thin, slim, little, bit, chip, sliver, chink, slip, sip, whit, tittle, wink, glint, glimmer, flicker, pigmy, midge, chick, kid, kitten, minikin, miniature.* Long *-o-* or *-oo-* may suggest melancholy or sorrow, as in *moan, groan, woe, mourn, forlorn, toll, doom, gloom, moody.* Medial and final *-are-* sometimes goes with the idea of a big light or noise, as in *flare,* *glare, stare, blare.* Medial *-att-* suggests some kind of particled movement, as in *splatter, scatter, shatter, chatter, rattle, prattle, clatter, batter.* Final *-er* and *-le* indicate repetition, as in *glitter, flutter, shimmer, whisper, jabber, chatter, clatter, sputter, flicker, twitter, mutter,* and *ripple, bubble, twinkle, sparkle, rattle, rumble, jingle.*

Most of these words do not refer to sounds, but all of them make sense to our ears: what they mean is embodied in their sound.

The roots of the sound-sense connection run deep. Linguists have discovered that in many languages unrelated to each other the word for mother has an "m" sound, which requires a formation of the lips identical to that of nursing infants. Words expressive of revulsion and distaste often have guttural sounds (hard "g" and "k"), which are formed in the same part of the throat where we *gag: garbage, crud, curse,* and quite a number of expletives are examples, and the childhood word kaka is a primal expression of this instinctive interplay between sound and sense. So is the way we pronounce disgusted when we really are.

Onomatopoeia is in fact an everyday phenomenon. When we announce that the weather is really "hhhhot" or "ffffrrreezzing," we are prompted by the same impulse that has long inspired poets and public speakers — and actors. We will use "onomatopoeia" quite generally to refer to all the ways in which a performer can make language sound like what it's about. For our purposes, then, Browning's use of "slushy," "spurt," and "quick sharp scratch" is onomatopoeia, and so is the way in which you can expressively speak these words.

Making a text sound like what it means builds sound sense into the stories our characters tell. Onomatopoeia is an important tool.

Grounding sound sense inside your character

Some acting teachers caution their students against the use of onomatopoeia, for fear that it encourages actors to stand outside of moments and to *describe* circumstances and events instead of living them. It is certainly true that onomatopoeia can be misused and overdone; the same is true of skills in every area of acting. But it is wrong to think that sound sense is somehow an imposition on dramatic language. Humans instinctively use sound sense in everyday life, and it would be odd if actors ignored this. Whether a

> play is poetic or naturalistic, moreover, it is art, and one expects language to be used expressively.
>
> Onomatopoetic impulses should come from your character's gut. The colors and textures of your language should be grounded in an urgent need to express precisely what happened in the story. When sound is essential to sense, it comes quite naturally from inside your character.

Here are the first two verses of a soundscape by Isabella Gardner that is unusually full of onomatopoeia in a strict sense. Other word choices echo and amplify those that imitate the sounds of summer.

Summer Remembered

Sounds sum and summon the remembering of summers.
The humming of the sun
The mumbling in the honey-suckle vine
The whirring in the clovered grass
The pizzicato plinkle of ice in an auburn
uncle's amber glass.
The whing of father's racquet and the whack
of brother's bat on cousin's ball
and calling voices call-
ing voices spilling voices...

The munching of saltwater at the splintered dock
the slap and slop of waves on little sloops
The quarreling of oarlocks hours across the bay
The canvas sails that bleat as they
are blown. The heaving buoy bell-
ing HERE I am
HERE you are HEAR HEAR

An actor attuned to sound sense would notice in the third line how the onomatopoetic effect of the "m"s in "mumbling" is extended by the nasality of ing and by the "n"s of "honey-suckle" and of "vine"; how the "r"s in the fourth line interact and reinforce each other; how "pizzicato plinkle" is one sound unit; how the "k" sound in "racket" anticipates the final sound of "whack."

the slap and slop of waves on little sloops
Why "sloops" and not "yachts" or "boats"?
9.16 *Speak this line so as to imitate the sound of water lapping against the side of a docked boat. Take care that the contribution of "sloop" to the overall effect is audible.*

Here is a famous poem by one of the great voices of the Harlem Renaissance, Langston Hughes. It was here that Lorraine Hansberry found the title for her 1959 play, *A Raisin in the Sun*.

Dream Deferred
What happens to a dream deferred?
    Does it dry up
    like a raisin in the sun?
    Or fester like a sore –
    And then run?
    Does it stink like rotten meat?
    Or crust and sugar over –
    like a syrupy sweet?

    Maybe it just sags
    like a heavy load.

Or does it explode?

This poem is not onomatopoetic in the strict sense, but its words are carefully chosen so that their sound helps to conjure the images. You would not want to be heavy-handed in realizing the sound sense of such a plain-spoken poem, but its language is richly sensuous.
9.17 *Explore the onomatopoetic value of each of the following words and phrases:*
dry up
fester like a sore
rotten
crust
syrupy sweet
heavy load

155

The phrase "syrupy sweet" should be as thick and sugary as maple syrup or molasses. And "crust" should not talk about the crunchiness atop the syrup but *be* it.

and his big, manly voice,
Turning again toward childish treble, pipes
And whistles in his sound (Speech 11, Appendix B)

Jaques, characterizing the old pantaloon *who* represents the sixth age of man, imitates the change in his voice.

9.18 Note how the "s"s of "pipes and whistles" are extended by those in "his sound." In fact, the full text about the pantaloon contains twenty-two "s" sounds: Shakespeare wants you to give this character a sibilance, perhaps because some teeth are missing. Start in your lower register and gradually slide up to the old man's high-pitched voice.

The effect is to make this passage an indirect quote.

Seeking the bubble reputation

9.19 Here Jaques coins a one-word metaphor: fame is a bubble, elusive and very ephemeral. In performance, it will help an audience to grasp this image if the word "bubble" lives a fragile instant and then bursts — perhaps as the soldier grandiosely reaches for it. Play with the "b"s so that they make your mouth a bubble.

Read Excerpt 21, Appendix A.

Sound sense is essential to Carol's vision of her final moments. Even the most ordinary language in this passage has onomatopoetic value.

with just a bloody stump for a neck

9.20 "Stump" and "neck" are a one-two punch and very evocative. Each ends bluntly and, in this context, rather violently. The "k" of "neck" is a gutteral: it should touch your neck and that of every person in the audience.

Then there'll be a long cold wind. A whistle, sort of.

9.21 There are several continuant consonants in "long cold wind," which allow you to hold onto these words so as to mimic the sound you are imagining. Work on sliding the wind right into the whistle, so that these two sentences are one unit. "Whistle" is a real onomatopoetic word. Note the function of "sort of," which is not simply colloquial junk language. The "s" of "sort" extends your whistle and holding onto the "f" in "of" continues the sound of the wind.

It'll start to snow a little bit.

9.22 The playwright may not have been aware that the short "i" of "little" and "bit" is a phonetic intensive suggesting smallness, but the sound-sensitive actor can give voice to the playwright's impulse to make this phrase tiny, as if a couple of scattered flakes were coming down.

A very soft easy snow.

9.23 What word here suggests how this whole phrase should sound? Use the language to conjure the thing itself.

All you'll see is this little red splotch of blood and a whole blanket of white snow.

9.24 "Splotch" — another sp- word — is wonderfully expressive. One can hear in it how the blood splatters and makes an irregularly shaped stain on the snow. Play with "splotch" to create in sound what you see in your mind's eye.

9.25 The short vowels of "little red splotch of blood" suggest that the phrase should sound small. Try this.

9.26 By contrast, "whole blanket of white snow" is dominated by long vowels and continuants (n, l, f, s). Stretch out the phrase to paint a vast panorama.

9.27 This line is like one of those movie shots in which the camera ascends from a close-up to a bird's-eye view. Create this scenic contrast in sound.

Verbal Actions

Because verbs name actions, making a verb sound like what it means is especially dynamic. Speaking the verb *is* the action. This variety of sound sense might be termed a verbal action.

9.28 How might the sound of each of the following verbs embody its

157

action? *Be specific about what you imagine you are doing. If you are
playing with "slap," for example, know where you are striking, and
with what force; you might even make up a simple scenario about
whom you are slapping, and in what circumstances. Experiment with
quite different versions of each verbal action.*

slap	insinuate
pinch	demand
tickle	decide
wrestle	vacillate
fondle	suspect
stab	surround

Does it stink like rotten meat? (Langston Hughes, "Dream Deferred")
*9.29 Focus on "stink" as a verbal action. How you speak this verb should
set the scene and make the event happen. Don't overdo it: this
poem is understated, because there is a lid holding down the energy
that might eventually explode. Yet the verbal action must be
sensuous enough for an audience to hear it.*

**Maybe it just sags
like a heavy load**
*9.30 Focus on "sags." If you start this sentence in your upper register and
finish it near the bottom of your voice, the vocal shape created as
your pitch "sags" is a metaphor for what the line means.*

In the opening of the storm scene in *King Lear* (III.ii), Shakespeare
relies on what the actor can do with the sounds of the text to create the
storm. Shakespeare's Globe had simple sound effects, but no synthesizers
or booming speakers, no lighting to flash on and off. On a bare stage in
late afternoon two actors enter, and their movements and voices are
meant to conjure the wind and rain, thunder and lightning. Lear's first
speech is a brilliant soundscape, and its power is diminished if it is simply
shouted over pumped-up special effects. The text is full of opportunities
to treat verbs as verbal actions.

Blow winds, and crack your cheeks! Rage, blow!
You <u>cataracts</u> and hurricanoes, spout   *downpours*
Till you have <u>drenched</u> our steeples, drowned the cocks!   *submerged*
You sulph'rous and <u>thought-executing</u> fires,   *quick as thought*
<u>Vaunt-couriers</u> of oak-cleaving thunderbolts,   *precursors*
Singe my white head! And thou, all-shaking thunder,
Strike flat the thick rotundity o'th' world!
Crack nature's molds, all <u>germens</u> spill at once   *reproductive seeds*
That makes ingrateful man! [...]
Rumble thy bellyful! Spit, fire! Spout, rain!

Two sounds predominate, and both appear in the first line: "Blow winds, and crack your cheeks! Rage, blow!"

The sound of the wind is written into recurrent "o"s and "u"s (back vowels that naturally engage the lower register). This effect is amplified and sustained by other long vowels and by continuant consonants that Lear can hold onto as he gives voice to the howling storm.

Blow, winds

9.31 *Use all the air of a deep breath taken into the bottom of your lungs to create the sound of the wind with these two words. When Shakespeare wrote "Blow winds, and crack your cheeks," he had in mind maps of the period that depicted the four winds as faces with bulging cheeks. Let your cheeks fill with air before you let go of the first "b." Hold onto each vowel and consonant as long as you can without losing the words. Note how muscular and expressive the "w"s are. Changing your pitch should be part of the aural effect. There is no need to shout or strain your voice. Make sure you support your voice with sufficient breath.*

9.32 *This wind blows throughout the speech. Use the following words to continue the sound sense of "blow winds":*

rage	*sulph'rous*	*rotundity*
hurricanoes	*thought*	*molds*
spout	*vaunt-couriers*	*rumble*
drowned	*thou*	*bellyful*

In sharp contrast, Shakespeare uses repeated "k" sounds to give the audience claps of thunder and the violent noise of lightning strikes.

crack your cheeks

9.33 Attack this phrase as if "crack" were in fact the sound of lightning striking. "Cheeks" echoes and reinforces this effect.

9.34 Speak each of the following words as part of the storm. In context some of these words will faintly echo the "k" sound; others will be booming claps. For now, play with varying degrees of volume. Do not shout; do not strain your voice. Support each word with breath channeled through a relaxed throat.

cataracts	*all-shaking*
hurricanoes	*strike*
cocks	*thick*
oak-cleaving	

9.35 Now read through the speech rather quietly, so as to experience the interplay of vowels and consonants that sustain this soundscape of wind and thunder and lightning.

Singe my white head!

9.36 Lear orders the lightning to burn his hair off. Play with "singe" as a verbal action. It is not volume but what you do with the word's component sounds that will create the imagined event.

Rumble thy bellyful! Spit, fire! Spout, rain!

9.37 The first sentence, which should sound as though it were indeed rumbling out of your belly, is a sustained note of ominous thunder. "Spit" and "spout" should spray the first several rows.

Lear's rage is quite literally built into the language of this speech. To voice these words with muscular commitment to their sound sense is to feel all that is required.

Bleeding

Unless a jarring or quite deliberate effect is desired, you should fade into and out of vocal colors, so that an audience does not hear where the sound sense began or ended. The text that precedes onomatopoetic language should gradually take on its quality of sound; after arriving at the key word or phrase, the text which follows should just as seamlessly fade out of it.

Fading in this way has an aesthetic payoff: more of your text becomes vocally expressive. Instead of a word or phrase having sound sense, progressively darker or lighter shades of vocal color imbue a clause, a sentence, even a paragraph. I call this phenomenon "bleeding" — vocal color centered on a particular word bleeds into adjacent language, as if a drop of blood were soaking into a tissue or a daub of dye were spreading in wet cloth. Fading in this way is also good craftsmanship, because you avoid calling attention to what you are doing.

They All Want to Play Hamlet[1] is a one-man show about acting Hamlet. At one point the actor talks to the audience about a major shift in interpretations of Hamlet.

I know it has become quite fashionable these days to neglect the nineteenth-century melancholy Hamlet in favor of the more volcanic Hamlet of Elizabethan revenge sagas.

Sound sense and bleeding make this mouthful playable and entertaining.

9.38 *Suppose that the word "melancholy" had triggered an onomatopoetic impulse. The word may not seem to be intrinsically expressive, but the continuants "m," "n," and "l" lend themselves to a languid reading. Sigh the word out, as if you were indeed a melancholy Hamlet.*

9.39 *Now bleed that energy into "Hamlet" (another "m," another "l," and an "H" that is heavy of heart). The phrase "melancholy Hamlet" is now a sound sense unit.*

9.40 *Now bleed the vocal texture back into "nineteenth-century."*

9.41 *Now start at the beginning of the sentence and gradually fade into the sound of "nineteenth-century melancholy Hamlet." Because "neglect" is closer to the source of the sound sense, it will be more melancholy than "these days" — and so on. Think of the line as a seamless descent into melancholy.*

9.42 *Perhaps the word "volcanic" has leapt out at you: play with speaking it as if it were an eruption.*

9.43 *Bleed the vocal quality of "volcanic" into the language that follows. "Hamlet" sounds entirely different in this context. Let this explosive*

---

[1]Conceived by Tim McDonough. Created in collaboration with Jon Lipsky and Vincent Murphy. © 1981 by Theater Works.

energy wane on "sagas," as if you had run someone through on the word "revenge" and were now just beginning to relax and gloat.

Converging on the story

If you voice "melancholy" so that it sounds melancholic but also sounds like Hamlet talking, is that moment onomatopoeia or indirect quote? If your approach to "the more volcanic Hamlet of Elizabethan revenge sagas" is to hop up on a box and pose as if you were stabbing someone, are you talking from inside an implicit scene, or using gesture and space, or characterizing a revenge hero?

The answer is "all of the above" — or whichever approach it is that helps you find your way inside the moment. The various topics we have covered — and others yet to come — do overlap at times. For an actor focused on telling the story, all roads lead to the other time and place; there is more than one way to get where you want to go — inside the story. And, of course, several approaches may combine in realizing a moment: gesture and sound sense, or space and characterization, etc.

On successive days you may pick up a different tool to work on the same moment. It is, in fact, good rehearsal procedure to stay open to what may be discovered by varied approaches as they converge on the story.

Scale in Sound Sense

As is in all areas of acting, there is a question of scale in the use of onomatopoeia — and in other aspects of sound sense. Sometimes the truthful and expressive choice is to play a character's onomatopoetic impulses quite strongly. When Romeo, fresh from the balcony scene, comes to Friar Laurence to announce out of the blue that he wants to marry Juliet (II.iii), the Friar is quite taken aback. "Holy Saint Francis!" he exclaims. "Is Rosaline, whom thou didst love so dear" — and about whom we saw Romeo sighing and groaning in his first scene — "so soon forsaken?" The friar proceeds to come down hard on Romeo for being fickle.

The sun not yet thy sighs from heaven clears,
Thy old groans ring yet in my ancient ears.

9.44 The sun hasn't even had a chance to burn off the mist created by all of Romeo's sighs for Rosaline! Explore making big choices for "sighs" and "groans" as a way of bringing this young fool to his senses.

After Friar Laurence gives Juliet a potion that makes her appear dead, he finds himself in the very awkward position of trying to comfort her grieving parents (IV.v). Since reason assures us that Juliet is in heaven, he tells them, our natural inclination to grieve should give way to happiness.

For though fond nature bids us all lament,
Yet nature's tears are reason's merriment.

9.45 In this delicate context the word "merriment" can hardly sound robustly light-hearted. But the friar might faintly color the word with the subdued happiness a true believer ought to feel. Since "tears" and "merriment" are opposites balanced against each other in a rhetorical device called antithesis, these two words should be voiced with the same degree of onomatopoetic sound sense.

Practice In Onomatopoeia

digs the beak into his throat
straightens legs and heaves
a red and blue vein out (Speech 5, Appendix B)

9.46 I'm sure you haven't forgotten the chicken. Suppose you want to treat "heaves" as a verbal action. If you were to do this suddenly, so as to POP the word out of its context, the effect would be rather comical — a choice which is not impossible in this context, since Billy the Kid thinks the story is, among other things, funny. Try this version, perhaps with some physical choice about the action.

In most cases, however, you will want moments of sound sense to develop gradually.

9.47 Work on carefully shaping how you fade into and out of "heaves." The first of these three lines is already en route to heaving. Each word in the second line should take another step toward "heaves" — even "and" must play its part in the fade. This vocal energy should

163

gradually subside on the next line. The onomatopoeia should sound perfectly natural — and true to the event.

Full often hath she gossiped by my side,
And sat with me on Neptune's yellow sands (Speech 13, Appendix B)
9.48 *What does it sound like if Titania gives only the word "gossiped" sound sense? This is a possible choice.*
9.49 *What if Titania subtly fades into a gossipy tone and sustains it though "by my side"? Try fading the energy out on the next line.*

Marking th'embarkèd traders on the flood,
When we have laughed to see the sails conceive
And grow big-bellied with the wanton wind
9.50 *Of course, they might still be gossiping as they check out the ships. Try this.*
9.51 *Popping into laughter only on the word that mentions it would sound unnatural. (Try it.) At some point before "laughed" you will want to start fading in their amusement, letting it grow as they gossip; "wanton wind" might climax the laughter which Titania is reliving.*

Note that working on this moment from the perspective of setting the scene might have converged on the same vocal choices.

He raised a sigh so piteous and profound
As it did seem to shatter all his bulk
And end his being. (Excerpt 12, Appendix A)
9.52 *Let us imagine that Ophelia is by this point so identified with Hamlet — having put her hand to her brow and nodded her head three times — that she now sighs along with him. Giving sound sense only to the word "sigh" would be unnatural. Speak these three lines as a sigh.*

The ninth year we went numb. We tasted war. But felt nothing. We smelled death. But felt nothing. We ate, drank, slept ... Nothing. The sand burned with more desire than we, the sundried meat.
(Speech 3, Appendix B)

9.53 We have already approached this text from the point of view of space. Suppose that another actor took a different path, and started working on this as an onomatopoetic soundscape. What does the ninth year sound like?

After the brawl that opens *Romeo and Juliet*, Romeo, who is lovesick because Rosaline will not give him the time of day, discovers blood on the street (I.i). This triggers a torrent of contradictory words and phrases that express his inability to relate to the feuding that preoccupies Verona.

Here's much <u>to do</u> with hate, but more with love.	*ado, tumult*
Why then, O brawling love, O loving hate,	
O anything, of nothing first <u>create!</u>	*created*
O heavy lightness, serious <u>vanity,</u>	*triviality*
Misshapen <u>chaos</u> of well-seeming forms,	*formless*
Feather of lead, bright smoke, cold fire, sick health,	
<u>Still</u>-waking sleep, that is not what it is!	*constantly*

If an actor simply rants these lines so that all the opposites are the same emotional color, the speech will not make much sense. It will work only if the actor imbues the opposing words with sound sense, so that the specific way in which each pair conflicts is audible.

9.54 Work through the opposites, giving them high-contrast vocal colors. This is a situation in which jarring effects will be truthful.

"Angels and ministers of grace, defend us!" That is what Hamlet exclaims when he first sees his father's ghost (I.iv). This apparition might be a devil in disguise, a possibility real enough to make Hamlet hesitate, though he longs for contact with his father, who died while he was away at school. Shakespeare has built Hamlet's momentary ambivalence into his language: the sound sense lets us hear him waver before he finally decides to speak to the ghost.

Be thou a spirit <u>of health</u> or goblin damned,	*wholesome*
Bring with thee airs from heaven or blasts from hell,	
Be thy intents wicked or charitable,	
Thou com'st in such a <u>questionable</u> state	*inviting questions*
That I will speak to thee.	

165

9.55 *Suppose that the sight of the ghost had dropped you to the ground. Position yourself kneeling or sitting on one hip. Lean toward the ghost when Hamlet speaks of it as benign; when he refers to it in negative terms, back off. As you speak the first three lines, map out this to-and-fro motion. That is Hamlet wavering, uncertain whether he should approach or flee.*

Be thou a spirit of health
9.56 *Hamlet is disgusted with life itself: he has already mentioned suicide. Melancholy has made his mood as black as the mourning clothes he refuses to stop wearing. If this apparition is indeed his father, the contact might cure him. Invest "spirit of health" with Hamlet's hunger for contact with his father. "Spirit" should radiate light and hope. How might you use the "h" of "health" expressively?*

or goblin damned
9.57 *Now the opposing possibility: the "g" of "goblin" is the "g" of "gag", and "damned" should have the onomatopoetic force of an expletive.*

Bring with thee airs from heaven
9.58 *Since his father's death and his mother's hasty re-marriage, life at court has been suffocating. Let "airs from heaven" be a breath of fresh air, a blessing, a healing dose of grace. Build this energy into the vowels and consonants.*

or blasts from hell
9.59 *How different the "h" of hell should be from the "h" of heaven! When we use "hell" as an expletive, it has lots of sound sense. The explosive force of "blasts" should knock Hamlet backward.*

Be thy intents wicked or charitable
9.60 *The line will make little sense in performance if the sounds of "wicked" and "charitable" are not in high contrast. "Wicked" has a lot going for it: the guttural "k" is very playable, and so is the "w" if you form it forcefully with expressively shaped lips. "Charitable" needs your help in making it as gentle and loving a sound as possible.*

9.61 Put the three lines together with your physical score.

Hamlet's ambivalence — the longing and the fear, the movement toward and away from the ghost — is right there in the language. If a Hamlet actor learns in rehearsal how to make sense of the sounds of this speech, his vocal score will carry him in performance.

A moment later Hamlet asks the ghost to speak. "O answer me!" he cries. Imagine a moment of silence.

Let me not burst in ignorance

9.62 Which is the onomatopoetically expressive word here? "B" and "p" are called "plosives" because of the explosive release of air. Yet "burst" is not the word that should be emphasized. Speak the line so that it bursts on "ignorance," meaning "not knowing" — that is what Hamlet can no longer stand.

9.63 Speak the line as you suddenly jump to your feet. "Suit the action to the word," as Hamlet later advises the players: coordinate your move with the sound sense.

Playing the sound sense of this line gives the Hamlet actor his beat — and the means to play it. The physical event of voicing "burst" puts you in the moment and gives you its emotion: one doesn't need to *feel* anything over and above full commitment to this language.

What the language can do to us
"What matters is not what we can do to the language, but what the language can do to us."[2]

Hamlet, to the consternation of his companions, follows the ghost, who reveals in a powerful narrative speech (I.v) that he was murdered by his brother: Claudius poured a vial of poison in the king's ear while he was taking a nap in the garden. The poison's effect on his blood was to "posset" and "curd" it. Both words mean the same thing — his blood began to clot the way milk does when something sour or acid ("eager") is

---

[2]The Irish actress Fiona Shaw, in a video about *As You Like It*, The Open University, 1996.

dropped into it.
And with a sudden vigor it doth posset
And curd, like eager droppings into milk,
The thin and wholesome blood.

9.64 *It is one thing to speak "curd" and "posset" as pejoratives, as if they simply meant "yucky"; it is another to treat them as verbal actions so that the audience hears lumps forming. The difference is a very big one: the choice is between playing what you feel (grossed out, for example) and giving the audience the event itself (and letting them be grossed out). An actor focused on the story is always prejudiced in favor of conjuring what happened rather than playing a reaction to what happened. Explore creating the clots.*

Hamlet's father's skin broke out in leper-like ulcers and scabs: the poison, he tells his son, covered "with vile and loathsome crust/All my smooth body." The juxtaposition of these two phrases is a great sound-sense contrast. The language is not merely descriptive: it is meant to embody the event of the king waking to discover what has happened to his skin.

with vile and loathsome crust

9.65 *"Crust" should not just be nasty-sounding: it ought to conjure the texture of what has happened to the king's skin. Make "crust" sound like what it means, and bleed that sound into "vile and loathsome" so that these adjectives express not a subjective reaction but the thing itself.*

All my smooth body

9.66 *In stark contrast to "crust," what is the sound sense of this phrase? What is its sensuous quality? (Note that the sounds that Blake used to change the energy in "The Tiger" are put to work here.) Take your time exploring these sounds: Shakespeare has given you long vowels and continuant consonants to work with — "l," "m," and "s" can all be sustained — and the whole phrase is monosyllabic, which also slows the pace.*

For Your Own Speech

Prepare five moments of onomatopoeia.

- Are there any examples in your text of onomatopoeia in the strict sense?
- If you are working on the sound sense of a verb, explore it as a verbal action. Speak it as though it were the action.
- Pay attention to the scale of your choices.
- Unless an abrupt change makes more sense, fade into and out of the onomatopoeia that you are working on. Being crafty should make your craft invisible. Note the expressive value of bleeding sound sense into adjacent language.
- Is there a section in your speech that might be developed as a soundscape, a sustained bit of sound expressiveness?
- Note opportunities to combine sound sense with other approaches.

Guidelines

Work sensuously so that the sound of your choices makes the story happen all over again in a vividly present way. How you affect the audience's ears should put them in touch with events and circumstances.

Remember that organic sound sense is not a descriptive impulse. It's not a question of the actor (or the character) standing outside an event and talking about it. The onomatopoetic impulse must come from your character's gut and from inside the moment: reliving the event makes you say this word or phrase just this way. Onomatopoeia should sound natural and necessary.

Unless the words you are working on are expressly about feelings, sound sense should focus on what happens in the story, not on emotional reactions to events.

Speaking sound sense should bring you into the moment. Hearing sound sense should bring an audience into the moment.

Chapter 10
Rhythm

English is inherently rhythmic. Our speech is made rhythmic by the interplay of accented and unaccented syllables, long and short vowels and consonants, emphasis and subordination, flow and pause. Even the most ordinary everyday English is to some degree rhythmical. "I have to brush my teeth and go to bed" is not only rhythmic, it is iambic pentameter — the meter which Shakespeare used and a natural rhythm for English speakers.

Rhythm is everywhere because it is quite literally organic — as organic as the heartbeat and the in-and-out of breath. Rhythmic impulses are pretty irresistible: our toes and fingertips start tapping involuntarily when we like the music's beat, and the nursery rhymes lodged in our heads are there largely because of their rhythmic hold on us.

In "The Barrel Organ," a poem of quite pronounced and varied rhythms, the English poet Alfred Noyes imagines that the instrument is playing a dance tune, and he gives us the beat in the following verse:

Go down to Kew in lilac-time, in lilac-time, in lilac-time;
Go down to Kew in lilac-time (it isn't far from London!)
And you shall wander hand in hand with love in summer's wonderland;
Go down to Kew in lilac-time (it isn't far from London!)

10.1 *Place your fingertips on the edge of a table or other surface and tap out the rhythm as you speak this verse. Set a brisk pace, and let your fingers dance to the beat. (Tap dancers should get on their feet.)*

This rhythm, which embodies the dance, contrasts greatly with that of an earlier verse, in which the barrel organ is playing tunes from tragic operas:

And there *La Traviata* sighs
Another sadder song;
And there *Il Trovatore* cries
A tale of deeper wrong

170

10.2 *There is plenty of opportunity for onomatopoetic sound sense in this verse. Explore.*

10.3 *What sounds contribute to slowing the rhythm?*

10.4 *Those who know these operas and how they are traditionally produced might imagine that they are playing a particular scene; some of the text might even be treated as quotes from the libretto. If you don't know the stories, speak the text as if you were a very unhappy lover at the climax of a heartbroken aria. Focus on how the rhythm embodies the scene you imagine.*

Rhythm is another kind of sound sense. Here is another poem with highly contrasting cadences, in which a great deal of the sense is in the rhythms.

anyone lived in a pretty how town
anyone lived in a pretty how town
(with up so floating many bells down)
spring summer autumn winter
he sang his didn't he danced his did

women and men (both little and small)
cared for anyone not at all
they sowed their isn't they reaped their same
sun moon stars rain

children guessed (but only a few
and down they forgot as up they grew
autumn winter spring summer)
that noone loved him more by more

when by now and tree by leaf
she laughed his joy she cried his grief
bird by snow and stir by still
anyone's any was all to her

someones married their everyones
laughed their cryings and did their dance
(sleep wake hope and then) they
said their nevers they slept their dream

stars rain sun moon
(and only the snow can begin to explain
how children are apt to forget to remember
with up so floating many bells down)

one day anyone died i guess
(and noone stooped to kiss his face)
busy folk buried them side by side
little by little and was by was

all by all and deep by deep
and more by more they dream their sleep
noone and anyone earth by april
wish by spirit and if by yes

women and men (both dong and ding)
summer autumn winter spring
reaped their sowing and went their came
sun moon stars rain

The contrast of rhythms in this e. e. cummings poem is not only *expressive* of the story, it virtually *is* the story. Visitors from outer space with no sense of rhythm might find it very difficult to grasp what it is about.

The conflicting energies are carefully crafted. Brisk polysyllabic rhythms contrast with slower monosyllabic lines, quick metrical feet of three syllables with slower two-syllable feet, short vowels with long vowels, clipped consonants (dentals and plosives) with continuant consonants which a speaker can prolong. An actor needs to be sensitive to the possibilities of such rhythmic building blocks.

anyone lived in a pretty how town

10.5 This line is constructed of the metrical foot called a dactyl, which has three syllables, the first accented, the next two unaccented: AN y one/LIVED in a/PRET ty how/TOWN. Whether or not you are conscious of this fact, it is important to sense that the line is crafted so as to be spoken briskly. Speak it as rapidly as you can while keeping your articulation clear.

The poet is creating a universe in which anonymous "busy folk" with names like "noone" and "anyone" rush through their lives without taking time to connect with anything or anybody.

10.6 Speak these words as briskly and clearly as possible: "busy folk," "anyone," "noone."

This is a world in which "children are apt to forget to remember" — another brisk dactylic line.

he sang his didn't he danced his did

10.7 I cannot hear this line without imagining a song-and-dance man like Fred Astaire or Gregory Hines tapping it out and finishing in a ta-dah pose. Try to get that sort of nimble energy into the line.

spring summer autumn winter

10.8 The busy folk who rush about this pretty how town are out of touch with this: a rhythm slow enough to suggest eternity. The line is so full of continuant consonants that it sounds as though it can go on forever. That this is not a sentence but a list in which each item is given equal weight heightens the effect: cummings gives us a solemn and stately progress of the seasons. As you speak the line, hold onto the consonants. Extend the final sound of each word before fading into the initial sound of the next. Take a deep breath and make this sound like a year.

sun moon stars rain

10.9 This is one of several variations on the slower rhythm established by "spring summer autumn winter." An audience should be able to recognize this rhythm and to sense that whenever it recurs, it speaks of the same dimension of reality. The monosyllables help to slow the tempo. *The consonants in this line should seem to last for days, weeks, months.*

women and men (both little and small)
cared for anyone not at all

10.10 Busy folk do not live their lives in the "sun moon stars rain" rhythm. They hustle and bustle and have no time for anyone. How briskly can you speak these lines?

It seems that "anyone" is at risk of rushing headlong through life without making contact with much of anything. Then a miraculous thing happens: noone grows to love anyone and the slower rhythm enters their lives.

when by now and tree by leaf
she laughed his joy she cried his grief
bird by snow and stir by still
anyone's any was all to her

10.11 Read this slowly, as if romance had suspended time. Notice how the component sounds let these lovers prolong their time together. Every moment is full, rich, sensuously savored.

10.12 One phrase in this verse is in the faster rhythm — which? The effect is to remind us momentarily of that other point of view, or rather that other mode of living. But the smallest detail about anyone — that others would rush by as quickly as you can say "anyone's any" — is "alllll to herrr," and we can hear in those long monosyllables how noone dotes on him.

Not everyone is so lucky.

someones married their everyones
laughed their cryings and did their dance
(sleep wake hope and then) they
said their nevers they slept their dream

10.13 What is the rhythm of the first two lines? Note how cummings mixes two-syllable trochees (/ ∪) with three-syllable dactyls (/ ∪ ∪). What happens rhythmically in the third line? What is the rhythm of the fourth line? Read this verse aloud so that the rhythmic changes make sound sense.

one day anyone died i guess
(and noone stooped to kiss his face)
busy folk buried them side by side
little by little and was by was

10.14 The interplay of the two rhythms is especially complex in this verse. Note the nonchalant tone of the first line: this is not noone's point of view but that of the busy folk. What is the rhythm of "one day anyone died i guess"? This line should catch the audience by surprise.

10.15 What is the rhythm of the second line? This rhythm is true to the event and helps to conjure the moment.

10.16 In the third and fourth lines, the two perspectives of the poem are juxtaposed. What happens rhythmically? How does E.E. Cummings achieve this effect?

10.17 The sense of this verse is embodied in its rhythms. What the rhythms say is more important than the facts that the words convey. What we should be able to hear is that noone and anyone have entered that other, slower rhythm — for good. Read the entire verse aloud, focusing on the interplay of the rhythms and on their sound sense.

all by all and deep by deep
and more by more they dream their sleep
noone and anyone earth by april

10.18 The rhythm of the first two lines is doubly significant. They are, of course, a dirge, solemn and mournful. But cummings also gives us the rhythm of eternity: decades seem to pass. How long can these two lines last? Rather than putting mini-pauses between the words, extend the sounds so that each blends into the next.

10.19 What is the rhythm of "noone and anyone"? Of the rest of the line?

How Does a Poem Mean? is the title of a textbook by the poet John Ciardi. The first and foremost way in which this cummings poem means is rhythm. The same is true of a two-line poem by Robert Frost, in which the very different energies of a puppy and an old dog are embodied in a remarkable rhythmic contrast.

The Span of Life
The old dog barks backward without getting up.
I can remember when he was a pup.

The old dog barks backward without getting up.
10.20 Onomatopoeia and rhythmic sound sense work hand in hand here. "Bark" is a true onomatopoetic word, and the four stressed syllables of "old dog barks backward" sound like four staccato barks. These stresses also slow the tempo. This line is as sluggish as the old dog: it embodies his energy.

I can remember when he was a pup.
10.21 Flashback! The very different energy of this line can be analyzed in terms of the type of metrical foot (three-syllable dactyls) and consonants that allow the line to flow smoothly and swiftly. What is important is that you sense the text's inherent rhythm. This sentence should not be about the puppy's energy; it should be the puppy's energy. Make the line as frisky as a puppy at play.

Imagine that fifty thousand years from now, with English a dead language, a rhythmically challenged scholar uncovers this poem and wonders why in the world it was ever printed. What it says seems to him quite unremarkable. Where is the poetry?

Here is the opening of Ralph Hodgson's rhythmically rich account of Eve's temptation. In the jaunty, buoyant rhythm established in the first verse, we hear how carefree life in Eden was before the fall of man.

Eve
Eve, with her basket, was
Deep in the <u>bells</u> and grass,   *bellflowers*
Wading in bells and grass
Up to her knees,
Picking a dish of sweet
Berries and plums to eat,
Down in the bells in grass
Under the trees.

Half of these lines are enjambed — that is, they flow without a break into the next line. You can spot such lines by the absence of punctuation at the end of them. The combination of brisk three-syllable feet and of enjambed lines moves the verse along, an effect heightened by repetitions reminiscent of nursery rhymes.

10.22 *Use the rhythm of the first verse to set the scene: Eve bounces through waist-high wildflowers and grass in a cloudless paradise. Note how short vowel sounds predominate.*

The second verse begins with a very different rhythm, which captures in sound the slithering motion of the serpent.

Mute as a mouse in a
Corner the cobra lay,
Curled round a bough of the
Cinnamon tall. ...
Now to get even and
Humble proud heaven and
Now was the moment or
Never at all.

10.23 *Longer vowel sounds and continuant consonants set the tempo for the first half of this verse. Explore how the rhythm embodies the serpent's stealthy energy: silent, still, watchful.*

10.24 *In the second half of this verse, the pace gradually increases as the serpent decides to make his move. A new rhythm embodies the urgency with which the serpent seizes this opportunity.*

10.25 *Read the whole verse from the serpent's point of view: watch Eve intently, then move in to tempt her.*

In the third verse the poet mixes the two rhythms he has established in a marvelously effective way.

"Eva!" Each syllable
Light as a flower fell,
"Eva!" he whispered the
Wondering maid,
Soft as a bubble sung
Out of a linnet's lung,

Soft and most silvery
"Eva!" he said.

10.26 The sinister slowness of each "Eva!" is heightened by the sprightliness with which the rest of the verse suggests that Eve is hearing the serpent's voice as yet another wonderful, innocent event in her untroubled world. The poet uses contrasting rhythms to capture the two points of view in dialog. Explore the rhythmic interplay.

A very soft easy snow. The squirrels might come down to see what happened. (Excerpt 21, Appendix A)

10.27 Carol is lying at the bottom of the hill, headless and every limb broken. The stillness of the scene is captured in part by the quiet, measured rhythm of the first sentence: most of the syllables end with vowel sounds that can be sustained for as long as the speaker wishes. In the second sentence there is a rather abrupt change of rhythm. It is as if we can hear the scurrying motion of the squirrels. Use the change in rhythm to conjure their entrance into the scene.

Perhaps we can say that rhythm embodies the energy and motion of an event: snowfall or squirrel, carefree Eve or stealthy serpent, old dog or frisky pup, busy folk rushing through life or lovers entering eternity, light-footed dance or tragic aria, etc.

Rhythm is another way to conjure what is happening in the other time and place. As in all of your work on narrative speeches, you should focus your exploration of rhythms not on what your character is feeling in the here and now, but on the energy of each event inside the story.

When the Ghost in *Hamlet* tells his son how he was murdered, he uses rhythm to conjure how quickly the poison moved through his system. He speaks of the drug as a "leprous distillment"

whose effect
Holds such an enmity with blood of man

That swift as <u>quicksilver</u> it courses through   *mercury*
The natural gates and allies of the body,
And with a sudden vigor it doth <u>posset</u>   *curdle*
And curd, like <u>eager</u> droppings into milk,   *sour, acidic*

Stanislavski and the truth of "tempo-rhythm"

At one point in his long teaching career, the great Russian theater artist Konstantin Stanislavski focused his students at the Moscow Art Theater on searching for what he called the "tempo-rhythm." It is impossible to play an action truthfully until you feel its pulse, he said; if you don't find the true tempo-rhythm of a scene or a speech, you can't get inside it. So convinced of this was Stanislavski — who regularly changed his mind about what was most important in acting — that for a time he brought a metronome into the rehearsal hall. He would set the instrument to a beat and ask the actors to "keep time" while playing the scene.

"Rhythm," says the Irish actress Fiona Shaw, "is the key to the subconscious."[1] It is also another way to enter a story.

This much is certain: a good narrative speech requires rhythmic variety, for two basic reasons. Rhythms must change in order to be true to the distinct energies of different events and circumstances. If your rhythm remains the same throughout a speech, moreover, the effect is a deadly monotony.

The thin and wholesome blood. So did it mine (I.v)

10.28 Four of these seven lines have no punctuation at the end of them and flow without a break into the next line. In a passage with so many enjambed lines, as you might expect, the forward motion of the text accelerates. Start slowly and gradually quicken the pace. The rhythm of this passage should let us hear how the poison spread through Hamlet Senior's bloodstream.

10.29 Do you hear how Shakespeare uses the monosyllabic phrase "So did it mine" to slow down this speeding passage? Each syllable is accented, and the effect is emphatic, as if each word were underlined: So — did — it — mine. Read the passage again: gradually depress the accelerator, then slam on the brakes.

---

[1] In a video about *As You Like It*, directed by Fiona Shaw, produced by Amanda Willet, The Open University, Rutledge, NY, 1996.

So did it mine,
And a most instant tetter bark'd about,
Most lazar-like, with vile and loathsome crust
All my smooth body.

The quick rhythm of the poison resumes after "So did it mine" and then another monosyllabic phrase slows the rhythm as the story of the poisoning comes to an onomatopoetically expressive close (see 9.66).

10.30 After the emphatic accents of "So did it mine," reestablish the rhythm of the poison, then let "with vile and loathsome crust" gradually slow into the long sounds of "All my smooth body."

"All my smooth body" is a short line, with five syllables instead of ten or eleven, which indicates a pause. No doubt the ghost is reliving that moment in the other time and place when he saw what had happened to his skin.

10.31 Suppose that you have raised both arms as if to show your son the "vile and loathsome crust." After "All my smooth body," slowly lower your arms in dismayed silence as you look at what has happened to you.

Tradition has it that Shakespeare himself played the ghost. If so, he gave himself a vocal score that can be played like music.

Naming rhythms

Rhythmic contrast is not simply a matter of faster or slower — that's far too generic. There's "slow" and there's "slow." There's legs-won't-move-anymore slow and chocolate-syrup slow, soaking-in-a-bubble-bath slow and shell-shocked slow, nothing-to-do slow, sexy slow, and so forth.

You should always consider the specific texture of a rhythm. If, as the dictionary tells us, a rhythm is "any wave-like recurrence," how might you draw the waves involved in slithering, scurrying, crawling, gliding, panicking, hesitating? Whether a rhythm is faster or slower is not nearly so important as its texture and quality of movement. Visualizing what silky smooth waves look like, as opposed to herky-jerky waves, may help you to hear the difference between two such rhythms.

It is good practice to name the rhythms you are working on. It is best to avoid emotional labels and psychological terms, which can mislead you into trying to play emotions and mental states instead of actions. Use verbs, interesting adjectives or metaphors instead. You can even talk about your rhythms in terms of metaphorical scenes: e.g., the rhythm of sneaking up on your brother to put ice down the back of his shirt, or of picking your way through a mine field with a baby in your arms. The very best terms will likely be suggested by your text. The rhythm of the ghost's lines about the poison in his bloodstream might be called "swift as quicksilver" or "coursing" or "sudden vigor."

Five Factors That Determine Rhythm

What makes a passage move briskly or slowly? Five factors may singly or in combination contribute to determining the rhythm of a text.

1. Polysyllables vs. monosyllables

In English, a string of monosyllables slows a line; it is as if each word were underlined and emphasized, as if each syllable were accented — and accented syllables go by more slowly than unaccented ones.

When Ajax strives some rock's vast weight to throw,
The line too labors, and the words move slow.

All but two words in this couplet from Alexander Pope's *An Essay on Criticism* are monosyllables, which is how the poet makes "the words move slow."

10.32 *Read these lines as if you were Ajax (a Greek warrior famed for his strength) in the act of lifting an enormously heavy rock. Let each vowel and consonant be part of the straining. It may help to mime Ajax's action with full muscular commitment: get the rock to your waist on the first line, to shoulder height by "labors," and over your head on the last half of the second line.*

181

The monosyllables here do more than echo the slowness with which Ajax lifts his rock: in large part they create that slowness; they *are* the slowness.

Polysyllables — with unaccented syllables that are more quickly spoken — move along more rapidly.

I know it has become quite fashionable these days to neglect the nineteenth-century melancholy Hamlet in favor of the more volcanic Hamlet of Elizabethan revenge sagas.

It is the profusion of polysyllables in this sentence which make it not only a mouthful but a text which can be spoken quite briskly — or as Hamlet would say, "trippingly on the tongue."

2. The rhythms of metrical feet

Spondees (/ /) move more slowly than iambs (∪ /) or trochees (/ ∪), which are not as brisk as dactyls (/ ∪ ∪) and anapests (∪ ∪ /).

When Romeo exclaims that Juliet's beauty "doth teach the torches to burn bright," the two accents of the spondee "burn bright" slow the phrase down. The jaunty quality of "Eve in the bells and grass" is due in large part to its dactyls.

3. Re-shaping the mouth and tongue between syllables

The old dog barks backward without getting up. (Robert Frost, "The Span of Life")

Something else slows this line besides its many heavy accents. Most of the syllables begin and end with a strong consonant sound or cluster of consonant sounds, so that the mouth and tongue have to change shape between syllables.[2] The more pronounced and frequent such changes, the more time it takes to say the line. This is why speaking tongue twisters rapidly is so difficult.

10.33 As you speak the line, give all the consonants full value. Focus on how your mouth changes between syllables.

---

[2] Cf. Laurence Perrine's analysis of this poem in *Sound and Sense*, Harcourt Brace Jovanovich, Third Edition, 1987, pp. 223-4.

The same principle is another reason that Alexander Pope's Ajax seems to struggle mightily. The muscular effort it takes to re-shape your mouth between sounds creates the impression that Ajax is straining:
When Ajax strives his rock's vast weight to throw,
The line too labors, and the words move slow.

When consonants and vowels flow into one another, on the other hand, language moves easily and briskly. Pope's very next lines, about a mythic woman so fleet of foot that she could run atop grain fields and the ocean, create a rhythm that really flies:
Not so when swift Camilla scours the plain,
Flies o'er the unbending corn, and skims along the <u>main</u>.   *ocean*

When a word ending in a consonant is followed by a word beginning with a vowel, the final consonant becomes the initial sound of the new word: "Flies o'er," "skims along." This creates an easy flow. The "o" of "so" and the final "a" of "Camilla" likewise slide into the sounds that follow. There is also an elision: scansion (see Appendix C) makes it clear that "the unbending" is pronounced "th'unbending."
Some sequences of consonants are easier to pronounce than others. As your lips form the sounds of the word "nimble," for example, the end of "m" is identical with the beginning of the "b" that follows. Juliet's phrase "nimble-pinioned doves" (Speech 14, Appendix B) has other sounds that are close in terms of where they are formed in the mouth — and so the phrase can be nimbly articulated, in keeping with its sense.

4. Rhythmic sound sense

When Jaques imagines a "whining schoolboy" who is "creeping like snail," the image clearly calls for a slow pace, embodied in the vowels and continuant consonants, and onomatopoeia helps to create the rhythm. These two kinds of sound sense often work hand in hand.
When Juliet generalizes about old folks, both the sense and the sounds are slow, though the rhythm is of a different quality than that of the whining boy who hates going to school.
But old folks, many feign as they were dead,
Unwieldy, slow, heavy, and pale as lead. (Speech 14, Appendix B)

Rhythms make the energy of events and images audible. In each of the following examples, the rhythm of the language mimics and embodies the rhythm of an event:

Not so when swift Camilla scours the plain,
Flies o'er the unbending corn, and skims along the main.
(Alexander Pope)

Love's heralds should be thoughts,
Which ten times faster fly than the sun's beams
(Speech 14, Appendix B)

I can remember when he was a pup.
(Robert Frost, "The Span of Life")

That swift as quicksilver it courses through
The natural gates and allies of the body,
And with a sudden vigor it doth posset
And curd, like eager droppings into milk,
The thin and wholesome blood.
(*Hamlet*, I.v)

Round and round she goes, where she stops nobody knows.

Ask about any moment in your story: Is the energy of this event or of this image relatively slower or faster? In what way? What is its rhythmic pulse?

Sound sense is a two-way street
Sound may reveal sense, or sense may inspire sound. The rhythm of a text may give you the rhythm of an event in your story, or the nature of the event may suggest how the text should be spoken so as to embody it.

---

5. Punctuation

Along with pauses and other stage directions, a playwright can use punctuation to orchestrate the rhythms of a speech. Long sentences and phrases are more likely to flow briskly. A sequence of short units produces rhythms that can be halting, hammering, frantic, catatonic, etc.

In Excerpt 16, Appendix A, a series of short phrases creates a specific rhythm, and the one relatively long phrase stands out: "Cement pilings. Prefab walls. Zombie architecture, owned by invisible zombies, built by zombies for the use and convenience of all other zombies. A zombie city! Right here! Right where we're living now." In Excerpt 17, Appendix A, a burst of fragmentary "sentences" creates a very different rhythm, as Weston falls asleep: "I flew giant machines in the air. Giants! Bombers, what a sight. Over Italy. The Pacific. Islands. Giants. Oceans. Blue oceans."

"My body will stop at the bottom of the hill with just a bloody stump for a neck and both arms broken and both legs." (Excerpt 21, Appendix A) The absence of punctuation produces a complex effect, in which the relentless march of the sentence is in tension with the staccato effect of the consonants and monosyllables.

The flow of "I could feel myself in my bed in my room in this house in this town in this state in this country" (Speech 7, Appendix B) is what musicians call *legato* — the sentence glides smoothly. In contrast, when his drunken father gets out of the car and walks toward the house, Wesley's short phrases give us a series of details separated by tense silences. "A pop of metal. Dogs barking down the road. Door slams. Feet. Paper bag being tucked under one arm. Paper bag covering 'Tiger Rose.' Feet coming. Feet walking toward the door. Feet stopping. Heart pounding." Punctuation creates the rhythm.

In verse, as we have seen, an enjambed line, which has no punctuation at the end, flows into the next:

Out, out, brief candle.
Life's but a walking shadow, a poor player
That struts and frets his hour upon the stage
And then is heard no more. (Speech 17, Appendix B)

After the half-line phrase "Out, out, brief candle," the relatively long phrase created by two enjambed lines changes the rhythm. When

Shakespeare wants to pick up the pace of a passage, he sometimes writes a sequence of enjambed lines that allow the actor to accelerate.

Acceleration and Deceleration

If your speech is a sequence of different rhythms, a craft question arises: how to make the transition from one rhythm to the next. There are two possibilities.

Let's call a sudden contrast in rhythm a *cut*, a term from cinematic editing.[3] When a movie cuts without fading from a playground to a battlefield, the blunt juxtaposition of high contrast energies is abrupt, arresting, jarring. One uses this effect sparingly, when it truthfully captures the unexpected nature of an event.

More commonly, an actor moves from one rhythm to the next gradually, by degrees, without any apparent break. Most rhythms evolve. In film editing — as in theatrical lighting and in sound recording — a gradual transition is a *fade*. A change in rhythm generally involves a quickening or slowing of the pace. Let's call fading from a slower to a faster rhythm an *acceleration* (adapting the musical term for quickening the pace, *accelerando*); let's call the opposite, fading from a faster to a slower rhythm, a *deceleration*.[4]

Acceleration and deceleration are valuable technical skills; they are also important tools for telling a story. When events snowball, when an idea or plan emerges and develops, when an emotion waxes, when a conviction or resolve grows, when anything at all becomes exciting — whenever the pulse quickens — the change in energy takes the form of an acceleration. When emotions are subsiding, when events are coming to a conclusion, when hopes are failing and a character is sinking into despair, when the pace of events is slowing after a climax — what happens rhythmically is a deceleration. These energy changes are an essential part of any story. Acceleration and deceleration are how we hear rhythms change: they are another kind of sound sense.

Acceleration and deceleration are potent tools because they do much more than simply signify change; they *cause* change, for both actor and

---

[3]A cut is "an abrupt transition from one scene to another without using an optical effect such as a dissolve, a wipe, or a fade. It is achieved by splicing the last frame of one scene with the first frame of the next." Ephraim Katz, *The Film Encyclopedia*, Third Edition, HarperPerennial, 1998.

[4]The musical term for this is *ritardando*.

audience. Acceleration is not only expressive of what happens when you get excited (adrenaline kicking up the heartbeat, speech and movement quickening, etc.) it actually *stimulates* such excitement, in you and in your audience. Accelerating affects performers and spectators quite physically.

The power to excite inherent in acceleration — and the calming effect of deceleration — are strongly in evidence in Wesley's speech about his parents' argument.

Read the end of Speech 7, Appendix B, from "Then I heard the door of the Packard open."

Wesley anticipates trouble, and the long acceleration that begins as his father approaches the house at first expresses his growing tension. As Wesley's pulse quickens, so does the text. But it is also the sequence of events that accelerates: the footsteps, his father's discovery that the door is locked, the calling, the kicking, and the escalation of violence. The quickening rhythm of the text, and later the deceleration, are expressive not only of emotional reactions to events but of the events themselves.

Feet coming. Feet walking toward the door. Feet stopping. Heart pounding. Sound of door not opening. Foot kicking door.
10.34 You are near the beginning of the acceleration. Start very, very slowly, with spaces between the words and between the short sentences. The pace quickens — slightly — as the footsteps come closer and Wesley's father reaches the locked door. The fight has a long way to go, so don't be in too much of a hurry. Keep in mind that Wesley doesn't want any of this to happen — he is in a way trying to hold events back. Focus on how a very gradual acceleration of this text helps you to feel Wesley's tension.

The truth of this moment, Stanislavski would say, is in its tempo-rhythm — and in how the rhythm is changing. Acceleration is a way inside the story.
10.35 This time start very quietly — as if you were listening for quiet footsteps and barely breathing. As trouble approaches, step by step, let your voice get slightly louder. Resist this: try to keep things quiet. Note the sound sense in this gradual increase in volume.

187

10.36 Starting at this point in the speech, accelerate gradually but continuously through "Mom screaming for police," about halfway to the end. Hold back so that you do not reach your maximum speed, which must still be intelligible, until you arrive at that phrase. Focus on how the acceleration helps you to create the stages of the fight's development. At the same time, gradually increase your volume; in music, this is called a change in dynamics. Do not peak until the very end of this section of text — on "police." If you actually screamed, the text would likely become a blur, so hold back a bit. Sharpen your consonants as you get louder; this helps to keep your speech clear.

10.37 Now begin a very gradual deceleration right through to the end of the speech. It will take Wesley a while to calm down, so take your time with the deceleration; the very slowest pace should not be reached until the last couple of words. Your dynamic fade is from very loud to very, very quiet. Accentuate your consonants as you use less voice.

It is not just a question of pace, of course. As trouble develops, several different rhythms occur, each with its own quality. The drunken footsteps have a plodding rhythm, perhaps; the fight's jagged rhythm is violent, "smashing," "insane"; the rhythm of the mother moving through the house in tears is quite fragile and brings us to the stillness of Wesley listening to the distant sound of cars on the freeway. Is that final moment exhausted and numb, or trembling and residually angry, or calm and oddly comforting? Each choice suggests a different rhythm, though all of them will be relatively slow.

Dynamic fades

As you explored rhythmic changes in Wesley's story about his parents' fight, you also faded up and down in terms of loudness and softness. This sort of dynamic fade frequently goes hand in hand with acceleration and deceleration, since we tend to get louder as we get excited and to "quiet down" afterward, but dynamics is a separate issue and a change in volume isn't essential to an acceleration or a deceleration.

By generalizing what we have learned from this example, we can formulate three principles with respect to rhythmic fades.

Three Principles for Accelerating and Decelerating

1. Change the rate of change.
The rate of rhythmic change in an acceleration is faster toward the end than at the beginning:

1 ——————2 ———3 —— 4—5–67 etc.

If we were to diagram a typical acceleration in a graph, we would see that there was continuous change, but that the rate of change increases, resulting in quite an organic rush at the finish:

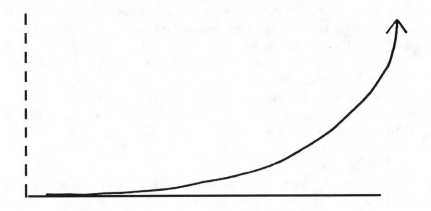

Similarly, a deceleration moves relatively slower — in graphic terms, it drops off more steeply — at the end than at the start.

2. Back off in the opposite direction.
You should back off as far as possible at the beginning of an acceleration or deceleration. Backing off is important for several reasons. In the first place, it gives you lots of room to fade from one rhythm to the next.

An effective acceleration is continuous. Your rhythm should be changing from moment to moment. But if you get where you are going too soon, the acceleration stops. In terms of the graph above, the rising arc of your fade stops rising because there is nowhere to go. Your performance becomes as flat as the ceiling it has reached. Flat is boring: nothing is happening, nothing is changing; on machines that monitor heartbeats, flat means dead. Backing off in the opposite direction (as far as you sensibly can) helps you to avoid getting there too soon.

If you start an acceleration too briskly, you are likely to be going way too fast by the end. Backing off in the opposite direction — to the slowest truthful rhythm — helps you avoid this pitfall. The absolute maximum speed (or volume) of which you are capable should in fact be avoided because the result is largely unintelligible. You should never really "max out."

Backing off is also a wonderful means of discovering expressive, truthful ways of playing the moments that precede and initiate a fade. In the case of Wesley's speech, backing off in the opposite direction (from the pandemonium of the fight) gives you a sensuous, truthful, effective way of playing both the footsteps and how Wesley listens to them. When you back off in the opposite direction, you should always ask yourself what the sense is in the backed-off energy — and how far you can possibly go in this opposite direction.

Because it encourages you to discover high contrasts between the beginnings and endings of your rhythmic fades, backing off also helps you to shape a speech that has variety and range.

3. Hold back.

You need to pace yourself when you perform accelerations and decelerations. Once you have decided at what point in the text an acceleration should finish, you must rehearse so that it concludes on the very phrase you intend. In order not to reach your destination too soon, you should hold back even as you move forward.

Does that seem contradictory? There are substantial reasons for this contradiction, as you shall see when we get to the topic of opposites. Suffice it to say at this point that a character is almost always being held back by internal and external forces. The tension this creates is the stuff of drama. There is always some difficulty in getting where you want to go!

If you are speaking too fast by the end of an acceleration, or if you are arriving at the endpoint of your acceleration too soon, the solution lies either in backing off farther in the opposite direction or in holding back more as you fade — or both. The same is true for decelerations.

190

Changing the rate of change, backing off, and holding back should become instinctive.

A study in conflicting rhythms

Let's look closely at a text which is a good example of contrasting rhythms, and which affords several opportunities to use acceleration and deceleration in order to fade from one rhythm to another. Juliet has sent her nurse to find out from Romeo when they will be married. This soliloquy opens the scene in which the nurse finally arrives with the news — three interminably long hours after she set out.

Read Speech 14, Appendix B.

Juliet consciously contrasts the energy of youth and love with that of old folks like her nurse. But there are other rhythmic contrasts in this speech. The images of nimble-pinioned doves and of wind-swift Cupid are polar opposites of the foot-dragging petulance with which Juliet enters the stage. The rhythm of her impatience ("O she is lame!") is very different from that of her doting when she imagines Romeo's reply ("And his to me") — though both these monosyllabic phrases are relatively slow.

We have already noted how Shakespeare uses clusters of monosyllables to slow the pace. It is as if nearly every word were accented and underlined, which creates quite an emphatic rhythm. For example, the couplet that concludes this speech, which you have already explored in terms of characterization (see 5.12-14), is mostly monosyllabic, and its heavy tread is slowed by onomatopoetic impulses and by the length of its component sounds.

But old folks, many feign as they were dead,
Unwieldy, slow, heavy, and pale as lead.

10.38 Read these lines as slowly as possible. Remember that Juliet is exasperated by all this waitinnnnng; her rhythm here may be exaggerated, but it's quite natural. It's not a question of pausing between words but of stretching the words like taffy. Extend each final sound so that it flows right into the initial sound of the following word.

The clock struck nine when I did send the Nurse.

10.39 The soliloquy starts with monosyllables. Speak the first line with a heavy accent on each word. The energy here is akin to that of the final couplet: this is the tedious rhythm of waiting for the old nurse.

10.40 Make a plodding, sulking, heavy-footed entrance as Juliet; choreograph your movement with the text.

and from nine till twelve
Is three long hours, yet she is not come.

10.41 This is another slow stretch. How might fourteen-year-old Juliet vocally exaggerate how long it's been?

The rhythm of Juliet's "warm youthful blood" — and of the romantic images that flood her imagination — is very different.

Love's herald's should be thoughts,
Which ten times faster glide than the sun's beams

10.42 Imagine that Juliet makes a quick, impatient, love-hungry movement — perhaps a long diagonal cross downstage. She moves as swiftly as light, as thought. Play this movement without speaking the text.

10.43 Now read the text with this movement in your voice.

Therefore do nimble-pinioned doves draw Love,
And therefore hath the wind-swift Cupid wings.

10.44 This is the same rhythm. These lines require nimble-tongued articulation.

· Warm your mouth up on "nimble-pinioned" — say it until you can make it fly.

· Explore the onomatopoetic possibilities in "wind-swift."

· Bleed the rhythm of "wind-swift" into "Cupid" and "wings." Pay particular attention to the sound of your breath as you speak these words.

10.45 Read these two lines in the rhythm suggested by its images.

10.46 Move with these lines as swiftly as a winged messenger of love.

To get from one of Juliet's rhythms to the other, there are, as we have seen, two possibilities. Let's look first at the effect of abruptly changing rhythms by way of a *cut*. Perhaps the first two lines could be shaped in this way.

The clock struck nine when I did send the Nurse.
In half an hour she promised to return.

10.47 Repeat the slow, heavy-footed entrance you created earlier. Try the second line as a sudden burst of exasperation, with a fast, impulsive movement downstage.

10.48 Imagine that at the beginning of the scene the lights come up to discover Juliet lying on a bench with one arm over her eyes. The first line is dry and expressionless; she is perfectly still. On the second line she jumps to her feet with a very different energy.

Perchance she cannot meet him. That's not so.

10.49 Imagine that on the first half of the line Juliet has an anxiety attack; then, she uses the three emphatic monosyllables of the next sentence to put the brakes on her panic.

More commonly you will fade from one rhythm to another, accelerating or decelerating. While cuts create discontinuities, rhythmic fades create a sense of flow, as one rhythm organically develops into a different one.

That's not so.
O, she is lame! Love's heralds should be thoughts,
Which ten times faster glides than the sun's beams

The rhythm of "Love's heralds ..." is very swift, but "O, she is lame!" is monosyllabic and continues the slower rhythm of "That's not so." Shakespeare is in fact directing you to back off in the opposite direction. If you ignore his actorly advice and blurt out "O, she is lame!" too quickly, you will have very little room to accelerate, and you will end up speaking much too quickly too soon.

10.50 What is the slowest truthful version of "O, she is lame"? Let your voice underline each word. This establishes the starting point for your acceleration: the next sentence will begin in the same rhythm. Instead of speaking "Love's heralds" at one quick pace all the way through, you will now — much more effectively — accelerate to a rhythm as swift as a sunbeam.

Therefore do nimble-pinioned doves draw Love,
And therefore hath the wind-swift Cupid wings.
Now is the sun upon the highmost hill
Of this day's journey, and from nine till twelve
Is three long hours, yet she is not come.

Earlier we looked at the text beginning "and from nine till twelve" as a quite slow section. Now we realize that in context it is actually part of a deceleration, and that the effect of the monosyllables here is gradually to slow the brisk passage that precedes it. It is more shapely and usually more truthful to fade from one rhythm to the next, rather than to play two distinct rhythms which are simply adjacent. It is also a more active choice to accelerate or decelerate: the audience hears that something is happening, that the energy is changing rather than remaining static. Movement and change are inherently interesting.

10.51 Start in the brisk nimble-pinioned rhythm and gradually slow down all the way through to the end of "yet she is not come." That last phrase is still decelerating: you should not hit the slowest point until the very last word.

yet she is not come.
Had she affections and warm youthful blood,
She would be as swift in motion as a ball.

10.52 By now you should be able to read the musical score which Shakespeare has written. Once again this section begins with slow monosyllables. From that backed-off starting point, gradually accelerate the next two lines.

Had she affections and warm youthful blood,
She would be as swift in motion as a ball.
My words would bandy her to my sweet love
And his to me.

10.53 In this passage you must come full circle: the acceleration of the first sentence fades right into the deceleration of the second. Juliet is slowing down romantically on the monosyllables "to my sweet love," but it takes the next phrase to bring her to a complete stop. During the pause indicated by the short line "And his to me," Juliet dotes on thoughts of Romeo.

10.54 Read the whole of Juliet's soliloquy. Focus on how she moves back and forth from one rhythm to the other. Look for variety: her monosyllabic moments should not all be the same, nor should her bursts of energy. Can you sense an overall shape to the speech?

Practice In Rhythmic Sound Sense

He falls to such perusal of my face
As he would draw it. Long stay'd he so. (Excerpt 13, Appendix A)
10.55 The apparently mad Hamlet has burst into Ophelia's chamber and now he stares at her. Note the long vowels and continuant consonants of "Long stayed he so." How does the rhythm of this phrase help to tell the story? The monosyllables "As he would draw it" start the deceleration. Play the moment as if Ophelia were reliving its tense stillness.

Small showers last long, but sudden storms are short. (John of Gaunt, *Richard II*, II.i)
The opposing images imply different rhythms. Shakespeare has also built the contrast into the language. The first half of the line is monosyllabic ("showers" is slurred as one syllable) and rich in continuant consonants (*s, m, l, sh, w, r*) it also requires substantial reforming of the mouth between syllables. The second half of the line is dominated by dentals (*d, t*) and plosives (*b, p*), which move more quickly.
10.56 Explore the sound sense of the contrasting rhythms in this line. How far can you go in each direction? Which is the more effective way to move from the first rhythm to the second, a fade or a cut?

Bloody, bawdy, villain!
Remorseless, treacherous, lecherous, kindless villain!
O, vengeance!
Why, what an ass am I! (*Hamlet*, II.ii)
10.57 Hamlet's tirade against King Claudius ends with a string of polysyllables: these enable him to accelerate to a fierce climax. After the pause indicated by the short line "O, vengeance," the speech cuts to a very different energy, which is clearly indicated by the shift to monosyllables, as Hamlet comments on his outburst. Explore the emotional sense in this rhythmic change.

Titania's votaress (the "she" of this passage) died giving birth to the young boy whom Titania now refuses to give over to Oberon.

Full often hath she gossiped by my side,
And sat with me on Neptune's yellow sands,
<u>Marking</u> th'embarkèd <u>traders</u> on <u>the flood</u>,   *observing; ships; the sea*
When we have laughed to see the sails conceive
And grow big-bellied with the <u>wanton</u> wind,   *roving freely (lustful)*
Which she with pretty and with swimming gait
Following, her womb then rich with my young squire,
Would imitate, and sail upon the land
To fetch me trifles, and return again,
As from a voyage, rich with merchandise.
But she, being mortal, of that boy did die;
And for her sake do I rear up her boy;
And for her sake I will not part with him.   (Speech 13, Appendix B)

10.58 Where does the rhythm change in this text? What is the sense in the new rhythm?

10.59 Explore decelerating into the rhythm of the last lines.

10.60 What scene is implied by "But she, being mortal, of that boy did die"? Explore speaking this line from inside the implicit scene. The resolute tone of the last two lines might be the echo of a vow made to the votaress on her deathbed.

Hermia, who is short in stature, believes that Helena has stolen her boyfriend. In this speech she imagines that Helena has added insult to injury by making a disparaging remark about her height.

Now I perceive that she hath made compare
Between our statures: she hath urg'd her height,
And with her personage, her tall personage,
Her height, <u>forsooth</u>, she hath prevail'd with him.   *indeed (ironic)*
And are you grown so high in his esteem,
Because I am so dwarfish and so low?
How low am I, thou painted maypole? Speak!
How low am I? I am not yet so low
But that my nails can reach into thine eyes.
(*A Midsummer Night's Dream*, III. ii)

10.61 At what points in this speech do monosyllabic lines or half-lines change the rhythm? Note the various kinds of expressive emphasis created in this way. Explore how these rhythmic changes develop out of the preceding rhythms.

The next text invites you to characterize "withered Murder." Macbeth is about to exit in order to kill King Duncan.

withered Murder,

<u>Alarumed</u> by his sentinel, the wolf,   *signaled*

Whose howl's his watch, thus with his stealthy pace,

With <u>Tarquin's</u> ravishing strides, towards his design   *(he raped Lucrece)*

Moves like a ghost. (II.i)

10.62 Imagine that in a performance at Shakespeare's Globe, Macbeth moves diagonally upstage, with an eye over his shoulder, towards Duncan's chamber door. The rhythm of the text — and of your movement — is not constant. Which phrases quicken, which slow the pace? How might you play the rhythmic changes physically and vocally? Consider both the circumstances and the images.

For Your Own Speech

1. Explore contrasting rhythms for several different sections of your speech.
- What event, motion, energy, or image does each rhythm seek to conjure? How does rhythm embody the sense of the text and help to tell the story?
- Name each rhythm. Avoid bland, cliché, generic labels, as they tend to inspire bland, cliché, generic work. Names for your rhythms should not refer to emotions or moods, since such terms lead to playing feelings rather than events. Verbs, interesting adjectives, and metaphors provide you with much better language for talking about your work. *The very best names for your rhythms — because they will guide you to work on what the author has in mind — are non-emotion words that come from your speech.*

- Don't settle for generically faster or slower: be specific about the texture of your rhythms. Remember that one way to define rhythm is "any wave-like recurrence." Draw each of your rhythms as a wave with a repeating shape.
- How does onomatopoetic sound sense interact with the rhythms you perform?
- How do long and short vowels and consonants contribute to shaping these rhythms?
- How can you put these rhythms into your body? The energy of each rhythm should be in your muscles, even if you are still.

Guidelines

Rhythm is another way in which sound sense makes audible what is happening in the story. Your goal is to shape your text so that it embodies the energy and motion of events — what Stanislavski called their tempo-rhythm.

Your rhythms should be expressive of what is occurring in the other time and place — not of your feelings now, as you tell the story. It is of course possible that the rhythms of your story may also embody your feelings in the here and now.

Work on developing rhythms that are sensuous enough to affect both you and your audience.

Consider both longer and shorter passages.

Make sure that you are not just speaking these rhythms but acting them.

2. For other sections of your speech, craft an acceleration and a deceleration. These may be consecutive or they may occur in separate sections of the speech.

- Name the rhythms that you are fading into and out of.
- How do your acceleration and deceleration help to tell the story? What events and energies do they embody?
- Fading is by definition changing. Once you begin a rhythmic fade, keep the fade going, from moment to moment.
- Back off in the opposite direction as far as you can, so as to give yourself room to fade into the rhythmic change. What is the sense in this backed-off position? Does backing off reveal to you an

interesting and truthful energy for the beginning of the text?
- Hold back even as you fade. Avoid going so fast or so slow that what you are saying is unintelligible. Shape your acceleration and your deceleration so that you don't reach the final speed or slowness until the very last words of the section of text you are working with.
- If you find yourself going too fast or too slow at the end of a fade, back farther off at the beginning, or hold back more as you fade — or both.
- Remember that the rate of rhythmic change in an acceleration is faster toward the end than at the beginning. Your acceleration should begin slowly, the rate of change should gradually increase, and there should be a bit of a rush toward the very end. Your deceleration should be a relatively slower at the end than at the start.
- After you have shaped your acceleration and deceleration, graph them. On your graphs, insert several key words or phrases so that you can see how the graph relates to the text you are working on.
- Read aloud the sections you have accelerated and decelerated while keeping one eye on your graphs. Make adjustments — to your graphs or to your performance — until the two are in agreement.

Guidelines

Work on the skill of continuously, gradually fading the rhythmic change even as you hold back. The tension in this contradiction is exciting.

One rhythm should develop organically into the text. Aim for a fade that is so seamless that it is impossible to hear where one rhythm ends and the next begins.

Dynamics (louder/quieter) and rhythm are separate issues. Not all accelerations involve a parallel fade from quiet to loud; not all decelerations go from some degree of forte to pianissimo. Dynamics and rhythm do tend to link up when the acceleration and deceleration are part of a build up to and down from a climax, as in Wesley's speech about the fight between his parents.

These rhythmic choices are tentative, but they will begin your exploration of expressive and varied rhythms for your speech.

3. Is there any point in your speech at which a cut — an abrupt change in rhythm — might truthfully express the unexpectedness, the suddenness of an event?

- A high-contrast juxtaposition of very different rhythms is warranted only if it helps you to tell the story.
- If you consider a cut, explore what the transition would be like if you faded from one rhythm to the other.
- What happens to your character when you play a cut?

Section Three
Shape Sense

Chapter 11
Fades and Builds

Shape sense

Shaping is the essential act of art: artists are all shapers. This is so because content cannot exist without form. A poem cannot speak without words, and the words must be shaped so that they mean *just this*. Song must find a voice, and that voice must shape its melody and lyrics if the song is really to sing. Shape is a vehicle of sense.

In order to shape your speech so that it embodies the story, you must:
- put together its parts and clarify how they relate to one another;
- subordinate what is incidental to what is most important;
- orchestrate events so that they culminate forcefully and truthfully in a turning point;
- explore the shapes given to you by the author and perform them so as to maximize their effect.

All that is shape sense.
- How do I get from this part of the story to the next?
- How do I act what happens *in between* the events of my story?
- What are the key words in my speech? What are the most important actions and events? How do I make these more important than the rest?
- Is there a turning point in my speech? A central event? Does a sequence of events build to a climax? How can I make such a moment a highpoint?
- What's the action, decision or realization that my speech leads to? How can I make it clear that it is the upshot of what has gone before?

Shaping skills will help you discover practical, effective answers to these questions. This chapter and the next focus on acting transitions from one moment to the next, what I call the "from/to" of acting.

From/to

A character reliving a story travels freely from scene to scene and event to event, shifts from one persona and point of view to another, moves from mood to mood. When you are acting a speech that tells a story, skills at getting from/to are essential.

When your energy changes abruptly from one moment to the next, the effect is jarring, explosive — and sometimes implosive, as when someone bursts into tears quite out of the blue. An eruption of new energy can be truthfully expressive of unexpected change. Or perhaps what an audience sensed was coming happens all at once. But sudden changes of this sort should be used sparingly: if overused, they lose their effectiveness. They also obscure how a character gets from one moment to the next by simply leaping into the new energy — without any transition.

More commonly, a character *fades* from one energy to another: this takes both actor and audience through intermediate stages that make visible (and audible) how the change occurs. Fading is the first and foremost means of shaping a transition from one acting moment to another.

Fades

A fade is a gradual and continuous change in energy. Whatever it is that you are fading becomes more and more, or less and less. This change in energy should happen seamlessly, as in one of those charts that go from black to white through every shade of gray. A fade should happen as smoothly as lights can fade up or fade out on a scene. Since it is often the case that one energy is waning as another is waxing, acting fades may be thought of as cross-fades, in which the lights go out on one scene as they come up on another — without any jumps. In this way a fade moves by degrees from energy A to energy B.

Fading is a major tool in acting — and in *Acting Narrative Speeches*. An actor accomplished in fading can take his or her audience anywhere.

The importance of fading

Actors and directors often discuss roles in terms of a *journey*: from a given starting point, a character moves through intermediate stages to wherever it is that he or she ends up. It is in the transitions from one moment to the next that an audience sees what specific steps lead from A to B, from B to C. It is in these transitions that a character journeys. Transitions tell the story.

The transitions that comprise a character's journey are in fact more important than the stopping points along the way, because they show us the character in motion. If we don't understand or believe how you got from A to B, the moments themselves are for naught.

We can't go with you on your character's journey unless you *take* us with you, from point to point. Fades make it possible to take us along. We not only see how your character gets from A to B, we vicariously experience the transition.

Fading keeps you honest about investigating precisely what happens between one moment and the next. It forces you to make sense of a transition and to make visible *how* you get from A to B. Fades are an antidote to mysterious jumps, inexplicable changes of heart, unearned moments for which there has been no preparation. There are certainly moments in life and on stage when emotions and actions erupt out of the blue, but it is more often the case that events and energies evolve and develop in discernible stages.

Being careful about fading will also keep you from bailing out on a moment so that the audience doubts the genuineness of what your character had been feeling. In theater as in life, the measure of a moment's grip on you is how long it takes the moment to fade. The stronger and deeper a moment, the longer the transition to the next moment. Imagine that you are playing a high school teacher who has just thrown two students out of class and sent them to the office. You have been standing in the doorway, yelling down the hall. You slam the door shut and immediately resume the lesson. It will seem bogus — even comic — if you are instantly calm and collected. It takes time for rage to subside. Your voice and your body will be residually angry for a while.

In rehearsal, fading is the actor's most useful tool for creating shapes both large and small. In performance, the skill of fading your acting impulses so as to create spontaneous shapes is essential to channeling inspiration.

Varieties of fades

You've already worked on fading in several different contexts. When you moved seamlessly into a moment of onomatopoeia, you were fading vocal colors and textures. You were fading rhythms when you worked on acceleration and deceleration. When Wesley's account of his parents' fight started very quietly and grew by degrees to be very loud, you were fading what a musician would call the dynamics of the speech.

Every sort of acting choice may be gradually introduced. The onset of a mood, the growing insistence of a gesture, the increasing speed or size of a movement, the emergence of a metaphorical image — all such developments may be faded into existence. You may also fade:

• from one tone or mood to another;
• from one character to another;
• from one action or event or scene to another;
• from one period of time in the story to another;
• from one emotional reaction to another.

You can fade from anything to anything, as long as you are clear about what you are fading. You must define for yourself what you are fading from and what you are fading to. If fading is becoming more and more (or less and less) fill-in-the-blank, it is important to fill in the blank. *What* is becoming more and more, *what* is becoming less and less? You must decide on your starting point and your ending point, and you must discover precisely what happens between the two. A fade must have specific content; otherwise it is just a formal exercise.

The best way to force yourself to consider what the poles of your fade are is to name each of them, not with psychological or emotional labels, but with language that comes from your text.

A fade may be physical or vocal or both. It may involve a paragraph, a whole speech, an entire scene, or only a few words. Fading from one moment in a story to the next may involve no great distance. But some fades cover a whole lot of ground — for example:

• from violence to tenderness;
• from intimacy to distance;
• from certainty to doubt;
• from hyperactivity to stillness;
• from excitement to stupor;
• from pleasure to pain;
• from shyness to exhibitionism;
• from pre-exam hysteria to sunning-on-the-beach calm; etc.

Fading from something to its opposite is awfully good practice, and for reasons that will be made clear in Chapter 15, this is an important skill in acting.

Principles for fading

These principles are familiar to you from your work on accelerating and decelerating rhythmic fades.

1. Back off in the opposite direction as far as is truthful.

This maximizes the room you have to fade. Backing off is also a discovery tool, which can lead you to truthful energies you might not otherwise have found.

Backing off also helps you to avoid forecasting what is about to happen when it is important to surprise both your character and the audience.

2. Hold back.

Don't be in a rush to make the transition. The point of a fade is to reveal all the stages in-between the energies you are fading from and to. You should not reach the endpoint of a fade until you get to the very last word of the text you are shaping. Once there is no longer any change in energy, the fade is over.

3. The rate at which you fade may change.

A fade may begin relatively slowly, for example, and gradually pick up speed as you move closer to the next moment.

Fading a gesture

In *Curse of the Starving Class,* Weston suspects that his wife is having an affair with a lawyer, and he talks about how easy it would be to kill them.

I was in the war. I know how to kill. I was over there. I know how to do it. I've done it before. It's no big deal. You just make an adjustment. You convince yourself it's all right. That's all. It's easy. You just slaughter them. Easy. (Excerpt 19, Appendix A)

11.1 *The rhythm of this text suggests that you might explore an action that repeats for each of the short sentences. Imagine, for example, a kitchen knife in your hand — you can use a pen or other substitute prop — and experiment with stabbing it into some surface. Start very small — just a light touch with the point. As you read the text aloud, fade this gesture so that it very gradually becomes larger and more muscular. The strongest point might happen around "You convince yourself ..." After that, fade back down to a tiny but pointed move at the end.*

You can also fade from one gesture to a different gesture by degrees. Suppose that as he starts this speech Weston is playfully sparring with his son. They trade light slaps, then go into a mock clinch, in which Weston goes through the motion of landing rabbit punches on the back of his son's head. As the father gives over to his grief and his need for comfort, imagine fading the rabbit punches into comforting pats, then into an embrace.

Fading movement

You can likewise fade a movement, so that it develops — in terms of speed and/or size — and you can fade from one quality of movement to another. In *Mr. Puntila and His Man Matti*, for example, the actor playing Puntila must at several points in the play fade from sober to drunk or from drunk to sober.

11.2 *When Puntila is sober, he is a stiff, cold, callous, suspicious, straight-laced, penny-pinching, authoritarian son-of-a-gun. When he hires workers, he feels muscles, looks at teeth. Walk about and put these qualities into your movement. That's what you're going to fade to. When Puntila is drunk, he is a smiling, generous, egalitarian fellow, fond of flirting and joking, who engages in lots of friendly physical contact. He manages to keep his balance with the grace of a ballet dancer. Establish the drunk Puntila and then slowly, seamlessly fade to his stern alter ego as you walk about. When you have established the sober Puntila, gradually fade back to the amiable drunk.*

Fading a metaphor

An actor might fade from one metaphor to another: from a bulldozer knocking down a wall to a feather floating in the wind; from a lithe jungle

208

cat stalking prey to a hyperactive rodent; from dancing a waltz to pounding a rock with a sledge hammer.

Imagine that as he begins the speech about his parents' fight (Speech 7, Appendix B), Wesley is frozen in the middle of the room: "I listened like an animal." That's your first metaphor, taken right from the text. Let's say that as the fight between his parents escalates, Wesley starts to move about, becoming more and more agitated until finally he is bouncing around the kitchen like a superball thrown into a stairwell. An actor might invent and explore such a metaphor to help him play the frantic, violent part of this speech.

I listened like an animal. My listening was afraid. Afraid of sound. Tense.

11.3 Start with this text and then do the rest of the fade without words. Your movement will develop in response to the stages of the fight: the sound of the car coming, the glare of the approaching headlights, the sound of footsteps, the first knocks, the kicks, the fist through the door, the screaming, etc. Get into a crouch, listening like a frightened animal — what kind? Imagine that by degrees, very small at first, Wesley animates. Start with the slightest turn of the head, in one direction, then another. Next your upper body turns, then the whole body. Your movement should still be relatively slow — you're fading gradually. Lean in both directions; take a half step one way, a full step the other. Fade this back-and-forth, don't-know-which-way-to-escape movement until Wesley is frantically bouncing off the walls and furniture like a superball.

Another actor, of course, might use a different metaphor to get at the truth of this scene. Wesley might start in a dreamy reverie, smelling the avocado blossoms, become more and more awake, until he seems to have had twenty cups of coffee, then lapse into something like a coma, hearing only the far-off sound of cars on the freeway.

Fading from scene to scene, event to event

Living in Exile imagines the nine years leading up to the events of Homer's *Iliad*.

Read in Speech 3 in Appendix B about the first two years of the siege of Troy.

In a text of this sort, one might be tempted to make a fresh start on each new year. But that would sidestep telling the story of how each year developed into the next, and how these nine years culminated in the events of the *Iliad*. Fading requires that you investigate precisely how you get from one moment to another.

If you fade into the second year, you will not be surprised out of the blue, but — as makes perfect sense — the whole second year will be a period of *becoming* more and more surprised.

We set out "to get us some."
In the second year, we were surprised, caught off guard, caught unprepared. We reevaluated our provisions. Who could've imagined it. After one whole year — no visit from the Goddess, Victory?

11.4 Your backed-off started point is the fierce, foolhardy confidence of the second year. The phrase "to get us some" echoes soldierly talk from the Vietnam War. Making the surprise of the second year a gradual development should take you through distinct stages; one scenario might start with an amused "Hunh!" and evolve through curiosity to uncertainty to a growing inability to comprehend, finally to dismay and perhaps panic. Explore.

Living through these stages makes the second year an event, one that the audience can experience along with you.

When Hotspur tells Henry IV why he didn't turn over some prisoners of war as requested (Speech 12, Appendix B), he begins his story by setting the scene.

My liege, I did deny no prisoners.
But I remember, when the fight was done,
When I was dry with rage and extreme toil,
Breathless and faint, leaning upon my sword

Shakespeare gives the actor only a few lines to travel from the here and now of addressing the king at court to the other time and place.

11.5 You are about to fade into the wounded exhaustion of the battlefield. Back off in the opposite direction: what might you discover by applying this principle? Perhaps Hotspur's response to being called on the carpet is typically hot-headed: if he flies off the handle at the

*outset, his energy will be very far from "faint." On "My liege," kneel
erect on one leg in front of the king with both arms out in vehement
protest. Speak with this same energy. Your fade is slowly to collapse
into leaning heavily on one leg. As you fade, hold back: you
shouldn't be fully arrived in the battlefield scene until the very last
word of this section. The rate of change should be more gradual at
the beginning of your fade than at the end. Even in the last line,
"Breathless" should not sound as faint as "sword."*

There you are on the battlefield. This physical adjustment might be
translated into leaning on a table or the back of a chair, leaning against a
wall, etc.

Hotspur's exhaustion in the other time and place is in fact an
interesting way to react in the here and now to what he feels is an unjust
accusation from the king: it wearies him, so that his whole body sags.

Fading from character to character

There are excellent examples of fading from one character to another
in Hotspur's speech, since his story centers on characterizing the king's
emissary (see 5.44-52). For much of the speech Hotspur goes back and
forth from his own point of view to that of the fop.

**Breathless and faint, leaning upon my sword,
Came there a certain lord, neat and trimly dressed,
Fresh as a bridegroom.**

*11.6 Fading into a characterization of this "certain lord" will serve as an
entrance for the fop. Start on the battlefield: wounded Hotspur is
breathless and faint, leaning heavily on his leg. This is the backed-off
starting point for your fade. Gradually and seamlessly, so that the
transition is invisible, transform into the fop, "fresh as a bridegroom."
Remember that a fade is slower at first — in this case because you
are weary and faint, and probably stunned by the appearance of the
fop. Start to rise as Hotspur and finish as the fop, who should not be
100% arrived until "bridegroom." What is the effect of holding back
on your rise so that you are erect only on the last word of your fade?*

Notice how this is just like a cross-fade in lighting: weariness fading
down, freshness fading up.

With many holiday and lady terms
He questioned me, amongst the rest demanded
My prisoners in your Majesty's behalf.
I then, all smarting with my wounds being cold

You might start these lines as an indirect quote, letting us hear the fop. The last line is certainly Hotspur. Where does the point of view change?

11.7 Sustain the fop characterization through the third line, and then abruptly change energy for the fourth.

That could work in this context. Sometimes a sudden change is truthful and expressive. Before you decide, you should experiment with a fade.

11.8 You might start becoming Hotspur somewhere in the second line. Try fading so gradually that there is no moment when the audience hears or sees the change. A seamless transition is often the ideal.

And as the soldiers bore dead bodies by,
He called them untaught knaves, unmannerly,
To bring a slovenly, unhandsome corpse
Betwixt the wind and his nobility.

11.9 From Hotspur looking at the bodies of his dead comrades — a heartfelt, devastated moment — fade into the fop's prissy annoyance at their smell. Don't be in a rush. "He called them" is still Hotspur: it will take him a while to pull himself out of that moment of grief and fade back into the characterization.

Remember that one measure of the depth of Hotspur's grief about his dead soldiers is how long it takes him — in theatrical time, of course, not real time — to escape its hold on him. If he hops right back into characterizing the fop, it will make his grief seem shallow.

Fading feelings

Feelings wax and wane. Your character can become more and more apprehensive, more and more embarrassed, curiouser and curiouser, calmer and calmer.

Suppose Athi (Excerpt 1, Appendix A) really loses it while he tells his mother that he won't take the fish and the butter because they come from the landlord's wife. He has strong political convictions about accepting gifts from the enemy. His passion is no doubt intensified by the fact that

212

he is so hungry — and perhaps so tempted by the food; saying no to *himself* may force him to go over the top.

> **but nothing could make him take the fish or the butter. He got mad and said: "Did you beg them from the landlord's wife? You can take it back with you, I don't want it."**

11.10 *Athi is not an actor in search of an emotion. He isn't trying to make himself angry. Imagine that, like many people in emotional situations, he makes an effort to stay calm. Anger takes hold of him despite the fact that he resists it. All the more reason, then, to back off in the opposite direction at the outset, to hold back, and to fade more gradually at first than at the end. Start as quietly and calmly as you can, given the inner turmoil. Try to keep a lid on your feelings. Don't be maximally enraged until "want it" — it is at the very end that Athi loses it.*

Note how fading helps you to build the anger in an organic way.

Builds

A build is a fade that rises to a climax: there is a gradual increase in the intensity of a particular energy until the highest, most forceful point is reached. A build can shape material so that it arrives at a turning point of some sort: an action or decision, a realization or admission, perhaps the resolution of a conflict. Some builds, both in classic and contemporary material, fade up to huge climaxes; but builds come in all sizes, and some culminate very quietly. So *climax* is a relative term. It means not the highest point of a play or an act or a speech, but the highest point of a build. A whole scene can be shaped as a build, or a large chunk of text, as in Wesley's speech about his Mom and Dad fighting. But a short list of three or four items can build; a single sentence can build to its final word; a phrase can build. The highest point of any build is its climax, however small.

Builds typically involve gradual changes in:
- pitch (upward);
- pace (faster);
- volume (louder).

None of these elements is absolutely essential to a build, but they are common: we tend to talk faster and louder and to get higher in pitch when we get excited. But it is possible to construct a reverse build, which starts relatively loud and fast and high-pitched, and then gradually quiets, slows, deepens in pitch.

Builds are inherently exciting. Something is becoming more and more and more, and this creates a palpable sense of anticipation. In music, it is anticipating the climax of a crescendo that makes it exciting. Reaching the climax ends the anticipation and relaxes the tension it creates. This alternation of tension and relaxation is fundamental to all artistic creation. It is the same in acting. What's exciting about a build is the tension of anticipating its climax. After the climax, excitement gives way to the arrival of what was anticipated. That is why the anticipation of events sometimes seems better than the events themselves.

The shape sense of a build

Passions rise. Ideas grow on you. Plans unfold. Circumstances mount. Events snowball. Arguments accumulate until they persuade. All such developments can be captured in a build. It is because builds happen in life that they can happen on stage. Builds are organic.

What is said or done at a climax is emphasized by the intensified energy at the top of a build. Playwrights shape their scripts so that speeches and dialogs, scenes and acts build to a central idea, a turning point, an important action. Builds are the sensible way to shape a speech so that what is most important is given its due.

> • Hotspur's speech builds explosively to a moment when he loses it all over again — and says quite clearly why the fop angered him so.
> **I then, all smarting with my wounds being cold,**
> **To be so pestered with a <u>popinjay</u>,**   *parrot*
> **Out of my grief and my impatience**
> **Answered neglectingly I know not what —**
> **He should or he should not — for he made me mad**
> **To see him shine so brisk and smell so sweet**
> **And talk so like a waiting gentlewoman**
> **Of guns and drums and wounds, God save the mark!**
> (Speech 12, Appendix B)

214

• Juliet grows so fearful of waking up in the tomb that she drinks the potion (Speech 15, Appendix B).

• Laureen builds to the central message of her fantasized encounter with her alter ego on the street: "YOU'RE ONLY IN MY HEAD!" (Speech 10, Appendix B)

• Titania builds to the death of her votaress, which is the reason why she will not give the changeling boy to Oberon (Speech 13, Appendix B).

These builds, and their climaxes, are true to the events, and they allow the audience to hear and see and feel what is most important.

Principles for Shaping Builds

1. A build should have specific content.

At the outset we will practice the technical skill of shaping a build, without taking much time to analyze the material. When you shape a text for performance, however, you must ask yourself "*what* is building?" What is it that is waxing, welling up, accumulating? You should know precisely what you are building and craft a shape specific to your speech. A build should help you to make clear what your text is about, what your character is experiencing, what is happening in the scene. It should quite literally make sense. If you rely solely on technique and outward form, you may fashion builds with the illusion of sense, but generic builds are in fact senseless.

2. Watch your language.

Avoid emotional and psychological labels for your fades and builds, as these tend to trap you into playing feelings instead of events and actions. Verbs, interesting adjectives, and metaphors are much more conducive to exploration and discovery.

The best vocabulary for talking to yourself about what you are building will be found in your speech — or elsewhere in the play. Using words and images from your text helps you stay close to your character, the story, and the playwright's intentions. In this way you avoid imposing concepts and importing issues which are not in the script.

In John Guare's *Six Degrees of Separation*, a character of considerable verve says that his "hair stood up" with excitement when he first read J.

D. Salinger's *Catcher in the Rye*. In the same speech this character speaks of an existential "paralysis" like that at the end of *Waiting for Godot*, when the characters seem unable to move. An actor who values staying close to the text might speak of fading from "*Godot* paralysis" to his "hair standing up."

3. Get inside your builds.

You have to act a build and its aftermath. When you are acting a speech that tells a story, a build means re-living the shape of events.

4. Back off in the opposite direction before beginning a build.

Since the formal components of a build often include accelerating the pace, rising in pitch, and getting louder, backing off typically involves starting slower, quieter, and lower in pitch. But your backed-off starting point should not be relaxed or casual; it should be full of potential energy, intensely concentrated. All that is about to unfold in the build is condensed in a densely packed moment that is like a star ready to explode. It is a build waiting to happen.

Feet coming. Feet walking toward the door. Feet stopping. Heart pounding.

11.11 *We applied the principle of backing off when we worked on acceleration in Wesley's speech about his parents' argument (see 10.34-37). The long fade that starts at this point is actually a build, and so Wesley should begin very quietly, slowly, at a low pitch — all of which makes perfect sense in the circumstances. But the tension that will unfold in the build and become the violence of the argument is already in Wesley's gut at the outset, like a clenched fist. You don't want this to happen!*

Backing off maximizes the room you have to develop the build and helps you keep from getting too big too soon.

It also discovers to you new energies (quieter, slower, lower pitched, and opposite-whatever-you're-building-toward) which you might otherwise not have found. Backing off generates variety in your acting score.

Back off as far as possible. Ask yourself: how far can I truthfully go in the opposite direction?

5. Hold back as you build.

Holding back is what keeps a build building. If you get fast, loud, high-pitched, and high-intensity too quickly, the consequence, as actors say, is that you have nowhere to go. You have reached the ceiling and as you move along it, your performance quite literally goes flat — and flat is dead, flat is boring, because nothing is changing. All your lines are performed on the same high level, which is monotonously shrill, and not nearly so exciting as a build. The energy of your build should not peak until the very end of the text you are shaping. Before you get to that point, you must hold back.

Even when you get to the climax, you should hold back a bit: screaming gets unintelligible, so does talking too fast or too shrilly.

There is always an opposing energy at work as you build, some force that holds back the emerging energy and in this way creates tension. Perhaps some circumstance inhibits you from releasing the energy, until you can no longer hold it back. In emotional situations, most of us don't *want* to get upset; we resist it, but it takes hold of us. Perhaps some part of you does not want to go where you are headed, even as you propel yourself forward. You will explore this sort of inner conflict in Chapter 15.

11.12 Imagine for a moment that you are in a situation in which you do not want to admit that you are angry. The more you are accused of being angry, the angrier you get — and the more you deny it. Improvise for a moment the stages that you might go through as you deny your anger: repeat "I'm not angry" while holding back. Try to keep the lid on your anger, even as the pressure inside you builds up.

There's lots of tension in that; it is often a relief when the lid finally blows off.

When Laureen sees her alter ego down on the street (Speech 10, Appendix A), she is intensely curious — and frightened — about what he might say. Part of her doesn't want to know, but another part of her crawls to the window to find out. Both her rising panic and her growing realization are embodied in the following build, and holding back helps you to create her inner conflict.

217

"Just let me live five minutes longer." Then you see him more clearly than before. You see for sure that he is you. That he's not pretending. He yells up to you in a voice you can't mistake. He yells at you so the whole street can hear him. **"YOU'RE IN MY HEAD. YOU'RE ONLY IN MY HEAD!"**

11.13 First back off in the opposite direction so as to give yourself room to build. Backing off often discovers a truthful, high-contrast way of starting a build — and sure enough, being vocally small and emphatically slow seems very right for Laureen's fervent wish: "Just let me live five minutes longer." Try this first line slow, low and quiet. Hold back, even as you continuously accelerate, rise in pitch and turn up the volume. There's no need to shout until the very last word. Hearing an actor build toward shouting is more exciting and effective than shouting itself. For our purposes, then, ignore the CAPS.

Keeping a build under control

If you find that you are getting too far along in your build too soon, the remedies are quite simple:

- back off more at the beginning;
- hold back more as you build;
- consider subdividing your build into two or more smaller builds, each of which is a step toward the biggest climax.

---

6. Gradually increase the rate at which you build to the climax.

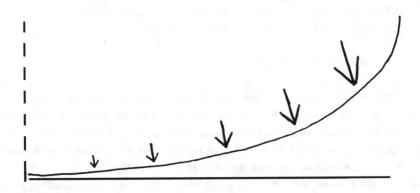

This is a graphic representation of a typical build. It begins as a slow ascent. The rate of change gradually increases. Late in the build, there is a bit of a rush to the finish line; only in its final moments does the ascent to the climax become steep. It is not until the very end — the last word of the text being shaped — that the highest point of the build is reached.

As we have seen, there is always some opposing force — represented here by downward arrows — which holds back the emerging energy. What precisely those arrows represent depends on the context.

7. Pull back periodically so that you can rebuild.

You cannot build and build. Very soon you would go through the roof. You must regularly pull back in order to build again.

Cutbacks and decrescendos, which you will explore later in this chapter as means of pulling back, have sound sense and expressive value in themselves. They also set up the next build.

Putting it all together: playing a build

The third act of *Curse of the Starving Class* begins with a narrative speech by the father. After his scalding bath, Weston is transformed. He is sober and clean-shaven, and as the lights come up, he is folding the family's laundry. In a pen next to the stove is a lamb sick with maggots, and Weston tells the lamb a story about an eagle, whose thrilling aeronautics this former flier has never forgotten. Why has this story stuck

219

with Weston? He sees in it an image that really speaks to him about something important which he can not otherwise articulate. For one thing, Weston identifies with the eagle's freedom in flight. Whether or not he is free to come and go is a central issue in Weston's life.

Read Speech 9, Appendix B.

Just like a thunder clap. Blam! He's down on that shed roof with his talons taking half the tar paper with him, wings whippin' the air, screaming like a bred mare then climbing straight back up into the sky again. I had to stand up on that one. Somethin' brought me straight up off the ground and I started yellin' my head off. I don't know why it was comin' outa' me but I was standing there with this icy feeling up my backbone and just yelling my fool head off. Cheerin' for that eagle.

Imagine a version of this passage that jumped immediately to the level of the climax: you would have nowhere to go.

11.14 Try doing four or five lines of this text on the same high level: loud and fast and high-pitched.

The effect is unpleasantly shrill, inexpressively one-note, and not nearly so exciting as a build. The sense of something happening, unfolding, *becoming* is lost in a wash of shapeless excitement. And "I started yellin' my head off" is a non-event if you've been shouting since the eagle landed.

Shape is the vehicle of sense. Shaping this text as a build is expressive of the "icy feeling" going up Weston's backbone, of the eagle's "climbing straight back up into the sky," and of Weston's impulse to "stand up on that one." Notice that I can use words from the text to name all these dimensions of what the build is about, and that this language is more specific, stimulating and playable than something generic like "excitement."

You are going to accelerate, gradually increase volume and go up a bit in pitch, all in service of building to that cheer. First, of course, you will back off. How far can you truthfully go in the opposite direction? Weston has planted the bait and is now breathlessly waiting for the eagle to come back: quiet and slow and low-pitched is perfect. This starting point is not relaxed or casual; as is usually the case, the backed-off moment is full of intensely concentrated energy.

11.15 Get down in a crouch. As you build, slowly rise: don't be fully erect till the very end. If the impulse seems natural, an arm might extend your rising motion. Perhaps the build begins in a well-articulated whisper: "Just like a thunder clap." "Blam!" should be part of the fade: give it sound sense but don't jump your volume. Hold back — that creates the build's tension. Focus on reliving the story all over again, here and now. It should feel as if you don't know what's coming. Remember that acting is reacting. Taking in these events should put you in a responsive, all-senses-alert mode: eyes wide open, mouth slightly open in wonder, nostrils flared, etc.

This is a lot of sense in this shape. When an author writes a build such as this, the actor must sensitively interpret how its rhythms, pitches, and dynamics help to tell the story.

Letting a shape lead you

One of the many paradoxes of acting involves the tension between what is fixed and what is spontaneous, between painstaking rehearsal and the illusion that everything is happening for the first time, between being in control of what happens next and abandoning yourself to the course of events.

The shapes that you create need to be so well rehearsed that you are free to do them a little differently each time. An honest performance lives and breathes — and therefore changes in many subtle ways, even as it stays true to the material and how it was rehearsed. In performance, you are in effect re-improvising the shapes you have scored for yourself.

Since acting is reacting, you should not think of a shape as something you make happen. A shape should happen to you. You should be led by it. This means that it is generally truthful for your character to be a few steps behind a build or other fade, rather than out in front of it.

In performance, the shapes you have constructed should quite literally take you places. Give yourself over to them. Follow their lead.

Pulling Back

You must regularly pull back in order to build again. From this perspective, a speech is a series of builds and pullbacks — of various sizes and shapes. As with all changes in energy, a pullback can be sudden or gradual.

Cutbacks and decrescendos

Cutbacks are sudden pullbacks. The intense energy of the climax doesn't disappear; just as in physics, energy may transform but it cannot diminish. For this reason, a cutback does not mean you can relax. On the contrary, the energy after you pull back sharply becomes concentrated, as if a star had collapsed into a dense mass.

An immediate, high-contrast change after a build can be powerful and it can be truthful, but you should use this arresting effect sparingly, lest it lose its expressive value.

More commonly, you will fade down from climaxes, more or less slowly. What waxes must wane, what goes up must come down, and after the climax of a story comes its denouement, when issues are victoriously resolved or characters accept defeat. In music, a gradual decrease in volume is called a *decrescendo*; we will borrow the term and use it in a more general sense to mean any gradual lessening of energy after a climax. A decrescendo, therefore, is the mirror opposite of a build; it often involves slowing the rhythm, becoming relatively more quiet and coming down in pitch. As with a build, the rate of change increases toward the end of the fade. How long a decrescendo lasts — how much text it encompasses — will vary: like builds, decrescendos come in all sizes.

Exploring whether to cutback or decrescendo

Whether you cutback or decrescendo after a climax is an aesthetic decision. What seems most truthful for the material you are working on? The alternatives should be actively explored.

After the build you have just done for the speech about the eagle, you have a choice about how to shape the next bit of text.

I was standing there with this icy feeling up my backbone and just yelling my fool head off. Cheerin' for that eagle. I'd never felt like that since the first day I went up in a B-49. After a while I sat

down again and went on workin'. And every time I cut a lamb I'd throw those balls up on top a' the shed roof. And every time he'd come down like the Cannonball Express on that roof. And every time I got that feeling.

11.16 Explore first a cutback. All the expansive release of "Cheering for that eagle" suddenly gets pulled back at "I'd never felt like that ..." Your energy should get very compact, like a tense fist — full of excitement, but quiet, slower in rhythm, and lower in pitch. Then do another, much smaller build to the end, one which echoes "that feeling" of cheering for the eagle.

You can mark a cutback in your text by drawing a downward arrow in front of the word that begins the sudden change. Note that a cutback automatically backs you off in the opposite direction for the next build.

The alternative way of pulling back after "Cheerin' for that eagle" is to fade the energy down so that it organically wanes.

11.17 Start "I never felt like that" at the same intensity as "Cheerin' for that eagle." Fade down slowly in terms of pitch and volume and pace. Since the rate of change increases, your fade should be more gradual at the outset, more pronounced toward the end.

In order to mark this in your script, you might draw the shape of your fade in the margin; it will look like an upside-down build. Or you might bracket the text you are fading down and in the margin put the symbol used in music for a decrescendo.

"... You can take it back with you, I don't want it." Hungry as he was, she had to wrap her presents up again. She said goodbye and went back home. (Excerpt 1, Appendix A)

After Athi explodes at his mother, you have to make a choice about how you shape the pullback.

11.18 If you cutback at "Hungry as he was," the energy of Athi's outraged refusal will get concentrated in an intense moment expressive of both his hunger and his mother's heartache. You will need a "beat" — a tiny pause — after the climax.

11.19 Now explore the option of shaping a decrescendo here. Start "Hungry as he was" with the same energy as the climax. Don't rush

223

this fade. It is as if the anger drains out of Athi — and out of the storyteller who is empathetically identified with him. To keep the fade going, hold back even as you decrescendo. Your rage should continue to wane till the last word: getting quieter, lower in pitch, and slower.

There are several powerful builds in the St. Crispin's Day speech in *Henry V* (IV, iii). The young king is rallying his greatly outnumbered army just before the battle of Agincourt, on the feast of St. Crispin. This speech is an excellent example of how narrative — the several scenes which Henry asks his men to imagine — may be used to persuade. There aren't many of us, he tells them, but victory will win each of us a bigger share of the glory, and when this feast day rolls around every year, we'll be toasting our neighbors and telling our kids what happened. Here is how the speech mounts to its stirring conclusion.

> **Then shall our names,**
> **Familiar in his mouth as household words,**
> **Harry the king, Bedford and Exeter,**
> **Warwick and Talbot, Salisbury and Gloucester,**   *(noblemen about to fight)*
> **Be in their flowing cups freshly remember'd.**
> **This story shall the good man teach his son;**
> **And <u>Crispin Crispian</u> shall ne'er go by,**   *two martyrs remembered on this day*
> **From this day to the ending of the world,**
> **But we in it shall be rememberèd;**
> **We few, we happy few, we band of brothers;**
> **For he today that sheds his blood with me**
> **Shall be my brother; be he ne'er so <u>vile</u>**   *low in rank*
> **This day shall <u>gentle his condition</u>:**   *make him a gentleman*
> **And gentlemen in England now a-bed**
> **Shall think themselves accurs'd they were not here,**
> **And hold their manhoods cheap whiles any speaks**
> **That fought with us upon St. Crispin's Day.**

There are two builds here. The first climax is at "But we in it shall be rememberèd" — important because this is the lasting glory that Henry is promising his army. What happens after that climax? It is certainly not impossible to fade down on the next line, but a sharp cutback is most likely Shakespeare's intention. The brotherhood that Henry is trying to forge — and that he genuinely feels as he addresses men he is asking to die for him — is embodied in a quiet, intimate reading of "We few, we happy few, we band of brothers."

11.20 Shakespeare has already backed you off in the opposite direction at the outset of this passage. "Then shall our names" establishes a slow, deliberate rhythm. Henry launches quietly into a roll call of the nobles fighting with him. Build this to the promise of lasting glory at "But we in it shall be rememberèd." Then there is a cutback: "We few ... " is hushed, emphatic, intimate, and taut with life-or-death urgency. This line's potential energy is released in the next build, to the speech's spear-shaking conclusion.

Then I could picture my Dad driving it. Shifting unconsciously. Downshifting into second for the last pull up the hill. I could feel the headlights closing in. Cutting through the orchard. I could see the trees being lit one after the other by the lights, then going back to black. My heart was pounding, just from my Dad coming back. Then I heard him pull the brake. Lights turned off. Keys turned off. Then a long silence. (Speech 7, Appendix B)

This passage builds to "just from my Dad coming back." This is not a huge climax — remember that builds come in all sizes. If you wanted to name this shape, you could call it something like "headlights closing in" or "Dad coming back."

11.21 First try a sharp cutback, becoming suddenly quiet and relatively slower for the monosyllabic "Then I heard him pull the brake." Continue at this hushed — but very tense — level through "Then a long silence." Here the flatness has shape sense.

Sometimes, as in the last example, there is a brief plateau at the top of a build or at the bottom of a pullback, before the next shape begins.

11.22 Alternatively, you might fade down after the climax. In this case "Then I heard him pull the brake" begins at the level of "just from my Dad coming back" and Wesley's pounding heart calms down as he becomes engrossed in figuring out what's going on. Hold back as you fade down. The last four sentences should only gradually get slower, quieter, and lower in pitch. The rate of this decrescendo itself slows.

"YOU'RE IN MY HEAD! YOU'RE ONLY IN MY HEAD!" Then he turns and walks away. You watch him go until you can't see him any more. Then you make a clean jump all the way to the bottom. And your life goes dancing out the window. (Speech 10, Appendix B)
Laureen's fantasy climaxes with what she imagines her alter ego yelling up to her. How should you shape the end of this speech?

11.23 First try a sudden cutback after the CAPS. Her volume contracts but that doesn't mean that Laureen's desperation disappears — unless you decide that she is in fact relieved and that her suicide is a kind of release. Should the next lines stay quiet or build a bit? Explore until you are satisfied that the shape makes sense.

11.24 Now explore fading down until the end of the speech. In this version, "Then he turns" should begin in CAPS and the text should gradually become lower case.

Fading down to "dancing out the window" — and slowing even more because it is the end of the speech — means that you will take time with the final phrase, which makes it sound as important as it is.

Your choice of whether to cut back or fade down may be influenced by the choices you have made about previous pullbacks: you want to avoid repeating the same shape too many times in a row.

You will discover that fading down is much more common. Passions and events generally take time to unwind. The occasional cutback is a bold effect, but only if you use it infrequently, so that its suddenness is really a surprise.

Steps

Most builds are fades, but a build can also happen in steps. A build of this sort intensifies its energy in distinct stages. Typically, each step increases in volume and pitch and tempo. Steps are particularly useful for lists — of words, phrases, clauses, sentences — which enumerate a series of attributes, events, reasons, etc.

You can make note of this sort of build by drawing steps in the margin of your text. You may wish to write a word over each step, so as to remind yourself where the changes happen.

In *A Midsummer Night's Dream*, Helena tells Hermia that she has not betrayed their friendship. She says it three ways.

I evermore did love you, Hermia,
Did ever keep your counsels, never wrong'd you (III, ii)

11.25 Start slow and low and quiet. What is the sense in this backed-off starting point? Perhaps Helena's initial energy is something like "Ooooh nooo, Hermia, I would never do anything to hurt you." The next two steps should be spoken a bit louder and at a higher pitch, and each can be spoken at a quicker pace.

Earlier in the play, Helena pleads with the man she loves in a series of steps.

Use me but as your spaniel; spurn me, strike me,
Neglect me, lose me; only give me leave,
Unworthy as I am, to follow you. (II, ii)

If you treat "only give me leave,/Unworthy as I am, to follow you" as three steps, that makes a total of eight. In longer lists like this, the interval between steps may gradually shorten, so that the overall pace of the build quickens.

11.26 Pitching your voice to its lowest comfortable note on "spaniel" positions you to climb many steps; it is also amusingly expressive of how low Helena stoops here. Use the monosyllables at the start to slow you down. As the list progresses, the interval between each step should shorten, and each phrase can be spoken a bit more quickly. Note how these steps build to what Helena wants permission to do: "to follow you."

Here is Petruchio in *Taming of the Shrew* asserting ownership of his unwilling bride, who has proved a formidable adversary:

Nay, look not big, nor stamp, nor stare, nor fret;
I will be master of what is mine own.
She is my goods, my chattels; she is my house,
My household stuff, my field, my barn,
My horse, my ox, my ass, my anything (III. ii)

This text might be shaped as two sets of steps, with the second line as a first, smaller climax. But let's explore it as one long build.

11.27 Each phrase that can sensibly be a new step should go up a notch in pitch and volume; and the overall pace of the list should gradually increase. By my count, there are fifteen steps. Each step needs to be small, therefore, but a step nonetheless. Start quite low in volume and pitch, so that you have lots of room to build. Note the rhythmic implications of the monosyllables in the first line. So that you have a specific content to play, imagine that Petruchio, after a long struggle with Kate, fades from exhaustion to exultant joy.

Just as you may shape steps ascending, you may shape steps going down.

11.28 Start Petruchio's list at a high pitch, and quite loud; your initial pace should be quite brisk. Decelerate as you come down in pitch and volume. Play the list this time as a fade from jovial celebration to a serious, calculated attempt to break Kate's spirit.

King Claudius plans to poison Hamlet's cup, and the audience knows this, so there is considerable tension in watching the King offer a toast to Hamlet before the duel in the final scene.

Give me the cups,
And let the <u>kettle</u> to the trumpet speak,   *kettle-drum*
The trumpet to the cannoneer without,
The cannons to the heavens, the heavens to earth,
"Now the King drinks to Hamlet." (V, ii)

11.29 These steps — calling upon drum, trumpet and cannon to sound in sequence — should ascend in pitch and volume to the heavens. Bring "the heavens to earth" back down a step in keeping with its sense, and let the last line be a lower step still.

My heart was pounding, just from my Dad coming back. Then I heard him pull the brake. Lights turned off. Keys turned off. Then a long silence. (Speech 7, Appendix B)

11.30 That the last four sentences are so short suggests another possibility for shaping the pullback after the climax at "just from my Dad coming back": descending in steps. Each sentence should come down a notch in volume and pitch and tempo. Explore making the interval between sentences a fraction longer with each step.

Steps bring variety to the shape of your speech. But the more important skill is building smoothly and seamlessly in a continuous fade that arcs up to a climax.

For Your Own Speech

1. Shape a fade that builds to a climax, large or small. Include the pullback that follows this climax: either a cutback or a decrescendo.
   - What is building in your build?
   - Does the build culminate in a key moment? Does its climax give special emphasis to a statement or event?
   - Back off in the opposite direction.
   - Hold back. Use this to create tension.
   - The beginning of your build should be a slow, gradual ascent. It should be steepest toward the end.
   - Consider pace, pitch and volume as elements of your build and pullback.
   - Explore both the cutback and the decrescendo version of your pullback.
   - Note for future reference how your pullback sets up the next build.
   - What is the physical life of this build? Explore on your feet.

2. Prepare a fade in which a specific energy gradually changes to a very different, high contrast energy.
   - You should be able to articulate clearly and succinctly the two poles of your fade. Name each energy with words drawn from your speech, preferably language that does not refer to emotions or psychological states.
   - What is the physical life of this fade? Explore on your feet.

Guidelines

Keep fading until the last word or phrase of the text that you are shaping.

Be careful not to go too fast, too loud, or too high in pitch: stay intelligible and believable. If you feel you are getting ahead of yourself, work on backing off further at the beginning, and on holding back.

Rehearsal is a laboratory in which you experiment with your material. Begin work on each of these fades with a hypothesis about what you are fading *from* and what you are fading *to*. Then investigate the hypothesis on your feet. What you discover as you rehearse these fades may change

229

how you think about the energies involved.

Stay a step or two behind your fades and builds. Let them take you where you are going. Let them happen to you.

Get yourself in touch with the content of your fades and builds.

Get *inside* the shapes of your speech. Each is part of your character's journey. *Act* your shapes. *Live* them.

Chapter 12
From/To

You have been working on moments and sections of your speech without worrying about transitions from one part to the next. In certain respects this piecemeal approach mimics a good rehearsal process, in which discoveries accumulate as you go off in a certain direction one day and take a very different tack the next. Exploring far and wide leads to performances with range and variety and depth.

While you are working on story sense and sound sense, some transitions will evolve without conscious consideration. Others you must explore at a later stage in your process, as you begin to pull things together. Developing a sensibility about the from/to aspect of acting — about what is possible as you move from moment to moment — will make your work on transitions easier and more sophisticated. It will also make your impulses shapelier, so that you can make instinctive choices about transitions as you work on other issues.

Shaping transitions that help to tell the story

When you are putting your speech together, what happens in the other time and place is, as ever, the paramount consideration. How you get from one bit of text to the next should help to tell the story. Each transition should be another step along your character's journey.

Getting specific about how and why your character moves from moment to moment can result in new insights about a story's events, reveal details that might otherwise have escaped you and your audience, and stimulate you to create new and meaningful actions. When the path from moment A to moment B is made visible, more of the character's journey is mapped out and more of the story is told.

Suppose that you are putting together a speech after exploring quite different approaches to it in several rehearsals. Or perhaps you have imagined bits and pieces in your head without bothering about how they fit together. You now find yourself standing on a chair, but you know that your next moment needs to happen on the floor. This is not a problem, but an opportunity for discovery. How might you get down from the chair so that this transition helps to tell the story? Well, it depends on the specifics of your speech. Getting down might become:

- an aggressive attack on an enemy;
- a celebratory, heel-clicking leap;
- a clumsy, self-conscious fiasco;
- a very cool, snap-of-the-fingers hop;
- a terrified descent.

Imagine, for example, a speech in which a young woman remembers going to her first prom. She is standing on a chair, having the hem of her dress fixed by her mom at the last moment. The next event is meeting her date at the door. The text mentions her heart pounding when his car drives up, but nothing is said about how she gets from the chair to the door. How might getting down off the chair help you to tell the story? Consider the range of possibilities!

Or imagine a story in which a character climbs up on the railing of a bridge to jump and then decides not to do it. Nothing is said about how he gets down; at the end of the speech he is sitting in his car. Suppose you got up on a chair to act the bridge scene. How you get down is an opportunity to tell more of the story. Actors often collaborate with playwrights by making what is unspoken visible.

How you get from one moment to the next may not come to you immediately. A transition may elude you for days and weeks. Meanwhile you should keep running the transition in exploratory fashion, staying open to impulses which might come from:

- what has just happened or what happens next (either of which may evolve or change);
- the circumstances at this point of the story;
- what's potential in your physical position;
- the space in which you're working.

Here's an example of how a transition that helps to tell the story might be discovered in a rehearsal situation. There is a speech in *Curse of the Starving Class* in which Weston talks about how and why he got into so much debt.

I remember now. I was in hock. I was in hock up to my elbows. See, I always figured on the future. I banked on it. I was banking on it getting better. I figured that's why everybody wants you to buy things. Buy refrigerators. Buy cars, houses, lots, invest. They wouldn't be so generous if they didn't figure you had it comin' in.

232

Why not make a touch here and there. They all want you to borrow anyhow. Banks, car lots, investors. The whole thing's geared to invisible money. You never hear the sound of change anymore. It's all plastic shuffling back and forth. It's all in everybody's heads. So I figured if that's the case, why not take advantage of it? Why not go into debt for a few grand if all it is numbers? If it's all an idea and nothing's really there, why not take advantage? So I just went along with it, that's all. I just played ball.

Now shady characters are out to kill Weston, and he realizes he has to run away. At the end of this speech, his son tells him, "You better go." And in a few minutes Weston does leave, apparently for good.

Imagine that several weeks into rehearsal, the actor gets on his feet to explore his final scene for the first time. He knows what the speech is about, but he has no preconceptions about how it should be staged, except for two ideas suggested by developments in the rehearsal process. He knows he wants to start with his back against the refrigerator, because the director has asked everyone to makes choices about contact with this central image. Let's call leaning against the fridge moment A. And he knows that he wants the end of the speech — "I just played ball" — to be the last in a series of playful moments inspired by the script's numerous references to baseball: an image of sliding into home plate. That's moment B.

In rehearsal, the actor leans against the fridge, without any idea of how he will get to that baseball moment — how he will make the transition from A to B. As he begins the text, it dawns on him: just slide very slowly down the fridge and hit the floor on the last line. He starts his descent, and immediately the movement makes sense. It is not just OK for the text; it seems perfect. Weston is "sinking into debt," and in the here and now his heart is sinking as well, as he realizes he is going down the drain for good. Weston hits the kitchen floor, with his arms in the air and his legs arcing as if to touch home plate. It is a last ditch effort to get "home" safely, another attempt to relate to his son, a final moment of horseplay as if everything's going to work out. The actor playing his son, who is now dressed in his father's baseball cap and black raincoat, looking rather like an umpire in the circumstances, crouches over his father. He sticks his thumb in the air in the baseball gesture that tells a player he is out. "You better go," he says.

Exploring the question of how to travel from point A to point B in your acting score can lead to discoveries large and small. In this example from *Curse of the Starving Class*, the significant action is metaphorical in nature, and suitable to the expanded realism of the play. But the transition from A to B may be more narrative in nature and more realistic.

Read in Speech 4, Appendix B, Briseis' account of the sixth and seventh years.

In *Living in Exile*, Jon Lipsky has imagined that the Trojan women taken captive by the Greeks formed a secret network, and in this speech Briseis tells us how the women fared in the nine years before the events of the *Iliad*. At the end of the sixth year we hear that most of the boys born to them that year were named Hector, after the greatest of the Trojan warriors. The seventh year begins with the statement that the women had become lunatics: "We went with animals, ate in rituals the wounded's severed limbs." What happened between these years? How did these women go from having babies to eating human flesh like scavengers? Why? Unless you abruptly jump from one year to the next, and thereby leap over the question, you will have to shape a transition from year six into year seven that makes narrative sense.

One actor discovered this connection: it was precisely because of the newborns that the women become so ferocious. They needed to feed themselves so that they could nurse and nourish their young.

Just about every boychild born that year was named by his mother: "Hector."

The seventh year we were lunatics. Sleeping by day, roaming at night. We went with animals, ate in rituals the wounded's severed limbs.

12.1 *Play the following scenario silently. Sit on the ground and use a pillow or a bundled garment as your baby. Imagine you're holding your newborn for the first time. He is just born. Give him his name: "Hector." He will grow up to be a great warrior and defeat these despicable Greeks. You look up in the fierce joy of believing that; to*

a Greek your expression might seem lunatic. Now the need to feed this infant dawns on you: it is less a thought than a biological urge. Gently put your baby down and slowly rise. How are you going to get enough food? Look about, perplexed. Start to move about, searching. Let your urgent mission develop into a ravenous hunger. Start hunting like an animal. You spot a limb cut from a wounded soldier. Move toward it.
12.2 Now play the basics of this scenario with the text.

Briseis doesn't have to be "lunatic" right away, for the whole of the seventh year. That year is about *becoming* lunatic, and becoming means fading. Shaping the transition in this way — or some other way that fills in the gap between the years — tells more of the story. The audience can see and vicariously experience how Briseis gets from her son's birth to roaming at night with the animals. The change in her does not happen — invisibly, inexplicably — in the silence between the sixth and seventh years.

Read in Speech 3 from Appendix B what Patroklos says about the second and third years.

What happens between those two years? How do those very "surprised" soldiers become "uncompromising, ruthless and professional"?

Who could've imagined it. After one whole year — no visit from the goddess Victory?
In the third year, we were uncompromising, ruthless, and professional. With deadly disciplined precision, we set out to get the job done.
As the second year ends, let's imagine, you are standing atop a chair with your arms extended in prayer to the goddess. This is the climax of the surprise that has been fading up since the end of the first year. We will call this image of dismayed prayer moment A. Let's say that the third year has already been explored in terms of an implicit scene: you sneak up on a sentry and slit his throat. The violence can happen as late as "get the job done." That's moment B. You might of course leap from the chair directly into the violence, or perhaps descend stealthily and move slowly into it. But neither of these choices gets to the heart of the matter. How does the

second year lead to the third? How does surprise become ruthlessness? What sort of transition might help to tell the story of how the Greeks got from A to B? Let's look at two different versions.

12.3 Perhaps you hypothesize that the Greeks' surprise becomes fear, which leads to violence. This fear is a new moment, a bridge between the second and third year. It suggests that the "deadly disciplined precision" is a consequence of feeling vulnerable: people who are scared can do terrible things. Perhaps the surprise at the end of year two is already tinged with fear, which fades into full-blown terror as the third year progresses. You may be so scared that the killing of the sentry gets really nasty. Explore this scenario.

12.4 Imagine that "In the third year ..." is a bargain with the goddess: I promise you I will be uncompromising, ruthless and professional if you will give us victory. You go from surprise to prayerful resolve to the act itself. Try this different scenario.

Exploring transitions is work that you must do on your feet. Yes, you sometimes *think* of a transition, a vision or concept pops into your head, but most from/to discoveries are triggered by being in the moment, where you can listen to your body for impulses.

Playing insignificant actions so as to make them significant

At the very least, you should go from A to B in the spirit of the moment, with expressive energy. Even if the action which you perform is not in itself significant (putting down a coffee cup while you relive the moment of breaking up with someone, for example), *how* you perform the action may be significant.

Imagine that you sit down as you conclude a story about an exhausting trip. There is nothing about sitting in the text, but if you sink wearily into a chair as you talk about finally arriving, this action becomes meaningful — as if it were part of an implicit scene — and helps you to tell the story. (Other details about how you sit might be inspired by the specific circumstances.) Or suppose that, in a different story, your line is "I couldn't wait for them to come." If you sit down expectantly, perched on the edge of your chair, this action, though not in the story, contributes to fleshing it out.

If you tell a story about making a difficult decision, you can sit in a way that embodies how hard it was to make up your mind. For that matter, almost any bit of business might be done indecisively, with expressive value. An emaciated prisoner of war who is remembering what it was like to eat chocolate might sit as if in physical ecstasy — or, in the same sensuous spirit, sponge his chest with a wet cloth, smooth the blanket on his cot, etc. In such cases, your action is not in itself meaningful; it is how you do it that makes it significant.

Sticking with strong moments

Don't be in a rush to leave a strong acting moment. Your text may move on to the next event, but you should stick with the energy and the physicality of a rich, powerful moment for a while. You should always be interested in how long such a moment might continue, how long its intensity might linger. If you move quickly out of every moment, the result is a sequence of short-lived events, none seemingly important enough to spend time with. If an event grips you, it is hard to shake. You can measure how strong and deep a moment is by how long it takes you to get free of it.

Removing the pauses

Pauses are sometimes necessary, but only sometimes. For the most part, speeches should flow continuously. You should be biased in favor of keeping language and action moving forward. All pauses should be challenged to see if they are really essential. If nothing is really happening in a pause — if the audience is simply left waiting for the next line or action — it should be cut. An effective pause must be active, not inert.

Sometimes an actor uses a pause to separate two moments when s/he should really figure out how they are connected. Instead of living through a transition, the actor stops and changes gear in the blank space between sentences. This sort of pause is a silence about what happens between A and B — and a sign that the transition from A to B needs to be explored.

I was very, very angry with you. (Pause) Then I got over it.
12.5 Read the first sentence in a ferocious rage. After a pause in which nothing seems to happen, smile and do the second sentence as if you hadn't a care in the world.

There's a comic effect in such a sudden change in tone. Part of what makes it funny is that we have no idea what happened to the anger. It dissipated in the pause, invisibly, absurdly. A habit of removing pauses can force from/to questions out into the open, so that more of the story becomes audible and visible. If you were so angry, how did you get over it? *How?*

like in them movies. But no, I lost my virginity in the attic of an old house in New Rochelle. (Excerpt 5, Appendix A)

12.6 Get yourself inside Rosie's movie fantasy (see 4.20). Do this in a chair. Take a pause after "like in them movies," in which you simply sit still for a long moment, frozen in the fantasy. Then stand up and resume talking. All the dreamy quality has drained from your voice, and you are 100% back in the here and now.

Rosie's pause here is inert. Nothing happens — or it happens invisibly, which amounts to the same thing. How you say "But no ..." might convey a change in Rosie's emotional state, but that is not the real question. What happens to her fantasy? How does Rosie let go of it and return to reality? How do these two dimensions of her life interact? If your character doesn't live through the transition, the audience doesn't either.

12.7 After "like in them movies," let Rosie, still in that romantic Greenwich Village apartment, gaze starry-eyed at the person she is speaking to. She expects to see a movie star but — where is she? Explore a silent moment of confusion as she takes in where she really is: a dingy old corner store. "But no..." should sound quite present, as if Rosie were just now understanding that it happened in New Rochelle.

In this case, Rosie's pause is active: something significant is happening.

When you start putting together your speech, it is natural that there will be pauses, many of them left over from picking the story apart and feeling your way through each moment. Most of these pauses you no longer need. You should presume that a pause is unnecessary and search for a version of the transition in which A develops directly into B. What happens in the story? How does B grow out of A? Run through the from/to repeatedly, staying open to spontaneous impulses about what happens in the transition. Whether the from/to in question involves two minutes or two months, you should live through what happened between A and B — and you should do it as you speak.

After you've removed all the dead spots you can, you may find that there is some pause you really can't do without, one which is meaningful and active because something is happening — happening not just for you but for the audience. This pause will be all the more effective because it interrupts a well-established flow. If you have stopped repeatedly and unnecessarily, one more pause is a non-event. But if you have moved the story along, an active pause can seem momentous. That is what actors and directors mean by "earning your pauses."

Acting on the line
Making a transition in silence is occasionally effective. But most of the time it is better to play a transition without a pause. If you make it a habit to remove pauses, this will force you to act "on the line," as directors so often encourage actors, rather than between the lines.

Other methods of crafting transitions

Unless an abrupt, jarring effect is what is truthful, transitions should be gradual and seamless. For this reason, fading is the actor's primary tool for creating transitions. Any list of methods for moving from A to B, therefore, must begin with:

Fade from A into B.
Other methods — several of which entail fading — can help when you are exploring from/to possibilities or putting a speech together.

Let A suggest B, and go directly from A to B.
What is happening in A may instinctively suggest what happens in B. The next moment is often implicit in the action, the physicality, the energy of the present moment.

When exploring a transition, it is critical that you stay tuned to what is happening *now*, which has a great deal to tell you about what happens *next*. Stay inside the present moment — don't relax out of it and think in the abstract. Look for clues about what might happen next in your physical position, your spatial location, the direction you are heading, what is around you, what you have in hand, the action you are engaged in, etc. What is possible given your present energy?

Avoid going to neutral between moments. If you go from A to neutral to B, the transition will happen invisibly. Insofar as possible, your energy and your physical life in this moment should develop right into the next. Go directly from A into B.

In Moliere's *Tartuffe*, there is a moment when Orgon, who has taken to excessively pious behavior, becomes so enraged by the interruptions of his outspoken maid that he tries to hit her. Suppose that in the heat of the moment he grabs his cane and turns around to find that she has knelt down and folded her hands in make-believe prayer. The gist of his next line is that he needs to calm himself by going out for a walk. Suppose you put the cane down and recompose yourself before you announce your intention to walk. This breaks the connection between A (the cane over your head) and B (exiting with the cane for a walk) by going to neutral in-between. The audience misses the fun of watching you struggle to get out of the awkward situation by pretending that you had grabbed the cane in order to go out. If you fade directly from A to B and take your time doing it — slowly lowering the cane and trying to act as if you had no intention of violence — then B develops organically, and amusingly, out of A. Staying in touch with the cane is the key to playing this transition. Orgon's line about going for a walk is implicit in the cane over his head.

And with his other hand thus o'er his brow,
He fell to such perusal of my face
As he would draw it. (Excerpt 13, Appendix A)

After seeing the ghost, Hamlet is either distraught or pretending to be distraught — or both. Ophelia has put her hand to her brow (moment A) to show her father how "mad" Hamlet looked when he burst into her room (see 5.1). Then she remembers how Hamlet studied her face so intently that he seemed like an artist getting ready to draw it (moment B).

12.8 What does the hand at your brow suggest about how to play what comes next? Ophelia is acutely aware of Hamlet's eyes on her. What is he looking at? Let her hand descend from her brow as if to find out. Hamlet is staring as if to draw her: this image suggests that Ophelia's fingers might trace the lines of her face as if drawing them.

The action for moment B is implicit in moment A. Following clues in what you are playing right now can lead you to discoveries about what happens next.

240

Of breaches, ambuscadoes, Spanish blades,
Of healths five fathom deep. (Speech 16, Appendix B)
12.9 Imagine that Mercutio's soldier has pantomimed a sword thrust on "Spanish blades." The text that follows is about making a toast (as in "To your health!") in a tavern. How might you develop A directly into B?

Going from A to neutral and then into B would be senseless in this case. Going from A right into B creates gestural flow and helps to tie this speech together as one evolving fantasy.

A man in a white robe, with two white wings reaching from the sky to the ground. He didn't tell me his name that day, but later on I found out that he was the blessed St. Michael. [...] (in the deep voice of the Archangel) — **Joan, go to the help of the king of France, and give him back his kingdom.** (She replies in her own voice.) **Oh sir, you haven't looked at me; I am only a young peasant girl [...]** (Speech 2, Appendix B)
12.10 Suppose that Joan of Arc gestures about the angel's wings with both arms. This action, nicely expressive of the young Joan's awe, is A. What does A suggest to you about how to play the next moment, in which the angel speaks to her? What happens to the wings gesture? How might B then develop into C, Joan's physical response to what the angel asks of her? Explore how you might flow from A into B into C.

When you fade from each moment into the next, events seems to evolve organically, and the story, even though the point of view changes, is unified.

what hits me across the eyes is this giant eagle. Now I'm a flyer and I'm used to aeronautics, but this sucker was doing some downright suicidal antics. Real low down like he's coming in for a landing or something, then changing his mind and pulling straight up again and sailing out away from me. (Speech 9, Appendix B)
12.11 Suppose that Weston gestures up toward the eagle when he first sees it. What does this suggest about how you might play the text that follows?

241

12.12 Suppose Weston doesn't gesture, but that his whole body flinches when he spots the eagle. What does this physical reaction imply about playing the rest of this excerpt?

Then I started to wonder who the owner was. I mean if I didn't feel like the owner, then who was the owner? I started wondering if the real owner was gonna pop up out of nowhere and blast my brains out for trespassing. (Speech 8, Appendix B)

Weston is walking around his property early in the morning. You have played with impulses for popping out playfully from some space in the kitchen (see 8.5).

12.13 Popping out in this way would mean that at an earlier point Weston gets behind something or another. Does such an impulse make sense for the previous text? Why might Weston be looking to hide? Perhaps the paranoid fantasy that someone is going to blast his brains out is already creeping up on him. Explore.

Sometimes an acting choice can tell you how to play the moment that precedes it. Sometimes A is implicit in B.

12.14 Explore this whole text as a fade:
- *from the odd sense that someone else is lurking about*
- *to impulses to hide,*
- *to popping out,*
- *to making a run for it.*

Knit the Seams: Delay Or Anticipate B.

When a story shifts scene, jumps in time, tells of a new event, switches to a different point of view, changes tone — whenever something ends and something new begins — there is a "seam" in the text. If you change your action and energy just where the text does, you call attention to that seam. The audience feels the discontinuity.

Occasionally this is desirable. If a new idea comes to your character all at once, or if an event comes out of the blue, it may be truthful and effective to change your energy abruptly. In such cases, discontinuity makes sense. For obvious reasons, this effect should be used sparingly.

Most of the time, a speech in which the seams are apparent is not good from/to work. Seams interrupt the flow of a speech. Actions seem to end, instead of developing into what happens next. A story with seams feels like swatches of fabric pinned together.

An actor can knit seams together so that they virtually disappear: the speech becomes one piece of whole cloth. The tool for shaping a smooth transition, of course, is a fade, but you must be careful about where you begin: if you start your fade right on a seam, you will accentuate it.

There are two possible ways to knit a seam together so that the action is continuous: you can anticipate or delay the new energy — that is, you can begin the fade before or after the seam. Which choice will better serve a particular text is a question you must answer by experimenting.

Not that it's fancy or anything, but it's peaceful. It's real peaceful up here. Especially at that time a' the morning. Then it struck me that I actually was the owner. That somehow it was me and I was actually the one walking on my own piece of land. And that gave me a great feeling. (Speech 8, Appendix B)

Do you see the seam? A new idea occurs to Weston. This event propels him into the house, where he climbs into a scalding tub. No doubt the "great feeling" is complex, but it is certainly exciting and full of new hope.

Here is a simple diagram of the seam. The lines above the text represent the contrasting energies that precede and follow the seam.

peaceful ... at that time of the morning I Then it struck me ...

Does the idea come to Weston all at once? To test that hypothesis, change your energy abruptly, right at the seam.

12.15 Situate yourself so that you feel "real peaceful." Then, like a bolt, it strikes you that this piece of land belongs to you. Try changing your physical position along with your vocal energy.

That is possible, but it is important to realize that this choice calls attention to the seam and heightens the discontinuity between energy A and energy B.

If you suspect that the idea creeps up on Weston, fade from A to B. If you start your fade with "Then it struck me," however, the seam will still be quite present.

12.16 Start a fade from your peaceful energy to the excitement of realizing you are the owner at "Then it struck me."

In this case, the excitement grows gradually, but we hear the fade kick in at the seam. In order to knit the seam so as to make it disappear, you will have to start fading *before* the seam or hold off starting the new energy *until* after the seam.

Instead of:

you can delay:

or anticipate:

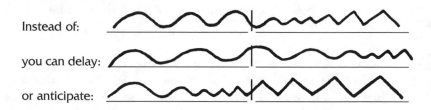

12.17 The new idea comes to you while you are deep into peaceful enjoyment of the morning, and only gradually does it change your energy. Start your fade after the textual seam. Stay "real peaceful" for the first part of "Then it struck me ..." Hold back: Weston is not fully excited until "great feeling."

12.18 Now anticipate the seam by starting to get the idea during "Especially at that time of the morning."

12.19 Try getting the first glimmer of the idea even sooner: "It's real peaceful up here."

I started feeling like I should be running or hiding or something. Like I shouldn't be here in this kind of a neighborhood. Not that it's fancy or anything, but it's peaceful. It's real peaceful up here. Especially at that time a' the morning. Then it struck me that I actually was the owner. That somehow it was me and I was actually the one walking on my own piece of land. And that gave me a great feeling.

Perhaps Weston's "great feeling" is nothing more than a profound sense of peace, peace in knowing that he is the owner. If so, then there isn't any seam — it really has disappeared!

12.20 Play the entire text as a gradual fade from paranoia to peacefulness. The idea that you are in fact the owner is what makes you peaceful.

Knitting the seams keeps you honest about how your character gets from one moment to the next. A seam jumps from A to B; knitting it forces you to fade, which means that you and the audience live through the transition.

If you anticipate a new energy before arriving at the seam, an audience senses, when you do get around to speaking about it, that what you say is true, because they have already felt it along with you.

One by-product of knitting seams by *delaying* the new energy is that the old energy hangs over into a new section of text. This is a truthful phenomenon, since it takes a while for strong energies to wane. Such a lingering effect helps to convince the audience that your character was genuinely, deeply gripped by the previous energy.

> **the breeze blowing through the curtains over the bed, like in them movies. But no. I lost my virginity in the attic of an old house in New Rochelle.** (Excerpt 5, Appendix A)

12.21 Return once more to Rosie's Hollywood fantasy. For the moment, she is in a Technicolor movie; your physicality should be romantic and glamorous. After "like in them movies," change your energy abruptly, breaking the spell.

That's possible. But you have the option of knitting the seam together by anticipating or delaying the new energy. In this case, anticipating the energy of "But no" would erase the wonderful movie moment, so try delaying the new energy.

12.22 "But no. I lost my virginity … " starts with Rosie deep in her movies fantasy. She is so lost in it that it fades away very gradually. By the end of this text, she has returned only part of the way to the here and now; part of her is still in the movies.

Staying with the energy of her fantasy as she admits what really happened makes the contrast more poignant.

> **In the second year we were surprised, caught off guard, caught unprepared. We reevaluated our provisions. Who could've imagined it. After one whole year — no visit from the goddess Victory?**
>
> **In the third year, we were uncompromising, ruthless, and professional. With deadly disciplined precision, we set out to get the job done.** (Speech 3, Appendix B)

Earlier we explored how the Greeks, surprised because victory did not come right away, became "ruthless" (see 12.3-4). Here's yet another approach, in the spirit of knitting seams.

12.23 Anticipate the third year. Imagine growing frustration and anger in year two, so that you're already in the spirit of the third year as it starts. As you play the second year, fade:

- *from knowing you'll win*
- *to not understanding what's wrong,*
- *to hating the Trojans for putting you in this fix.*

By the time you begin the third year, you are already in a ruthless mood.

12.24 You are giving a party and having a great time. Someone has just told a very funny story. The phone rings and you are laughing as you pick it up. You start getting unexpected bad news. Slowly your grin fades — slowly. For a good while, you're still grinning as you listen to the bad news.

That's not only good from/to work, it's good listening. Before we react to events, we must take in what is said or done. If what we're taking in is a surprise, we may be slow to react. When you are acting such a moment, you should fade into your response. The bigger the shock, the more time it may take to register.

Transform A into B.

Jaques' "Seven Ages of Man" is a speech with at least seven seams. Let's look at the transition from the whining schoolboy to the lover.

creeping like snail
Unwillingly to school. And then the lover,
Sighing like furnace (Speech 11, Appendix B)

12.25 The schoolboy walks dejectedly, sulking. Continue this same walk as the lover, who sighs as he walks.

In this case, one walk serves both A and B. The action remains the same, but the text changes what it means. The schoolboy's walk transforms into the lover's.

12.26 The schoolboy stops in protest on "Unwillingly" and folds his arms, which on the Elizabethan stage was a sign of melancholy, a condition to which unhappy lovers were prone. Stay in this pose for the lovesick sigh.

246

12.27 Imagine that the schoolboy leans despairingly against a wall as he spits out the word "school." The lover starts in exactly the same physicality, the same energy.

If you make the end of A identical with the beginning of B (or very nearly so), A "transforms" into B. What you are playing remains the same, but what it means changes as the text changes. There is great economy in such transitions, and the ease with which A becomes B is very satisfying.

The method is simple: shape the last moment of A so that it is the first moment of B — or very close to it.

And one man in his time plays many parts,
His acts being seven ages. At first the infant
12.28 Suppose you had the impulse to make two fists and to shake them the way infants do when they cry. You can set this image up by gesturing on the previous line so that your hands are already in position. At "seven ages" bring both hands, with palms facing up, to either side of your face as if to say "What else but seven ages, as tradition has it." The transformation of this gesture into the infant's fists will seem quite natural. Explore.

In this way you can anticipate an action you want to play and make it seem an artless, simple development of what preceded

then I filled the whole tub up again but this time with ice-cold water. Just sat there and let it creep up on me until I was in up to my neck. Then I got out and took a shave (Speech 8, Appendix B)
12.29 Imagine that you gesture about the ice-cold water rising in the tub. How might you do this so that your hand arrives at your face just as you talk about the shave?

and you've had yourself whipped with a big bundle of them, or in the morning as you lie in bed. (Excerpt 2, Appendix A)
12.30 Perhaps a gesture about the whipping becomes an image of Puntila lying abed with an arm under his head. Explore.

or in the morning as you lie in bed. Where else do you get such smells? Or a view like this? I like it best when it's hazy, it's like sometimes when you're making love, you half close your eyes, everything's blurred. (Excerpt 2, Appendix A)

12.31 As Puntila fantasizes about lying in bed in the morning, let your arms slowly rise and stretch, as if you've had a luxuriously long sleep. As you fade into the love scene, explore how your arms might become part of it.

The morning image and the metaphor of making love have become one evolving bed scene.

and with my head resting against his beating heart, we both sat in silence, he thinking of the wreck of all his hopes in the loss of a dear son (Excerpt 8, Appendix A)

12.32 Explore how Elizabeth Stanton might transform into her father.

Un-punctuate

Written and spoken language are processed in different areas of the brain. When we are speaking, we structure language differently than we do on the page, where punctuation marks are placed in accord with grammatical conventions and the tastes of authors and editors. Many of the ways in which we *vocally* punctuate and shape our thoughts cannot readily be put on paper. The difficulty of reading transcripts of recorded conversations makes this quite clear.

It is certainly true that an author's punctuation ought to be carefully considered, and much of it should be realized in performance. But speaking so as to honor every period on the page creates tiny pauses — fractions of silence — between all the sentences. Commas and colons and semi-colons can also become impediments to flow. Some of these hitches are unnecessary and unfaithful to the way we talk, and they can get in the way of making from/to connections.

I was a narc. All I knew was drugs.

12.33 Speak these two sentences without any period between them. Removing the period also removes any downward inflection on "narc."

Many contemporary Americans might vocally punctuate this text as one thought, although grammatically there are two sentences.

You asked me. I told you. What's your problem?
12.34 Shape these three sentences as one unbroken thought.
You might, of course, speak this as three separate sentences — for example, in a heavily emphatic tone. In the midst of a heated exchange, however, a character might spew these out as one unit, as if there were no periods.

I go home. I read a magazine. I cook something. Wash the dishes. Go to bed.
12.35 Imagine that a depressed character bemoans the lonely tedium of everyday life in a lethargic rhythm. Link these little sentences by holding on to the final sound of each sentence until you begin the next. The flow of sound should be continuous.

When you are speaking in one of those slow rhythms in which sounds become longer, lengthening the final sound of one sentence as a bridge into the next is often sensuously expressive and true to the way we speak. This effect is possible only if periods are removed.

They told me what kind of pain I'd have. How the spasms would come. How to deal with the pain. How to push. (Excerpt 22, Appendix A)
12.36 Create a rhythm for this text that embodies the spasms and leaps over the periods. Each "How" is a stab of pain. Extending the final consonant sounds of "have," "come," and "pain" will give you rhythmic flexibility.

When Shakespeare begins a new sentence in the middle of a line, the actor should usually move right into the new sentence without any pause.

And all our yesterdays have lighted fools
The way to dusty death. Out, out, brief candle. (Speech 17, Appendix B)
12.37 Leap into exclaiming "Out, out, brief candle." Be sure to articulate

"death" without cutting it off, but there should be no space between the end of the first sentence and the beginning of the next.

12.38 In the following examples, remove the period in front of any sentence that begins mid-line.

As is the night before some festival
To an impatient child that hath new robes
And may not wear them. O, here comes my nurse. (Excerpt 11, Appendix A)

Leaping into the new energy heightens the amusing change of mood.

He falls to such perusal of my face
As he would draw it. Long stayed he so. (Excerpt 13, Appendix A)

Note how the monosyllables help to create the long moment of Hamlet staring at Ophelia. The rhythm here is slow, but Ophelia should go right on to "Long" as if to attach this very important detail to the previous line.

How if, when I am laid into the tomb,
I wake before the time that Romeo
Come to redeem me. There's a fearful point! (Speech 15, Appendix B)

There is sense and naturalness in taking out the period before the last sentence.

Even when written punctuation accurately reflects how the playwright hears a text, decisions must be made about interpreting it. It is one thing to take on the speech patterns of a character, period, or milieu; it is another to let punctuation impose an acting choice which does not suit the performer or the moment. An actor cannot be expected to speak a line precisely as it was spoken in the theater of the author's mind. When written punctuation gets in the way of spoken truth, it should be altered or eliminated.

Whenever an actor speaks text so as to remove the mini-pauses created by the punctuation that separates sentences, clauses, and phrases on the page, s/he is "un-punctuating": that is, speaking as if the punctuation marks were not there. The objective is to create a truthful, shapely flow of spoken language.

This has nothing to do with rushing the text. When you are un-punctuating, be careful not to speed through the periods, exclamation points, and question marks. Don't start running when you see the end of the sentence coming. You should simply keep moving at whatever pace embodies the energy of the moment. Even the slowest pace can flow through printed punctuation.

When characters get excited, and when events are moving swiftly, there is no time for leisurely punctuation in the voice. Sentences tend to snowball: accelerations flow right through periods and other markings.

In Wesley's speech about his parents' fight, there might be expressive spaces between sentences before the text accelerates, but as the argument gets up a head of steam, the punctuation tends to disappear. Shepard is following the conventions of written English, which makes the passage clear to a reader, but in performance some of the punctuation should be removed.

12.39 Start about three-quarters into Speech 7, at "Foot kicking hard through door. One foot right through door." Read some of this text with periods in your voice, little stops between each sentence.

This creates a staccato rhythm that might be effective for some of the text, but hammering like this would soon get very repetitive. Stopping for periods gets in the way of creating a build. It's as if you kept hitting the brake while trying to accelerate.

12.40 Try the same section, unpunctuated, as a build.

Moving through punctuation while reading a text aloud can help you to discover precisely how sentence A flows into sentence B. Your voice knows a great deal about how to punctuate what you say, and you should listen to it in search of spoken sense.

12.41 As an exercise in un-punctuation, read aloud Excerpt 2, taking out the periods. You might eventually discover, of course, that certain periods are essential to sense and shape. But assume for now that there is a sensible way of flowing from each sentence directly into the next. Experiment with rhythms and inflections. If you don't find an effective path the first time you try to connect two sentences, go back and try again — and again. Look for a variety of ways to un-punctuate as you work your way through this text. Be careful not to rush unnecessarily.

Sometimes a little rush into the next sentence is truthful, as when a new idea pops into your head, for example, but most of the time there's no need to hurry.

**the berries for instance. After the rain. And the birch leaves, when
you come home from the sauna and you've had yourself whipped**
(Excerpt 2, Appendix A)

*12.42 Take your time as you "bask" in the imagined smell of the berries.
Hold onto the final sound of "instance" until you begin "After the
rain" in the same languid rhythm. Then the smell of the birch leaves
pops into your head: jump on that memory and develop this change
of pace into the vigorous energy of being whipped after a sauna.*

Hitching

Micro-pauses at the ends of sentences are sometimes less effective
than expressive hitches *within* sentences. Hitching within a sentence —
which gives the following word emphasis — might embody a hesitation,
a search for the right word, a calculated little pause, an avoidance of
something difficult to talk about, etc. *This must be done sparingly,* or else
you end up rewriting a text with just as many micro-pauses, all of them in
unexpected places. This creates not flow but an eccentric herky-jerkiness.

**I went to visit Mavis in Memorial Hospital. She was dying of
everything.** (Excerpt 4, Appendix A)

*12.43 Play the period between these two sentences. Use the little pause
it creates to gather yourself before you say that Mavis was dying.*
That is certainly a possible choice.

*12.44 Take out the period. Note that the final consonant of "Hospital" is a
continuant; if you wish, you can extend it a tiny bit as you flow into
the beginning of the next sentence. Explore three possibilities for
hitching inside the second sentence. Hitch before:*
 • *"everything";*
 • *"dying";*
 • *"was."*

Those are three different effects. Going through the period "buys" you
this little internal pause.

Un-punctuation can help you to keep the text flowing and to create
rhythms, accelerations, builds and from/to connections. You should
observe written punctuation in your voice whenever sense and expressive
effect require, which is a great deal of the time. But you should move

through written punctuation — un-punctuate — when that is more truthful and when it facilitates moving from one bit of text to another. Memorizing a text with the written punctuation in your voice can be an impediment to spontaneity and discovery. The shape of your text should remain flexible in rehearsal, so that you are free to explore, even if this eventually leads you back to the playwright's punctuation.

Practice in From/To

12.45 Choose two years from Living in Exile *(Speeches 3 and 4 in Appendix B). What happens as the first of these years develops into the next? Tell the story of this transition. How and why is B a consequence of what happened in A?*

· *Do at least the last half of text A and the first half of text B — as much as you need to execute your from/to.*

· *Memorize the text and explore on your feet.*

· *The transition should appear to be seamless: the physicality, the action, the mood of one year should flow sensibly and revealingly into the next.*

For Your Own Speech

1. Develop three from/to moments, each with a brief text, in which you go:
   · from one gesture or movement or space to another;
   · from one action to another;
   · or any combination of these.

2. Develop two transitions, using as much text as you need, in which you go:
   · from one scene or event to another;
   · from one time period to another;
   · from one mood or tone or textual color to another;
   · from one character to another;
   · from one feeling to another;
   · from one metaphor to another;
   · from anything to anything else;
   · or any combination of these.

253

- As you work on these transitions, keep in mind all the methods we have considered. For each of your transitions, experiment with several approaches. You will certainly shape several fades. It is probable that the physicality of A will at some point suggest B, so that you move from A directly into B.
- As an exercise in applying other methods to your speech, use each of the following approaches at least once:
  - Knit a seam by anticipating or delaying the new energy.
  - Transform A into B by shaping the end of one moment so that it is identical (or nearly so) with the beginning of the next moment.
  - Remove an unnecessary pause.

Guidelines

The main issue is shaping transitions that help to tell the story. What does each of your transitions make visible about your character's journey?

Transitions that are problematic or rich in diverse possibilities should be run repeatedly in an exploratory spirit. Stay open to impulses from the story, from what has just happened, from your own body, from the space in which you are working, etc.

Stick with the energy and the physicality of strong moments. Let them linger even as the text moves on to talk of the next event.

Can you make any insignificant bit of blocking more significant by playing it expressively in the spirit of the moment?

3. Work on 6-8 lines of your speech as an exercise in un-punctuation.
- Explore how you might move directly from each sentence into the next.
- *Don't rush* — especially as you move through periods (or question marks or exclamation points).
- If you do hitch for breath, do so inside a sentence, expressively. Don't overdo this; the point is flow.
- Which periods do you really need for sense and for shape?

Guidelines

When you read through the section of text which you have un-punctuated, the transitions should sound necessary and perfectly natural.

Find the flow, the spine or arrow which runs through this section: that is, find its from/to shape sense.

Chapter 13
Putting Together the First Draft

Focusing on process

Sometimes a writer sits down and a poem, a scene, a story, a play pours out. The rest of the creative process consists in editing and minor revisions. At other times, it may take hundreds of pages of exploration to get to the point where the real writing can begin. Some authors engage in a period of research and gestation before they write: making notes, jotting down phrases and fragments that come into their heads, sketching details and passages in a journal, outlining shapes and listing possibilities.

Rehearsals, both private and collective, are similarly various. Sometimes a speech comes all at once and needs little reworking — every artist is grateful to be inspired. Sometimes it comes in bits and pieces, fits and starts. Many a good rehearsal process, after weeks of exploration, has created a wealth of choices which have not as yet been pulled together. An actor may have worked on alternative versions of moments, speeches, whole scenes. There is considerable value in staying open like this: decisions are made late on, when you really understand the material. Why make up your mind at the outset, when you know so little?

You have explored your speech from many different perspectives. Like a writer who's ready, an actor gets to a point when it's time to put together a first draft.

After you have that first draft on its feet, you will continue to work on your speech, developing opposites and layers (in Chapters 15-17), and revising along the way. Some moments from your first draft may stick; others will grow, evolving over time; some parts of your speech may undergo radical revision. The *process* of developing a speech should remain more important than the product, even after a show has opened. A given performance is you, at this moment in your artistic life, working on this material, at this stage of its development. Not to mention that you are acting on a particular day, for a specific audience, responding to all the nuances of a one-time-only performance.

Goals for putting your speech together

The first draft of your speech should have:

- *Story sense:* Moments in which you set the scene, characterize, and indirect quote should have sensuous specificity. Gesture, movement, and space should make events visible and very present.
- *Sound sense:* Onomatopoetic colors should let an audience hear what happens, and varied rhythms should truthfully embody the energies of different events.
- *Shape sense:* How you transition from one moment to the next should be an important part of how you tell the story.

Why is your character telling the story?

As you put your speech together, remind yourself why your character is telling the story — and reexamine the question in search of a deeper understanding of the story's relevance. You should assume that there is some *need* to tell the story. It is not just interesting or amusing or a way to pass the time. The stakes should be high: telling the story, and getting it right, must matter. It is likely that some event or situation in the here and now has triggered the story and made it not only relevant but essential.

One sort of Shakespearean soliloquy starts with a question, confusion, moral dilemma, or predicament: the character does not know what to do or think or feel or believe. The soliloquy is an attempt to think through the problem and arrive at some resolution: the character articulates his misgivings, speculates, weighs alternatives, and perhaps makes up his or her mind. This model is a good framework for many narrative speeches.

In some cases, a character has a clear motive in telling a story: it is meant to persuade, comfort, shame, explain, etc. An objective of this sort suggests the light in which events should be cast and which details need emphasis.

But the purpose of telling the story may have as much to do with your character's own needs as with any other-directed motive. A great many stories are told in an effort to understand some issue or experience. When this is the case, there is an exploratory quality to the story, a questioning of details as they are recalled. A character may not even grasp that the story relates to his or her present circumstances. Perhaps the connection will be discovered in the course of the speech. If so, this insight or realization — what literary critics call an *epiphany* — is a real event and should be played as a moment of important discovery. This approach to a story makes it urgent. It helps you to play the speech from moment to moment in a spirit that feels quite present, because your character is searching. It is as if the story were a mystery that your character is trying to solve. The point of the story is not something your character already knows. Sometimes a speech ends on an unresolved note: the mystery is unsolved, an important question is left hanging.

Some stories seem to rise unbidden, as if they have a will of their own. Even if your character does not know why s/he is remembering these events, you should ponder how the story embodies the themes of the play and explore how to make its relevance visible.

For what context are you preparing?

You may be preparing material for performance in a rehearsal, a production, a class, an audition — or for no audience at all, if you are working on your own. Some of these contexts may have specific needs or requirements that will influence choices about how you put together your first draft. But the issues and suggestions that follow will be useful in most contexts.

Space and your speech

At the end of your process, you may wish to develop a version of your speech in which you perform with nothing more than a chair or two, so that you can use it for auditions. But for now you are free to experiment with production values — a simple set, a few props, perhaps a costume element (or substitutes such as might be used in rehearsal) — if you think that they will help you to get inside the story.

Given the room you are working in, where might your speech be staged most effectively? Can some corner of the space serve you, or a window, a doorway, a pillar, any of the available furniture? How you insert your body into space — how you play it — is as important as space itself.

Where should you place your audience? What should its spatial relationship be to specific events and moments?

The first picture

You should begin your speech with an engaging, evocative picture. Your physicality — how you shape your body, where you are in space, perhaps a gesture or movement — should pull an audience into your speech even before you speak. It should do the same for you. How you begin should place you inside your first moment.

Your first picture, whether still or in motion, should have tension, specific energy, visual interest — and narrative significance. It should begin to tell the story. Starting from neutral, from outside the story, is not nearly so interesting as hitting the ground running. Aim to start inside the story, or at least in touch with it.

If your opening sentences are introductory in nature, scan ahead to the first real action, event, or image in your text. Put yourself into the physicality of that moment — as if the real beginning of the story were already in your body and prompting you to speak. If you do this, your text will "catch up" to your first picture, which meanwhile intrigues us.

Here are some examples of how this sort of physical anticipation of the text might work:

First picture: You are sliding down a wall with an arm over your eyes.
Text: I had a nasty dream last night. Couldn't wake myself up. All
    night I was sinking ...

First picture: You are doubled over in pain.
Text: I got really scared yesterday. You never called. By midnight I was
    having cramps ...

First picture: You are tracing a vein in your forearm with one finger.
Text: I understand how you feel. How fragile life is. How vulnerable. I
    used to be a surgeon. Vascular. I specialized in collapsing veins.

First picture: Your back is arched and your head is turned slightly to
    one side as if to look over your shoulder. One hand holds a
    strand of hair. Your voice is hushed, tense.
Text: I was almost ready to leave, just needed to brush my hair. I was
    wondering if it was going to rain, and whether I should get a
    trim, when I felt the gun in my back.

First picture: You are leaning as if exhausted, but your body is tense, "dry with rage."

Text: My liege, I did deny no prisoners. / But I remember when the fight was done, / When I was dry with rage and extreme toil, / Breathless and faint, leaning upon my sword...

In this case, jumping ahead to begin inside the story suggests that — in the here and now — the King's accusation wearies and enrages you.

Freeze framing: the last moment

A movie audience is often given a final image to stare at while the credits roll and the final moments sink in. One technique for doing this is to stop the action so as to focus on a single frame. Your speech should end in a carefully crafted picture that crystallizes how your story finishes. Where do you want to leave your audience? In what moment? With what energy? It is while the audience stares at your freeze frame that the story will settle.

What final image is apt for your story? It may be the last action, but you might also return to an earlier moment or create a new snapshot. This moment should be resonant, re-echoing what has happened.

You should hold your freeze frame for a slow count of three. An audience needs this time to catch up after the text ends. When you relax out of this last image, don't comment on your performance with words or body language.

Taking in

Acting is reacting. It is less about what you do than about what is done to you — and about the responses triggered by statements, actions, events, circumstances, concepts, memories, revelations. None of these can affect you unless they are taken in. You can't react to something if it doesn't act on you. That is one reason why actor training places such importance on listening and responding. Nothing can really get to you unless you listen — with all your faculties.

- We take in by way of the senses: seeing, hearing, tasting, smelling, touching, and kinesthetic perception are all modes of taking in.
- Whenever we become aware of, notice, perceive, or discover something, we are taking in.
- Understanding is taking in: when we learn, realize, comprehend, or absorb ideas or information.

· Watching and listening are active modes of taking in.

In all its forms, taking in is a receptive state. The eyes, however subtly, tend to widen, perhaps the nostrils flare, the mouth opens a bit, and when we are shocked, the jaw drops so as to leave us agape. All channels are open. The body language is that of a person caught with his or her defenses down. When you are taking in, you and your character are quite vulnerable.

A take-in moment is followed by a more or less gradual fade as a feeling — or an urge to action — wells up. Taking in backs you off in the opposite direction and positions you to live through the emergence of your response. When what you take in is a shock, your character may be so stunned that the take-in moment lasts quite a while.

Taking in is what allows honest emotions to arise in performance. If you attempt to make emotions happen, they tend to flee you. An emotion is not something you do. When you become emotional, you are not active but acted upon. Emotions are physical reactions to things said and done to your character; they are involuntary responses to what you take in. If you fail to take in, you cut yourself off from being moved — and trap yourself into faking feelings or using extraneous devices to stimulate them.

When you are working solo, it is especially important to position yourself so that you take in all the things that *happen* to you. As you create for yourself and for your audience the events of the story, you must make sure that your character takes them in so that s/he can respond and react.

Moments of *taking in* fuel your performance. If you are only putting out and never taking in, you will sooner or later run out of gas.

You should incorporate into your performance moments in which you and your character are taking in.

Knowing and not knowing what's going to happen

When your character begins a story, s/he should travel back to that point in time when s/he did not know what was going to happen. When a story is relived all over again, your character must take in each development as it occurs.

On the other hand, of course, your character knows all too well what is going to happen. S/he may even attempt to evade what is coming or to fabricate events.

There is a powerful tension in narrative speeches between knowing and not knowing what is about to occur. That tension should be palpable for actor and audience. As you put your speech together, make sure your character returns to a time when s/he does not know the outcome — and explore the tension between knowing and not knowing how the story will end.

Eye contact with other characters

If your character is already inside the story as it begins, you may not be looking at the person(s) you are talking to. In such a case, you should find a moment fairly early in the speech when you make eye contact. This establishes the existence and location of whomever you are addressing.

More often a character starts speaking in the here and now and is in eye contact at the outset. Eye contact gets broken as the story takes hold of you. You may for a short time stare at nothing in particular as your character remembers, then begin to "see" events as you journey into the other time and place. You may, of course, relive eye contact with characters inside the story.

You may occasionally reestablish contact with the person(s) to whom you are speaking. This can be useful in making transitions from one part of your story to another. You might fade out of a scene, talk for a moment to your audience, then fade back into the story.

But eye contact with someone in the here and now does not mean that you have to leave the other time and place. There are powerful occasions when someone deep inside a story looks at us and we see that they are not really with us: they are elsewhere, even as they speak to us. This makes us feel we are right there in the story.

Just as in scene work, eye contact at a carefully chosen point can be very telling, both inside and outside the story. Not looking can be just as significant. You can make things quite uncomfortable for your character by being skittishly evasive of eyes. You should consider when to make eye contact with other characters and when not to, and rehearse this as part of your acting score.

When you perform solo, it is now customary to place the character(s) to whom you are speaking out in the audience — whether it is a real audience or a group of fellow actors in a class or workshop. This is generally more effective than talking to an empty chair or to an invisible person off to one side, and it directs your energy out. You might speak directly to audience members, or imagine someone in an empty seat, or place another character at a fixed point just above people's heads.

At some point in your rehearsal process, you should play your speech to one or more live bodies. You are certain to discover acting values by exploring eye contact. For one thing, eye contact engages your natural instincts about how to talk to people.

Many auditioners don't want actors to play directly to them, so playing to an imagined character in the audience is the safest choice in auditions. If others are in the audition room, it seems to me that they are fair game.

Who is the audience?

Before theatrical realism erected a fourth wall between characters and audiences, those who had come to watch and listen were very present in performances. Audiences were directly addressed in asides, ad libs, soliloquies, prologues, and epilogues, and in any number of other ways.

Sometimes they were cast as a character. The audience became part of the chorus of elders whom Clytemnestra defies or of the English army whom Henry V rallies before a battle. In a contemporary solo performance, they might be addressed as the military officers sitting in judgment at a court martial or as fellow participants in a group therapy session.

Whether you are directly addressing the audience or pretending that it does not exist, you can secretly cast it as whoever you think will help you act your speech. For a guilty story about the death of a fellow soldier, for example, you might imagine them to be his angry platoon buddies or his grieving family. Do you expect the audience will understand why your character behaves as she does in the story? Do you imagine they share your character's values or are they hostile? What tone should you take with them? Are you hiding anything from them? How does the way in which they respond to some admission or revelation affect you? How might you interact with them? All such questions invite you to be specific about the identity of your audience.

> When you are performing a speech out of context, it is sometimes helpful to imagine circumstances quite different from those of the play — including whom you are speaking to. A story originally told to one person might be told to several, even to the whole audience. In such cases you should consider how to cast them. It matters a great deal who they are.

Eye contact with an audience

True monologs are usually addressed to the audience. Shakespearean soliloquies were originally played to the audience, and this is again in fashion. In both cases the audience is your scene partner, and you can take in its responses, both real and imagined. You can also play moments to particular audience members.

When you are speaking to the audience, your eye contact with it should be genuine. An audience can sense when you are merely looking in its direction. Real eye contact connects you to your audience, so that it directly receives your energies. It also allows you to take in an audience's responses.

If you address the audience, carefully considered eye contact should be part of your acting score. If you rehearse this ahead of time, the arrival of a real audience will be less of a shock. When it does finally appear, you will find that solid eye contact is actually calming, since it eases the tension generated by shying away from an audience's eyes.

> #### Living in two worlds
>
> Characters who are about to tell a story are often restless or distracted, as if their minds were somewhere else. They are already en route to the other time and place. But in most cases they do not leap into reliving events to the full.
>
> A character's first steps inside a story are often somewhat tentative. Initial actions may be incomplete or sketchy, as if the story were a photograph just beginning to develop. "It happened *like this*" is the spirit in which many stories start. Ophelia's "And with his other hand *thus* o'er his brow" (Excerpt 13, Appendix A) is a gesture that happens partly in the scene with her father, partly in the story that she is telling him. She has a foot in two worlds: here and now she demonstrates what happened, even as she reexperiences what Hamlet did a short while ago in her bedchamber.

Each moment in your speech fades another few percentage points inside the story. How far along are you at any given point? How faintly or fully should each action be played? You must carefully calibrate the scale of your choices as events become more and more present. Near the climax or turning point, it is as if everything were happening *now, here* — which is to say that you are almost a hundred percent in the other time and place. To get there, you must walk yourself step by step inside the story — and in that way take your audience with you.

And yet a character who travels inside a story continues to inhabit the circumstances in which it is told. The power of a narrative speech, like the power of all theater, resides in the audience's perception that you are living in two worlds. Your behavior as you relive what happened in the other time and place should seem natural and believable in the here and now of telling the story. You need not compromise your storytelling impulses, but you must keep them credible. The audience must understand how and why actions in the story are repeated in the here and now. A Greek messenger, for example, might collapse to the floor as some character in the story does; in the here and now, it may be that the messenger is overcome by grief and collapses for that reason. The collapse takes place in both worlds. At the climax of a story, a character is often so deep inside it that the question of the here and now may not arise — because the audience is also, for the moment, completely absorbed in the events of the other time and place.

For Your Own Speech

Put together a first draft of your speech.

- Decide on how to stage it in terms of space.
- Develop a first picture and a final freeze frame. Hold the last moment for a count of three.
- Your first draft should have at least one important take-in moment; it may well have several.
- Make specific choices about the audience for your story. To whom are you talking? Where do you want to place him or her or them?
- Make at least two choices about eye contact which help you to tell your story. The quality of each eye contact should be quite specific.

Guidelines

How is your character in touch with the story as your speech begins? What has triggered the story? Why does the character need to tell it?

How fully are your first moments in the story played? Does your character start tentatively? Does he or she struggle to remember or to envision? Are any of your initial actions an effort to demonstrate what happened (or will happen)?

In order to map your fade from the here and now into the other time and place, estimate in terms of split percentages (80/20, 60/40, 50/50, 10/90, etc.) how far your character has traveled into the story (and perhaps out of it) at various stages of your speech.

How you relive the story should be believable in your character's present circumstances.

Preparations for rehearsing your first draft

1. Warming up

Exercises that you might use to relax, energize, and warm-up include:
- Shake out hands and arms, ankles and legs.
- Jump up and down while flopping as if you were a rag doll.
- Bend over from the waist with knees flexed and with arms and head hanging freely, in which position you might sway, shake, hum from the top to the bottom of your voice, and do a bit of text.
- Relax your characteristic tensions with relaxation exercises for the neck, shoulders, jaw muscles, etc.
- Do some deep breaths on your back, then on your feet, so that your abdomen expands and contracts, but your shoulders do not rise.
- Use vocal and articulation exercises to play with your text.

2. Dropping in on moments

You need to get yourself ready to *play*, to be impulsive, to be instinctive, not to "do it right." A performance should not be set in stone. For all that you are crafting a very specific vocal and physical score for your speech, the only "right" version is one that is true to the moment: that is organically, spontaneously in touch with the variations and nuances of a particular performance. A speech that is live has to be (more or less) different each time.

To get yourself ready to perform with spontaneity, it is helpful to run bits and pieces of your speech, on impulse, in any order, and with full commitment. This exercise is called *dropping in*. Move about the room as you improvise moments and sections of your speech. Interact with your environment. Let yourself have impulses toward the walls, windows, doorways, furniture, etc., even if this leads you to play moments differently from the way you planned to do them in your first draft. Focus on grounding yourself solidly in each physical and vocal impulse. You might, for example, do the following moments, one after the other, in any order that comes to you:

- a gesture from your score without text;
- a movement with text;
- your last moment with text (hold the freeze frame: one Mississippi, two Mississippi, three Mississippi);
- the first 2/3 of a build (don't finish it, so that you leave yourself hungry to do it when you act the whole speech);
- a moment you especially like — one which is true, shapely, funny, striking, important to you;
- a tricky or revealing from/to moment;
- a take-in moment;
- an eye contact moment with one or more persons in your audience (really look and see them);
- your first picture and opening lines (get yourself really grounded in the moment which begins your speech).

3. Get ready to debrief

Have paper and pen available to you, so that you can make notes immediately after you run the speech. What should you hold onto? What moments, issues, and directions should you work on, and how? Later chapters will introduce new approaches aimed at further development of your speech, but the overall process of refining, rethinking, and reworking is up to you.

4. Dedicating your work

Your goal is to relive the story. *Why* you do this is critical to how you perform. What's important to you in these events and in your interpretation of them? Dedicate your work to that. On some occasions you may want to dedicate a performance to a person or event that you associate with the material.

Chapter 14
Architecture

Before you work on any of these new shaping issues, you must have gotten to the stage at which you can perform the speech on your feet, with story and sound and shape sense.

Pace

After careful exploration of each and every moment over weeks of rehearsal, your work may be too evenly paced, because you are taking the same amount of time with small details as you are with important events. All or part of your speech may be too slow and deliberate.

In order to deal with this issue, experiment with *up-pacing* your speech all the way through. Which parts seem truthfully and naturally to move along at a brisker pace? Why? Which parts must go slower — and why? What is the sense in each of the rhythms?

Each new scene, each event, each character in your story might initiate a new rhythm, a different pace. Note accelerations and retards as you build to climaxes and then fade down from them. Note how you need to fade from one pace to another as your story shifts into different gears.

Do not rush anything with which you need to take time. But it is moving things along that makes it possible to take time here and there.

Speed-throughs

Directors sometimes ask an ensemble to speed-through a scene or act, even a whole play. These are sometimes called "Italian run-throughs." What is surprising about this exercise, which usually starts at what seems to be an absurdly fast pace, is that it inevitably discovers sections that in fact should go that fast. It also has the value of quickening the overall tempo of the acting after weeks of painstaking work on moments and details.

Subordination

In working on the first draft of your speech, you have given most everything careful attention. As a result it may seem that every moment is equally important. Of course, this is not so. Some events and actions are

269

central, others less so. Even though you may have worked hard and long to craft a small detail, in performance the powerful move may be to toss it off lightly.

What parts of your speech should get special emphasis? What details, while played just as specifically, should be subordinated to the bigger events? Presumably everything counts, but not equally.

One way to subordinate less important details is to treat them as if they were inside a parenthesis. An aural parenthesis typically involves a downward change of pitch (such as you might use right now to read this parenthesis aloud) and often a quickening of pace (because you want to move along briskly and get back to the main point). This format — pitch change and up-pacing — will often serve to differentiate a subordinate clause or a less important detail from the main idea. You can mark a bit of text that you want to subordinate with your own parenthesis.

Framing

The most essential, expressive moments in a speech — those which are especially important to the story and its meaning — need extra emphasis.

To *frame* a moment is, in the first place, to take time with it. When you do that, the audience senses that the moment is especially significant — and is given time to experience what it signifies. It is as if theatrical time has been slowed; an action may go into something like slow motion. You can even freeze-frame a moment on stage — as the curtain falls, as the lights fade, or simply until movement is resumed.

Framing is not only a question of time, however. All of theater's resources may be used toward this end of giving heightened emphasis to key moments.

You can, for example, frame a gesture, movement, or action by making it larger.

Space may quite literally be used as a frame: locating a moment in a doorway or a window, in the space under a table, even between two characters, may serve to put a frame around it. Using a surface such as a table top or the seat of a chair as a little stage can focus an audience on any action that you place on it. Using space in a novel, unexpected fashion can also lend emphasis to a moment.

Text may be shaped so that a particular line or word is framed. Actors

and directors sometimes speak of putting a "box" around a crucial bit of text. You may do this in one or more of the following ways:
- slowing the rhythm;
- substantially raising or lowering the pitch of your voice;
- stressing what you say heavily;
- giving the word(s) expressive vocal texture or color;
- increasing the sharpness of your articulation;
- taking a little pause before the language you wish to frame;
- making the text louder or quieter;
- choreographing a nonverbal event so that it emphasizes the text: a gesture, movement, or facial expression, an arresting action or a striking bit of staging.

A phrase or sentence may also be framed by placing it at the top of a build or at the bottom of a decrescendo, so that it is the culmination of a textual shape.

The Central Moment

Most speeches develop toward a central moment, which may be an action, an event, a decision, a realization, or an admission. Whether or not the central moment is a climax, it is the crucial moment, the turning point. Once you become aware of this moment, you are in a position to orchestrate the rest of your speech so that it leads up to and away from this central moment.

You will no doubt take more time with this moment than with others.

Architecture

A speech should have an *architecture* that orchestrates its builds and cutbacks and decrescendos into a coherent whole. You should eventually sense how each component shape contributes to the overall structure of the speech.

The builds and pullbacks that are the building blocks of a speech's architecture should be various. Builds come in all sizes and shapes and degrees of intensity. Not every climax is a Himalayan peak; some are smaller mountains, some are hills. Nor should every cutback or decrescendo pull you down to the depths.

The architecture of a speech, therefore, should *not* be shaped so that the highs and lows are all at the same level. The various rises and falls might look like this — or some such shape:

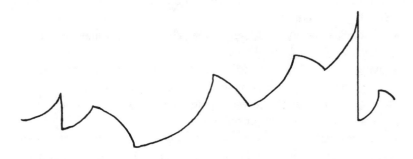

A speech should be shaped so that everything leads toward its central moment. It is in fact the whole speech that builds — if not to a climactic event, then to an epiphany, a decision, some sort of turning point, perhaps the resolution of the character's inner conflict, or the knowledge that there is no resolution. If your speech does have a central climax, its builds should collectively build up to it — and perhaps away from it on the other side.

How can your voice, your use of body and of space, your changes of energy shape the various stages of your character's journey to the story's central moment? That is the task of discovering the architecture of your speech.

In the margin of your text, you can mark for each section its particular shape. When you have finished your shaping work, you should be able to "draw" the structure of the entire text: its architecture.

Playing the Architecture of Your Speech

Most actors realize that the old debate about whether to work from the inside out or from the outside in was misguided. It is a two-way street. Playing a character's body and behavior can take you inside; playing a character's motivations and values and personal history can create his or her physical life.

Just as playing a character's outside can take you inside, performing the overall shape of your story is a way to get inside it. Architecture is the body of your speech's soul, the form of your content. In performance, you should set out to play the shape of your material. It will carry you through each performance, as the shape of a carefully rehearsed song carries a singer, as choreography carries a dancer. It is quite often the shape of a speech or a scene that stirs both actor and audience.

The architecture of your speech must be rebuilt in every performance. No matter how closely you follow your blueprint, of course, the structure will always turn out a bit differently. That is the excitement of a lively performance. A carefully crafted speech must also be spontaneous: as if the shapes were happening for the first time, as if you were improvising what you have so diligently rehearsed.

Smudging the lines

Just as an artist sketching in charcoal will use a finger to smudge a line, so you can soften the edges of your architecture by making sure that every event has its own specific energy. Shapes should never be generic or monochromatic. The architecture of your speech must house all the contrasting colors and textures you have discovered in your story. The illusion that your story's events are happening for the first time will be heightened by two sorts of roughness that you can bring to your architecture: unexpected, idiosyncratic choices and the small spontaneous impulses that are inevitable if you live each shape from moment to moment.

For Your Own Speech

1. Do two brisk run-throughs, in search of moments and sections that are more truthful and natural at a brisker pace. Your speech should be varied in tempo. Precisely how does each slower and brisker pace help you to tell the story?

2. Using a 1-10 scale, rank in the margin of your text the details and moments in your story which are more important (10 is highest) and those which are less so. Draw a simple shape for your speech that places the highest numbered moments highest and the lowest numbered lowest. What does this reveal to you about the shape of your speech?

3. Where is the central moment in your speech? This may be the biggest climax or a quieter, more introspective moment. It may be an

273

action or event, a moment of realization, a decision, a turning point, the resolution of the character's inner conflict, etc. How should you shape the speech so that it culminates at that point? How do the component parts of the speech move toward this moment?

4. Shape at least two builds of markedly different sizes. The decrescendos that follow them should also be different from each other. Are there any sudden cutbacks in your speech?

5. Shape a moment in which one thought is vocally subordinated to another.

6. Frame a phrase or a line in your text by taking more time with it. You may also use any other theatrical means to heighten the moment.

7. Once you have made shaping decisions on your feet, annotate a copy of your speech so as to indicate your shaping decisions. You may use the markings I have suggested and/or graphics of your own, both in the margins and in the text itself. Marks that make sense to you are useful tools, so you should give them some thought.

8. Draw the architecture of your performance score. A simple two-dimensional graph will do, but your visual imagination may suggest another form. Major highs and lows should be labeled with a word or phrase from the text so that it is clear where you are at that point. Indicate the central moment, subordinated texts, and what you wish to frame.

9. With the drawing of your speech in front of you, do a sit-down reading of your speech at performance level, taking the same amount of time with each moment as you would if you were on your feet. Are you in fact playing the shapes that you have put on paper? If there are discrepancies, is it your drawing or your performance that should be adjusted? Checking yourself in this way can clarify the architecture.

10. Get on your feet and perform your speech with a focus on playing its architecture. Make the shapes spontaneous by living through each moment. Give yourself over to the shapes. Let them lead you. They should happen to you more than you make them happen.

Section Four

Opposites and Layering

Chapter 15
Opposites

A Vocabulary for Inner Conflict

Life, in case you haven't noticed, is complicated, full of conflict and confusion. Pushed and pulled by ambivalent feelings, we journey indecisively through a succession of crossroads that keep us guessing whether we've taken the right path. Along the way our constant companions are the contradictions within us: warring impulses, irreconcilable needs, incompatible goals. Even our strongest values and beliefs may be inconsistent. To escape all that for even a moment — to be completely at one with what we are doing or feeling — is not only a blessed relief, it is bliss. Wholeness is the goal of many a spiritual quest, and to achieve it is to experience ecstasy. The root meaning of "ecstasy" is to "stand outside" oneself. Why is ecstasy so intensely joyful? Because we are momentarily released from the state of inner conflict which is the human condition. One reason actors act is that performance — when all is going well — is just such a heightened state of being perfectly in tune with the moment.

Theater can respond to life's complications by simplifying so as to clarify. Fables, farces, and commedia dell'arte, for example, can charm us with characters who are full-blooded incarnations of a particular passion or vice. Lechers, gluttons, misers, and braggarts pursue the one thing they want single-mindedly. But the great characters of western drama, whether comic or tragic, are full of conflict. While conflict *between* characters may drive the plot, it is conflict *within* characters that makes them compelling. Characters who are not inwardly conflicted are one-dimensional, lacking in depth. It is as if they were cardboard cutouts: looking behind them discovers nothing. There is no tension between appearance and reality, between surface and what lies beneath. Minor characters such as servants and messengers may be sketched in this simplified way, but dimensional characters must be fleshed out so that the audience perceives how opposing forces define their lives. Acting work that aspires to any complexity must discover the conflicts within a character and heighten them.

Fine actors know this, of course. They acquire a habit of mind that looks for the conflict within and shape performances that have the inner

277

struggle requisite for powerful roles. An ability to create divided selves is an essential qualification for moving center stage. It also sustains a theater capable of holding a mirror up to the complexities that plague us. Though drama may not be able to resolve our most basic conflicts, it can tell us yet another story about our painful, comical, incurable condition. Among the mysteries which theater investigates are the issues we will never solve, the knots we will never unravel.

As a systematic approach to developing inner conflict, I propose that you explore *opposites* — radically different versions of the speech you have already developed — and then *layer* together two (or more) opposites so as to create a conflicted speech.

I stumbled on this approach while teaching a follow-up class for graduates of a workshop on acting narrative speeches. The consistently powerful, illuminating, surprising results led to my including it in all acting classes as an indispensable consideration. Opposites are the key to exploring and structuring conflict *within* characters: the divided self is divided by opposites.

Actors need language to talk to themselves and their directors about this work, and they need guidelines and tools for exploring and shaping conflict. There is not much in print. Uta Hagen's *Respect for Acting* discusses how conscious and unconscious objectives may be at odds. There are two pages in Michael Shurtleff's *Audition* that present opposites as one of his "guideposts," and he writes forcefully about their importance:

> Through the years of teaching I have found that this concept of opposites is the most remarkable for actors. Once it permeates their thinking, they regard it as such an essential that they wonder how they existed before without it. In truth, they probably did not exist without it, but their consciousness level was very low and their ability to summon it when needed was minimal. But opposites exist so strongly in every human being that one would have difficulty avoiding it. [...] There are opposites in every scene. The actor may have to dig for them, for the playwright may well have implied them under the surface of the character and not have written them into the dialogue at all; but they are always there for the digging. They are well worth digging for; the result is the most interesting kind of acting: the complex.[1]

---

[1] Michael Shurtleff, *Audition*, Bantam Books, 1979.

The concept of opposites has so little currency that a theater critic for *The New York Times* could write in a review of a George C. Scott performance that "I have an acting theory to propose this morning," which "for want of a better term" he calls "the theory of contradictory impulses." He goes on to describe the power of playing opposites as if he'd never heard of the concept before.

Each emotion, you see, contains its opposite. In consuming love, there are the seeds of implacable hate. Courage is cowardice overcome. And since gregariousness is often one of timidity's covers, the loudest banter can serve to define the shyest person. [...] [Mr. Scott is] always giving you both sides of an emotion at the same time — the upward tug *and* the downward pull; the dark colors and the bright shadows. [...] Just when he most desperately wants to be held and comforted, what do we see in those limpid blue eyes of his? Fear that he won't be held, panic that his needs won't be met. That's why his acting invariably appears so rich, so full: he moves effortlessly back and forth between seemingly contradictory impulses. [...] Where a single spare emotion would look false and overstated, he comes up with a double exposure — desperation wedded to glee; arrogance tempered by insecurity; fear and fearlessness hand in hand. It makes all the difference. Our eyes keep going back to him.[2]

The tone of genuine discovery here is an index of how little the issue has been discussed. It is as if the reviewer needed to coin terms in order to describe the many colors of a richly layered performance. Unfortunately, he's right: we do lack concepts and methods for working on this fundamental issue. We need a vocabulary.

Opposites As a Starting Point

Some speeches are so focused on the clash of energies within a character that an actor must begin work on them from an opposites point of view. Consider, for example, Friar Laurence, the man who takes it upon himself in the conflict-ridden world of *Romeo and Juliet* to marry a Montague and a Capulet. When he first appears onstage, it is very early morning and the friar, basket in hand, is out picking herbs for the potions he mixes in his laboratory. In order to introduce us to this character and

---

[2]David Richards, "Opposites Attract When One Actor Shows Two Sides," *The New York Times*, February 28, 1993.

how his mind works, Shakespeare uses in a very pronounced fashion the rhetorical device called antithesis, in which opposing words are balanced against each other. The words and phrases which I have italicized in Friar Laurence's soliloquy are antitheses — or double antitheses, as in the first line, where "night" balances "morn" and "smiles" contrasts with "frowning."

> The grey-eyed *morn smiles* on the *frowning night,*
> Check'ring the Eastern *clouds* with streaks of *light;*
> And <u>fleckled</u> darkness like a drunkard reels   *dappled*
> From forth day's path and <u>Titan's fiery wheels.</u>   *sun-god's chariot wheels*
> Now, ere the sun advance his burning eye
> The *day* to cheer and *night's dank dew* to *dry,*
> I must up-fill this <u>osier cage</u> of ours   *wicker basket*
> With <u>*baleful*</u> *weeds* and *precious-juicèd flowers.*   *deadly, evil*
> The earth that's nature's *mother* is her *tomb,*
> What is her burying *grave,* that is her *womb* (II.iii)

The Friar goes on in this antithetical fashion, showing us a particular blossom in which

> *Poison* hath residence, and *medicine* power;
> For this, being *smelt,* with that part *cheers* each part,
> Being *tasted, slays* all senses with the heart.

And by way of analogy:

> Two such opposèd kings encamp *them* still   *themselves*
> In *man* as well as *herbs* — *grace* and *rude will.*

What are we to make of this rather obsessive weighing of pluses and minuses, positives and negatives? Is Friar Laurence a marvelously balanced man who adheres to the middle way? That is a less dynamic conception of his nature than Laurence's telling image of darkness reeling like a drunkard out of the way of oncoming day. The Friar careens from one reckless improvisation to another — marrying the young lovers, giving the potion to Juliet, consoling her grieving parents, rushing to the tomb, and then running away in fear. This is a man who cannot locate any center ground, who lives in a world where accommodation and compromise do not exist. The audience is alerted by his very first speech that Friar Laurence is a man who lives on the one hand and on the other hand about almost everything. So opposites would be the place to start work on this speech and on this character.

Opposites are also the starting point for a Juliet speech that is full of another rhetorical device involving opposites. An oxymoron combines what would seem to be contradictory words in a single phrase ("sweet sorrow," "making haste slowly"). When Juliet learns that Romeo has killed Tybalt, she experiences the confusion of being madly in love with her new husband and at the same time deeply outraged at his murder of her cousin:

O serpent heart, hid with a flow'ring face!
Did ever dragon <u>keep</u> so fair a cave?   *live in*
Beautiful tyrant! Fiend angelical!
Dove-feather'd raven! wolvish-ravening lamb!
Despisèd <u>substance</u> of divinest <u>show</u>!   *reality; appearance*
Just opposite to what thou justly seem'st –
A damnèd saint, an honourable villain!
O nature, what hadst thou to do in hell
When thou didst <u>bower</u> the spirit of a fiend   *lodge*
In mortal paradise of such sweet flesh?
Was ever book containing such vile matter
So fairly bound? O! that deceit should dwell
In such a gorgeous palace! (III.ii)

Can wonderful, beautiful, loving Romeo really be full of Montague vileness? The girl who asks this is Romeo's bride, but she is also a Capulet, and at this moment she feels with Goethe's Faust that:
    "In my breast two souls have taken their abode,
    And each is struggling there for mastery."
So an actor might begin work on this speech by exploring Juliet's opposing reactions to the news of Tybalt's murder.

Exploring Opposites for a Speech Already Worked On

While you may have occasion to start your work on a speech from the point of view of opposites, it is more commonly the case that you take up the issue of opposites after your initial work on a text. Let's consider how opposites may add new dimensions to the first draft of a speech by working briefly on two examples.

Joan of Arc's vision

Joan of Arc's story about an angel appearing to her in the fields when she was a young girl is the central event of her life; a narrative speech makes it part of Jean Anouilh's play.

Read Speech 2 in Appendix B.

Suppose you had worked on this speech and gotten a good first draft on its feet. The Archangel makes his request of Joan and her response is quite negative: she is fearful and seems certain that she is incapable of what is asked of her. "I am only a young peasant girl ... please pity me ... I've never had to be responsible for anything, except my sheep. ... I am small, and ignorant ... I should always remember I had killed them." In the text this flurry of excuses is unremitting: apart from her return to the field on the night of the first vision, there is scarcely a hint of anything but refusal.

It is certainly possible to play the speech in this single-minded way: young Joan says no, no, no, but the angel takes "no pity." But one wonders how a shepherd girl could become Joan of Arc if nothing in the angel's command appeals to her. How could she put on armor and lead the armies of France to victory if she had no interest at all in doing so? Granted that the God of France has chosen an unlikely candidate, would he really settle on someone entirely unwilling? That might ensure a disinterested Joan, but hardly the strongest candidate — nor the most credible one, unless we forego any exploration of her character and simply shrug our shoulders at the miracle of what she accomplished.

A more dynamic approach would be to reexamine the speech from an opposites point of view by investigating actions and energies that run counter to choices in the first draft, even if they seem to contradict the words. (Once again, the issues are unisex enough that everyone can

282

explore the moments; and male actors should remember that Clytemnestra — the next character we'll look at — was originally played by a man.) Let's play with a few lines from Joan's speech.

I've never had to be responsible for anything, except my sheep.
You need to give yourself some sense of what a first-draft version of this line might feel like. There are of course many ways to play such a moment.

15.1 Try, for example, to make yourself as small as possible, as if to hide or to make yourself an insignificant speck. Perhaps you sink into a squat on your haunches as you say the line.

15.2 Try this same move again as if it were a slow descent into despair — a collapse into resentment at the limited horizons of the world you were born into. Such a choice already suggests that Joan is not really content with her station in life, but that she doesn't believe in the possibility of escaping it.

15.3 Try sinking into a crouch once more, this time playing self-disparagement, as if young Joan does not believe in herself.

All these imagined first-draft choices, and other impulses you might have, go with the grain of the text. Now let's explore choices which go *against* the grain of the text.

15.4 Start in a crouch.

   • *As you speak the line, rise slowly to your feet as if joy were surging from deep inside you. Let the joy come ever so slightly into your eyes and into the shape of your mouth.*

   • *Play the moment again, letting your joy be brighter.*

   • *Once more, and this time Joan's face should be as radiant as the light emanating from the angel.*

15.5 Suppose that Joan is feeling an unaccustomed, very pleasurable glow of pride. You can use your narrative skills to create this energy. For example, play the line as if Joan were slowly standing up in court; she imagines that her sheep are courtiers bowing to her.

15.6 This time play the moment as if Joan were a sort of Cinderella transformed by a magic wand and wearing for the first time a splendid suit of armor. How might she move?

15.7 Try yet a different approach. Stay in the crouch through "I've never

*had to be responsible for anything," then pop up quickly. How you
get to your feet as you say "except my sheep" should mean: "Yes!
Me! I can do it! I've dreamed of doing it! I'm your woman!"*

Note that these alternative versions of the moment seem quite
credible, even though the actions and line readings say something
"opposite" to what the text says. Actors do not, of course, have license
perversely to contradict every line of a text, but when the larger truth
requires, we are called on to explore *what* else may be true in addition to
what our characters say. It is certainly true that young Joan is fearful and
dubious, which is why her words rang true when you sank into a crouch.
But an opposites perspective may lead you to discover that a very
different energy is true as well — which in this case is entirely unspoken,
although many speeches provide textual clues about the forces generating
inner conflict.

What is remarkable about good opposites work is that after being fully
committed to the interpretation fleshed out in a first draft, we may explore
a radically different, opposing version *which also seems true.* Joan may
have more than one response at the same time. This is simply to suggest
that she is like most of us at moments of crisis: ambivalent. We all know
how very human it is to be saying one thing — and meaning it — while
feeling or doing another. That is why an actor can so convincingly play an
action in opposition to the words.

One part of Joan is fearful and thinks that she is not up to leading the
armies of France, and that is the part of her that formulates the words
spoken to the angel. An actor can "give voice" with all the other
languages at her command — action, gesture and movement, facial
expression, sound sense, etc. — *to another part of Joan* who reacts very
differently to the angel's instructions.

If you believe that visions like Joan's are really projections from within,
then it is really Joan herself who is demanding that she save France. There
may indeed be "two souls" inside her, two halves of a divided self.
Opposites work can make both Joans visible.

We are not yet concerned with how to put opposite energies together
so as to portray ambivalence. We will consider that process when we focus
(in Chapter 17) on *layering,* which is the term I use for integrating
opposites in a conflicted speech. For now we are interested in developing

an opposites sensibility — a mindset about inner conflict — and in acquiring a set of tools for proposing and exploring opposites for a speech.

I am only a young peasant girl, not a great captain who can lead an army.

15.8 *Suppose that in your first draft you had backed up on these words. Explore this, adding any other impulses to hide or run away. How you use space here might be expressive. The energy is "No, no, no ... "*

15.9 *If the thrust of your first version of the speech was saying no and backing away, then you might begin your opposites exploration by moving toward the angel as if to say yes. What other positive physical responses might Joan have?*

15.10 *Imagine that young Joan had used a stick for herding. In the here-and-now of telling the story she has in hand a substitute prop (whatever might be available) which she impulsively uses as if it were her old stick. As she moves forward on this line, toward the angel and her calling, her arm slowly rises as if it were holding a sword. Time this gesture so that it completes as you say "an army."*

15.11 *You might go further with this imagined moment on the battlefield: leap onto a rock or slash an opponent in combat.*

Note how the tension between Joan's action and what she is saying energizes the moment. A strong opposites choice stimulates the audience because it asks them to read what you are playing vis-à-vis the text.

Clytemnestra's revenge

For ten years, ever since her husband Agamemnon sacrificed their daughter Iphigenia to the gods so that the Greek ships might sail to Troy, Clytemnestra has dreamed of revenge. When Agamemnon returns, she welcomes him home. After he takes a bath — perhaps with her wifely assistance — she wraps him in a large robe and hacks him to death with a double-headed ax.

The murder happens offstage, as death always does in ancient Greek drama. It is not that the Greeks avoided bloodshed: their theater is full of slaughters and sacrifices, suicides and assassinations. These are reported by messengers, who conjure offstage events in splendid, and quite graphic, narrative speeches; so it is just as true to say that they happen right in front of the audience. Here Clytemnestra plays messenger to her own deed. Agamemnon's bloody body is onstage, rolled out on a wagon used in Greek tragedies for just such occasions. She now must face the horrified chorus — the elders of her city, Argos.

Read Speech 1, Appendix B.

Suppose that your first draft of this speech focused on Clytemnestra's rage and her vengeful satisfaction in what she has done. She glories in the deed, just as she says.

and then I strike him
once, twice, and at each stroke he cries in agony
15.12 *So that you have a physical score to work with, start in a standing position and raise one fist as if you were wielding a short-handled ax. On the words "once" and "twice," deliver blows; as you say "and at each stroke he cries in agony," go slowly to your knees as if Clytemnestra is following the slumping body down. (Be careful of your knees in this series of explorations: control your descent.)*

She did it and she's glad — that's certainly true. But a one-dimensional rendition of the murder — she hated him and killed him, *period* — risks making Clytemnestra so monstrous that audience members cannot identify with her. They might find it all too easy to distance themselves from such a brutal act. "That's not me up there; I could never be so cold-blooded; I would feel so many other things — I'd feel guilt, I'd be nauseous, I'd be too frightened. I'm not at all like her." In this way we may inadvertently let an audience off the hook.

I am convinced that the first order of business in playing a villain, or any character who does something horrible, is to make visible the hurt that is ultimately the source of the deed. Actors cast in such roles would do well to think of themselves as the victims of the play, who commit crimes only to relieve their pain. An actor must get herself and her audience in touch with Clytemnestra's heartache, the suffering that drives her to kill Agamemnon. Vulnerability in a character elicits a measure of sympathy from the audience, and a willingness to identify. (This presupposes that the character is not a cartoon villain or a psychopath with no redeeming qualities and no motives with which we can sympathize.)

The second order of business in playing a character like Clytemnestra is to complicate the crime by exploring opposites. What energies within the character conflict with the impulse to do what she does? The very things an audience member might feel if he or she were killing a spouse may be layered into Clytemnestra as opposites.

Both these steps make it possible to identify not only with the victim but with the perpetrator of the crime. If an audience is positioned to empathize with Clytemnestra, it can accompany her on her journey to the murder. They will do this if she is not a monster but a human being who feels the range of emotions that they feel — and yet she does what she does! The implication, of course, is that we too might commit such a deed: on stage, but for the grace of God, goes every one of us.

What else, then, might Clytemnestra be experiencing as she relives the murder she has just committed? As is so often the case, there are quite a few possible opposites, a whole spectrum of other energies that might be investigated — who knows how many? Determining which of these will become prime candidates depends on the interests of the actor (and director) and on the thrust of a particular production. Let's improvise some of these possibilities, quickly sketching what would be explored more extensively in rehearsal.

15.13 *In this version, Clytemnestra feels that she is not really inside the person who is murdering Agamemnon. It is as if she were watching herself from above. After years of imagining the deed, she now feels nothing: her voice is distant, her face shows no affect. Use the blocking imagined for your first draft: two blows, then down to your knees.*

If the whole speech were played out from the point of view of this opposite, what about the lines about reveling in the murderous shower of Agamemnon's blood? This is not a problem but a creative opportunity. It may be, for example, that Clytemnestra is *trying* to feel something and asserts what is not really true. Or perhaps by that point — in a layered version of the speech that includes both opposites — the violent act has jolted her into joyful release.

15.14 This time let Clytemnestra experience nausea as she approaches Agamemnon, raises the ax, delivers the first blow, sees the gaping wound, raises the ax again, etc. Take your time with this. Why and how does she go to her knees in this opposite version of the moment?

15.15 Now feel the eyes of each chorus member on you as you recount the murder. Go from face to face: you see shock, horror, disgust. The oldest faces are frightened and bewildered, like children. Imagine that unexpectedly you spot the pain in your daughter Electra's face, and her hatred for you, which hurts. In these expressions you see — as in a mirror — what you have done. Play your reaction to these faces. In this way you can begin to sense the force of public shame, so powerful in ancient Greece, which Clytemnestra might feel despite herself.

15.16 Place yourself against a wall and imagine that you are yourself being murdered. Register the first two blows; when you go to the floor, sliding down the wall, it is because you are dying. Try this a couple of times, speaking the text from inside the events.

Could you possibly play being murdered while addressing the elders of Argos? Yes, if you play this scenario subtly, as if Clytemnestra were empathetically and involuntarily feeling each blow of the ax.

15.17 Your actions should be just as specific as in the previous exploration, but smaller, and not as literal. If before you were clearly warding off blows, now you may appear to be flinching as you relive what happened. Instead of going to the floor, you might collapse against a wall, sink into a chair. You are still being murdered, but what you are secretly playing should make sense as Clytemnestra's physical reactions to Agamemnon's murder. Every move, every tone must read true in the here-and-now of speaking to the chorus.

15.18 Kneel behind a chair with a back that you can wrap your arms around. The chair is a surrogate for Agamemnon. He is your spouse, and there was a time when you fiercely loved him. Suppose that as you help him bathe, you unexpectedly feel both tenderness and pity. He has aged, and his back is scarred from the war; he is ten-years weary, and he dozes as you hold him. This is your good-bye hug. Put your head against his. Then, so as not to disturb his nap, reach for the ax and pick it up. As you raise it, hold him even tighter. After two blows, lower him gently to the floor.

Still other opposites might be explored. It would be interesting, for example, to rehearse the speech while tenderly soaping Agamemnon's back. One Clytemnestra actor might focus on being afraid of her warrior husband, another might imagine a scene of sexual passion, a third might be interested in the pain of feeling betrayed by her mate.

Toward and away from

Opposites create a tension between moving toward and away from an action, a decision, a choice, etc. One or more forces drive your character toward it. Other forces push or pull you in a very different direction, away from it.

When Agamemnon returns, Clytemnestra certainly feels rage. She wants to kill him and she will; she even believes, or at least a part of her believes, that it is the right and just thing to do. But now, in the bath, she sees that he has been scarred by the war and by time: after ten years on the battlefield, he looks much older. Let us imagine that she unexpectedly feels other things besides rage. She wants to kill him but she also:

- pities him;
- feels guilty for deceiving him and planning his murder;
- is on the verge of fainting;
- feels not the satisfaction she expected but numbness;
- is oddly happy to see him;
- feels the old intimacy;
- senses his grief for what he has done and wants to comfort him;
- wants to make love to him;
- wants to baby him tenderly in the bath;
- is afraid of Agamemnon and of the city at large.

And so forth. None of these possible opposites will negate Clytemnestra's vengeful rage, but each adds dimension to her character and complicates her act by pulling her away from the murder.

Substantial, dimensional speeches will generally provide the actor with multiple clues about opposites, in word and in action. So far, however, we have explored speeches for which, in the absence of conflicts spelled out in the text, we have supplied a range of possible opposites. Some may object that it is anachronistic to introduce a contemporary sense of inner conflict into a character like Clytemnestra. The point is quite debatable. When Clytemnestra asks Agamemnon to step down from his chariot and walk into the palace on red cloth, a tempting invitation to an act of excessive pride, it is clear that he is conflicted. In any case, whatever the playwright's thinking may have been, opposites are truthful to our present understanding of the human condition. The classics are not frozen in time, after all; they live in history and must evolve to stay alive. It is doubtful that the opposites we have been exploring would be so playable if they violated the material.

Choosing an Opposite for the Whole Speech

Exploring opposites is a delicate, complex business, full of subtleties and surprises. But the task is fundamentally simple: to investigate radically different approaches that might be truthful for your material.

In order to get a feel for opposites, we have explored moments and played brief texts. But taking an opposites approach to a speech does not mean piecing together moment-to-moment choices which run counter to what you played in the first draft. It is not a question of thinking, "I hit him on this line so now I'll hug him," or "this section was quiet before, now I'll do it loud." An opposites approach is a very different direction for the whole speech.

You are searching for stimulating, dynamic, *truthful* opposites to what you've already developed. Consider "opposite," high contrast choices for playing:

- the events of the story;
- its overall tone and energy;
- the temperaments, motivations and values of each character;
- your character's responses to what happens.

You can trigger notions for opposites to explore by listing actions, reactions, energies and moods that you are presently playing, and proposing opposites to each of these. You don't have to know where you are going with this exercise — it is a discovery tool that can provoke unexpected insights.

Every aspect of your first draft may be looked at from the point of view of opposites.

- You might propose a radically different energy for your *character*. If your Henry V has the passionate conviction of an ambitious leader, you might look for the doubts that make him terribly insecure.
- You might reexamine your character's needs and goals and discover a *motivation* that conflicts with actions in your first draft. What new actions might this opposite motive inspire?
- *Relationships* may be reversed. An insecure beginner may become confident and successful while the established figure who formerly dominated her becomes more and more dependent (I am thinking of David Margulies' *Collected Stories*).
- Even the *circumstances* of a scene may be experienced in an entirely different way. What had previously seemed elegant and refined may now seem tawdry and excessive.

Logical opposites should be your starting point. The opposite of being sure is doubting; the opposite of rebelliously defying is submitting, meekly or fearfully; the opposite of shy is some variety of bold or assertive; the opposite of being locked in is being locked out; the opposite of leaving is staying; the opposite of being chased is chasing; the opposite of believing is doubt or disbelief.

- If Athi (Excerpt 1, Appendix A) has in your first draft steadfastly refused to take the fish and butter, now is the time to make the food seem so delicious, to make Athi so tempted to accept it for himself and for his fellow prisoners, that he clings to his mother's present.
- If your Laureen (Speech 10, Appendix A) has had no clue what the fellow down on the street means by pointing to his head and then up to her, you ought now to play the speech as if she knows precisely what he means — but dreads the implications. If your Laureen has been focused on staying alive ("Just let me live five minutes longer!"), now you ought to investigate the part of her that wants to die — this is, after all, a fantasy about jumping out a window.
- Suppose that your Rosalind (Excerpt 14, Appendix A) doesn't believe in romantic love, because she fears it is all madness and play-acting. You might next focus on how powerfully smitten she is with Orlando. To explore this opposite, you might play the whole speech

291

in very intimate circumstances. Rosalind might snuggle up next to Orlando and whisper the text as if she were indeed his mistress; she might tenderly touch his hair, eyes, cheek, etc. This opposite might be called the "mad humour of love." A different approach would be to oppose the common-sensical skepticism of your first draft with a Rosalind who is herself driven mad by her out-of-control feelings for Orlando — an opposite which you might call her "living humour of madness."

Opposites As a Spectrum of Radically Different Directions

Exploring sources of conflict for Joan and for Clytemnestra has taught us that for a given speech there is a spectrum of possible opposites. While one or another of these may seem to be a polar opposite, others will angle off in various directions. If A represents the first draft of a speech, then the possibilities for Z might be diagrammed like this:

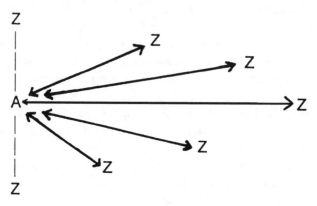

In this light we must broaden our definition of opposites to mean *very different directions,* even if some of those directions are not what we would conventionally understand as opposites. We will continue to use the word "opposites" as shorthand for this range of energies or impulses in conflict with the thrust of your first draft.

Imagine a love scene in which one character is feeling a strong romantic attraction to another. Perhaps the text indicates an impulse toward a specific action: "I want to hold you." But the same character might be pulled in a number of "opposite" directions. I want to hold you, *but:*

- my past experience tells me I'll get hurt;
- physical intimacy frightens me;
- I'm sure you'll reject me (because I'm not worthy of love);
- I don't trust men (or women);
- it will make me feel guilty;
- I hate you for what you did to my family;
- I'm repulsed by your deformity;
- others are watching and I feel too exposed.

Such a list might go on and on: opposites conflict us with infinite variety.

Not Caring Is Not an Option

The one thing an opposite can *never* be is any variety of "I don't care." If your goal is to infuse a speech with powerful opposites energy, the proposition that your character "doesn't care" is a non-choice. It contributes nothing in the way of conflict — or good sense — to propose that on the one hand your character is committed to thus-and-such very strongly, but on the other hand it doesn't really matter. The "I don't care" trap can take many forms:

- It's not that important. It doesn't matter to me. It doesn't bother me.
- I'm uninterested, indifferent.
- I'm nonchalant, cool, unperturbed. I'm in a state of calm equilibrium.
- I'm doing just fine, everything's hunky-dory — no problem!
- I'm in control of the situation. I'm on top of it.
- I am above all this and I look down on the issue scornfully. (This is the message of playing sarcasm.)
- This situation can be easily handled and is no real threat. (That is the implication of being flippant about your circumstances.)

All of these stances spell death to opposites work. If your character doesn't really care about what you worked on in your first draft, there is no push or pull in an opposite direction. Not caring has no direction at all, and no energy; it simply undercuts your previous work. Clytemnestra's situation cannot be: I want to kill you for sacrificing our daughter, but on the other hand it doesn't really bother me what you did.

Dramatic characters cannot help but care about their opposites. Their conflicts concern what is most important in their lives, and the struggle within them is so intense that they are never indifferent. The push-pull of opposing energies puts them off balance, and they are rarely on top of the situation. Conflicted characters feel like underdogs.

Masks

It is of course possible for conflicted characters to *act as if* they don't care. People do hide their conflicts by pretending that everything is OK: they put on a mask. In opposites work we are interested in revealing inner conflict — and in removing any mask that disguises it.

On the night before the battle of Agincourt, Henry V visits his greatly outnumbered and dispirited troops (*Henry V, Act IV*). He may smile, joke, comment on a card game, banter with bravado. This is the mask he puts on for his men, cheering them with "a little touch of Harry in the night." It may also comfort Henry to act as if his troops were not likely to be slaughtered the next day. But the king's mask is not an opposite. His opposites are at war *behind* the mask. Perhaps the young king's guilt for leading his men to their death is in conflict with his ambition to defeat the French. His spirits may waver as he weighs the stark reality of their doomed situation against his vision of a victory celebrated forever after on St. Crispin's Day. On the one hand, he is steeling himself for battle; on the other, he feels a tender intimacy for the "happy few" who will fight with him. Fear and rage, exhaustion and energy, the diametrically opposed spirits of the two father figures in his life — all these may be combatants in one or another actor's portrayal of Henry V at this point in Shakespeare's story.

If a character wears a mask that hides inner conflict, do not mistake the mask for one of the opposites. Inner conflict is the struggle between opposites *behind* the mask.

Opposites of Equal Intensity

An opposite must be a strong, active impulse in a very different direction from what you have been working on in the first draft. It must be powerful enough to put up a real fight inside your character. Opposites should therefore be of roughly equal intensity. On the seesaw of life, opposites sit at either end, where all the up-and-down action is; at the center of the seesaw, there is little action and no drama. A strong opposite cannot take a middle-of-the-road, neutral stance — another reason why "I don't care" is not a viable opposite.

In Robert Anderson's *Silent Night, Lonely Night,* a naval officer in WWII learns that he will be shipped out in the morning, a few days before Christmas. He tries to call his wife, but he cannot reach her. He needs "to say good-bye to someone, some girl. It was a big thing. I was going off to war, and I wanted to say good-bye." He gets in touch with the only woman he knows in town, whose husband is on a ship in the Pacific; he drops by with gifts for her and her child. They drink some champagne and listen to music. He begins to feel, as she does, that something might happen. His hunger is innocent enough: lonely and frightened, he needs to be held, comforted, reassured. But at the same time he feels terribly guilty about his impulse to betray his wife, this woman, and a fellow officer. The two opposites — for purposes of shorthand, let's call them guilt and desire — must be strongly felt, and pretty equally felt, for this situation to be dramatic. If he can take it or leave it, there is no tension: if his misgivings are weak, he will do it; if his neediness is negligible, he will walk away easily. But if at the moment of truth, when he must either go or stay the night, he is pulled with equal force in both directions, then this will be a difficult and telling decision.

We mustn't make things easy for our characters; on the contrary, we need to make their conflicts very tough on them. The stakes must be high. Clytemnestra must kill Agamemnon *at some cost* — precisely what that cost is can be explored in opposites work. What it costs a daughter to stand up against her father's fascist politics will depend on how devoted she is to him in other respects — how much she *doesn't* want to hurt him. And vice versa: the deeper her affection for her father, the more she will be angered and hurt by his political stance. (This story is in William Styron's novel *Sophie's Choice* and in the screenplay.) Lives uncomplicated by inner struggle may be relatively peaceful, and one-dimensional characters may be a lot happier, but the stuff of drama is high-stakes conflict between opposites that are equally matched — at least until it is time for the curtain to fall.

Developing an Opposite from a Moment

A moment or section in your first draft may already contain the germ of an opposite for your whole speech, in which case you should explore what that moment's energy might mean for every other moment.

Suppose, for example, that in a first draft of Weston's speech about the eagle (Speech 9, Appendix B), you had focused on the thrill that this former pilot experiences as the eagle takes off: he starts cheering for the bird's "suicidal aeronautics." But your first draft had a very different energy when the eagle's shadow passed over Weston the first time, "huge and black and cold like": Weston was spooked. That moment might inspire you to explore whether an ominous energy of this sort might be true for the speech from beginning to end. Such an opposite might prompt you to start the story with a sense that something dreadful is going to happen, to deepen Weston's distaste for castrating, to heighten his fearful reaction to the eagle's swooping, and to end with an "icy feeling" running up your backbone that is more terror than thrill.

Perhaps your first draft of Joan of Arc's speech is a terrified retreat from the angel and the notion of leading the French army. But the moment of feeling a hand on your shoulder seems intensely pleasurable, because you are being touched by an angel. Maybe you tremble along with your sheepdog, as saints sometimes do when having a vision. A moment like this might lead to a very different version of the whole speech, and it suggests a specific, quite physical approach to exploring in an opposite direction.

In *A Woman Alone*, a monolog by Dario Fo and Francesca Rame, Maria is unhappily married. Her conventional morals result in strong feelings of guilt when a young man falls in love with her. She breaks off contact with him, then discovers that up and down her street he has painted "I love you, Maria" in red letters a foot high. Perhaps in your first draft you discovered that Maria was exhilarated and very moved by this declaration of love. Now you might revisit the whole story in light of this moment. Is Maria romantically inflamed from the get go, despite her misgivings?

Is there a moment or section in your first draft that already contains an opposite that you might explore for the whole of your speech?

Characters in Conflict with Themselves

Inner conflict must be grounded in the particular issues of your material. But there are mindsets, questions, and vocabularies that are useful whenever you are talking to yourself about opposites.

The first step, and the most important, is to develop a sensibility attuned to the many ways in which characters can embody the clash of forces within a play. You must learn to think in terms of opposites. Considering a range of roles will provide you with practice — and may even suggest possibilities for your own material. Here are thumbnail studies of six characters in conflict with themselves.

CAVALE: *ugly duckling — pretty swan*
In Sam Shepard's *Cowboy Mouth*, Cavale tells a story about being cast in a school play as the ugly duckling (Excerpt 15, Appendix A); "but I didn't mind 'cause at the end I'd be that pretty swan and all." But the story has no such happy ending for Cavale, because "this real pretty blonde-haired girl dressed in a white ballet dress rose up behind me as the swan." If she is merely sarcastic about the incident, it will seem that Cavale looks down on being pretty and on moving like a ballerina, as if it were beneath her. But it cannot be that Cavale doesn't really care about playing the swan. The whole point of an ugly duckling existence is one day to be transformed, and part of her still longs to be the swan. An audience should catch glimpses of Cavale in this softer light throughout the play. Just as Richard III leans into playing the villain role that he feels has been thrust upon him by birth, tough-talking Cavale leans into playing the ugly duckling. What is masked by her bad-girl, rock-and-roll swagger is her belief that she is unattractive and unlovable, which is the real opposite. Self-image is one inroad to character opposites: the contrast between how a character sees herself and the ideal that she longs to be.

HAMLET: *being — seeming*
When his mother asks him why he seems so grieved by his father's death, Hamlet protests vehemently: "Seems, madam! Nay, it is; I know not 'seems' " (I.ii). In fact Hamlet cannot bear people who pretend, who seem to be what they are not. This theme runs through the entire play (and through much of Shakespeare's drama). Hamlet's conflicts with the King and Queen, with Ophelia and her father, and with his seeming friends Rosencrantz and Guildenstern are imbued with this issue; so are his doubts about the validity of the ghost and his fascination with acting. Why should Hamlet be so sensitive about *seeming*? Quite possibly, from an opposites point of view, because he feels he is the biggest seemer of them all — an

approach which would make the tension between being and seeming a source of internal conflict for the central character.

LEAR: *blindness — seeing, covering up (clothing) — stripping away (nakedness)*

Shakespeare fleshes out each of his major themes with lines, images, and actions. The text of King Lear, for example, is filled with references to eyes, sight, and both physical and psychological blindness. The old king habitually refuses to see what he does not want to, but the circumstances of the play force him to moments of insight about his daughters, his court, mankind, the universe, himself. What is remarkable is that the central character, who by play's end has seen so much, goes to his death struggling with this issue. His last act is to demand that those on stage and in the audience see that his daughter is still breathing. Yet Lear knows that his daughter is "dead as earth." He sees the terrible truth but cannot bear to look at it. I was so struck by this conflict of impulses when I first played Lear that I chose to cover my eyes as I spoke his last words: "Look at her. Look, her lips. Look there. Look there." (V.iii) This moment of "seeing" is really a final act of blinding himself. An actor might shape other moments in the play so as to collaborate with Shakespeare in developing this theme. Lear might, for example, react to the outrage of seeing Kent in the stocks by covering his eyes. When Lear wakes from his madness, he might stare at Cordelia as if seeing her for the first time. A director might introduce a game of blind man's bluff into one of the scenes, or have the Fool cover Lear's eyes as he challenges the old king with riddles. In the parallel subplot, Gloucester is blinded just as he begins to see the truth about how he has been deceived; and Edgar's eyes are opened when he is betrayed by his brother and forced to flee for his life.

There are more references to clothing in *King Lear* than in any other Shakespeare play. It is a world in which the small vices of "poor naked wretches" are plainly visible, while for the privileged "furred gowns hide all," including a multitude of secret sins. Many *cover up* who they really are and what they really think; they flatter and deceive. Only the truth-sayers in *Lear* are who they appear to be. Lear learns that honesty and self-knowledge demand that he *strip away* everything that hides his true self and his "true need." A great many moments in *Lear* embody the tension between covering up or stripping away: Lear takes off his crown in the abdication scene which begins the story; he tears off his clothes when he recognizes man's true condition in Poor Tom's nakedness; he fashions a simple crown for himself when he is mad; very near his death, he asks that somebody "undo this button." Lear and Edgar — and quite possibly other members of the ensemble — must in word and action play the opposition of *clothing* and *nakedness*.

PUNTILA: *drunk — sober, buddy — boss*

Bertolt Brecht's Puntila is a generous, amiable fellow when he is drunk, but when he sobers up he transforms into a tight-fisted, abusive landowner. This remarkable metamorphosis occurs onstage several times in the course of the play. Puntila is in fact a dual personality. So is the central character in Brecht's *The Good Person of Setzuan,* in which Shen Te's natural kindness gets her into such trouble that she must develop an alter ego: she disguises herself as a mean uncle who shows up whenever she needs to be selfishly tough with people.

ROSALIND: *infatuation — distrust*

In *As You Like It,* Rosalind disguises herself as a man, with comic consequences when she forgets who she is supposed to be. Conflict between face and mask, male role-playing and female identity, old self and emerging self, is typical of this sort of "britches" role. It is in this context that Rosalind — as Ganymede — confronts Orlando, who has been proclaiming his love for her. She tests his feelings — evidence that she does not trust them — by arguing that love is a madness that must be cured, and she explains just how she would go about it (Excerpt 14, Appendix A). At the same time she is feeling madly attracted to him, and the tension between her infatuation and her distrust makes the scene edgy and complex — and as much about Rosalind's inner conflict as about her relationship to Orlando. She is in dialog with herself as well as with him.

WESTON: *leaving — staying*

In *Curse of the Starving Class,* the father's central conflict is that he can't stand it at home, but he can't stay away; he has to break loose, but he needs to feel connected. However the individual actor states these opposites — and the best choice would be to use language from the play — we must see in Weston impulses toward leaving and toward staying. An actor might, for example, play with variations on packing and unpacking, and stake out the doorway as the space to which Weston ambivalently gravitates.

Polar Opposites

Thinking in terms of polar opposites can trigger insights into your character's conflicts. Basic categories such as the following may stimulate you to formulate more specific opposites for a speech.

pro — con	manic — depressive	flee — pursue
yes — no	sour — sweet	flee — fight
up — down	inside — outside	push — pull
off — on	inferior — superior	admire — despise
now — then	hard — soft	hide — reveal
here — there	light — dark	conform — rebel
never — always	morning — night	forgive — revenge
lost — found	simple — complex	hope — despair
backward — forward	stranger — kin	belief — doubt
same — different	masculine — feminine	reality — appearance
present — absent	adult — child	pleasure — pain
empty — full	clear — confused	attraction — repulsion
hot — cold	wise — foolish	innocence — guilt
black — white	visible — invisible	freedom — necessity
colorful — colorless	asleep — awake	comfort — discomfort
public — private	vain — self-conscious	tension — release
rich — poor	passion — apathy	selfish — other-directed
habitual — new	stable — unstable	meaningful — meaningless
heaven — hell	chaos — order	I can't go on — I go on

This list might be endlessly extended. An actor eventually evolves certain categories that speak to his or her own imagination and experience.

You may also brainstorm metaphorical opposites that are entirely specific to your material. The goal is to provoke yourself to think freshly about conflicts within your character.

We have seen that there is a spectrum of possible opposites for any speech and that you may well decide to explore a radically different direction which is not a logical opposite for the thrust of your first draft.

But considering polar opposites may stimulate you to define more precisely the energy you wish to investigate.

Questions That Can Generate Opposites

Certain questions are consistently useful in thinking about opposites for your character.

• *How is your character a divided self?*

How would you characterize the two selves? How would each of them tell the story of your speech?

• *What part of himself/herself is your character talking to?*

Whether or not a character is talking to someone else on stage, she may also be telling herself what some other part of her needs to hear. A speech about the necessity of acting bravely, for example, may be addressed to the scared part of herself: what is bravado but a display of courage by a frightened person? Such a character is speaking in the first place to herself.

Imagine a speech which goes on insistently about the rock-solid reasons for believing that something will happen; this may well be your character's attempt to convince the part of himself that is doubtful.

Thinking about the self-directed dimension of a speech leads you to realize that Lear and Hamlet and St. Joan and Blanche DuBois are often saying to themselves what some other part of them needs to hear. You must find ways to embody that other part of your character — by exploring in the spirit of opposites. You must play both parts of a self in dialog with itself: the part who is speaking, and the part spoken to — who are on differing sides of the issue at hand.

If an argument is going on inside you, how would you name the two points of view?

• *Who does your character aspire to be?*

This question points you toward a variety of possible conflicts.

• A character's self-image may be radically different from his or her real self.
• A character may be conflicted about who he thinks he *ought* to be as opposed to who he is.

- A character may lead a double life, in which her everyday self periodically gives way to a fantasy self.
- Part of a character may emulate a parent or idolized role model, while another part rebels against this influence.
- Some people behave as if they lived in circumstances very different than the reality in which they find themselves. When a very hungry Charlie Chaplin cooks a shoe in *The Gold Rush*, he proceeds to eat it as if he were having a gourmet meal.

And so on. In each case, both aspects of the character need to be fleshed out.

- *What is your character hiding?*

The premise of a guarded secret has long served drama as a plot device leading to climactic revelations, but the power of secrets is of more general significance to actors. Once an audience senses that a character has a secret, it begins to read appearance against reality, outer against inner, surface against undercurrent. This empowers and stimulates an audience. It also endows the character who has a secret with mystery and depth. What your character is hiding may be an opposite.

- *What is your character's true identity?*

A character may hide not just a secret, but a secret self. In such a case, your character's identity may become an opposites issue.

When a character puts on a mask simply to hide his or her true self, this façade is not an opposite because it does not generate inner conflict. But when a character's public face is really an alternative self — with values and needs that conflict with those of a hidden self — such a mask is much more than a disguise.

In classical Roman theater, the mask worn by an actor was called a *persona*. To create a character whose outer and inner personalities are in conflict, you must play two different masks — two different incarnations of your character. If your inner conflict is to be strong, then the two masks must lay claim to being your character's true identity with equal validity.

This concept of multiple masks was familiar to the ancient Greeks, whose actors changed characters by changing masks. The god Dionysos, patron of theater, was thought to be a succession of masks, with no face beneath. This suggests a dynamic way to think about the rival identities that conflict certain characters: they cannot choose between masks, and deep down, they have no identity.

• *What energy is your character suppressing? What is your character keeping a lid on?*

This is another question about what is hidden. Here the focus is not on persona but on the dynamics of a character who is trying to control feelings and impulses that have built up considerable pressure within. When your character is suppressing a dangerous impulse or stifling a passion, it is as if an old-fashioned pressure cooker were ready to explode: your character is struggling to hold the lid down.

What specific energy is building up pressure inside your character? If some of it escaped from under the lid, what might it look like, behave like?

And what form does the lid take? What behaviors keep the hidden forces from exploding?

• *How are your character's opposites visible in body, voice and behavior?*

If an opposite were completely hidden, how would the audience even know it existed? If an opposite is to have any reality for the audience, it must be visible in a character's behavior.

Long established opposites are embedded in a person's physical and vocal manner. A young man may habitually stand as if he expects at any moment to be hit; presumably a history of being beaten has left its mark on his body. But he may also behave aggressively by way of compensation, with chest or groin thrust forward. A young woman's impulse to hide may be visible in her spatial choices and in her body language, while opposing behaviors insistently call attention to her.

A person's voice may characteristically ask questions, give orders, seduce, gossip, ridicule, sound surprised, tiptoe, etc. A voice — and how text is shaped — can be a window into what sort of a world a character thinks he lives in. If a character has more than one "voice," they may be opposites in conflict.

Opposites may thus be written into the body and voice, and behaviors can be created so as to make inner conflict visible.

• How is your character off balance?

Characters in conflict with themselves rarely achieve equilibrium. Subject to the tug-of-war of contrary impulses, they teeter this way and that, struggling to keep their footing. Opposites keep characters off balance. When central characters in drama arrive at a balancing point, it is either a temporary reprieve or the end of the play. A character who is perfectly in control of the situation is no longer dramatically interesting.

An actor's nervous urge to be in control of what happens in performance should not get in the way of playing the conflicted condition of not being in control.

The value of not being in control

It is natural enough that actors should want to be in control of their performances. So many things can go wrong: we are constantly at risk of appearing foolish. And don't we all want to be brilliant the first time we rehearse a scene or speech? We long to be on top of our material.

Good actors eventually learn that rehearsal is a process of putting themselves off balance in order to make discoveries, and that their liveliest performances are those in which they are moved by forces that can be shaped but not controlled.

How to Talk to Yourself about Opposites

What kind of language you use to talk to yourself about your work has real consequences for your acting. Speak to yourself in generic terms, for example, and you will likely do generic work. Learning acting, I am convinced, is in very large part learning how to *talk* to yourself about acting.

The use of emotional labels can be especially problematic. The danger is that you may end up emoting instead of doing. Talking about a moment in terms of its emotion can lead you to playing generic feelings such as "angry" or "afraid" and to "making" emotions instead of letting them happen, organically, truthfully. Emotions are *reactions* to events and circumstances and the by-product of playing an action; they are not something actors *do*.

The same is true of psychological language in general. Talking about your character's psychological state can lure you into indicating his or her condition instead of playing actions that embody specific conflicts.

Emotional and psychological labels are useful only as shorthand for talking about the spirit of an action, situation, or event. I sometimes use them in coaching to save time, with the proviso that actors must translate my shorthand into the sort of language that generates action choices. But I prefer to talk in other terms entirely. It is always more stimulating to use the language in which actors should become fluent: language that puts them into action.

How you talk to yourself about opposites is critical. Opposites may most effectively be stated in terms of:

- actions (stated as verbs);
- objectives (also verbs);
- metaphors;
- non-psychological, non-emotional adjectives (mostly metaphorical).

Actions

Your function as an actor is to act, not to emote or indicate or otherwise circumvent your proper role. Verbs should be central in your dialog with yourself, because verbs name what you *do*.

When you talk to yourself about the thrust of your first draft and about possible opposites, you may use opposing verbs:

cling — push away	flirt — flee
praise — condemn	believe — doubt
submit — refuse	threaten — comfort
punish — forgive	leave — stay

And so on.

If, for example, you perceive that for much of the first draft your character is begging, you may propose to yourself a spectrum of possible opposites: demanding, ordering, taking, giving up hope, offering help as if the other person were the beggar, etc.

If your first draft does not seem to suggest one verb, consider the action you are playing at a strong moment in your story. Are there other moments in the speech when that same action is what your character is doing, however implicitly? Might the speech be played as if that were your action all the way through? If so, what would be an opposite action?

Objectives

You may wish to think about opposites in terms of motivation. What is it that each character in your story wants and needs? How does that affect behavior? Are any characters confused or conflicted because they have two motives that are incompatible?

Since Stanislavski, actors have addressed questions of motivation in terms of objectives and actions. An objective is what one character wants another to do. An action is anything that a character does to get his or her objective.

When you are working on a narrative speech, you should focus first on objectives inside the story, rather than on your motives for telling the story in the here-and-now (which may be a later consideration).

A character's objective may be in conflict with an opposite objective, whether conscious or "unconscious."

to get him to leave — to get him to stay
to force her to confess — to get her to deny she did it
to make you choose me — to make you choose for yourself
to help you advance yourself — to keep you beneath me
to make Dad respect me — to make him admit his politics are wrong

If you decide that your character's inner conflict should be explored in terms of opposing objectives, first articulate what seemed to have been your primary motivation in the first draft. Then re-explore the story with this objective as your only focus. In how many different ways might you - try to get what you want? What new impulses arise as you work single-mindedly toward this objective? What lines can help you? How should they be spoken?

Each word, tone, gesture, movement, and spatial choice should count. Look at every moment as an opportunity to get other characters in the story to give you what you need. Monitor your progress along the way: at any given point, are you closer or farther from your goal? You must take in the success or failure of your efforts so that it affects you.

Should you consider the objective of other characters in your story? What do *they* do to get what they want?

When you propose an opposite objective, it too must be explored from moment to moment. It will motivate an opposing set of actions — which will more than likely conflict with actions in your first draft.

Metaphors

All of the following metaphors might be played as opposites for Wesley's story about the fight between his parents (Speech 7, Appendix B):

tightly compressed coil spring — wet rag
catatonic — superball careening in a stairwell
exhausted — too many cups of coffee
block of ice — house on fire
engine that won't turn over — speeding car
model plane swaying very gently — bulldozer crashing through walls
heavy hangover — out-of-control drunk
avocado-blossom paradise — desert hell
stand-up comic — horrified reporter — cheering sports fan
tantrum — mother comforting a crying child
horror movie terror — cartoon violence

And so on. Many of these metaphors are suggested by the text; others are examples of what an actor might bring to the story as a way of playing its events.

Once you've gotten a metaphorical inspiration, don't convert it into an abstract idea or a psychological concept. Analyzing a metaphor in this way reduces it to its "meaning," and while this may give you insight, you will be no farther along in developing your acting score. If, for example, you propose that a particular wife relates to her husband as a worried mother does to a sickly child, this metaphor is full of potential actions; you could improvise such an image for hours and days to unpack all its implications. To reduce the "worried mother and sickly child" metaphor to "anxiety" or "protectiveness" or any such abstraction constricts its meaning drastically and drains the sensuous life out of it. You end up with a ho-hum *idea*, whereas working directly with your metaphor *on its own terms* can spur you to discover surprising, revealing actions. Do not translate your metaphor into a concept; translate it into actions. *Explore the metaphor, not what it means.*

Non-psychological, non-emotional adjectives

The adjectives most useful to an actor are metaphorical in nature. These provoke more surprising, sensuous, and specific choices than psychological and emotional terms, which label moments in all-too-familiar terms. Boring actors reduce what might be remarkable or extraordinary to the commonplace and the comfortable; they talk about their work in whatever clichés are current, and this blinds them to fresh insights and discoveries. They are prisoners of what they already know.

An interesting actor looks for what is unique, intriguing, and unexpected even in the most everyday experience. You should search for what is strange about the familiar in order to encounter it afresh. Metaphorical adjectives can generate novel, stimulating approaches to scenes and speeches.

centrifugal — centripetal	arid — soaked
helium-filled — leaden	bubbly — flat
rich chocolate — sugarless bland	silken — scruffy
slapstick — balletic	corroded — stainless steel
angular — curvy	feline — canine
evergreen — deciduous	rubbery — brittle

And so on. What are the most evocative adjectives in your text? Do any of these suggest a way to play the whole speech?

Watch your language!

How you talk about a piece of material is critical to guiding your work. Watch your language while talking about opposites — or any other aspect of acting, for that matter. Practice the creative skill of translating emotional shorthand and generic psychological labels — all our boringly familiar cultural blah-blah — into stimulating, action-oriented, playable language that proposes what you should explore. For example: not "stupid" but "lobotomized" or "like an alien from another planet in shock"; not "sad" but "waking up the morning after the burial" or "picking up a pen to sign the divorce papers." Note that the last two examples are narrative in nature, and metaphorical: this moment is like a moment in such-and-such a metaphorical scene.

In Tennessee Williams' *The Glass Menagerie*, Amanda discovers that her daughter has not been going to her business school classes. She is not angry/sympathetic, let us say, but she shakes/caresses, hisses/cajoles, threatens/comforts, ridicules/encourages, plays prosecutor and best buddy. When the young peasant girl who will become Joan of Arc is told by an angel that she must save France, she is not afraid/interested, let us say, but she sees the angel as both her fairy godmother and as a demon tempting her. She listens to the angel's injunction as if she were being sentenced to burn at the stake, or as if she were ascending to heaven with an angel at each elbow, or marching at the head of a victorious army cheered by every citizen of Paris.

The very best terms for naming opposites — and for talking to yourself about every aspect of your acting work — will be found in your text. You must learn to speak its language.

Learning the language of the text

A play is a foreign country, in which words and actions have quite specific meanings. In a good rehearsal process you learn to speak not just lines but a whole language.

Every story has its own vocabulary. You should use the language of your text to talk to yourself about its themes and conflicts.

In Chekhov's *The Seagull*, Nina's speeches in the last act are a struggle between profound enervation and surges of fresh energy that she seems to will into existence.

> I was afraid you might hate me. I dream every night that you look at me and don't recognize me. If you only knew! Ever since I came I've been here walking about … by the lake. I've been near your house often, and couldn't make up my mind to come in. Let's sit down. (*They sit*) Let's sit down and let's talk, talk. It's pleasant here, warm, cozy. … You hear … the wind? There's a place in Turgenev: "Happy is he who on such a night is under his own roof, who has a warm corner." I … a sea gull … no, that's not it. (*Rubs her forehead*) What was I saying? Yes … Turgenev. "And may the Lord help all homeless wanderers." It's nothing. (*Sobs*) […] It's nothing. It will make me feel better. I've not cried for two years. … You are an author, I … an actress. We have both been drawn into the whirlpool. I used to be happy as a child. I used to wake up in the morning singing. I loved you and dreamed of being famous, and now? Tomorrow early I must go to Yelets in the third class … with peasants, and at Yelets the cultured merchants will plague me with attentions. Life's brutal! […]
>
> Why do you say you kiss the ground I walk on? I ought to be killed. (*Bends over desk*) I'm so tired. If I could rest … rest. I'm a sea gull. No, that's not it. I'm an actress. Well, no matter. … (*Hears Arkadina and Trigorin laughing in the dining room. She*

listens, runs to the door on the left and peeps through the keyhole) And he's here too. (*Goes to Trepleff*) Well, no matter. He didn't believe in the theater, all my dreams he'd laugh at, and little by little I quit believing in it myself, and lost heart. And there was the strain of love, jealousy, constant anxiety about my little baby. I got to be small and trashy, and played without thinking. I didn't know what to do with my hands, couldn't stand properly on the stage, couldn't control my voice. You can't imagine the feeling when you are acting and know it's dull. I'm a sea gull. No, that's not it. Do you remember, you shot a seagull? A man comes by chance, sees it, and out of nothing else to do, destroys it. That's not it. ... (*Puts her hand to her forehead*) What was I ... I was talking about the stage. Now I'm not like that. I'm a real actress, I act with delight, with rapture, I'm drunk when I'm on the stage, and feel that I am beautiful. And now, ever since I've been here, I've kept walking about, kept walking and thinking, thinking and believing my soul grows stronger every day. Now I know, I understand, Kostya, that in our work ... acting or writing ... what matters is not fame, not glory, not what I used to dream about, it's how to endure, to bear my cross, and have faith. I have faith and it all doesn't hurt me so much, and when I think of my calling I'm not afraid of life.

On the one hand Nina talks spiritedly of going for walks, "growing stronger every day," becoming "drunk" onstage because she is in such a "rapture," waking up singing as a child, dreaming of fame. Her calling as an actress makes her feel "not afraid of life." But she also speaks of the brutal life of an actor and of feeling "small and trashy," losing heart, knowing that her acting has become dull, traveling in third class and being plagued by admirers, being "so tired" and needing a rest. She ought to be killed!

How should you talk about these opposites? You might name one *the dying seagull*, since Nina keeps referring to herself as a seagull and recalls how one was shot earlier in the play. The other opposite might be called *how to endure*: "what matters is not fame, not glory, not what I used to dream about, it's how to endure ... "

Everything in the speech can be explored in terms of these opposites. You can play each narrative event as a moment of dying or enduring. Nina's conflicting energies should influence how you play the poetry she quotes, the images that well up in her, what she says about her failed relationship with Trigorin, how she sits and bends wearily over the desk in contrast to her spurts of physical restlessness.

Another actor might choose different language to title her opposites and to focus her work on Nina's inner conflict. She might, for example, play the speech as a rapturous performer, "drunk" with the delight of being on stage; then as a clumsy, insecure, dull actor who feels like she's "dying out there" when she's on stage. Yet another actor might explore the speech from the point of view of the Nina who says "I have faith" and then flesh out the part of her who admits "I quit believing in it myself."

It is possible to interpret a character's conflict with terms drawn from literary criticism, historical or philosophical or psychoanalytic perspectives, or issues close to your own heart. But the first order of business is to examine closely what the text itself has to say about themes and oppositions. *You must learn to speak the language of your story.* If you use words from the text to talk to yourself (and to your director) about what you are working on, you keep yourself in touch with your material.

One method of close textual analysis is simply to read through a fresh copy of your text and underline key words and phrases with an eye toward possible opposites. Particular attention should be paid to:

- central events and actions — with special emphasis on verbs;
- images and metaphors;
- non-psychological, non-emotional adjectives;
- differing points of view;
- conflicting objectives and needs;
- contrasting feeling states and sensations;
- competing self-images.

Recurring words, images, and actions are especially noteworthy. There may be families of words and clusters of images that collectively embody an opposite.

Let's look at a speech in Peter Shaffer's *Equus*. Dysart, a psychiatrist, is treating a young man whose cure, it seems, will rob him of the one passion in his life, a quasi-religious relationship with the spirit of horses.

311

Dysart feels conflicted about "sacrificing" his patient on the altar of normality; hence the disturbing dream he recounts in this speech. Words which suggest an opposites perspective are underlined.[3]

That night, I had this very explicit <u>dream</u>, In it I'm a chief priest in Homeric Greece. I'm wearing a wide gold <u>mask</u>, all noble and bearded, like the so-called Mask of Agamemnon found at Mycenae. I'm standing by a thick round stone and holding a sharp knife. I'm officiating at some <u>immensely important ritual sacrifice,</u> on which depends the fate of the crops or of a military expedition. The sacrifice is a herd of <u>children</u>, about five hundred boys and girls. I can see them stretching away in a long queue, right across the plain of Argos. I know it's Argos because of the red soil. On either side of me stand two assistant priests, wearing masks as well: lumpy, pop-eyed masks, such as also were found at Mycenae. They are enormously strong, these other priests, and absolutely tireless. As each child steps forward, they grab it from behind and throw it over the stone. <u>Then, with a surgical skill which amazes even me, I fit in the knife and slice elegantly</u> down to the navel, just like a seamstress following a pattern. I part the flaps, sever the inner tubes, yank them out and <u>throw them hot and steaming</u> on to the floor. The other two men then study the pattern they make, as if they were reading hieroglyphics. It's obvious to me that <u>I'm tops</u> as chief priest. It's this <u>unique talent for carving</u> that has got me where I am. The only thing is, unknown to them, I've started to feel distinctly <u>nauseous,</u> and with each victim, it's getting worse. My face is going green behind the mask. Of course, I redouble my efforts to <u>look professional</u> — cutting and snipping for all I'm worth: mainly because I know that if I ever let those two assistants so much as glimpse my distress — and the implied <u>doubt that this repetitive and smelly work is doing any social good</u> at all — <u>I will be the next across the stone.</u> And then, of course — the damn mask begins to slip. The priests both turn and look at it — it slips some more — they see the <u>green sweat</u> running down my face — their gold pop-

---

[3] I am indebted for this analysis to a former student, Marilynne McKay.

eyes suddenly fill up with blood — they tear the knife out of my hand ... and I <u>wake up.</u>

One part of Dysart — the part of him that *is* the mask — seems quite impressed with his "surgical skill" and "unique talent for carving" as he officiates at this "immensely important" sacrifice. Another part of him finds this "repetitive and smelly work" barbaric: what he is doing makes him nauseous. His paranoia about being found out suggests that he is having a nightmare. From this menacing perspective, perhaps it is the knife itself that does the slicing, while Dysart watches helplessly. Whereas the "professional" Dysart might throw the hot and steaming innards on the ground with poise and ritual grace, the Dysart who is "green behind the mask" might handle this messy, sickening chore quite clumsily.

Is waking a sudden relief or a horrified realization? Both versions of the final moment might be true. While the beginning of the dream is clearly more positive than the end, it is the interplay between the opposite energies — their confusing, disturbing coexistence — that expresses Dysart's moral dilemma.

Dysart's fear that he will be "the next across the stone" suggests that part of the speech might be played from the point of view of the children. One part of Dysart identifies with his victims.

A close reading of this text suggests numerous pairs of opposites — and how to name them. Of course, it is also possible to articulate opposites not expressly named in the text. The *pride* implicit in "I'm tops" and "unique talent" may, for example, invite an actor to consider whether *shame* might be an avenue to explore, so that the nausea becomes as much self-disgust as physical revulsion. The assistant priests might be both admiring *colleagues* and threatening *enemies.* The entire speech might be played as a compassionate *mission* to save young souls or as an orgy of *mutilation* inspired by envy and hatred of youthful passion. The dream is on the one hand a glowing *vision* and on the other a menacing *nightmare.* All of these possibilities stay close to the story and the issues it raises.

In John Guare's *Six Degrees of Separation,* an imaginative young man named Paul, who seems full of life and possibility, delivers a stirring speech about the death of the imagination, which he calls "the passport we create to take us into the real world." But he also speaks about emotional and intellectual "paralysis" and plays out "the extraordinary last lines of *Waiting*

313

for Godot — 'Let's go.' 'Yes. Let's go.' Stage directions: 'They do not move.'" Could you invent a better name for this dark undercurrent in the speech than "paralysis" or "*Godot*" or "They do not move"?

Another approach to talking about opposites is to use physical actions to "name" them. The paralyzed stillness with which Paul plays that line from Godot might be the real "title" for this opposite. Dysart's opposites might be two physical actions: slicing elegantly on the one hand, disgustedly tossing guts on the other. An actor playing Nina might think of one opposite in terms of the way she leans exhaustedly on the desk, as if she were dying; an exhilarated spin as she talks about being "drawn into the whirlpool" might define the other. (Or does the whirlpool suck her down into another tearful collapse?)

The truest terms for naming opposites will be language taken from the text. The next best vocabulary will be coined by the actor in the spirit of the story — not to impose concepts on the text, but to name what is implicitly there.

Mining Your Speech for Opposites Moments

After you have identified an opposite, the next step is to explore how it might be played for the whole of your speech. How might you approach each moment from this perspective? You are looking for every possible way to play your opposite. Or rather, since you believe the opposite is right there in the material, you are looking for every moment that embodies it. You might think of this process as mining your speech, as if the opposite were a vein of precious ore running through your text.

Suppose that in your first draft of Ophelia's speech about Hamlet coming to her room (Excerpt 13, Appendix A), you had focused on how "affrighted" she was: his behavior was terrifying. Now you are interested in an opposite that you call "the very ecstasy of love," borrowing a phrase from Ophelia's father, who is convinced that Hamlet has been driven mad by unrequited love for his daughter. So you work your way through the speech in search of every moment that might be played as part of this opposite.

And with his other hand thus o'er his brow
He falls to such perusal of my face
As he would draw it.

You have played this text with Ophelia's hand coming down from her brow to trace the features of her face (see 12.8). It is as if her fingers were his. In your first draft, let's imagine, you wanted to pull your face away from the "touch" of Hamlet's eyes, but were too afraid. Now you might play this contact as a little "ecstasy of love."

15.21 In obedience to your father, you have not seen Hamlet in quite a while. Lean into his hand, hungry for his touch. As his fingers trace your features, the quality of the contact is romantic, perhaps erotic.

In this spirit you might work your way through the speech, mining it for other moments that can be played as part of your opposite. "He took me by the wrist and held me hard" might be a little rough but sexy, for example. As Hamlet turns to leave the room, he stares back at Ophelia: his eyes "to the last bended their light on me." Those last two words might end the speech on an ecstatic note, as Ophelia takes intense pleasure in Hamlet's attention.

Mining your speech means trying to make sense of everything from the perspective of the new opposite. How might each word, each move, each event contribute to fleshing it out? It is often the case that certain lines come into their own as you explore opposites. Words and phrases and statements leap out because they are spoken in a context that brings them alive: they belong to the opposite.

Playing against the grain of the text

Remember that actions not only speak louder than words, they can say opposite things. That makes it possible to play against the grain of the text.

- If Joan of Arc adroitly brandishes her staff as if it were a weapon while she protests that she could never lead an army, we see that she might fight very well indeed (see 15.10-11).
- Imagine that Cavale moves into a simple, exquisite pose when she remembers how the pretty blonde-haired girl rose up behind her as the swan (Excerpt 15, Appendix A; see 5.4). If she stays in this pose when she says, "It was really shitty, man," the tension between the line and the action will help to tell the story.

• In *The Seagull*, as we have seen, Nina concludes by saying that "I have faith and it all doesn't hurt me so much, and when I think of my calling I'm not afraid of life." But we know that her acting career has gone badly, and that she cannot talk about her recent life without bursting into tears. Chekhov has written this line so that the actor can play against the grain of the text.

After reliving the murder of her husband, Clytemnestra defiantly tells the chorus that they should rejoice along with her. You might explore the possibility that she says this precisely because she herself does not feel joy.

Rejoice if you can rejoice — I glory. (Speech 1, Appendix B)
15.22 Look down at the butchered body of Agamemnon. You are flooded by memories of a time when you loved him. Gently wipe some blood off his face. When you look up at the chorus, all eyes accuse you, and the greater part of you agrees that you have committed a horrible crime. What you say is an attempt to deny what you feel. Try it once as a feeble effort and then as a painful cry from the heart.
We hear not triumph and pride but shame and defeat.
Imagine that as an opposite for Juliet's "The clock struck nine when I did send the Nurse" (Speech 14, Appendix B), you decided to explore how Juliet's dark premonition that things might turn out badly — which occurs at other moments in the play — might manifest itself in this speech.

Love's heralds should be thoughts,
Which ten times faster glides than the sun's beams,
Driving back shadows over <u>louring</u> hills.   *dark, gloomy*
Therefore do nimble-pinioned doves draw Love,
And therefore hath the wind-swift Cupid wings.
15.23 Accelerate the first two lines and move quickly forward, then slow the third line and back up to a wall as Juliet takes in the threatening darkness of those hills. The next lines seem to be brighter and brisker, but mining your speech might lead you to play them darkly, as a continuation of the "louring hills" energy. Slide down the wall: you are momentarily frightened. Speak the last two lines as a feeble protest against your sense of impending doom.

For Your Own Speech

1. Choose an opposite to explore for the whole of your speech.

Guidelines

Consider the range of possible opposites for your material and for the approach that you have taken to it in your first draft.

Re-read your speech with performance energy — or do a thoughtful walk-through on your feet. What qualities and energies predominate in what you are playing now? If you were an audience person, what would be your biggest impressions of the story? An opposites approach needs a big idea relative to your whole speech. What have you been working on so far? What is the thrust of your first draft?

Underline key words in your text which might suggest opposites.

With the first draft of your speech in mind, review the sections "Polar Opposites" and "Questions That Can Generate Opposites." Make notes as possible opposites occur to you.

Watch your language. Don't trap yourself into playing an emotional label or a psychological type instead of the story. Talk to yourself in terms of actions, objectives, metaphors, and adjectives that are not psychological or emotional. Above all, talk to yourself in the language of your text.

Remember that "opposite" means a spectrum of very different directions. The polar opposite of love is hate, but for our purposes love has a spectrum of opposites: mistrust, fear of being hurt, a bad self-image, moral qualms, a hunger to be independent, self-consciousness about the opinion of others, etc. Any approach that conflicts with what you have been playing may be considered an opposite.

No doubt there will be several opposite directions that you might explore for a given speech. Sort through your list of possibilities, consolidating those that are parallel and similar. Zero in on an opposite you are particularly interested in playing. The opposite you work on should strike you as important and stimulate you to examine issues you care about.

You will have more than one opportunity to investigate opposites for your speech. Where do you want to start?

2. Develop a new draft of your speech that focuses on the opposite you have chosen to explore. Play the whole speech fromt he point of view of your opposite — as if this very different direction were the whole truth.

- Avoid I-don't-care, it-doesn't-bother-me, I'm-on-top-of-it choices like the plague. Your character should not be in control of the situation; on the contrary, you should be trying to keep your character off balance. An effective opposite must be a strong, active push or pull in a very different direction from what you are playing at present.
- Start with the basic blocking of your first draft, but adjust it to accommodate new actions inspired by your opposite. Start your opposite draft with a different first picture and end it with a different freeze frame.
- Try to make sense of everything in the speech from the perspective of the new opposite. Presume that there is a version of every moment in which the opposite is somehow true. In this way you'll push yourself to discover the full truth of the opposite. Mine the speech for every nugget relevant to this opposite. How might each word, each move, each event contribute to fleshing it out?
- For now, there is no need to integrate this opposite with what you've played until now. Ideally there should be nothing of your first draft's energy in this opposite draft.Good opposites work requires the flexibility to go all the way with a new opposite, to play it as single-mindedly as possible, from beginning to end. Since you are focusing on one opposite, there will be no inner conflict in this draft.

In search of the whole truth

This opposite draft is an exercise in exploring how a very different direction might apply to every moment of the speech. Be open about this; don't anticipate that your opposite won't work for this or that part of the speech. Prejudging what's going to happen will cut you off from discoveries. There may be surprises in store.

But don't despair if your opposite doesn't work for every single moment. You are, after all, leaving out its opposite — the thrust of your first draft. Your opposite draft is not the whole truth, but a good opposite will have something to teach you about the entire speech.

The very best result would be that, upon seeing this new draft, others feel that it is a valid version of the speech. Strong opposites will often stand on their own, because they are just as true as the original draft.

Develop your opposite draft before dealing with the rest of this chapter.

A New Pair of Opposites for Your Speech

After developing an opposite draft, you will probably want to investigate other opposites.

- When you are working on rich material, there are many directions to explore. You may need to decide between several possible opposites, and this choice should be made after experimenting on your feet.
- You may be dissatisfied with the direction taken in your opposite draft, or the experience of working on it may have suggested another way to go.
- If you are working with others, you may be prompted by feedback or inspired by someone else's work to explore in another direction.
- Sometimes a speech can be developed in terms of two pairs of opposites.

How might you decide on new directions to explore? In the first place, of course, you should revisit the process in which you engaged earlier.

- Go back to the list of possibilities considered for your opposite draft.
- Return to the exercises for generating opposites in search of fresh inspiration. Play with listing polar opposites, review the "Questions That Can Generate Opposites," look at the key words and phrases underlined in your text, etc.
- Is there a particular moment that conflicts with the overall thrust of your first draft — or of the opposite draft you have just created? You might explore the whole speech from that perspective.
- What's missing from your speech? Is there an issue you're not getting at? A possible conflict within your character that has not been addressed?

Why you are doing opposites work: a few reminders

You're trying to tell the whole story.

You're bringing to light the forces that push and pull your character — energies that might otherwise lay hidden beneath the surface.

You're making visible how your character's responses to the story's events are in conflict.

You're figuring out the specific ways in which your character is a divided self. Opposites work positions you to understand how your speech is one part of your character talking to another part. To do this, of course, you have to define and play the two opposing parts.

You're laying the groundwork for playing a character who is off balance, not on top of the situation, not in full control — a character who is dramatically interesting.

What we can learn from working on opposites goes far beyond acting. Dissecting inner conflict can lead us to a deeper understanding of ourselves, and can make us more forgiving of others, including the characters we play.

1. Choose:
   - a new pair of opposites which conflict with each other; or
   - two radically different, high-contrast directions that conflict with your first draft, if not with each other.

2. Put aside the blocking developed for your first draft. Create two very different scenes that position you to explore these new opposites. Play half of your speech.
   - The two scenes should be specific but simple situations that help you to play the opposite energies in which you are interested.
   - What you play as the context for each of these opposites may be realistic or metaphorical. It may be suggested by something in the text or it may come wholly from your imagination.
   - You may venture far beyond the circumstances of your story and of the play from which it is taken. Feel free to be anachronistic and to cross national, cultural and class boundaries.

• It is useful to play the same half of your speech for each opposite, so that you can compare how the opposites change each moment.

Guidelines

The goal is to put yourself in touch with precisely the energy you want to investigate — and to free yourself from the horizons of your previous work.

Your new opposites should inspire vividly contrasting approaches to your material.

Play each opposite as if it were the whole truth. How does it affect your character from moment to moment?

Watch your language. Don't trap yourself into playing a generic emotional label.

Give yourself something specific and substantial to act: a situation to play, an action or relationship to explore, an objective to work at. The scenes you create should be simple but carefully detailed. Position yourself so that you are reacting to very particular circumstances. This will help you to avoid playing a generic emotion.

You may wish to focus on a single moment or event. For example:

• You imagine your character on a ledge, about to jump, and you improvise that scene and its energies very specifically — edging out, looking down, getting panicky, preparing to push off — as you play your text.
• In contrast to the polite reserve of your original draft, you imagine that several people are holding you back from physically attacking another person, at whom you bellow your text.
• Toward the end of *Curse of the Starving Class*, Weston confesses that he felt imprisoned by family life: "I couldn't stand it here. I couldn't stand the idea that everything would stay the same. That every morning it would be the same." (Excerpt 20, Appendix A) Imagine that an actor working on opposites for this speech wants to explore the outsider part of Weston that never really felt like he was part of the family. The actor experiments with different ways to position himself so that he is locked out of the house and full of longing to be inside.

321

- He does the speech with his nose pressed against the outside of a window watching his family eat dinner.
  - Then he kneels at a keyhole and whispers a plea to be let in.
  - Next he pounds on the door and loudly demands to be let in.
  - Finally, he walks into the house like a ghost and has very specific contacts with each family member as he speaks.
- A woman who is telling how she shot her husband does so:
  - as if she were a little girl making excuses when caught doing something naughty, then as a hardened criminal in prison;
  - as if she were remembering a blissful, magical dream, then living through a terrifying nightmare;
  - as a suffragette campaign speech, then as a recipe for a delicious hors d'oeuvre;
  - as an act of self-defense by a woman who fears for her life.
- A woman's speech about her relationship with her mother might be investigated for opposite energies by doing it as:
  - a little girl delighted because her mother is fixing her hair;
  - a mature woman feeding an aged, frail, dying parent;
  - a teen-ager caught lying about skipping school, or mortified by being grilled about sexual activities, or in a rage about being denied permission to go on a trip with friends.
- You are working on Henry V's St. Crispan's Day speech (*Henry V*, IV.iii), rallying the troops to battle. In order to position yourself to play Henry's guilty fear that he may be leading all his men to destruction, you do the speech:
  - holding a young boy mortally wounded in the battle;
  - walking through a field hospital lifting sheets off the disfigured bodies of old friends;
  - saying good-bye before the battle to all your buddies, one by one.

Your job is to explore, not to be right.

In acting, as in all creative endeavors, your job is not to be right, but to carry out your exploration with full commitment. I still remember the day I first realized this liberating truth. I was a young actor and part of an ensemble that in one exhilarating rehearsal improvised nonstop for almost two hours. When we had finished, the director told us quite straightforwardly that the direction in which we had raced so zealously was "exactly wrong." I was crushed, and not at all consoled by the thought that going "wrong" had taught us something. That night I realized that I had been wholly inside the improvisation, listening and responding honestly and inventively to my fellow actors. I had done my job, which was to explore wholeheartedly.

What is most important in your opposites work is not that you have got the right opposite, but that you thoroughly investigate what you have proposed to yourself. Staying open to discoveries as you head off in a radically different direction is much more valuable than being "right" — which is something you have plenty of time to do. Setting out to be "right" inhibits exploration.

Chapter 16
Single Images

A single-image approach

You have been working on stories in which a character journeys through a variety of moments that must be shaped into a coherent whole. This is the usual case with narrative speeches.

Sometimes, however, a shorter speech (or perhaps part of a longer one) can be acted as if your character were suspended in time and reliving one action or event or metaphor — a *single image* that captures the essence of some aspect of your story. This approach is a valuable rehearsal tool, useful for positioning yourself to investigate specific dimensions of your speech in a focused, economical way.

Is there an aspect of your speech that you feel you have not yet explored? Does some issue now seem underdeveloped? Is there another opposite you want to investigate? These questions can be addressed by doing your speech while playing:

• a single instant in the story;
• one action or event;
• one metaphor;
• one moment in your first draft or opposite draft;
• an entirely new moment which focuses on one dimension of your material.

What you play might be realistic or metaphorical. You are free of the constraints of probable behavior in a conventional production. There are no boundaries or rules for creating a single image, except that you should keep what you are doing single, and in that sense simple. If you develop a scene with several different actions or a variety of events, you are getting away from the value of singleness. *Single* means *one*.

The speech should be spoken afresh from inside your single image. It should not sound the same as in your previous drafts, nor should it be spoken neutrally, as if you were a narrator doing a voiceover. Your tone and rhythm ought to be inspired by whatever you are playing.

If your single image anticipates something that happens late on in the text, there will be a moment when your text catches up to the image and brings it into focus. If you had an audience, it would at that moment realize what you are playing and how it relates to your story.

What might you get out of this exercise?

- Perhaps experimenting with a single image will help you to play a moment in your first draft more fully.
- What was a moment in an earlier draft may now become what you play for a section of text.
- An issue or undercurrent running through your speech may gain weight and depth.
- You may discover a new moment, action or energy, which you can incorporate in a new draft.
- It is quite likely that playing your speech as a single image will teach you something about the shape of your text.
- You may use this technique — as you will — to explore a new opposite.

There are several different approaches to playing single images.

Snapshots

Many years ago I was visiting elementary school classrooms as part of an arts-in-education initiative. I would invite the children to tell a story while "frozen" in a snapshot of one moment in the story, and I asked them to speak as if they were really living that moment now. One young girl told us about sleeping over at her best friend's and waking up in the middle of the night to discover that the apartment building was on fire. She created a remarkable sequence of three snapshots. In the first, she played the arsonist as he crouched down, match in hand, to set the fire. She told the whole story in a surreptitious whisper: "I was spending the night at my girlfriend's place ... " Then she gave us a snapshot of her friend in a hospital bed, recovering from burns. The same story came out haltingly this time, as if she were in a lot of pain. Lastly, she played herself as she was awakened that night by shouts of "Fire!" She spoke in a loud rush, in the panic of the moment. Her three single images explored three points of view — each of which might be incorporated into a version of the story that moved from event to event.

A young actress, using the same format, curled up on the floor in a twisted position and began a story about her cat having kittens. She came home one day to find one of the litter dead in the living room, then another in the bathroom, two each in the kitchen and the bedroom — all killed by their mother. Only gradually did those of us watching realize that we were staring at a snapshot of a dead kitten. There was indeed something dead in the tone of this story, which also captured how stunned the cat's owner had been as she discovered the bodies.

In *Red Cross* (Excerpt 21, Appendix A), Carol fantasizes that her migraine-prone head will explode some day while she's out skiing. The playwright's final image suggests a snapshot for the entire speech: "My body will stop at the bottom of the hill with just a bloody stump for a neck and both arms broken and both legs." How might playing this one moment (see 8.14) shape the whole speech? It is possible that, as the migraine begins, your voice would register a faint twinge of pain, and that this would build as Carol falls and her bones start breaking; after the climax, her suffering might subside as she slips quietly, blissfully into death's release from pain. But this "happy" outcome might also lead you to play the entire speech as a thrilling, invigorating escape from her affliction.

Snapshots are still, but they must have inner life. Your body must have a tension that positions you inside a moment full of energy, so that you don't feel inert. A single image should put you into action — even if your image does not move. If a snapshot feels dead or neutral or flat-footed, work on it until its physicality is specific, electric, and playable.

It is not difficult to sense the difference between an inactive image and a lively one.

16.1 For a snapshot of someone in danger of falling from a high cliff, strike a pose of being off-balance in the middle of the room. Now go to a wall (or to some interesting space available to you), reach up and grab something as if you were hanging by your fingertips. Lift one leg in an attempt to climb up, and twist your torso so that you can look back over your shoulder at the rocks below.

The second version has more detail and physical life in it, both for you and for the audience.

16.2 For a single image of a character lying dead on a battlefield, lie out flat. Speaking from this inert pose might sound pretty flat. Now arch the middle of your body off the floor as if in an agony of pain; imagine that your text is spoken as a death rattle, or as an urgent attempt to say something important before it is too late.

Sometimes it is interesting to allow the stillness of a snapshot to animate for one moment. This should happen on impulse.

Footage

If a still image is like a photograph, footage is like a snippet of film that has been looped, so that one event plays continuously as you improvise a variety of actions inspired by the image.

Imagine doing the whole *Red Cross* speech (Excerpt 21, Appendix A), with its extended description of skiing, as if you were speeding downhill: polling, leaning from side to side, crouching in an egg position, etc. There would be interesting tension between the vigorous action of this image and the broken stillness of the last bit of text. An alternative image might have Carol tumbling down the mountainside as her limbs break.

In William Mastrosimone's *The Woolgatherer*, a young woman named Rose has suffered physical abuse as a child. "Every day he would find some new reason to hit me, every single day." In response to this text an actor might develop footage of Rose being beaten by her father, receiving blow after blow, each in a different part of her body. The same image might be played for a passage that is not explicit about the violence in her past — for example, a speech about not trusting men. In this way, a single image can be used to explore a subtext — thoughts or images that lie below the surface of a text and influence how it is played.

At one point Rose tells a story about watching helplessly as a gang of boys stone to death a flock of flamingoes. For this speech an actor might explore footage in which one of those birds is hit again and again by rocks, or she might play the image of Rose being beaten and in this way explore how the events are connected.

An Action That Repeats

Another approach focuses on an action that repeats over and over. In Sam Shepard's *Buried Child*, a drunken character repeatedly tosses beer bottles violently into the wings; his speech is punctuated by the sound of breaking glass.

You faded into a stabbing gesture for the last part of Excerpt 19, Appendix A (see 11.1): "I was in the war. I know how to kill. I was over there. I know how to do it. I've done it before." In a single image version of the whole text, in which Weston talks about killing his wife because she's run off with a lawyer, you might use a stabbing action to punctuate Weston's threats with a rhythmic pulse:

> I'll track them all down. (*stab*) Every last one of them. (*stab*) Your mother, too. (*stab*) I'll track her down (*stab*) and shoot them in their bed. (*stab*) In their hotel bed. (*stab*) I'll splatter their brains (*stab*) all over the vibrating bed. (*stab*)

And so on. This action might repeat at the same intensity, or it might fade up and down, in which case it would exemplify the next possibility for a single image.

An Action That Builds

Many years ago on PBS I saw a play (its title is lost to me) in which an African-American actress had developed a speech in terms of the ecstatic shaking that happens in some church services. She began the action as a faint tremor, almost imperceptible, and built it, in a curve familiar to you, to a climax of convulsive spasms before she collapsed.

You took this approach to Wesley's story about the fight between his parents when you faded your movement from the stillness of listening like an animal (a possible snapshot for that speech) to bouncing off the walls (see 11.3). This action is metaphorically inspired: Wesley is a superball (or a pinball, a subatomic particle, etc.).

An Unfolding Image

A single image may develop through different stages and include a few simple changes of action, as long as it is focused on the unfolding of one image.

A single image for Weston's story about the bath (Speech 8, Appendix B) might involve his slowly lowering himself into the hot tub, putting one leg forward at a time, then sitting back, perhaps sinking deeper, etc.

Throughout *Buried Child*, a character named Tilden, whose perceptions seem none too trustworthy, has talked about what's growing in the garden out back of the house. Everyone else in the family knows that they haven't had a garden in years. Near the end of the play, his mother Halie reports that a garden has indeed sprung up.

Read Speech 6, Appendix B.

Imagine playing this text as an unfolding single image: starting in a crouch, then rising ever so slowly; perhaps finding a moment when the sprout breaks through into the air; near the end, raising your arms toward the sun.

Internalizing a Single Image

There are times when a single-image exercise provides you with just the right energy for a section of text, but for some reason you do not want to make the image visible in performance.

- Perhaps physicalizing the image is not feasible given the style or the resources of your production.
- Perhaps your image is so wildly metaphorical or anachronistic that it would call attention to itself.
- Perhaps you want to play the energy of your single image but you are interested in other staging.
- Perhaps the image, which has put you in touch with an undercurrent in your speech, needs to remain below the surface as your subtext.

When you are interested in performing a single image without acting it out physically, you can *internalize* it — that is, play it in your imagination while you remain still (or perform other actions). The single image should continue to energize and shape the text, so that it sounds just as it did when you played the image full out.

In this way, actors can secretly play an image (or implicit scene) as the driving force behind any scene or speech.

When you are internalizing an image, you can consider playing one or two small actions inspired by it.

Using a Single-Image Approach to Explore Opposites

Once you have zeroed in on an opposite, you must decide how you want to explore it.

- You can use the blocking of your first draft as a starting point and allow your opposite to inspire differences not only of mood but of action, as in your opposite draft.
- You can create an entirely new set of circumstances as the context for playing an opposite, as you did when you explored a new pair of opposites and played half of your text.
- Or you can use a single-image format to ground you in the opposite energy that you want to explore.

In *A Streetcar Named Desire*, Blanche DuBois tells the story of her young husband's suicide. If an actor were interested in exploring the part of Blanche that feels responsible for his death, she might play the speech while holding a gun on him as if she were about to pull the trigger.

When you use single images to explore opposites, you might use half of your text or less, the same section for each image. This is an economical way to get a feel for a new direction before you fully commit to it — in which case you must then play the opposite for the whole speech.

Playing part of your speech as a single image is a useful format for warming up opposites before you work on putting them together (the focus of Chapter 17).

For Your Own Speech

1. Create two very different single images for your speech. Use a third to a half of your text, the same section, whether from the beginning, middle, or end.

2. Explore one new opposite by using a single-image approach.

3. Perform your choice of these single images in a sit-down version, in which you literally sit on your hands. Internalize the single image you have chosen so that it energizes and shapes your text. Warm the image up on your feet — play it full out — right before you internalize it. If you wish, you can make one physical move inspired by the image.

Guidelines

Your text — and how you have been playing it — is the most likely source of single image possibilities. Consider images and events and moments in your story. This is an opportunity to explore your speech in light of one element.

A single image may be implicit in your text's reference to a past or future event.

It is also possible to create an image of your own in order to focus on a particular issue.

If you want to get in touch with an energy that lies below the surface of your speech, what single image might you play?

Focus on playing the circumstances and the action of your images — not on playing emotions.

A single image should provide you with a simple and active way to investigate something that has caught your attention. You may not know at first why it interests you. Rehearsing is the art of positioning yourself to discover something you don't know.

Chapter 17
Layering

Layering is the term we will use for the process of putting opposites together. The result is a layered speech, in which opposites have been combined and carefully orchestrated, so that the interplay between them embodies your character's inner conflict.

Layering is a further evolution of your work so far, not a complete departure. Return to your first draft and build on it. Use as much of your previous blocking as makes sense; perhaps the spine of your first draft is still quite playable, even with the addition of conflicting energies.

Your physical score will certainly change to some degree. New actions discovered in your exploration of opposites and of single images will replace moments in your first draft. New impulses may emerge as you return to your earlier work. Feedback from others may lead to adjustments. At the farthest extreme, you may be inspired by recent developments to make a fresh start on the blocking, retaining only actions that insist on sticking with you. But the first draft remains your starting point, and you should make changes selectively.

You must continue to attend to the central task — reliving the story. Be careful not to lose specificity about what happens from moment to moment.

Work-throughs

Playing your score for a speech or a scene with one issue in mind is a necessary and valuable skill for actors. I call such explorations *work-throughs,* and they can be about any acting issue, not just opposites. You might work through a speech, for example, looking for spatial impulses, rhythmic variety, or opportunities to speak directly to the audience. In the vocabulary of scientific research, a work-through isolates the variable that is the focus of your experiment.

A work-through is part performance, part stop-and-start exploration. You work your way from moment to moment, experimenting with impulses inspired by a specific question you have posed to yourself.

Up to now, you have focused on opposites one by one. You have worked through your speech as if each of them were the only truth; this allows you to examine moment by moment how a particular opposite might find expression. In Chapter 15 this process was referred to as *mining* the speech, as if an opposite were a mineral vein running through your performance. This brings us to the geological metaphor implicit in the term layering.

You've probably seen one of those schematic drawings of the different layers of sediment and rock that lie under the surface of the earth.

This is one way to think about how different opposites co-exist in a speech: there is a surface layer, with one or more strata underneath. These hidden layers make themselves known to us by how they shape the surface. Just as a geologist knows that a layer of rock underlies a hilly area because of its configuration, so most of us can see, for example, the anger beneath a smile.

17.1 Imagine that you are very angry with someone. What does this do to your face? Now try to hide your anger beneath a smile. Stay infuriated, but smile very broadly as your cover.

Note how the surface smile is shaped by the underlying anger. Smiling can also, of course, be layered with other energies.

17.2 Imagine a simple set of circumstances in which:
- you make a brave effort to smile while terrified;
- your smile is layered with sadness.

We all learn how to read such terrain, how to see through the surface to what lies below.

When an under-layer surfaces — when a stratum of rock is exposed, or jealousy reveals itself — we know that this layer existed below the topsoil before it became visible. An emotion doesn't come out of nowhere. It builds up below the surface and rises toward it. If it is repressed or resisted — if anger, for example, has a lid on it — then there may come a moment of explosion, when feeling erupts like a volcano.

Non-geological metaphors may be more apt for some opposites.

Weston's impulses in *Curse of the Starving Class* to flee his family and then return to them may seem more like a tug-of-war or the attraction/repulsion of magnets than like geological layers. You might think of certain opposites as threads of different colors running through a tangled weave. But we will use the term *layering* for the process of putting together opposites of every sort.

You have already worked on the first two steps of the layering process.

Step 1: Consider possible opposites.

You have already explored several opposites. You may wish to continue working with these, though perhaps in a different combination than you had first imagined. You might, for example, pair the energy of your first draft with an opposite you investigated in circumstances far removed from those of your script, or you might combine the thrust of your opposite draft with the direction you developed in a single-image format.

It's also possible that you want to keep exploring. Your understanding of the opposites on which you have worked may have evolved or radically changed. Two of them may have coalesced into one. New directions may have occurred to you. You may wish to return to the process outlined in Chapter 15 to search for other opposites to explore.

Step 2: For each of the opposites you are interested in, play the speech as if that opposite were the whole truth.

Before layering opposites together, it is essential that you work through the whole speech to investigate how each opposite might manifest itself moment to moment, from beginning to end. Play everything in the speech from the perspective of the opposite you are working on. Success in developing strong layers depends on your openness to the possibility that there is an opposite version of every moment — that some sense can be found in approaching any part of your speech from the point of view of the radically new direction you are considering. As you begin the layering process, you should remain unprejudiced as to what's A and what's Z.

Your goal is to create, for each of your opposites, a series of moments that make it a layer running through the entire speech. Even if it comes to light only periodically, a layer is always present, shaping the surface.

Step 3: Decide which opposites you wish to include in your speech as layers.

What's your A, what's your Z? You should focus on the central conflict(s) of the speech. Which tensions seem most important, most revealing, most intriguing?

The opposites with which you will develop a layered version of your speech may not be polar opposites, nor even logical opposites, but they should be radically different energies that put your character into conflict with himself or herself. They may be more like A and H or A and Q than A and Z, but for shorthand purposes, we will refer to the opposites that you are layering as A and Z.

You will most likely work with two opposites. Occasionally you may decide to work with three layers or with two pairs of opposites.

Your opposites should be named with language from your text, and you should use that language to think and talk about your layering work.

If you decide to continue with an opposite that you have already explored, dig deeper and "mine" more moments. Put yourself back in touch with the moment-to-moment truth of your opposite.

If you decide to work with a new opposite, or with one that you explored for only part of your text, you should develop it in a work-through of the whole speech, as you did for your opposite draft.

Layering A and Z Together

When you are putting your opposites together in a layered draft, there are three possibilities at any given point: a moment may be essentially A or Z, or it may be A/Z, both at once.

Alternating A and Z

Let's consider first how a character may go back and forth between A and Z. As A and Z alternate, there may be short moments and longer sections:

A———Z—A–Z————A–Z–A–Z———A————————Z——

Of course, not all A and Z moments will be of the same magnitude. There's a considerable difference between a climactic Z moment and a little twinge of z. So the spine of a layered speech might be more like

335

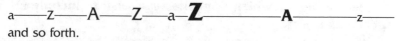

and so forth.

Occasionally the transition from one opposite to another is a sudden, high-contrast change of energy. Most of the time, getting from A to Z will involve a fade — a cross-fade, as A wanes and Z waxes. Some A to Z fades, of course, will be shaped as builds or decrescendos. A truer graphic representation of a layered speech might look like this:

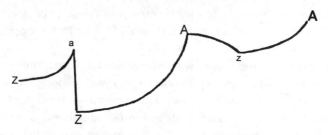

In this hypothetical shape, the second change is a sudden cutback from a lower-case "a" moment to strong "Z" moment.

Fading from A to Z

How many times you fade from A to Z to A depends on your material and on how you interpret it in terms of the opposites you are working with. Some fades are longer and some quite short, though no less carefully shaped. Living through each moment of an A-to-Z fade is critical to acting your character's conflict.

Imagine a trader on the floor of the New York Stock Exchange who engages daily in an adrenaline-drenched frenzy of buying and selling, yelling and signaling. Let's call this energy A. Energy Z is total relaxation, as he or she sits in a patch of sun in a green area on a gorgeous spring day, savoring lunch and dreaming of some activity which is very un-A. Here's a scenario for a gradual journey from A to Z and back again.

17.1 *Begin on the floor of the Exchange, bellowing, waving valuable pieces of paper, reacting viscerally to the ups and downs of the market. Time for lunch: you stomp off the floor, slamming doors open with enough force to knock a football player over, lunge down the stairs onto the sidewalk, taking no notice of the day or anyone around you. At the corner, you rip your wallet out and slap some money down for a hotdog and a soda. A block later you plop yourself down on a bench and tear the wrapping off your hotdog as if not getting it open right now could cost your clients a bundle. Your first bite is like a predator biting off its victim's head. You choke it down. Slowly, very slowly, the adrenaline drains out of your body. You actually take the time to chew your second bite, and you begin to taste it: it tastes good. You start to notice what a gorgeous spring day it is. You feel the mix of temperatures on your face. The air is like a bath. You whip your jacket off — there is still a lot of A energy in you, because it takes a while to loosen its grip. You sit back on the bench and relax your weight against it, a few pounds at a time. And so on. Perhaps you think about the vacation you will take next month or about seeing the person you're in love with tomorrow night. At the height of Z, the hotdog is the best you've ever eaten, and you savor it like a gourmet meal. You can't remember a more beautiful day in New York City. You approach bliss. When you look at your watch, you notice, with the trace of a smile on your face, that it is time to get back to the Exchange. You love your job. You amble back in an entirely different rhythm than when you left, jacket over your shoulder. As you pass the hotdog stand, you smile at the vendor, who doesn't recognize you, since you are an entirely different person. As you turn a corner and see the Exchange, a tiny change takes place in your system. At first the change is imperceptible, but gradually your pace begins to quicken and your smile to stiffen. This fade back toward A is held back by the strength and attraction of Z, even as your relish for A draws you forward. You arrive at the stairs leading up to the building's entrance. With each step the rate of your transformation changes. In the hall you grab your messages and rip open a half dozen envelopes with an energy that is more and more A. You arrive back on the floor of the Exchange and begin trading. It takes a while to get back up to speed, but at the very end there is a rush to a climax of A energy.*

This scenario is actually much simpler than the dilemmas of most dramatic characters. Imagine a trader who is torn between work and play: who longs to be in the park when s/he is on the floor of the Exchange, and who, when s/he finally gets there, can't wait to get back to work.

Moral dilemmas

In *Macbeth* the morality of the conflict between ambition and murder is relatively clear. But one can imagine a Claudius who is a better king (and a better husband to Gertrude) than Hamlet's father was; that does not make murdering his brother less wrong, but it complicates the crime to think that some of its motives may have been well intentioned. Richard II is ruining the country, but he is king by divine right; is it morally permissible for anyone to dethrone him?

A and Z are not necessarily good and evil, right and wrong, the high road versus the low. Your opposites may represent the conflict between alternatives that are both good. Should you devote a decade of your adult life to taking care of an ailing parent or should your pursue your career as a civil rights lawyer? Should you go on the Habitat for Humanity trip to build housing for the needy or should you prepare carefully for Tuesday's rehearsal? Should you obey your father and pretend to read a book so that the king can eavesdrop on Hamlet, or should you alert your lover that he is being spied on, as some Ophelias do? Should Athi take the fish and the butter that his mother has carried all this way and share the food with his fellow prisoners, or should he stick by his political convictions and refuse? Dramatic characters are often torn by competing obligations and by virtues in conflict with each other.

A/Z: ambivalence

Layering may lead to the discovery that a moment or section of your speech is A and Z at the same time. A/Z moments are moments of ambivalence. *The Random House College Dictionary* defines ambivalence as "uncertainty or fluctuation, especially when caused by [...] a simultaneous desire to say or do two opposite things." This is a perfect way to define the agitated, off-balance, highly conflicted state of being A/Z: *a simultaneous desire to say or do two opposite things.* Characters can be ambivalent with respect to opposing impulses, reactions, objectives — and most everything else.

Conflicted characters are in fact rarely 100% A or Z — at defining moments and climaxes, perhaps, and then only briefly. Most of the time they live somewhere between their opposites. In this light, characters are more or less ambivalent most of the time. Mixing larger and smaller percentages of opposites (90/10, 80/20, 70/30) results in moments which are essentially A or Z but which have strong undertows or faint nuances of the conflicting energy. In such cases, A/Z might be written A/z or a/Z. Layering makes it possible to put backspin on any line or action, so that your character is moving in one direction but spinning in the other.

At times of crisis, as your character approaches a turning point with respect to his or her inner conflict, the mix of A and Z may be 50/50, which can be electrifying. Just as opposite colors of equal intensity seem to vibrate when placed next to each other, A/Z moments vibrate with opposites energy when the push and pull are equal.

In moments of 50/50 ambivalence, it is as if your character were balancing on a thin edge where two steeply inclined slopes — your opposites — meet. On such an edge, as on a tightrope, it is difficult to balance: you wobble and teeter. You might fall either way. Putting your character on an edge is a great way to get him or her off balance.

If you further imagine that this edge is quite sharp, and that it is not level but slanted, so that you start to slide, you are then, in the immortal words of the satirical songwriter Tom Lehrer, "sliding down the razor blade of life."

Another way of picturing ambivalence is to imagine your character straddling a fence, with one leg on each side. Suppose that the fence is higher than your character's legs are long: that uncomfortable condition of not being able to put both feet down is very like the inner conflict of an ambivalent moment.

Whether a given moment should be scored as A or Z or A/Z is a question of interpretation.

the murderous shower
wounds me, dyes me black and I, I revel
like the Earth when the spring rains come down (Speech 1, Appendix B)

17.2 *Imagine that in a first draft of this speech you had developed a score in which Clytemnestra, on her knees, revels in the blood by rubbing it on her face, her arms, her torso. It is as if the last ten years had been a drought and now she bathes in the blessed rain. Work on this for a few moments.*

339

The power of opposites often lies in quite straightforwardly making an about-face and exploring actions that lie 180 degrees in the other direction. Here, for example, Clytemnestra has been rubbing the blood into her skin. What action would be a polar opposite? The answer is obvious, and it is in fact justified by the text, in which Clytemnestra says the "murderous" shower of blood "wounds" her and dyes her "black." There is a dark undercurrent beneath the joyous image.

17.3 *Now Clytemnestra wants to get the blood off her. She rubs her face, her arms, her torso, but this time she is trying very hard to wipe herself clean. It may help to endow the blood with hideous sensory properties that are best left to the individual imagination. Don't even think about what she is feeling — let your action define what is going on inside her.*

How might these opposites be layered together?

17.4 *Go back to the first version: rubbing the blood in. As you speak the text, let this action gradually fade into its opposite, wiping the blood off. Here Clytemnestra begins by celebrating, then takes in what is happening, and — in stages — becomes horrified. "I, I revel" is what she wants to feel but cannot. The first impulse to get the blood off you should be small, evolving as seamlessly as possible out of its opposite. Try this fade a couple of times.*

17.5 *Try fading in the other direction: start in the getting-it-off beat, as if Clytemnestra's initial reaction were quite naturally to recoil, then let her fade by finely calibrated degrees into bathing in the blood.*

Both these approaches are valid and interesting. A third possibility is that the two impulses are simultaneous, in which case Clytemnestra is wiping the blood off and rubbing it in at the same moment. Such an ambivalent reaction would not be surprising in these circumstances: just as she is experiencing the triumphal climax of her revenge, blood spurts all over her and, let us imagine, puts her in touch with the horror of what she has done.

17.6 *How might your hands contact your body if you were rubbing Agamemnon's blood into your skin and trying to get it off you at the same time? Approach this in experimental fashion. Establish one action and maintain it while mixing in the other. Try it the other way* around. *Each recipe will be unique. In performance one sometimes re-improvises the mix of simultaneous opposites which have been defined in rehearsal.*

**It is right and more than right. He flooded
the vessel of our proud house with misery,
with the vintage of the curse and now
he drains the dregs. My lord is home at last.** (Speech 1, Appendix B)

Let us imagine a Clytemnestra whose triumphant joy (A) is mixed with grief (Z) as it dawns on her that her husband is really dead. In order to confront the chorus, she might well try to resist her grief until she can no longer hold it off.

17.7 *Imagine that Clytemnestra approaches Agamemnon's body as she finishes her speech. "It is right and more than right" is spoken to herself as much as to the chorus: she is talking to that part of her that feels it is not right. Grief is welling up in her despite herself, but still she tries to rejoice. On "My lord is home at last" she sinks to her knees, half exulting, half grieving. Get yourself on that edge.*

You can take it back with you, I don't want it. (Excerpt 1, Appendix A)

17.8 *Athi is in prison because of his political opposition to the land-owning class. He refuses to take the fish and the butter from his mother because it comes from the landlord's wife. Get something you can hold as if it were a parcel of food.*

* *A: Thrust the food away from you. It comes from the enemy and is salt in your wounds. Remember Athi's rage.*
* *Z: You're starving and your fellow prisoners are starving. Maybe the morally responsible thing to do would be to take it. This is precious nutrition, and very tempting. Hold onto it as if it were worth a fortune.*
* *A/Z: Explore both impulses simultaneously. Try this several times.*

**He falls to such perusal of my face
As he would draw it** (Speech 17, Appendix B)

17.9 *You have imagined playing this moment — as Ophelia's hand traces her own features — with two radically different energies (see 15.21).*

* *A: Hamlet's stare freaks her out. Her face is tense and ever so slightly*

recoils from the "touch" of his perusal.

• *Z: This is the first time she's seen Hamlet since her father made her break off with him. She leans into the touch, which is a sensuous caress.*

• *A/Z: Explore playing both at once: she is ambivalent.*

You have already met Johnny from Athol Fugard's *Hello and Goodbye*: he's the fellow who tried to get his father to eat "warm buttered toast with the silver little fishes" (see 4.1-4). For his entire youth, Johnny has nursed his invalid father night and day. He has had no life of his own — no job, no relationships, nothing that gets him out of the house for more than a few hours. At the climax of the play he reveals that his father died a few weeks ago, and it hits him like a ton of bricks that he is on his own for the first time. "From now on it's you," he says to himself, "— just you."

There are many possible directions to explore in such a complex moment. It is certain that Johnny has more than one response to his new circumstances. In order to get inside his ambivalence, first you need to get solidly in touch with each of the opposites.

Translating emotion words

For purposes of the following exercise, I use words that name emotions as shorthand — as directors sometimes do. It will help you to translate these words into actions, implicit scenes and images that you can play.

• What does Johnny do as he has these various reactions? Placing yourself in specific physical circumstances will generate impulses to action.

• Use your narrative imagination to translate emotions into scenes that will put you in touch with what the character is feeling. In order to play Johnny's grief, for example, you might place him at the funeral or in his father's empty room. Implicit in Johnny's excitement is his discovery of all the possibilities now open to him: you might imagine him racing up and down a busy street full of exciting nightlife. Whether you play such circumstances physically (with adjustments for your present circumstances) or internalize them is up to you. A narrative approach helps you to situate yourself in a character's emotional terrain.

> • Metaphorical images may also help you to get inside what a character is feeling: Johnny is a kite free to go this way or that, as the wind blows; he is buried alive in his father's coffin; he is on a roller coaster, just approaching the scariest peak.

You're on your own, Johnny Smit. From now on it's you — just you.

17.10 The play takes place in a kitchen; the father's empty bedroom is right next to it.

• *A: Play this moment as a quiet surge of joy. You're free!*

• *Z: Now say these words with a sense of loss and emptiness. You're terribly alone.*

• *A/Z: Joy and a lonely feeling of loss.*

• *Try a different Z: as if an anxiety attack were welling up.*

• *A/Z: Joy and anxiety.*

• *Yet another Z: anger that his youth has been wasted and anger that his father is dead.*

• *A/Z: Loss and rage.*

he made me mad (Excerpt 12, Appendix A)

17.11 Hotspur's reaction to the foppish courtier is characteristically hotheaded. It is certainly possible that this is a moment of pure anger. But an actor interested in going beyond character type might well decide to make visible other dimensions of Hotspur — and other energies inside the story.

• *A: Put Hotspur's anger into your body. How does Hotspur behave? Implicit in his movement might be an impulse to knock the courtier down, for example. Use the facial expression created by those three m's as part of your physicality.*

• *Z: Eleven lines earlier, Hotspur mentioned that the courtier had continued to smile and talk "as the soldiers bore dead bodies by." We imagined Hotspur looking at fallen comrades at that moment (see 11.9). Let us suppose that his grief has not evaporated, and that it is a layer present through the entire speech. Play this line as if Hotspur were standing in a graveyard, gently placing a flower on the grave of a friend who died in the battle.*

• *A/Z: Rage and grief. What happens as these mix?*

There is another layer to be explored in this speech. Accused of not handing over the prisoners as requested, Hotspur's defense is to make people laugh with him about how it happened.

- *How would this line sound if you were approaching the climax of a really funny story?*
- *Explore mixing all three energies: rage, grief and laughter. This is a story about being infuriated by an absurdly funny character in very sad circumstances.*

The hyphenated quality of life

There is no such thing as pure anger, wrote anthropologist Jules Henry in *Pathways to Madness*. Anger is always hyphenated with something: there is anger-grief, anger-embarrassment, anger-hurt, anger-shame, anger-guilt, anger-jealousy, etc.

Actors might well generalize that principle. We rarely feel pure emotions; our reactions to events are usually more complex. Actors should attend to the hyphenated quality of life. The simple format we have used to explore ambivalent moments can be used to hyphenate speeches, scenes, characters, and whole performances.

Step 4: Work through your speech several times, playing A and Z and A/Z moments on impulse.

How do you go about deciding what's A and Z and A/Z? The process should be intuitive, not analytical. It's not a question of figuring out what's right so much as discovering, on your feet, which version of each moment and section seems truest, most revealing, and most relevant to your interest in the material. Move from layer to layer on impulse.

Remaining open

How many transitions your layered draft will have, how long they will be, precisely where they begin and end — these are empirical questions. You must experiment on your feet, because impulses may lead you to surprising discoveries. But how can you surprise yourself if you have already made up your mind about what's A and what's Z? You must remain open to the possibility that a given moment might be either A or Z — or, as is very likely, somewhere in between.

In which layer should you start? Trying it one way, then the other, will eventually give you the answer. Each time you work through the speech, make note of moments and sections that strike you as especially A or Z, but stay interested in what happens if you play them as part of the opposite layer. When a moment doesn't seem to work one way, play it the opposite way in the next work-through.

As you begin to make decisions, you will already be attached to certain possibilities. Some parts of your speech will feel right when played as A, others as Z. Most of these choices will go with the grain of the text, but a few, in the surprising way of opposites, may strike you as truthful because they contradict or belie the words. You may have discovered points at which it seems truest to play both opposites at once, so that your character is ambivalent.

But it is likely that a good number of moments will play truthfully either way; you will have to make choices as you put your layered draft together. If it is not yet clear how your opposites relate to certain sections, you can leave them as unmapped terrain until later steps in the layering process.

Each occurrence of A and Z should be explored in terms of relative duration and intensity. Some sections will be longer, some shorter; some moments will be of greater or lesser magnitude. Eventually all this will be carefully shaped, but at this stage you needn't worry about from/to considerations. Exploratory work can be rough; leaps and loose ends are for the moment permissible.

Be on the lookout for highly ambivalent moments, when both layers are strongly in play at the same time and your character teeters, precariously balanced on an edge. Such moments occur especially at turning points — at moments of crisis and decision, when A and Z are rather equally matched in their struggle for your character's soul.

When you have tentatively mapped out the terrain of your speech in terms of A, Z, and A/Z, you are ready for from/to considerations.

Step 5: Work through the speech several times, focusing on transitions from one layer to another and back again.

Improvising transitions from one opposite to another is a process that can lead to discoveries. Stay loose. Work impulsively. Everything is provisional. Even moments you feel sure about might change. Stay open to surprising yourself.

Some transitions may be fairly sudden. Cave-ins, eruptions, impulsive decisions, comic switches, and hysterical swings all find truthful expression in abrupt changes of energy.

Most transitions from one layer to another will be fades, some relatively short, others quite long.

Because you are fading from one opposite to another, you are really cross-fading two different energies: as A waxes, Z wanes, and vice-versa.

Transitions should happen not in pauses but on the lines: fade as you speak.

Knitting the seams between opposites

All the from/to methods discussed in Chapter 12 may be used in shaping transitions between opposites. In general, you should focus on how one opposite develops directly out of the other. You may, for example, find opportunities to knit the seams between your opposites.

In the soliloquy which opens *Richard III*, Shakespeare is careful to root Richard's villainy in the pain he has suffered as a result of his deformities. Suppose that you were interested in working on Richard as victim and as villain. In the following passage, there is a seam between these opposites at "And therefore, since I cannot prove a lover ... "

I, that am curtailed of this fair proportion,	
Cheated of feature by <u>dissembling</u> nature	*deceitful*
Deformed, unfinished, sent before my time	
Into this breathing world, scarce half made up –	
And that so lamely and unfashionable	
That dogs bark at me as I <u>halt</u> by them –	*limp*
Why I, in this weak piping time of peace,	
Have no delight to pass away the time,	
Unless to spy my shadow in the sun	
And <u>descant on</u> my own deformity.	*talk cleverly about*
And therefore, since I cannot prove a lover	
To entertain these fair well-spoken days,	
I am determined to prove a villain	
And hate the idle pleasures of these days.	

17.12 Shape your reading of this passage so that Richard's evil resolution grows out of a vulnerability with which an audience can sympathize.

Start in pain: he was born a monster that dogs bark at, he will never be loved by a woman, even his mother rejected him at birth. Move gradually toward the energy of "I am determined to prove a villain." Anticipate the seam.

Living through this transition between opposites tells in miniature the story of how Richard became a villain.

Playing a substratum

Whenever an opposite surfaces, you know that it has been running below the surface for some time as a substratum. Playing a substratum before it surfaces makes good from/to sense and enriches your speech by layering one opposite under the other.

Suppose that Z surfaces and you realize that it must be a substratum under the preceding A section. A good technique in such a situation is to play part of your speech that is strongly Z, then loop back immediately to the beginning of the A section you're exploring and play Z as an undercurrent, faint at first, then growing stronger until it comes to light.

17.13 Return to Richard III *and play his last two lines very strongly, full of a villain's determination to hurt those who he feels have hurt him. Then go right back to the beginning of this text and play Richard's pain. His vulnerability, as is usually the case, should make him quite young and innocent. Under this, play a hunger for revenge ever so slightly at first, as if resentment were welling up in a child; let this gradually mature until the substratum surfaces as a grown-up villain.*

When you are layering, playing a substratum is an alternative way of thinking about knitting seams. Playing Z under A anticipates Z's emergence. It also gives your work an edge, since Z, however faintly, is played at the same time as A. The result is true to the hyphenated quality of life: Richard's villainy is really anger-hurt.

Just as Z might in this case be layered under A, a substratum of vulnerability might be layered under moments of villainy. Staying in touch with Richard's pain makes it possible for the actor to sympathize with him, and for an audience to feel for Richard even as his actions horrify them. If he is played one-dimensionally, an audience is likely to dismiss him out of hand as an evil person whose story is not relevant to their lives.

Understanding the relationship between layers

Carefully crafted transitions are essential for achieving flow. But they are not merely a formal consideration, a matter of polish. Conflict is embodied and revealed in how your character goes back and forth between opposites. A conflicted speech is not about A and Z so much as it is about the interplay and the movement between the two: that is where the real action takes place. It is in the from/to of a layered speech that the audience sees your character's divided self.

Why does your character move toward and away from this A and this Z? What makes them wax and wane? In what specific way do these opposites trigger each other? Is there a pattern in how your character moves between layers? It is the relationship between your opposites that you must act. You need to develop a feel for the dynamics of your character's inner conflict.

Inventing a psychology for your character

In Chapter 15, the section called "Questions That Can Generate Opposites" suggests how you might think in general terms about the interaction of your A and Z. One part of your character may be trying to convince or calm or motivate another part, for example. Your character may exhibit flashes of what he or she aspires to be. Perhaps your character hides a secret self, an alter ego with a different personality and conflicting values.

Out of the specifics of your story you must create a unique portrait of a divided self. You must *tell yourself the story* of how your character moves back and forth between the opposites that conflict him or her.

Finding the particular push-pull, yin-yang of your opposites is a complex, rich, fascinating process. It is in this way that creative actors invent the psychology of their characters, rather than pigeonholing them in conventional categories.

The relationship between your layers will depend on the particulars of your material. The suggestion that Richard III is a child when he feels vulnerable, and that he "grows up" vengeful whenever he does something evil (see 17.12-13), is an example of inventing a psychology based on opposites.

Imagine a person whose opposites make her extremely shy sometimes and exhibitionistic at others. How might she get from A to Z to A again? What story might you tell yourself about such a character? What metaphors might help you explore this sort of from/to? Does her shyness sprout like a weed and quickly bloom into exhibitionism, or does she struggle out of a homely cocoon? Does she peel off her shyness like a stripper? Does the exhibitionist wilt? Become self-conscious? Act as if she suddenly felt naked? Hide? Maybe you create this metaphorical psychology: her shyness becomes so intolerably dull that she bursts into a vivid, shocking color; this makes her feel so exposed that she fades like a chameleon to a color that blends into her surroundings, until she disappears.

Step 6: Shape the journey.

After you have determined when your character is A and Z and A/Z, and after you have explored transitions, you must make some decisions about the overall shape of your layered speech. Presumably you know where your character begins and ends with respect to the opposites, and you have worked out a good deal about what happens in-between. You know whether the conflict gets resolved or is left hanging.

But what is the relative strength of A and Z throughout the course of the speech, and what does this teach you about its shape? Is there a turning point when one opposite gains the upper hand? Does the speech march toward a resolution of the inner conflict? A layered speech can sometimes be shaped as a series of builds, each ascending higher, to a final, climactic opposite.

Does your character go through a period of fluctuation? Some speeches are roller coaster rides, with a variety of ascents and descents, and lots of twists and turnabouts. Hysterical, unstable, and highly ambivalent characters, for example, are prone to rapid switches from one energy to its opposite.

Other speeches have fewer transitions but more edges and undertows. At the furthest extreme, a speech might be one long fade from A to Z, with many carefully calibrated stages in-between.

Three exercises can help you to map your character's journey through the speech.

- In the margin of your text, estimate the relative strength of A and Z in terms of percentages: 80/20, 60/40, 30/70, 10/90, etc. Note where each layer is strongest and weakest.
- Then graph the speech in terms of its opposites. Two possible formats are a single-line graph in which A is up and Z is down; or a two-line graph, in which separate lines for A and Z cross and intersect. Label the major highs and lows with words or phrases from your text. What do you see? Is there a progression, a pattern? Sit and monitor your graph as you read your speech with performance intensity. Does what you are playing correspond to what is on paper? Make adjustments — either to your graph or to your performance.
- "This is the story of a character who ... " Finish this sentence in terms of your opposites.

You should then be ready to relive the story in terms of your character's inner conflict.

Principles of Layering

Although the specifics will differ for each character you create, several general principles are useful guidelines for the process of putting your opposites together. They are as relevant to scene work and role development as they are to work on speeches. These principles should become an instinctive part of your work on inner conflict.

A. The more ..., the more ...

The more your character feels the pressure of A, the more s/he moves toward Z, and vice versa. Opposites feed each other. For example:

- The more time he spends with his family, the more he feels claustrophobic. The more time he spends away from them, the more he misses them.
- The more frightened she is, the more bravely she talks about what she's going to do. The more bravely she talks, the more she scares herself.
- The more reservations the soldier has about the morality of following his orders, the more brutally he carries them out — and the guiltier he feels.

350

• The more she insists that something is true, the more she doubts it. The more uncertain she feels, the more dogmatic she becomes.
• The more attracted Jill is, the more she shies away from Jack. The less she looks at him, the more attractive he becomes.
• The poorer his self-image, the more he acts superior — and the more he feels foolish.
• The wilder his fantasies, the more rigidly he controls his behavior. The more he denies himself, the more he desires.

I coil him round and round
in the wealth, the robes of doom, and then I strike him
once, twice, and at each stroke he cries in agony
17.14 Imagine that as you watch Agamemnon being wrapped in towels after his bath, you raise your double-headed axe. But you are beset by a potent combination of pity for Agamemnon and horror at what you are about to do. You feel that you will not be able to carry through what you have dreamed of for ten years. You feel as if your arms were being held back. It takes a tremendous effort to overcome the opposing energies, and this translates into a series of brutal blows.

The violence is proportional to all that holds Clytemnestra back. The more she doesn't want to do it, the harder she strikes.

Malvolio in Shakespeare's *Twelfth Night* is a perfect embodiment of how opposites provoke each other to extremes. He is an exceedingly strict overseer of his mistress's household, and nearly everyone thinks of him as a puritanical kill-joy. When Malvolio is tricked into believing that his mistress is in love with him, his transformation into a ridiculous lover reveals and releases what has been bottled up inside him. In hindsight, we realize that his severity was a way of keeping a lid on his own wild desires. The more this servant senses that his aspirations to be a master would turn the existing social order on its head, the more he insists on adhering to rules. In the same way, Malvolio's superior airs are in proportion to his sense of inferiority, and his arrogance is a measure of his insecurity.

B. Since A and Z drive each other in the opposite direction, layering them together should never involve compromise.

Inner conflict is a seesaw: when A is up, Z is down. It is of course at the two ends of this seesaw that dramatic highs and lows happen. A character whose opposites have been compromised sits near the fulcrum, where there is relatively little movement. Such a character is much too balanced to be interesting.

If opposites creep toward each other, they become weak, pale and tepid. Strong opposites incite each to extremes. Keep your opposites in high contrast. The swing from one extreme to the other becomes especially volatile at moments of crisis, as warring opposites fight for their lives. Until they come to a peaceful resolution — or one opposite is defeated — your opposites should energize each other, so that internal conflict remains high.

Making opposites roughly equal

Opposites need to be worthy opponents, roughly equal in intensity.

In Jane Martin's *Talking with …*, a collection of monologs for women, one character talks about growing up around snake handling at her family's church. Imagine that after working on your first draft, you realize that its main thrust is that snake handling is a positive experience, quite exciting. That's A. For an opposite, you pick up on another energy in the monolog by focusing on an incident in which her father gets very ill from a snake bite. In your opposite draft, you play the whole speech from the perspective that snake handling is absolutely terrifying, that it makes you nauseous even to think about it. That is your Z. When you are ready to layer these two opposites together, you realize that your A is not proportional to your Z:

$$A \longleftarrow\!\longrightarrow \mathbf{Z}$$

"Quite exciting" is no match for absolutely terrifying. You need to push the A energy of your first draft further in the opposite direction.

352

A is now much more than exciting. It is ecstasy, an experience of the sacred, a high that no drug can match, something you can't live without. Such an A is strong enough to hold its own against the terror of snake handling. A's intensity is in fact fed by Z: the more terrifying snake handling is, the greater the ecstasy of those who practice it.

We have seen that Richard III has, to put it mildly, a very bad self-image, and with good reason: his mother loathes him, dogs bark at him, and every mirror tells him why. But the character that Shakespeare gives us also has an enormously inflated ego. He is a megalomaniac, prone to grandiose fantasies, and he looks down on others just as much as he despises himself. There is even a part of him that seems to treasure his deformity, since it sets him apart from the mass of men. The pluses and minuses are all in due proportion.

Weston is out castrating the lambs when he feels a shadow cross over him. "I could feel it even before I saw it take shape on the ground," he says.

Felt like the way it does when the clouds move across the sun. Huge and black and cold like. So I look up (Speech 9, Appendix B)

17.15 Suppose that in your first draft, which sensibly focused on building to the energy of "Cheerin' for that eagle," this moment had not seemed particularly significant. Play it with a workaday sense of "Hmm, what's that?" Look up casually.

Now suppose that your opposites work has led you in a much darker direction. Weston does not enjoy castrating, and watching the eagle fly off with those "fresh little remnants of manlihood" might well make any man wince. There is something threatening in such a predatory image, and the eagle's swoops seem "downright suicidal." Perhaps you call this new opposite "huge and black and cold-like."

17.16 Play this moment as if the angel of death has just flown over you. Bright morning turns dark. Freeze. You hold your breath. What could that possibly be?! The knife drops from your hand. It takes a lot of effort to make yourself look up.

This new version has enough weight to be put in a scale opposite the excitement and high spirits of "Cheerin' for that eagle." And the whole story becomes much more complex.

C. Damned if you do, damned if you don't: inner conflict can be a vicious circle.

When each opposite is both positively and negatively charged, your character gets trapped in a vicious circle.

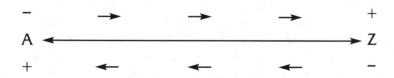

In this hellish state of endless vacillation, your character moves back and forth between A and Z, attracted by the positive charge of each pole, then repelled by its negative charge.

This sort of vicious circle may or may not be escaped in the course of the play. Tragic figures fall victim to their conflicts. Happy endings mean that the cycle is somehow broken, the conflict somehow resolved.

The young Joan of Arc is reluctant to leave her family, her fields, the security of her simple life, all that she knows and loves: this is A. It is positively charged and has a strong hold on her. To undertake what the angel asks of her seems impossible, moreover, and terrifies her — she has lots of reasons for not wishing to become a military commander. Z is negatively charged. On the other hand, the prospect of serving God, saving France, and having a great mission must be terribly attractive: Z is also positively charged. And if part of Joan resents the narrow horizons of her present life, if she would be happy to escape her father ("who wasn't easy"), then A is negatively charged.

Consider Clytemnestra's inner conflict about taking revenge on Agamemnon: on the one hand, a plus and minus if she kills him; on the other, a plus and a minus if she spares him and lives with her grief and her rage. She is damned if she does and damned if she doesn't. It's a no-win situation.

Consider the general case of any outsider — one of the great themes in Western literature. The specifics are very different for hunchbacked Richard III; Malvolio, the servant who longs to be a master; and Cavale, who feels like an ugly duckling. But the vicious circle they are trapped in is the same. Outsiders despise insiders and feel superior to them: because they stand apart, outsiders see themselves as exceptional and take pride in not being one of "them." On the other hand, being excluded tells outsiders they are somehow inferior, unworthy, unwanted. Being locked out is no fun. Part of every outsider wants in.

If an outsider does manage to get inside, she may not feel like herself anymore, since her identity was defined by being different. Becoming an insider may even lead to guilty self-loathing. And the inside may feel confining and claustrophobic in contrast to the freedom from constraints that an outsider has. If, on the other hand, an outsider remains locked outside, he may feel isolated, lacking in identity, despicable in his own eyes, freakish. Outsiders are damned if they don't get inside, and damned if they do.

Within the limits of one speech, you may not always have enough room to play this level of opposites work. When you work on a role — with entire scripts as your playing field — you have sufficient material to trap your character in a vicious circle. To play a layered version of your speech, it will suffice that your character lives the push/pull of real conflict. But do consider the possibility that your opposites may be both positively and negatively charged.

D. Take your time with transitions between opposites.

There are multiple reasons for taking your time while moving between A and Z.

• Each opposite has a strong grip on your character. It is therefore hard to leave A and hard to go toward Z — and vice versa.

If your character is unstable or approaching an ambivalent moment of crisis about a conflict, s/he may flip-flop between opposites rather suddenly. But for the most part movement between opposites is a struggle that takes time. Even as your character is pushed forward, there is a pull from behind in the opposite direction. Even as your character retreats, there is a strong attraction pulling him forward. A person does not move easily or quickly in such situations. Traveling between two opposites is full of hesitations and misgivings. There is a lot of friction holding back movement. One foot is on the accelerator, the other on the brake.

Actors and directors talk about making the stakes high for a character:

whether something happens or not must matter — a lot. The way to raise the stakes in layering work is to make sure that each opposite is very strong.

- An audience measures the strength of a moment's hold on your character by how long it takes you to fade out of it.

You have encountered this principle before. If you move away from an opposite too briskly, too easily, you create the impression that it is not very strong. Rushing a transition between layers weakens the sense of conflict.

- It is in the transitions between their opposites that dramatic characters live their conflicts, and it is precisely there that you should focus your attention.

Transitions between A and Z are the stuff of layering. More important than A or Z is the struggle which takes place in between A and Z: most of your acting should happen there, in the back-and-forth from layer to layer.

A well-layered speech spends more time with transitions than with either of the poles. Something like 80% of your performance might be spent fading from A to Z and back again, and the remaining 20% might consist of moments that are strongly A or Z or ambivalent.

An audience needs this transitional time as much as you do. If they are to have a good look at your character's inner conflict, you must slow the action as you fade between opposites.

If you live through your transitions honestly, moreover, you will discover that a section you had thought of as A is really about *becoming* A and that the Z text that precedes it is really about *leaving* Z.

E. Struggle.

Layering is not just a question of alternating your opposites. Every transition between A and Z should be a struggle. Even as you move toward Z, A holds you back. Part of you resists each push and pull. No matter which way you turn, the conflict does not go away. Your character should be off balance most of the time.

Inner conflict involves a good deal of confusion. If it is hard for *you* to put your opposites together, imagine what it is like for your character! Sometimes your own confusion is a clue to the turmoil inside your story: if you have a real question about whether a moment is A or Z, perhaps your character does as well. There may be times when your character doesn't know what to think or feel, much less what to do.

F. You must play A in order to play Z, and vice versa.

Every time your character asserts A, it is because Z is right there, as a temptation, an inclination, a fear. It is only because of Z that your character tries to be A.

- It is because Clytemnestra feels wounded by the murderous spray of Agamemnon's blood that she insists on reveling in it as if it were a spring rain. (Speech 1, Appendix B)
- It is because Rosalind is so attracted to Orlando that she must test him and question whether love is "merely a madness." (Excerpt 14, Appendix A)
- It is because Weston is so attached to his family — so unable to exist without it — that he keeps leaving it. At the end of *Curse of the Starving Class*, we hear about an eagle that has seized a cat. Up in the air, they fight to the death, because each is unwilling to let go of the other. Weston's relationship to his family is a struggle like that.

And so on. This principle is implicit in all the others, but it is later on in your layering process that you are in a position to grasp its truth — and how to play your speech in light of it. In order to play an A moment, you must be in touch with Z. Every Z moment is an effort to resist, deny, escape A. A exists because of Z, and vice versa.

but nothing could make him take the fish or the butter. He got mad and said: "Did you beg them from the landlord's wife? You can take it back with you, I don't want it." (Excerpt 1, Appendix A)
17.17 Get yourself in touch with A: your hunger and the temptation to take this food. Play Z — your principled and forceful refusal — as a way to overcome A.

and this real pretty blonde-haired girl dressed in a white ballet dress rose up behind me as the swan. It was really shitty, man. (Excerpt 15, Appendix A)

17.18 It is because Cavale still wants to be the swan that she works so hard at being a rock 'n' roll version of the ugly duckling. A is the moment of imagining herself as that real pretty girl rising in a white ballet dress (see 5.4). Play the last line as a way to escape the hunger to be the swan by being as ugly duckling as you can: black leather, heavy boots and a foul mouth.

he pulled something out of me that looked like a walnut all blackened and cracked. "What you see here is the proof," he said. I tried to tell him it was just my stomach shriveled up by hunger (Excerpt 10, Appendix A)

17.19 Part of Dorothea has always known what the angel shows her. Her grief at not having children is A. It is because of this pain that she insists that what the angel has removed is just her stomach. Get in touch with A so that her denial is necessary. The clearer the proof, the stronger the denial.

In each of these examples, playing Z makes sense only because the character is feeling A. You must play A in order to play Z.

For Your Own Speech

Create a layered version of your speech.

Guidelines

You will probably return to the spine of your first draft, improved by impulses about telling the story more fully and clearly, and perhaps by feedback. New moments discovered in the course of exploring opposites and single images may be incorporated. It is also possible to make radical changes in the staging of your speech, retaining only some elements of your first draft.

If you decide to continue with an opposite that you have already explored, dig deeper and "mine" more moments. Put yourself back in touch with the moment-to-moment truth of your opposite.

If you decide to work with a new opposite, you must explore the entire speech in light of it. How might this new energy affect how you play each moment?

Layers should be named with language from your text.

As you talk to yourself about your work, translate emotion words into actions, implicit scenes and images that you can play.

Explore alternative modes of moving from A to Z and back again. Occasionally you might cut suddenly from one to the other. Most transitions will be fades.

Take time with most of your transitions. Hold back as you fade. Perhaps the rate at which you fade will change as you approach an opposite.

Consider the relative size of A and Z moments. They should not all be of the same magnitude.

Note how A wanes as Z waxes. How far are you from A and Z at any given point?

When you notice a seam in your text where one opposite ends and another begins, consider whether you really want to change your energy on the seam. How might you knit the seam so that one opposite develops out of the other?

When an opposite energy emerges, experiment with playing it under the previous text as a substratum that rises to the surface.

Are any moments in your speech A/Z? If so, what is the relative strength of each opposite? Is one of them a strong undertow? Or a faint nuance?

Is there a moment when your character teeters on an edge? Is there a turning point at which your character's ambivalence is a struggle between energies of equal strength?

Does opposite energy put backspin on any moment?

Don't compromise your opposites. Let them drive each other further in the opposite direction: "the more ..., the more ... "

If you use one of the energies in your first draft as an opposite, does it need to be more extreme so as to balance the new opposite? The force with which A and Z push and pull your character should be roughly equal.

Do A and Z trap your character in a vicious circle, because each opposite is both positively and negatively charged?

Why do your opposites trigger each other? Tell yourself the story of how your character moves back and forth between these opposites. Do you see any patterns? What psychology might you invent for your character in terms of the interplay between his or her opposites?

It is not enough to *indicate* which parts of your speech are A and which Z; you must really get inside your opposites — and inside the way they interact with each other — in order to play a conflicted character.

Shape the journey of your speech. Where do you start with respect to your opposites and where do you end? Does the conflict you are working on get resolved? Is the question left hanging?

Sketch a graph of your layered speech and check its accuracy against your performance.

Focus on the struggle within your character, the push-pull of these opposites. Each transition is difficult and unsettling. Get your character off balance.

Is your character ever confused?

As you play A moments, make sure you are in touch with Z so as to resist it. Get in touch with A in order to play Z. The two exist because of each other.

As a warm-up for layering, drop into a few moments of each opposite on impulse. Get in touch with your A and your Z and ready to play.

Epilogue
A Narrative Approach to Acting

Learning how to live the story of a speech is learning how to live the story of a play. Entering another time and place is the very heart of acting, and the many skills involved in acting narrative speeches can be used in every aspect of performance.

The broadest implication of the work outlined in this book is an approach to acting which is focused not on motivation or psychology or the summoning of emotional states, but on something much more fundamental: on the story of your character's journey.

The story you tell yourself about how your character gets from moment to moment and from scene to scene needs much more detail than the script provides. Filling in the blank spaces between the lines is in large part how actors collaborate with playwrights. When you are developing a role, you must create a story that encompasses every part of your performance, including your relationships and interactions with other characters. This story is your roadmap through the play.

A lively narrative imagination is essential to actors. We are storytellers.

Learning how to talk to yourself about acting

Becoming an actor is not a matter of learning how to have feelings and impulses, how to respond to the pressure of circumstances, or how to imagine: we are all wired to do those things instinctively.

It is true, of course, that accomplished acting requires physical and vocal skills that habits and tensions hamper: training is important. It is also true that some performers are conditioned by experience to be exquisitely adroit at manipulating how they are perceived, and that others have natural endowments which make their presence powerful: what we call talent matters. But all who are seriously interested in acting can take comfort in the knowledge that humans are actors by birthright. Our urge to identify with others is biological and cultural. Our minds and bodies quite naturally respond to imagined circumstances. Is the study of acting, then, merely a question of acquiring technique? What is it that actors must learn?

Principles and guidelines are important because they define the issues on which actors must focus. Acquiring a comprehensive set of questions to ask yourself about your material makes it possible to explore far and wide, and to make discoveries. Learning how to act means developing a vocabulary for rehearsing and performing.

How to walk yourself inside each stage of your character's journey is the most important skill to master. Learning how to act is essentially a matter of learning how to talk to yourself about where you've come from, how you found your way to this moment, and where you want to go. Narrative skills enable you to locate your character's whereabouts and to go there. Once you have told yourself an evocatively detailed story about where you are, what is happening, and what is at stake in terms of the opposites that conflict you, you will have impulses to act and to interact in response to your situation. Knowing how to act is knowing how to position yourself.

Actors learn in part by internalizing how teachers talk about acting, and by integrating and adapting various approaches until the inner voice is their own. Learning acting is learning how to tell yourself your own stories.

Personalizing

If you are to get inside dramatic material, it must speak to you, which means that you must tell yourself the playwright's story in a way that resonates with your experience. You must come to understand how your character's story really is your own story — and the story of everyone in the audience.

The specific circumstances and events of a play may be different than anything you have personally encountered, but narrative skills make it possible to experience them vicariously. Bringing a story closer to home should not lead you to substitute your own experiences for those of your character, but your character's story can be personalized by weaving into it additional details — some of which might be autobiographical — that speak to your imagination.

The process of formulating opposites is an opportunity to discover how your character's conflicts and confusions, whatever the circumstances, are like your own.

When directors attempt to inspire you, you may need to translate their input into a story or an image that connects with you and that elicits the behavior they are trying to draw out of you.

362

Interactive scene work

What makes for good ensemble work? What joins a group of actors in a unified effort? In the first place, it is the story that brings an ensemble "together." A director's task is to get every member of a cast into the same production of the same story — and to keep them listening to each other as the story unfolds.

When actors talk to each other about what is going on between their characters at a particular point, they are really in dialog about where they are in the story. They do well to stay focused on what happens, rather than to distance themselves from events by analyzing them in psychological terms.

Every impulse in scene work is an act of storytelling: *this is — provisionally — what happens next.* What actors say to each other about a moment, and what a director says to them, ought to focus on how it contributes to the developing story line.

Metaphorical scenes and images: narrative tools for non-narrative materials

When you developed a second pair of opposites for your speech, you created for each a simple set of circumstances that positioned you to explore a different direction. Imagine a speech in which a former orphan remembers spending a day with a couple interested in adoption. You might play this story as:

- a glowing eulogy at a funeral service for your adoptive parents years later;
- a late-night gripe session in the dorm after a disastrous day — those awful people will certainly not adopt you, and good riddance;
- a counseling session in which you are certain that the whole event was your fault, and that there is something terribly wrong with you.

The same technique can be used for speeches that are not narrative. A speech in which your character vents emotions, for example, might profit from metaphorical thinking about the circumstances in which you are speaking. Suppose your character is apologizing for some terrible act of betrayal. There is no story, only a flood of feelings. You might explore the speech as a confession, as an attempt to defend what you did, as a triumphant celebration, or as your last thoughts as you prepare to end your life. Each of these approaches involves an implicit scene to define the circumstances in which youa re speaking and to whom.

The rhetoric that Henry V uses to rally his troops before the battle of Agincourt (*Henry V*, IV.iii) might be explored as:

- a celebratory reunion speech in a tavern years later;
- intimate words of comfort to a soldier who is recovering in a hospital;
- an address to the parents of soldiers who died under his command;
- a harangue in the midst of hand-to-hand combat.

Each of these scenes can be created with the skills required for narrative speeches.

When you used a single image to explore an opposite for your speech, you created a simple action that positioned you to play a specific energy. That approach can be used with non-narrative material, and in every sort of acting situation. Images (which are stories in miniature) are quite playable, and can be internalized if necessary.

A narrative approach to acting enables you to play a playwright's images along with the events of the plot and to embody a play's central images in your character.

A narrative approach to roles

A good play is a unique universe, with its own logic and its own psychology. It speaks its own language, and actors must learn its vocabulary and its grammar if they are to act it fluently and sensibly.

Entering the world of a play requires in the first place an understanding of what it is about. A play is about the issues and conflicts that recur in it, which constitute its themes. Every member of an ensemble should shape his or her role in terms of the play's major themes, because these define the universe in which all the characters live. Playing a role is more than playing a character; it is playing a play — that is, playing what it is about.

Even the most basic facts in a script must be understood in light of what the play is about. In Chekhov's *Three Sisters*, Masha's love for Vershinin is no generic human emotion, identical with the "love" experienced in other plays. What Masha feels is best understood in terms of what all the characters in this particular universe are searching for: her love is a hunger to escape meaninglessness, a search for purpose, and Vershinin is someone to live for.

When you are developing a role, you should take note of recurring words, actions, and images, and then outline the themes of the play — most of which will involve the conflict of opposites. For each theme, you should develop over the course of rehearsals a series of actions that embody it: a *throughline* of moments which flesh out that particular issue. Every moment in your performance — everything you say or do, every character choice and transaction with others — should be part of one or another throughline. If the play is about X and Y and Z, anything that does not contribute to these themes, or some combination of them, is extraneous and should be cut. In this way you create a performance focused on the issues with which your character struggles.

A role, then, is a fabric woven of thematic threads called throughlines, each of which tells the story of one of your character's inner conflicts. A carefully constructed throughline is a version of the play, a partial account of your character's journey. Each throughline has a beginning and an end; it probably has one or more moments of crisis; it may or may not have a resolution.

Developing a role is discovering how to play the story of each throughline. This is an essentially narrative process. You map your character's journey through the play by telling yourself the story of precisely where you are, with respect to each issue, from moment to moment.

Internalizing

While working on single images, you went through the exercise of internalizing a simple action that you had explored on your feet. You can in the same way internalize the whole of a narrative speech, by playing the circumstances and events of the story without physicalizing them. For a production of Sophocles' *Electra*, I once played the long messenger speech about a chariot race quite still, an approach that suited the style of the production, the director's taste, and the fact that the story is a lie. But the narrative I internalized was just as detailed, specific, sensuous, and active as it would have been in a production in which the messenger had been free to move. This sort of internalizing can be useful when telling a story in film and video.

For instructional purposes, the exercises in this book have asked you to make active, physical choices, because actors must learn how to play on their feet what they may later choose to internalize. What training requires may differ from the needs of a particular production, and the tastes of some performers may lead them to use narrative skills in a less explicit manner. Some actors need less in the way of active, physical choices to ground them in a story than others, though they must imagine events just as vividly — and play them internally.

You can internalize images, circumstances, and scenarios not only when working on narrative materials, but in all other areas of acting. If you imagine circumstances to ground yourself for a non-narrative speech, you can internalize them and let them secretly inform what you are saying. For a speech in which an angry daughter is venting at her mother, for example, you might develop another layer by imagining that she is saying all this at her mother's grave or as she discovers something hurtful in her mother's belongings. It helps, of course, to play the imagined scenario on your feet before internalizing it.

Two or more actors can internalize a metaphor for their characters' relationship, a set of imagined circumstances for an interaction, or an image as the subtext for a particular scene. Narrative elements can be internalized in any acting situation.

Shape sense and opposites

Shaping is just as important in scene work and in developing a role as it is in speeches, and the principles are the same. Two actors can jointly execute a build, for example, as can a whole ensemble, and not only for a scene, but for an act, even an entire play. A role is an intricate series of builds and pullbacks, which give each throughline its own shape. The overall architecture of a well-shaped performance puts every part in a specific relationship to the whole.

Opposites and layering are an important dimension of scene work. Relationships are living entities subject to inner conflicts just as individuals are, and the conflict *between* characters can be layered in just the same way as the conflict *within* characters.

Solo performances

Dramatic monologs, one-person shows, narrative song lyrics, certain styles of performance art, and stand-up comedy all require the skills you have been developing in your work on narrative speeches. Each of these genres asks you to set the scene, live through a sequence of events, play multiple characters and points of view, and shape stories.

Narrative and emotions

At the end of Shakespeare's *Twelfth Night*, Malvolio finds out that he has been duped. He learns that Olivia, the lady he serves, is not in love with him, as he had been led to believe, and that his rather cruel deception was done as a joke. Imagine that your Malvolio is upset by this discovery — not comically distressed, but quite genuinely hurt. What will get you to that point in every performance?

You must get yourself inside the character's circumstances, of course, which includes a commitment to his dreams and his hungers. You must take in what is said and done to you in the course of the play, right up to the last moment. And you must follow Malvolio's story, both as actor and as audience to your own performance. It is in large part because his *story* is sad that Malvolio is sad.

That may seem like heresy to some. How can actors who are inside their characters be following the story? But actors never cease to be themselves, and they are never unaware of the fictional nature of a play's events. Our sense that a story is sad or infuriating or hilarious is an important component of our identification with our characters, just as in life we feel kinship with others when we hear what has happened to them.

Imagine that Malvolio's mistress Olivia is saddened when she learns about the deception of her servant. Why is she sad? Because Malvolio's story is sad. Might not the *actor* playing Olivia be moved by his story in the same way? Of course she can, and she can play her response to Malvolio's sad story in performance. And so can the actor playing Malvolio.

The emotions you feel about events in the play are not always identical with your character's emotions — you may even have to resist being moved and play against it — but your performance is fueled by how you respond to your character's story.

Appendices

Appendix A
Excerpts

1. Bertolt Brecht, *Mr. Puntila and His Man Matti*

BOOTLEG EMMA: She [Athi's mother] hadn't seen Athi in two years, first the civil war and then the camp, and he was very thin. "So there you are, Athi, and look, here's a fish and this butter, the landlord's wife gave it to me for you." Athi said hello and asked about her rheumatism and some of the neighbors, but nothing could make him take the fish or the butter. He got mad and said: "Did you beg them from the landlord's wife? You can take it back with you, I don't want it." Hungry as he was, she had to wrap her presents up again. She said goodbye and went back home.

2. *Mr. Puntila and His Man Matti*

PUNTILA: Do you see that little one [a lake] and the tugboat with a chest like a bulldog and the tree trunks in the morning light? The way they float in the cool, clear water, all stripped and bundled, a small fortune? I can smell fresh timber five miles away, can't you? Ah, the smells we have here in Tavastland, I could bask in them all day. The berries, for instance. After the rain. And the birch leaves when you come home from the sauna and you've had yourself whipped with a big bundle of them, or in the morning as you lie in bed. Where else do you get such smells? Or a view like this? I like it best when it's hazy, it's like sometimes when you're making love, you half close your eyes, everything's blurred.

3. John Guare, *Landscape of the Body*

BETTY: We got down to South Carolina two days after what a night at the Olde Dixie Hotel. Durwood wasn't kidding all right. We came down this alley of trees and he says, "Close your eyes and now turn 'em on." He had this farm with white fences. I never saw so many white fences.

4. *Landscape of the Body*

BETTY: I went to visit Mavis in Memorial Hospital. She was dying of everything. They had cut off her breasts and she had lots of radiation treatment and her hair had gone. And I came to visit her. She was down to about sixty pounds and she wouldn't die. And I said, "Mavis, is there anything I can do for you?" And she said, "Yes, there is this new book: The Sensuous Woman. Bring it. Read it to me." And I went all that summer in Boston.

5. William Hanley, *Slow Dance on the Killing Ground*

ROSIE: And New Rochelle, of all places. At least if it'd been in some nice apartment in the Village, say, with the sounds coming through the window of traffic and people, the breeze blowing through the curtains over the bed, like in them movies. But no. I lost my virginity in the attic of an old house in New Rochelle.

6. Hugo von Hofmannsthal, *Electra*

ELECTRA: This time is given to you that you may taste and know
What agony is that of shipwrecked men
When their vain cry devours the night of clouds
And death, this time is given that you may envy
All that are chained to prison walls and cry
In darkness from the bottom of a well
For death as for deliverance.

7. Eugène Ionesco, *Exit the King*

KING: On top of everything else, I've got a headache. And those clouds! I thought I'd banished the clouds. Clouds! We've had enough rain. Enough, I said! Oh! Look at that! Off they go again! There's an idiotic cloud that can't restrain itself, like an old man, weak in the bladder. What are you staring at me for? You look very red today. My bedroom's full of cobwebs. Go and brush them away.

8. Eve Merriam, Paula Wagner, and Jack Hoffsiss, *Out of Our Fathers' House*

ELIZABETH: I recall going into the large darkened parlor and finding the casket, mirrors and pictures all draped in white, and my father seated, pale and immovable as he took no notice of me. After standing a long while, I climbed upon his knee, when he mechanically put his arm about me, and with my head resting against his beating heart, we both sat in silence, he thinking of the wreck of all his hopes in the loss of a dear son — and I wondering what could be said or done to fill the void in his breast.

9. *Out of Our Fathers' House*

ELIZABETH: I began to study Latin, Greek and mathematics with a class of boys in the Academy, many of whom were much older than I. For three years one boy kept his place at the head of the class, and I always stood next. Two prizes were offered in Greek. I strove for one and took the second. One thought alone filled my mind. "Now," said I, "my father will be satisfied with me." I rushed into his office.

10. Juan Rulfo, *Pedro Páramo*

DOROTHEA: But all the angels' faces were the same blank faces, no expression at all, as if each face were pressed from the same blank mold. And I kept begging them to tell me where my son was, but they'd walk right past me like I wasn't even there, and then all of a sudden one of those angels walked right up to me and without saying a word sank his fist deep into my stomach as if he were sticking it in a big mound of wax, and he pulled something out of me that looked like a walnut all blackened and cracked. "What you see here is the proof," he said. I tried to tell him it was just my stomach shriveled up by hunger but he just shook his head.

11. William Shakespeare, *Romeo and Juliet,* III.ii

JULIET: So tedious is this day
As is the night before some festival
To an impatient child that hath new robes
And may not wear them. O, here comes my nurse […]

12. *Romeo and Juliet,* II.ii

[Juliet: A thousand times good night! *Exit.*]
ROMEO: A thousand times the worse, to want thy light!
Love goes toward love as schoolboys from their books;
But love from love, toward school with heavy looks.

13. William Shakespeare, *Hamlet,* II.i

OPHELIA: He [Hamlet] took me by the wrist and held me hard;
Then goes he to the length of all his arm,
And with his other hand thus o'er his brow,
He falls to such perusal of my face
As he would draw it. Longed stayed he so.

At last, a little shaking of mine arm,
And thrice his head thus waving up and down,
He raised a sigh so piteous and profound
As it did seem to shatter all his bulk
And end his being.

14. William Shakespeare, *As You Like It*, III.ii

ROSALIND: He was to imagine me his love, his mistress; and I set him every day to woo me. At which time would I, being but a moonish youth, grieve, be effeminate, changeable, longing and liking, proud, fantastical, apish, shallow, inconstant, full of tears, full of smiles; for every passion something, and for no passion truly anything, as boys and girls are for the most part cattle of this colour; would now like him, now loathe him; then entertain him, then forswear him; now weep for him, then spit at him; that I drave my suitor from his mad humour of love to a living humour of madness, which was to forswear the full stream of the world and to live in a nook merely monastic. And thus I cured him [...]

15. Sam Shepard and Patti Smith, *Cowboy Mouth*

CAVALE: Once I was in a play. I was real glad I was in a play 'cause I thought they were just for pretty people, and I had my dumb eyepatch and those metal plate shoes to correct my duck foot. It was *The Ugly Duckling*, and I really dug that 'cause of the happy ending and shit. And I got to be the ugly duckling and I had to wear some old tattered black cloth and get shit flung at me, but I didn't mind 'cause at the end I'd be that pretty swan and all. But you know what they did, Slim? At the end of the play I had to kneel on the stage and cover my head with a black shawl and this real pretty blonde-haired girl dressed in a white ballet dress rose up behind me as the swan. It was really shitty, man.

16. Sam Shepard, *Curse of the Starving Class*

WESLEY: It's a zombie invasion. Taylor is the head zombie. He's the scout for the other zombies. He's only a sign that more zombies are on their way. They'll be filing through the door pretty soon. [...] There'll be bulldozers crashing through the orchard. There'll be giant steel balls crashing through the walls. There'll be foremen with their sleeves rolled up and blueprints under their arms. There'll be steel girders spanning acres of land. Cement pilings. Prefab walls. Zombie architecture, owned by invisible zombies, built by zombies for the use and convenience of all other zombies. A zombie city! Right here! Right where we're living now.

17. *Curse of the Starving Class*
WESTON: I am sleeping! I'm sleeping right here. I'm falling away. I was a flyer, you know. […] I flew giant machines in the air. Giants! Bombers, what a sight. Over Italy. The Pacific. Islands. Giants. Oceans. Blue oceans.

18. *Curse of the Starving Class*
WESTON: He doesn't know what he's dealing with. He thinks I'm just like him. Cowardly. Sniveling. Sneaking around. He's not counting on what's in my blood. He doesn't realize the explosiveness. We don't belong to the same class. He doesn't realize that. He's not counting on that. He's counting on me to use my reason. To talk things out. To go out and have a business lunch and talk things over. He's not counting on murder. Murder's the farthest thing from his mind.

19. *Curse of the Starving Class*
WESTON: I'll track them all down. Every last one of them. Your mother, too. I'll track her down and shoot them in their bed. In their hotel bed. I'll splatter their brains all over the vibrating bed. I'll drag him into the hotel lobby and slit his throat. I was in the war. I know how to kill. I was over there. I know how to do it. I've done it before. It's no big deal. You just make an adjustment. You convince yourself it's all right. That's all. It's easy. You just slaughter them. Easy.

20. *Curse of the Starving Class*
WESTON: I just went off for a little while. Now and then. I couldn't stand it here. I couldn't stand the idea that everything would stay the same. That every morning it would be the same. I kept looking for it out there somewhere. I kept trying to piece it together. The jumps, I couldn't figure out the jumps. From being born, to growing up, to droppin' bombs, to having kids, to hitting bars, to this. It all turned on me somehow. It all turned around on me. I kept looking for it out there somewhere. And all the time it was right inside this house.

21. Sam Shepard, *Red Cross*

CAROL: My body will stop at the bottom of the hill with just a bloody stump for a neck and both arms broken and both legs. Then there'll be a long cold wind. A whistle, sort of. It'll start to snow a little bit. A very soft easy snow. The squirrels might come down to see what happened. It'll keep snowing very lightly like that for a long time until my whole body is covered over. All you'll see is this little red splotch of blood and a whole blanket of white snow.

22. Sam Shepard and Joseph Chaikin, *Tongues*

SPEAKER: Everybody tried to prepare me. They told me how to breathe. How to relax. How to think about something else. They told me what kind of pain I'd have. How the spasms would come. How to deal with the pain. How to push. Nothing they told me was like this. I don't know whose skin this is. I touch the skin. Soft head. Is my hand the same skin. My fingers. I touch the head. Soft head. Just washed. Nothing they told me. This blood. This blood from me. Just washed. Nothing they told me was like this. Just born. My arm is his bed.

23. *Tongues*

SPEAKER: There was this moment. This moment where I vanished. This moment where the whole of me vanished. The whole of my thoughts. Vanished. The whole of my feelings. Vanished. The whole of my self. Vanished. The whole of what I call myself. Vanished. The whole of my body was left.

24. Tennessee Williams, *Orpheus Descending*

VAL: But those little birds, they don't have no legs at all and they live their whole lives on the wing, and they sleep on the wind, that's how they sleep at night, they just spread their wings and go to sleep on the wind like other birds fold their wings and go to sleep on a tree. ... They sleep on the wind and ... never light on this earth but one time when they die!

Appendix B
Speeches

1. Aeschylus, *Agamemnon*

CLYTEMNESTRA: I have said so many things to serve the moment.
Now it makes me proud to tell the truth.
How else to prepare a death for deadly men
who seem to love you? How to rig the nets
of pain so high no man can overleap them?

I brooded on this trial, this ancient blood feud
year by year. At last my hour came.
Here I stand and here I struck
and here my work is done.
I did it all. I don't deny it, no.
He had no way to flee or fight his destiny —
our never-ending, all-embracing net, I cast it
wide for the royal haul, I coil him round and round
in the wealth, the robes of doom, and then I strike him
once, twice, and at each stroke he cries in agony —
he buckles at the knees and crashes here!
And when he's down I add the third, last blow,
to the Zeus who saves the dead beneath the ground
I send that third blow home in homage like a prayer.
So he goes down, and the life is bursting out of him —
great sprays of blood, and the murderous shower
wounds me, dyes me black and I, I revel
like the Earth when the spring rains come down,
the blessed gifts of god, and the new green spear
splits the sheath and rips to birth in glory!

So it stands, elders of Argos gathered here.
Rejoice if you can rejoice — I glory.
And if I'd pour upon his body the libation
it deserves, what wine would match my words?
It is right and more than right. He flooded

the vessel of our proud house with misery,
with the vintage of the curse and now
he drains the dregs. My lord is home at last.

2. Jean Anouilh, *The Lark*

May I begin wherever I like? [...] I like remembering the beginning: at home, in the fields, when I was still a little girl looking after the sheep, the first time I heard the Voices, that is what I like to remember. ... It is after the evening Angelus. I am very small and my hair is still in pigtails. I am sitting in the field, thinking of nothing at all. God is good and keeps me safe and happy, close to my mother and my father and my brother, in the quiet countryside of Domremy, while the English soldiers are looting and burning villages up and down the land. My big sheep-dog is lying with his head in my lap; and suddenly I feel his body ripple and tremble, and a hand seems to have touched my shoulder, though I know no one has touched me. [...] I turned to look. A great light was filling the shadows behind me. The voice was gentle and grave. I had never heard it before, and all it said to me was: "Be a good and sensible child, and go often to church." But I *was* good, and I *did* go to church often, and I showed I was sensible by running away to safety. That was all that happened the first time. And I didn't say anything about it when I got home; but after supper I went back. The moon was rising; it shone on the white sheep; and that was all the light there was. And then came the second time; the bells were ringing for the noonday Angelus. The light came again, in bright sunlight, but brighter than the sun, and that time I saw him. [...] A man in a white robe, with two white wings reaching from the sky to the ground. He didn't tell me his name that day, but later on I found out that he was the blessed St. Michael. [...] *(in the deep voice of the Archangel)* — Joan, go to the help of the King of France, and give him back his kingdom. *(She replies in her own voice.)* Oh sir, you haven't looked at me; I am only a young peasant girl, not a great captain who can lead an army. — You will go and search out Robert de Beaudricourt, the Governor of Vaucouleurs. He will give you a suit of clothes to dress you like a man, and he will take you to the Dauphin. St. Catherine and St. Margaret will protect you. *(She suddenly drops to the floor sobbing with fear.)* — Please, please pity me, holy sir! I'm a little girl; I'm happy here alone in the fields. I've never had to be responsible for anything, except my sheep. The Kingdom of France is far beyond anything I can do. If you will only look at me you will see I am small, and ignorant. The realm of France is too heavy, sir. But the King of France has famous Captains, as strong as you could need and they're used to doing these things. If they lose a battle they sleep as soundly as ever. They simply say the snow or the wind was against them; and they just cross all the dead men off their role. But I should always remember I had killed them. Please have pity on me! ... No such thing. No pity. He had gone already, and there I was, with France on my shoulders. Not to mention the work on the farm, and my father, who wasn't easy.

3. Jon Lipsky, *Living in Exile*

PATROKLOS: In the first year we were daring, reckless. Inspired by war, we thought we were immortal. We *were* immortal. We were babies. We set out "to get us some."

In the second year, we were surprised, caught off guard, caught unprepared. We reevaluated our provisions. Who could've imagined it. After one whole year — no visit from the goddess, Victory?

In the third year, we were uncompromising, ruthless and professional. With deadly disciplined precision, we set out to get the job done. How we longed for home.

In the fourth year, we resigned ourselves. To the relentless tedium of an endless siege. Regulations were relaxed. Truces were declared. New rules were instituted. Ha-yaa, the Games began.

In the fifth year, we took our ease. The truces, the games, the rules we instituted, were now institutions. We did our job. Enjoyed our leisure. Living day-to-day, each day seemed full. We were — there's no other word for it — happy.

In the sixth year, things began to fall apart. We became sloppy, forgetful. The face of that old friend ... That well-known maneuver ... Obscured were old memories. Planning seemed impossible.

In the seventh year, we became desperate. The rules became rigid, the fighting monstrous. The enemy seemed implacable. We became cruel.

The eighth year was mutinous. Comrade abandoned comrade. There were no allies. Some cheered the elegant victories of our enemy. Self-mutilation became a source of glory. Suicide, though despised, was commonplace.

The ninth year we went numb, We tasted war. But felt nothing. We smelled death. But felt nothing. We ate, drank, slept … Nothing. The sand burned with more desire than we, the sun-dried meat.

4. Jon Lipsky, *Living in Exile*

BRISEIS: In the first year, we were oblivious: harvested our figs and olives in the morning, in the evening entertained our grandmothers with sentimental songs of love while black ships slipped through the wine dark sea.

In the second year, we were prisoners of shock, locked in our shame, chained to our inexpressible grief. At night we lay tearless where we were told. Didn't even howl at the moon.

In the third year, we guarded jealously the nests we clawed out in the wounded landscape. We shared no common dialects, blood bonds or expressions of respect. Shared even less our scraps of food, scrounged from our owners.

In the fourth year, we followed the fortunes of war. Learned to appear after victories, disappear after defeats. We identified the crazed men from the not-yet-crazed, and used every seduction to bed down with the not-yet-crazed.

In the fifth year, we came into our power. Our blacksmiths, our milkmaids, our musicians were held in high esteem. Our beauties became the arbiters of prizes, whose disdain could destroy the men we called "The Meat." It was — there's no other word for it — exciting.

In the sixth year, we imagined for the first time the possibility of a future. A few followed their masters into battle. Some died escaping through the swamps. Most dreamed of rescue. Just about every boychild born that year was named by his mother "Hector."

The seventh year, we were lunatics. Sleeping by day, roaming at night. We went with animals, ate in rituals the wounded's severed limbs. Our wombs became breeders of jealousy and envy, torturers of desire.

The eighth year blazed with plans for the great uprising. We set up our women's network, our secret road. We made contact with our enemies, And lived for our revenge.

The ninth year, we gave up hope. The jackals owned our gardens. The children scavenged battlefields. We let ourselves become unbeautiful. The Three-Faced Goddess walked among us, we believed, but in disguise, out of spite.

5. Michael Ondaatje, *The Collected Works of Billy the Kid*

After shooting Gregory
this is what happened

I'd shot him well and careful
made it explode under his heart
so it wouldn't last long and
was about to walk away
when this chicken paddles out to him
and as he was falling hops on his neck
digs the beak into his throat
straightens legs and heaves
a red and blue vein out

Meanwhile he fell
and the chicken walked away

still tugging at the vein
till it was 12 yards long
as if it held that body like a kite
Gregory's last words being

get away from me yer stupid chicken.

381

6. Sam Shepard, *Buried Child*

HALIE'S VOICE: Dodge? Is that you Dodge? Tilden was right about the corn you know. I've never seen such corn. Have you taken a look at it lately? Tall as a man already. This early in the year. Carrots too. Potatoes. Peas. It's like a paradise out there, Dodge. You oughta' take a look. A miracle. I've never seen it like this. Maybe the rain did something. Maybe it was the rain. [...] Good hard rain. Takes everything straight down deep to the roots. The rest takes care of itself. You can't force a thing to grow. You can't interfere with it. It's all hidden. It's all unseen. You just gotta wait til it pops up out of the ground. Tiny little shoot. Tiny little white shoot. All hairy and fragile. Strong though. Strong enough to break the earth even. It's a miracle, Dodge. I've never seen a crop like this in my whole life. Maybe it's the sun. Maybe that's it. Maybe it's the sun.

7. Sam Shepard, *Curse of the Starving Class*

WESLEY: *(as he throws wood into wheelbarrow)* I was lying there on my back. I could smell the avocado blossoms. I could hear the coyotes. I could hear stock cars squealing down the street. I could feel myself in my bed in my room in this house in this town in this state in this country. I could feel this country close like it was part of my bones. I could feel the presence of all the people outside, at night, in the dark. Even sleeping people I could feel. Even all the sleeping animals. Dogs. Peacocks. Bulls. Even tractors sitting in the wetness, waiting for the sun to come up. I was looking straight up at the ceiling at all my model airplanes hanging by all their thin wires. Floating. Swaying very quietly like they were being blown by someone's breath. Cobwebs moving with them. Dust laying on their wings. Decals peeling off their wings. My P-39. My Messerschmitt. My Jap Zero. I could feel myself lying far below them on my bed like I was on the ocean and overhead they were on reconnaissance. Scouting me. Floating. Taking pictures of the enemy. Me, the enemy. I could feel the space around me like a big, black world. I listened like an animal. My listening was afraid. Afraid of sound. Tense. Like any second something could invade me. Some foreigner. Something undescribable. Then I heard the Packard coming up the hill. From a mile off I could tell it was the Packard by the sound of the valves. The lifters have a sound like nothing else. Then I could picture my Dad driving it. Shifting unconsciously. Downshifting into second for the last pull up the hill. I could feel the headlights closing in.

Cutting through the orchard. I could see the trees being lit one after the other by the lights, then going back to black. My heart was pounding. Just from my Dad coming back. Then I heard him pull the brake. Lights go off. Key's turned off. Then a long silence. Him just sitting in the car. Just sitting. I picture him just sitting. What's he doing? Just sitting. Waiting to get out. Why's he waiting to get out? He's plastered and can't move. He's plastered and doesn't want to move. He's going to sleep there all night. He's slept there before. He's woken up with dew on the hood before. Freezing headache. Teeth covered with peanuts. Then I hear the door of the Packard open. A pop of metal. Dogs barking down the road. Door slams. Feet. Paper bag being tucked under one arm. Paper bag covering "Tiger Rose." Feet coming. Feet walking toward the door. Feet stopping. Heart pounding. Sound of door not opening. Foot kicking door. Man's voice. Dad's voice. Dad calling Mom. No answer. Foot kicking. Foot kicking harder. Wood splitting. Man's voice. In the night. Foot kicking hard through door. One foot right through door. Bottle crashing. Glass breaking. Fist through door. Man cursing. Man going insane. Feet and hands tearing. Head smashing. Man yelling. Shoulder smashing. Whole body crashing. Woman screaming. Mom screaming. Mom screaming for police. Man throwing wood. Man throwing up. Mom calling cops. Dad crashing away. Back down driveway. Car door slamming. Ignition grinding. Wheels screaming. First gear grinding. Wheels screaming off down hill. Packard disappearing. Sound disappearing. No sound. No sight. Planes still hanging. Heart still pounding. No sound. Mom crying soft. Soft crying. Then no sound. Then softly crying. Then moving around through house. Then no moving. Then crying softly. Then stopping. Then, far off the freeway could be heard.

8. *Curse of the Starving Class*

WESTON: I got up and took a walk around the place. Bright and early. Don't think I've walked around the whole place for a couple a' years. I walked about and a funny thing started happening to me. [...] I started wondering who this was walking around in the orchard at six-thirty in the morning. It didn't feel like me. It felt like some character in a dark overcoat and tennis shoes and a baseball cap and stickers coming out of his face. It didn't feel like the owner of a piece a' property as nice as this. Then I started to wonder who the owner was. I mean if I didn't feel like the owner, then who was the owner? I started wondering if the real owner was gonna' pop up out of nowhere and blast my brains out for trespassing. I started feeling like I should be running or hiding or something. Like I shouldn't be here in this kind of a neighborhood. Not that it's fancy or anything, but it's peaceful. It's real peaceful up here. Especially at that time a' the morning. Then it struck me that I actually was the owner. That somehow it was me and I was actually the one walking on my own piece of land. And that gave me a great feeling. […] So I came back in here, and the first thing I did was I took all my clothes off and walked around here naked. Just walked through the whole damn house in my birthday suit. Tried to get the feeling of it really being me in my own house. It was like peeling off a whole person. A whole stranger. Then I walked straight in and made myself a hot bath. Hot as I could stand it. Just sank down into it and let it sink deep into the skin. Let it fog up all the windows and the glass on the medicine cabinet. Then I let all the water drain out, and then I filled the whole tub up again but this time with ice cold water. Just sat there and let it creep up on me until I was in up to my neck. Then I got out and took a shave and found myself some clean clothes. Then I came in here and fixed myself a big old breakfast of ham and eggs.

9. *Curse of the Starving Class*
WESTON: *(to lamb as he folds clothes)* There's worse things than maggots ya' know. Much worse. Maggots go away if they're properly attended to. If you got someone around who can take the time. Who can recognize the signs. Who brings ya' in out of the cold, wet pasture and sets ya' up in a cushy situation like this. No lamb ever had it better. It's warm. It's free of draft, now that I got the new door up. There's no varmints. No coyotes. No eagles. No — *(looks over at lamb)* Should I tell ya' something about eagles? This is a true story. This is a true account. One time I was out in the fields doing the castrating, which is a thing that has to be done. It's not my favorite job, but it's something that just has to be done. I'd set myself up right beside the lean-to out there. Just a little roof-shelter thing out there with my best knife, some boiling water, and a hot iron to cauterize with. It's a bloody job on all accounts. Well, I had maybe a dozen spring ram lambs to do out there. I had 'em all gathered up away from the ewes in much the same kinda' set up as you got right there. Similar fence structure like that. It was a crisp, bright type a' morning. Air was real thin

and you could see all the way out across the pasture land. Frost was still well bit down on the stems, right close to the ground. Maybe a couple a' crows and the ewes carrying on about their babies, and that was the only sound. Well, I was working away out there when I feel this shadow cross over me. I could feel it even before I saw it take place on the ground. Felt like the way it does when the clouds move across the sun. Huge and black and cold like. So I look up, half expecting a buzzard or maybe a red-tail, but what hits me across the eyes is this giant eagle. Now I'm a flyer and I'm used to aeronautics, but this sucker was doin' some downright suicidal antics. Real low down like he's coming in for a landing or something, then changing his mind and pulling straight back up again and sailing out away from me. So I watch him going small for a while, then turn back to my work. I do a couple more lambs maybe, and the same thing happens. Except this time he's even lower yet. Like I could almost feel his feathers on my back. I could hear his sound real clear. A giant bird. His wings made a kind of cracking noise. Then up he went again. I watched him longer this time, trying to figure out his intentions. Then I put the whole thing together. He was after those testes. Those fresh little remnants of manlihood. So I decided to oblige him this time and threw a few a' them on top a' the shed roof. Then I just went back to work again, pretending to be preoccupied. I was waitin' for him this time though. I was listening hard for him, knowing he'd be coming in from behind me. I was watchin' the ground for any sign of blackness. Nothing happened for about three more lambs, when all of a sudden he comes. Just like a thunder clap. Blam! He's down on that shed roof with his talons taking half the tar paper with him, wings whippin' the air, screaming like a bred mare then climbing straight back up into the sky again. I had to stand up on that one. Somethin' brought me straight up off the ground and I started yellin' my head off. I don't know why it was comin' outa' me but I was standing there with this icy feeling up my backbone and just yelling my fool head off. Cheerin' for that eagle. I'd never felt like that since the first day I went up in a B-49. After a while I sat down again and went on workin'. And every time I cut a lamb I'd throw those balls up on the top a' the shed roof. And every time he'd come down like the Cannonball Express on that roof. And every time I got that feeling.

10. Sam Shepard, *Suicide in B^b*

LAUREEN: You struggle to the window. You hold yourself up by both elbows and stare down at the street, looking for your life. But all you see down there is yourself looking back up at you. You jump back from the window. You fall. You lay there gaping at the ceiling. You're pounding all over. You crawl back for another look. You can't resist. You pull yourself up to the window sill and peer down again. There you are, still standing down there on the street. Still looking straight back up at yourself. Your terror drops for a second. Long enough to start getting curious. You look hard at yourself on the street. You check out all the details. You examine yourself in a way you never have before. Not to resolve any conflicts but only to make an absolute identification. You check the face, the hands, the eyes, the turns in the mouth. You look for any sign that might give him away to you as an impostor. A man in disguise. But then you see him signaling to you from the street. He's pointing to his head, to his own head, then pointing back to you. He keeps repeating this over and over as though it's very important. As though it's something you should have understood a long, long time ago but never did. You pick up the gesture from him and start repeating it back to him. Pointing at your head first then pointing down to him on the street. He starts to nod his head and smiles as though you've finally got the message. But you're still not clear what he means. You pry open the window with the last strength you've got and the shock of cold air almost kills you on the spot. "If only I don't die before I find out what he means!" You say. "Just let me live five minutes longer." Then you see him more clearly than before. You see for sure that he is you. That he's not pretending. He yells up to you in a voice you can't mistake. He yells at you so the whole street can hear him. "YOU'RE IN MY HEAD! YOU'RE ONLY IN MY HEAD!" Then he turns and walks away. You watch him go until you can't see him any more. Then you make a clean jump all the way to the bottom. And your life goes dancing out the window.

11. William Shakespeare, *As You Like It*, II.vii

JAQUES: All the world's a stage,
And all the men and women merely players.
They have their exits and their entrances,
And each man in his time plays many parts,
His acts being seven ages. At first the infant,

Mewling and puking in the nurse's arms.   *crying*
Then the whining schoolboy with his satchel
And shining morning face, creeping like snail
Unwillingly to school. And then the lover,
Sighing like furnace, with a woeful ballad
Made to his mistress' eyebrow. Then a soldier,
Full of strange oaths and bearded like the pard,   *leopard*
Jealous in honor, sudden and quick in quarrel,
Seeking the bubble reputation
Even in the cannon's mouth. And then the justice,
In fair round belly with good capon lined,
With eyes severe and beard of formal cut,
Full of wise saws and modern instances,
And so he plays his part. The sixth age shifts
Into the lean and slippered pantaloon,   *foolish old man*
With spectacles on nose and pouch on side,
His youthful hose, well saved, a world too wide
For his shrunk shank, and his big, manly voice,
Turning again toward childish treble, pipes
And whistles in his sound. Last scene of all,
That ends this strange, eventful history,
Is second childishness and mere oblivion,
Sans teeth, sans eyes, sans taste, sans everything.   *without*

12. *Henry IV*, Part I, I.iii

HOTSPUR: My liege, I did deny no prisoners.
But I remember, when the fight was done,
When I was dry with rage and extreme toil,
Breathless and faint, leaning upon my sword,
Came there a certain lord, neat and trimly dressed,
Fresh as a bridegroom, and his chin new reaped   *beard newly trimmed*
Showed like a stubble land at harvest home.   *at the end of harvest*
He was perfumèd like a milliner,
And 'twixt his finger and his thumb he held
A pouncet box, which ever and anon   *perforated perfume box*
He gave his nose, and took't away again,
Who therewith angry, when it next came there,   *(his nose) (with a smell)*

387

Took it in snuff; and <u>still</u> he smiled and talked;   *continually*
And as the soldiers bore dead bodies by,
He called them untaught knaves, unmannerly,
To bring a slovenly, unhandsome corpse
Betwixt the wind and his nobility.
With many <u>holiday and lady</u> terms   *affected and effeminate*
He questioned me, amongst the rest demanded
My prisoners in your Majesty's behalf.
I then, all smarting with my wounds being cold,
To be so pestered with a <u>popinjay</u>,   *parrot*
Out of my grief and my impatience
Answered neglectingly I know not what —
He should or he should not — for he made me mad
To see him shine so brisk and smell so sweet
And talk so like a <u>waiting gentlewoman</u>   *lady-in-waiting*
Of guns and drums and wounds, <u>God save the mark!</u>   *scornful oath*
And telling me the <u>sovereignest</u> thing on earth   *greatest*
Was <u>parmacity</u> for an inward bruise,   *ointment (from whales)*
And it was great pity, so it was,
This villainous <u>saltpeter</u> should be digged   *(used in gunpowder)*
Out of the bowels of the harmless earth,
Which many a good <u>tall</u> fellow had destroyed   *brave*
So cowardly, and but for these vile guns,
He would himself have been a soldier.
This bald unjointed chat of his, my lord,
I answered <u>indirectly</u>, as I said,   *without thinking*
And I beseech you, let not his report
<u>Come current</u> for an accusation   *be accepted as true*
Betwixt my love and your high Majesty.

13. *A Midsummer Night's Dream,* II.i

[OBERON: I do but beg a little changeling boy
To be my <u>henchman</u>.]   *page*

TITANIA: Set your heart at rest.
The fairyland buys not the child of me.
His mother was a <u>vot'ress of my order,</u>   *(bound by a religious vow)*

And in the spicèd Indian air by night
Full often hath she gossiped by my side,
And sat with me on Neptune's yellow sands,
<u>Marking</u> th'embarkèd <u>traders</u> on <u>the flood</u>,   *observing; ships; the sea*
When we have laughed to see the sails conceive
And grow big-bellied with the <u>wanton</u> wind,   *roving freely (lustful)*
Which she with pretty and with swimming gait
Following, her womb then rich with my young squire,
Would imitate, and sail upon the land
To fetch me trifles, and return again
As from a voyage, rich with merchandise.
But she, being mortal, of that boy did die;
And for her sake do I rear up her boy;
And for her sake I will not part with him.

14. *Romeo and Juliet,* II.iv

JULIET: The clock struck nine when I did send the Nurse.
In half an hour she promised to return.
Perchance she cannot meet him. That's not so.
O, she is lame! Love's heralds should be thoughts,
Which ten times faster glides than the sun's beams
Driving back shadows over <u>louring</u> hills.   *dark, gloomy*
Therefore do nimble-pinioned doves draw Love,
And therefore hath the wind-swift Cupid wings.
Now is the sun upon the highmost hill
Of this day's journey, and from nine till twelve
Is three long hours, yet she is not come.
Had she affections and warm youthful blood,
She would be as swift in motion as a ball.
My words would bandy her to my sweet love,
And his to me.
But old folks, many feign as they were dead —
Unwieldy, slow, heavy, and pale as lead.

15. *Romeo and Juliet,* IV.iii

JULIET: Farewell! God knows when we shall meet again.
I have a faint cold fear thrills through my veins

That almost freezes up the heat of life.
I'll call them back again to comfort me.
Nurse! What should she do here?
My dismal scene I needs must act alone.
Come, vial.
What if this mixture do not act at all?
Shall I be married then tomorrow morning?
No, no; this shall forbid it: lie thou there.   *[Laying down a dagger.]*
What if it be a poison which the friar
Subtly hath ministered to have me dead,
Lest in this marriage he should be dishonored
Because he married me before to Romeo?
I fear it is; and yet methinks it should not,
For he hath <u>still been tried</u> a holy man.   *always proved*
How if, when I am laid into the tomb,
I wake before the time that Romeo
Come to redeem me? There's a fearful point!
Shall I not then be stifled in the vault,
To whose foul mouth no healthsome air breathes in,
And there lie strangled ere my Romeo comes?
Or, if I live, is it not very <u>like</u>   *likely*
The horrible <u>conceit</u> of death and night,   *thought*
Together with the terror of the place,
As in a vault, an ancient receptacle
Where for all this many hundred years the bones
Of all my buried ancestors are packed;
Where bloody Tybalt, yet but <u>green in earth</u>,   *newly buried*
Lies festering in his shroud; where, as they say,
At some hours in the night spirits resort —
<u>Alack</u>, alack, is it not like that I,   *(expression of dismay)*
So early waking, what with loathsome smells,
And shrieks like mandrakes torn out of the earth,
That living mortals, hearing them, run mad —
O, if I wake, shall I not be distraught,
Environèd with all these hideous fears,
And madly play with my forefathers' joints,
And pluck the mangled Tybalt from his shroud,

And in this rage, with some great kinsman's bone
As with a club, dash out my desperate brains?
Look! Methinks I see my cousin's ghost
Seeking out Romeo, that did <u>spit</u> his body   *impale (as on a spit)*
Upon a rapier's point. <u>Stay</u>, Tybalt, stay!   *stop*
Romeo, Romeo, Romeo, I drink to thee.

16. *Romeo and Juliet*, I.iv

MERCUTIO: O then I see Queen Mab hath been with you.
She is the fairies' midwife, and she comes
In shape no bigger than an agate-stone
On the forefinger of an alderman,
Drawn with a team of little <u>atomies</u>   *tiny creatures*
Over men's noses as they lie asleep.
Her chariot is an empty hazel-nut
Made by the joiner squirrel or old grub,   *(both hollow out nuts)*
Time out o' mind the fairies' coachmakers.
Her wagon-spokes made of long <u>spinners'</u> legs,   *spiders*
The cover of the wings of grasshoppers,
Her traces of the smallest spider web,
Her collars of the moonshine's wat'ry beams,
Her whip of cricket's bone, the lash of <u>film,</u>   *fine filaments*
Her wagoner a small grey-coated gnat,
Not half so big as a round little worm
Prick'd from the lazy finger of a maid.   *(lazy maids had wormy fingers)*
And in this <u>state</u> she gallops night by night   *(seated like a queen)*
Through lovers' brains, and then they dream of love;
On courtiers' knees, that dream on <u>curtsies</u> straight;   *bows*
O'er lawyers' fingers, who straight dream on fees;
O'er ladies' lips, who straight on kisses dream,
Which oft the angry Mab with blisters plagues,
Because their breath with <u>sweetmeats</u> tainted are.   *candies*
Sometime she gallops o'er a courtier's nose
And then dreams he of smelling out <u>a suit;</u>   *a fee for lobbying*
And sometime comes she with a <u>tithe pig's</u> tail,   *(paid as parish dues)*
Tickling a parson's nose as <u>'a</u> lies asleep,   *he*
Then he dreams of another <u>benefice.</u>   *church office (income)*

Sometime she driveth o'er a soldier's neck,
And then dreams he of cutting foreign throats,
Of breaches, <u>ambuscadoes,</u> Spanish blades,   *ambushes*
Of <u>healths</u> five fathom deep; and then <u>anon</u>   *toasts; suddenly*
Drums in his ear, at which he starts and wakes,
And being thus frighted, swears a prayer or two
And sleeps again. This is the very Mab
That plats the main of horses in the night,
And bakes the <u>elf-locks</u> in foul sluttish hairs,   *hair tangled by elves*
Which, once untangled, much misfortune bodes.
This is the <u>hag,</u> when maids lie on their backs,   *nightmare spirit*
That presses them and learns them first to bear,
Making them women of good <u>carriage</u>.   *a pun: posture; pregnancy*
This is she —

17. *Macbeth,* V.v

MACBETH: She should have died hereafter.
There would have been a time for such a word.
Tomorrow, and tomorrow, and tomorrow
Creeps in this petty pace from day to day
To the last syllable of recorded time,
And all our yesterdays have lighted fools
The way to dusty death. Out, out, brief candle.
Life's but a walking shadow, a poor player
That struts and frets his hour upon the stage
And then is heard no more. It is a tale
Told by an idiot, full of sound and fury,
Signifying nothing.

Appendix C
If You Are Working
on a Speech by Shakespeare . . .

If you are working on a speech by Shakespeare or one of his contemporaries, your work on the text, before you get on your feet, should include the following considerations. Some of these apply to other periods and styles of dramatic verse and to "heightened" texts in general. If your speech is in prose, you need not scan it, but you may want to consider some of the rhythmic issues involved in verse, since they are also relevant to prose.

Scansion

To analyze the structure of a Shakespeare speech in verse, you must scan it. Scanning provides you with clues to pronunciation, emphasis, rhythm and shape.

The first step is to divide each line of verse into feet (/) and above each syllable mark whether it is

/   accented (long), or

∪   unaccented (short).

Shakespeare's verse is basically iambic pentameter: that is, five feet (/) of iambs (∪ /). A Shakespearean line is usually 10 or 11 syllables.

> 10: a "masculine" line: ∪ / / ∪ / / ∪ / / ∪ / / ∪ /
>
> 11: a "feminine" line: ∪ / / ∪ / / ∪ / / ∪ / / ∪ / / ∪

A feminine ending is softer, less emphatic. Sometimes it gives the impression of thoughtfulness or uncertainty. When a line has no punctuation at the end, a feminine ending helps it to flow into the next line. The main function of a feminine line, of course, is to accommodate final words in which the last syllable is not accented.

A. A system for scansion

1. Count the syllables first.

Are there ten or eleven syllables? If there are ten, proceed to step three. If there seem to be eleven syllables, go to step two.

2. Determine if the last syllable is accented or not.

If there are eleven syllables and the last is naturally unaccented (as in "nature," "honest") or if the last word is a monosyllable which is an unlikely candidate for emphasis (such as a preposition or a linking verb), then the line has a feminine ending. Mark that last syllable unaccented and put a slash before it, as at the end of the feminine line above. Proceed to step three.

If there seem to be eleven syllables but the last is definitely accented, double-check your count. If you still get eleven, then there are three possibilities:

- your syllable count is wrong because of a *slur* — a monosyllabic pronunciation of what seems to be two syllables (for some examples, see the discussion of slurs under step five);
- the half-line before the caesura (defined below at B) has a feminine ending;
- there is a three-syllable foot somewhere in the line — something which is relatively rare.

3. Mark off feet from the rear of the sentence, assuming each foot is two syllables.

4. Pencil in iambs.

Assume that a Shakespearean foot is an iamb unless you are forced to think differently by:

- pronunciation (the accents of a word may not fit the iambic scheme);
- sense (which may indicate that a monosyllable needs emphasis and should therefore be accented);
- spondaic alliteration or monosyllabic emphasis (discussed below).

Little words, prepositions especially, *can* be accented. Such accents are light; they are relative to the unaccented syllables preceding and following. This is true in everyday English speech. These four lines in praise of England as an island nation protected by the sea (*Richard II*, II, i) have four examples of lightly accented prepositions (here underlined):

This pre / cious stone / set <u>in</u> / the sil / ver sea,
Which serves / it <u>in</u> / the of / fice of a wall,
Or as / a moat / defen / sive <u>to</u> / a house,
Against / the en / vy <u>of</u> / less hap / pier / lands

5. Read the line as marked.
Is your scansion at odds with the usual pronunciation of any polysyllables?
Does your scansion accent those monosyllables which sense requires you to emphasize?
Solve problems. You may have to research how Elizabethans pronounced a word in terms of accents and articulation.

Elizabethan speech
❏ Pronunciation differences
For Elizabethans, "heaven" and "spirit" were generally monosyllabic; one sees "heav'n" in some texts. "Hour," a monosyllable for us, is normally two syllables in Shakespeare. "Fire" is normally two syllables, but is sometimes slurred as one.

Occasionally the suffix -*tion* scans as *tchi-on*, two syllables:

O for / a muse / of fire / that would / ascend
The bright / est heav / en of / inven / tion.

In this text, "fire" is one syllable and "heaven" scans as two.
Most directors prefer not to use archaic pronunciations and do not worry about what modern pronunciations do to the scansion.
Elizabethan *word accents* may be different: e.g., "persével," "revénue."

❏ Elisions
In verse, elision is the omission of a vowel at the end of a word when the next word begins with a vowel: th'embattled plain, th'orient, look to't.

O swear / not by / the moon, / th'incon / stant moon.

Here, in the fourth foot, "th'in-" is one syllable, which makes the line regular. This elision is "corrected" in some modern editions, changing the scansion and the pronunciation.

❏ Slurs

Pronouncing a word indistinctly — as speakers of English often do in everyday speech — may compress two syllables into one (or nearly one). An Elizabethan might slur "flower" as one syllable and "glorious" and "hideous" as two syllables, just as we do. Romeo's name scans sometimes as two, sometimes as three syllables, as the verse requires.

There are not eleven but ten syllables in

Small showers / last long, / but sud / den storms / are short.

"Showers" is slurred as one syllable.

He raised a sigh so piteous and profound
That it did seem to shatter all his bulk,
And end his being; that done, he lets me go...

In the first of these lines, "piteous" is slurred as two syllables. You might scan the third line with a feminine ending on the first half of the line:

And end / his be / ing; / that done, / he lets / me go.

But I suspect that an Elizabethan would slur "being" as one syllable just as we do, and that the line is ten syllables and regular.

Note the slurred syllables underlined in the following lines:

Light van / ity, / insa / <u>tiate</u> cor / morant (*RII*, II. i)
Against / the en / vy of / less hap / <u>pier</u> lands (*RII*, II. i)
Are clam / <u>orous</u> groans / which strike / upon / my heart (*RII*, V. v)

Slurs can be marked in your text with a half-moon arc under the word.

❑ **-ed**

This suffix is sometimes voiced as a syllable (in some texts this is marked -èd) and sometimes slurred (in which case it may be printed as 'd, as in "tripp'd," "call'd"). In texts that do not indicate how to pronounce -ed, scansion will tell you that a syllable is missing and indicate that the -ed should be spoken as a separate syllable.

The good is oft interred with their bones. (*JC*, III. ii)

Counting the syllables reveals that "interred" must be three syllables.

The time is out of joint; O cursed spite... (*H*, I. v)

Scanning — and pronouncing — "cursed" as two syllables makes the line entirely regular.

B. Take note of irregularities in the scansion.

Iambic pentameter establishes a regular pattern, but the majority of Shakespeare's lines are not regular, and the longer he wrote, the less regular his verse became. Variations on the basic meter are significant and have expressive value. Iambs can be replaced by other feet which change the rhythm and give particular emphasis to important words and phrases.

Other metric feet commonly encountered are the spondee and the trochee.

/ / spondee

When Romeo first sees Juliet, he exclaims:

O she / doth teach / the torch / es to / burn bright! (I. v)

In context, it seems clear that "burn bright" is a spondee, which means there is an accent on each word, and the actor should emphasize both. Spondees are commonly alliterative — that is, both words begin with the same consonant — and often monosyllabic.

Small showers / last long, / but sud / den storms / are short (*RII*, II. i)
Hold hard / the breath... (*HV*, III. i)

In general, don't mark a spondee unless you see alliteration or repetition ("on, on", "out out"). A spondee must be aurally necessary, not a mere expressive impulse.

/ u trochee

Shakespeare frequently uses a trochee at the beginning of a line in order to give special emphasis to a word.

In the midst of iambs, a trochee is a rhythmic change of pace that grabs the ear:

DaDUMdaDUMdaDUMdaDUMdaDUM
DAdum!

Can you hear how, in the following lines spoken by wrongly accused Hermione (*WT*, III. ii), the accent on the first syllable of "Tremble" gives the word special force?

I doubt not then but innocence shall make
False accusation blush, and tyranny
<u>Tremble</u> at patience.

How are you to know that "Tremble" is a trochee? It's pronounced that way! Scansion must always be checked against pronunciation, so that you catch an error such as scanning "tremble" as if it were an iamb.

In the following lines spoken by Hotspur (Speech 12, Appendix B), "Breathless" and "Fresh as" are trochees at the beginning of a line. This tells the actor to emphasize these words. Trochees also occur, with the same emphatic effect, at the beginning of the second half of some Shakespeare lines, as here with "leaning" and "neat (and)." Read this excerpt aloud to see how the rhythmic change of pace quite naturally energizes the underlined words and gives them extra bite. The whole passage really lands on "Fresh," which heightens the contrast of the fop's crisp energy with Hotspur's battlefield exhaustion and rage.

But I remember when the fight was done,
When I was dry with rage and extreme toil,
<u>Breathless</u> and faint, <u>leaning</u> upon my sword,
Came there a certain lord, <u>neat</u> and trimly dressed,
<u>Fresh</u> as a bridegroom…

Here is a quiet use of trochaic feet to give a gently optimistic pulse to the first lines out of Friar Laurence's mouth in *Romeo and Juliet* (II. iii). Scan the lines to spot the rhythmic variations.

The grey-eyed morn smiles on the frowning night,
Check'ring the eastern clouds with streaks of light

There are two trochaic feet, which give rhythmic emphasis to "smiles" and "Check'ring." Note how the trochees energize these images.

Short lines

A line with less than ten syllables (if the line is not completed by another character) is Shakespeare's way of indicating a pause, either for a silent beat, in which a character decides, grieves, imagines, etc., or for an action such as kneeling, handing over a key, drinking poison.

Here is Juliet complaining about how long it is taking the Nurse to get back to her with news from Romeo:

Had she affections and warm youthful blood,
She would be as swift in motion as a ball;
My words would bandy her to my sweet love,
And his to me.
But old folks, many feign as they were dead —
Unwieldy, slow, heavy and pale as lead. (Speech 14, Appendix B)

"And his to me." With this short line, Shakespeare has built in a pause, in which Juliet seems to dote on the notion of what words Romeo might send her.

Juliet takes out the potion given her by Friar Laurence in a short-line pause. Perhaps she opens it and raises it to her lips.

My dismal scene I needs must act alone.
Come, vial.
What if this mixture do not act at all? (Speech 15, Appendix B)

C. Scan monosyllabic lines and half-lines (and some monosyllabic phrases) with accents on every word.
Monosyllabic lines have two major effects.

❏ A monosyllabic line *slows* the rhythm.
As Alexander Pope put it:

And ten low words oft creep in one dull line.

Shakespeare uses monosyllables to create these heavy, mournful lines spoken by Lear (V. iii) as he enters with Cordelia dead in his arms:
Howl, howl, howl, howl! O you are men of stones.
Had I your tongues and eyes, I'd use them so
That heaven's vault should crack. She's gone forever.
I know when one is dead and when one lives.
She's dead as earth.

A line accelerates, on the other hand, with the use of polysyllables and metrical feet like the anapest (∪ ∪ /) and the dactyl (/ ∪ ∪), which have more short or unaccented syllables.

By combining these principles, Shakespeare can orchestrate the rhythms of a speech.

Absent thee from felicity a while,
And in this harsh world draw thy breath in pain. (*H*, V. ii)

Here the relative briskness of the first line's reference to carefree happiness sets off the heavy-hearted monosyllables of the second.

❏ A monosyllabic line *emphasizes* each word.
A monosyllabic line stresses virtually every syllable. It is as if each word were underlined.
Shakespeare often treats momentous, heartfelt moments in this way.

Much of Lear's speech over dead Cordelia is monosyllabic.

> And my poor fool is hanged! No, no, no life.
> Why should a dog, a horse, a rat have life,
> And thou no breath at all? Thou'lt come no more.... (*V.* iii)

He dies speaking monosyllables.

Lovesick Duke Orsino is very melancholy, and a bit of sad music has touched him to the quick when he asks Viola:

> How dost thou like this tune? (*TN*, II.iv)

It is not at all a casual question, which is signaled by the monosyllables. Try it with every word underlined: that is Shakespeare's direction.

D. Mark (||) the caesuras.

A great majority of Shakespeare's lines have a caesura — a point about midway where the line may sensibly be divided into two half-lines. A half-line is the smallest possible unit in speaking Elizabethan verse, but it is not usually spoken as a separate phrase. A caesura in Shakespeare does not indicate a pause or break. Half-lines are vocal units within a line that should, as a rule, be spoken continuously.

Speaking a text with attention to its caesuras does much to clarify sense: each phrase and syntactical unit can be given a distinct vocal shape within the flow of the text. A caesura also permits Shakespeare to give emphasis to the last word of the half-line and, when he wishes, to the first word that follows it.

Here are the caesuras for the beginning of Hotspur's story about the courtier who outraged him (Speech 12, Appendix B):

But I remember || when the fight was done,
When I was dry with rage || and extreme toil,
Breathless and faint, || leaning upon my sword,
Came there a certain lord, || neat and trimly dressed,
Fresh as a bridegroom. || He was perfumèd ...

The caesura is a form of punctuation more reliable for the actor than editorial decisions about Elizabethan punctuation or the lack thereof.

Sometimes there is no caesura, as when Lear, in trochaic pentameter, mourns that dead Cordelia will "come no more": "Never, never, never, never, never."

E. After marking the accents and caesuras in your text, read it aloud several times.

Ride the meter: let the iambic pulse move you forward. Shakespeare's verse should have momentum. There should not be a full stop or pause at the end of a line unless you have come to the end of a complete thought, as indicated by a period, question mark, or exclamation point. In the absence of such punctuation, move on.

But you should not run through the end of a line into the next with no vocal acknowledgment of the line structure. Whether or not there is punctuation at the end of a line, there should be a slight poising of the final word. The actor holds onto the last syllable for a split second, then transitions from this sound into the first syllable of the new line. For a fraction of a moment the last syllable — if there is not a full stop — is lifted and held, yet forward movement continues. It is as if you bounce off the energy of each line's last word into the next line, but pass through a moment of suspension in the air.

In this way the end of a line serves as a *springboard* into the next. It should feel as though the flow of language is continuous even though the end of a line is subtly acknowledged. Coming to a halt should be a significant event.

Emphasis

The importance of emphasis

Speaking Shakespeare's verse requires special skills. It is heightened, elevated language. It needs a style of speaking that gives voice to its intricate builds, its rhetorical shapes, its musical rhythms. Speaking blank verse naturalistically, with the impulsive inflections of everyday speech, not only fails to do the language justice, but makes it very difficult to understand what is being said. You can certainly speak Shakespeare in contemporary tones, provided they make expressive sense, but you must first shape the language so that people can hear what the text says.

You must speak the *structure* of each thought. The syntax must be audible: subject-verb-object, above all. Modifiers should modify, not take center stage. Subordinate clauses should sound subordinate; parallel structures should be vocal parallels; lists should aurally accumulate; climactic conclusions should be the pinnacle of carefully constructed shapes.

The most important words must be lifted so that the audience can *hear* what is most important. Finding the right emphases in a Shakespeare speech is like focusing a lens: what was blurry becomes crystal clear.

All this must have been as true in Shakespeare's day as now. Structuring the sense of what is said is a good part of an actor's work in every period. The first step is figuring out precisely which words to emphasize. This work starts up front and must be continued throughout rehearsal, so that the text comes into progressively clearer focus. Deciding what to emphasize — and how — may require weeks, in which you explore the shape of each sentence and the overall structure of the speech and of the scene in which it occurs.

Sometimes you must simplify and edit impulses in the later stages of rehearsal: nothing should get in the way of sense.

Knowing what you are saying.

Deciding which words to emphasize assumes that you understand what your text is saying. If the sense of a line is not clear to you after considering the notes in your edition, you should look up any unfamiliar words. Pay attention to meanings that a modern dictionary terms "archaic," "rare" or "obsolete." You might need to consult a specialized resource, such as a Shakespeare lexicon or a more heavily annotated edition of the play (e.g., Arden, Cambridge, Oxford), where difficult lines are often discussed at some length.

Emphasize the spine of the sentence: the fewest possible words.

The key to speaking Shakespeare clearly is emphasizing the words that the audience needs to hear to make sense of the text. A good rule of thumb is to emphasize the minimal number of words essential to comprehension: these comprise the spine of the sentence. In this spirit, actors and directors often refer to the *operant* words.

403

All the rest of your text should be spoken without undue emphasis — lightly and (as Hamlet would say) "trippingly on the tongue." Emphasizing unessential words clouds the meaning: texts become unintelligible if too many words are emphasized.

Focus on nouns and main verbs, above all on *nouns.*

Resist emphasizing pronouns, negatives, adjectives and adverbs, prepositions and conjunctions, except when they are part of an antithesis or essential to telling the story.

Pay special attention to the endwords.

In Shakespeare's verse, a word's location in the line is the best guide as to whether you should emphasize it. Shakespeare structures his verse so that the important words are placed in an emphatic position — especially as *endwords.* Most of the words needing emphasis in Shakespeare are at the end of a line, or at the end of the first half of a line (the last word before the caesura).

Look at Speech 17 in Appendix B, Macbeth's soliloquy after hearing the news that his wife is dead. The eminent British actor Ian McKellen commented that the endwords of these lines "say it all": hereafter, word, to-morrow, day, time, fools, candle, player, stage, tale, fury, nothing.

The last word before the caesura is the endword for the first "half" of a line. In Macbeth's tomorrow speech, the half-line endwords (here in italics) flesh out the previous list in this way: hereafter, *time,* word, to-morrow, *pace,* day, *syllable,* time, *yesterdays,* fools, *death,* candle, *shadow,* player, *frets,* stage, *no more,* tale, *idiot,* fury, *nothing.* That gives us most of the operant words in the speech, its spine. All these words need emphasis, some more lightly than others.

This structure enables actors to speak the verse quite clearly and enables audiences to hear the important words and therefore to follow the story, the rhetoric, and the imagery. Actors who attend to the design of Shakespeare's verse by emphasizing endwords make it much easier to follow what is being said. Trust the endwords, and underline them in your text.

Careful consideration of why Shakespeare has placed a word at the end of a line or half-line will lead to discoveries large and small. It is useful throughout your rehearsal process to check whether you are neglecting endwords — and the sense that they make audible. Insights about endwords continue throughout the course of rehearsing and performing Shakespeare. In one sense, work on his plays is a process of exploring precisely how to emphasize the endwords. What is the right quality and the right degree of emphasis for each particular endword in your speech? The emphasis given to each endword should be specifically suited to its sense in the context. Actors of Shakespeare should be virtuosi of endword emphasis.

Attention to endwords should be balanced with the urge to move the thought along to the end of larger units. Even as a half-line or line culminates in its endword, that word should springboard an actor into the next line.

Underline metrically emphasized words.
❑ Trochaic firstwords
Shakespeare quite frequently uses a trochee at the beginning of a line in order to give its first word emphasis. Let's call these "trochaic firstwords" and underline them along with endwords.

In Macbeth's "To-morrow" speech there are these examples: *Creeps, Life's, Told, Signifying.* If these words are added to the endwords listed above, the spine of the speech is virtually complete.

A trochee that begins the second half of a line — that is, a trochee following the caesura — also directs you to emphasize that word. When a caesura splits an iambic foot in half, the second half of the line begins with a new word and an accented syllable. The result (sometimes, not always) is what we might call a quasi-trochaic effect: even though the foot in question is an iamb, there is a rhythmic pulse whereby Shakespeare gives the word which begins the half-line emphasis. There is an example in the next to the last line of the "Tomorrow" soliloquy:

Told by / an id / iot || <u>full</u> / of sound / and fu / ry.

Here the caesura divides the unaccented second syllable of "idiot" and "full," which is given emphasis by its accent.

❑ Monosyllabic lines
In the same Macbeth speech, after the self-important "player" struts and frets a while, he leaves the stage for good, and Shakespeare

405

emphasizes the finality of every man's exit by slowing the next line with monosyllables. As we have seen, you should scan such lines as if every syllable were accented, with the aural effect of underlining each word:

And then is heard no more.

This new rhythm continues with It is a tale, but each of the next three half-lines begins with a trochee, which energizes the conclusion; instead of slowing to a doleful close, Shakespeare wants bite.

Many memorable lines have been etched into our minds because their monosyllables are quite naturally emphasized:

We are such stuff / As dreams are made on (*T*, IV, i)
What a piece of work is a man! (*H*, II, ii)
The course of true love never did run smooth. (*MND*, I, i)
… and what's his reason? I am a Jew. Hath not a Jew eyes? Hath not a Jew hands … (*MV*, III, i)

The last example, we should note, is prose, where monosyllabic emphasis is just as possible as in verse.

❑ Spondees
When Macbeth exclaims "Out, out, brief candle!" the natural urge to emphasize both the first and the second "out" means you should scan this foot as a spondee, with both words accented and emphasized.

When Romeo first sees Juliet, he exclaims:

O she doth teach the torches to burn bright! (I, v)

Spondees in Shakespeare, as we have seen, are commonly alliterative: hard heart, wide world, etc.

A good rule of thumb is to mark a spondee only if the foot involves alliteration or repetition.

Consider by way of summary this excerpt from Juliet's speech before she takes the potion (Speech 15, Appendix B). I have underlined the endwords (both at the end of lines and before caesuras), the trochaic firstwords (two of which follow caesuras), and the monosyllabic half-line at the climax: "Here's drink — I drink to thee." Read aloud just the underlined words: they pretty much tell the story!

> Alack, <u>alack</u>, ‖ is it not like that <u>I</u>,
> So early <u>waking</u> ‖ — what with loathsome <u>smells</u>,
> And <u>shrieks</u> ‖ like mandrakes torn out of the <u>earth,</u>
> That living <u>mortals</u>, ‖ <u>hearing</u> them, run <u>mad</u> —
> O, if I <u>wake</u>, ‖ shall I not then be <u>distraught</u>,
> <u>Environèd</u> ‖ with all these hideous <u>fears</u>,
> And madly <u>play</u> ‖ with my forefathers' <u>joints,</u>
> And pluck the mangled <u>Tybalt</u> ‖ from his <u>shroud</u>,
> And in this <u>rage</u>, ‖ with some great kinsman's <u>bone</u>
> As with a <u>club</u> ‖ <u>dash</u> out my desperate <u>brains</u>?
> O, <u>look</u>! ‖ Methinks I see my cousin's <u>ghost</u>
> <u>Seeking</u> out <u>Romeo</u>, ‖ that did spit his <u>body</u>
> Upon a rapier's <u>point</u>. ‖ Stay, Tybalt, <u>stay</u>!
> Romeo, Romeo, <u>Romeo</u>! ‖ <u>Here's</u> <u>drink</u> — <u>I</u> <u>drink</u> <u>to</u> <u>thee</u>.
> [or, in another edition (Q1):
> Romeo, I <u>come</u>! ‖ <u>this</u> <u>do</u> I <u>drink</u> <u>to</u> <u>thee</u>!]

Certain juicy words might tempt you to emphasize them (*loathsome, hideous, madly, mangled, desperate*), but they are not essential to the spine in the same way as the words underlined. As adjectives and adverbs, they are on the to-be-avoided-for-emphasis list. So it is not "<u>hideous</u> fears," but "hideous <u>fears</u>"; not "<u>mangled</u> Tybalt," but "mangled <u>Tybalt</u>"; not "<u>madly</u> play," but "madly <u>play</u>." In each case it is much more important to hear the noun or verb than the modifier. Note that most of these tempting words have so much sound sense that they take care of themselves and do not need additional emphasis.

Read this section of Juliet's speech. The words which are not emphasized should be spoken quite lightly so that the emphasized words stand out.

When Shakespeare wants you to emphasize a word which would not ordinarily be emphasized — such as an adjective or an adverb or a pronoun — he puts it in an endword (or other metrically emphasized) position. Here are several examples in one passage:

    And gentlemen in England, ‖ <u>now</u> a-bed,
    Shall think themselves <u>accurs'd</u> ‖ they were not <u>here</u>
    And hold their manhoods <u>cheap</u> ‖ whiles any speaks
    That fought with <u>us</u> ‖ upon St. Crispan's Day. (*HV*, IV, iii):

A line of verse which has no punctuation at the end continues a thought into the next line. The final word of such a line is not always important to sense.

    … But howsoe'r you have
    Been jostled from your senses, know for certain
    That I am Prospero… (*T*, V, i)

The final word "have" is not so important to sense as to warrant emphasis. It should not be underlined. But a case could be made for underlining "certain," in which case Prospero speaks it emphatically. When a line of verse flows into the next without punctuation, you must determine from the context whether the final word should be emphasized.

You should not emphasize both a verb and its direct object: e.g., "I want you to <u>make</u> the <u>bed</u>." We do talk in that emphatic way when we're aggravated, but in Shakespeare, where emphasis is critical, "I want you to make the <u>bed</u>" will suffice. Given a prejudice for emphasizing nouns over verbs, you should generally emphasize the direct object. You should not, therefore say "to <u>save</u> a brother's <u>life</u>" but "to save a brother's <u>life</u>."

    Then will he strip his <u>sleeve</u> and show his <u>scars</u> … (*HV*, IV, iii)

In this example, Shakespeare has placed the direct objects as endwords.

If two words are linked which have essentially the same meaning, they should be treated as a unit, with only the second word emphasized on behalf of the whole phrase. E.g.:

    The slings and <u>arrows</u> of outrageous fortune (*H*, III, i)
    To grunt and <u>sweat</u> under a weary life (*H*, III, i)
    'Twould be my tyranny to strike and <u>gall</u> them (*Measure*, I, iii)

Emphasis can have its effect only if unnecessary emphases are avoided.

Emphasize <u>important</u> words.

Shakespeare usually situates important words so that the structure of his verse will emphasize them. Words that in one way or another are *really* important should be double-underlined and given special emphasis.

1. Emphasize words important to *telling the story* because they:
   - name characters and tell us who they are and what they are up to;
   - define where and when the scene is taking place;
   - give essential information about the plot;
   - make clear the nature of a crucial transition from one moment or idea to the next;
   - state conclusions, morals, turning points, epiphanies, critical decisions, upshots — the central moment to which the text leads.

2. Emphasize *topic* words and phrases which announce what the next section of text is about.

Tell me, my daughters —
Since now we will divest us both of rule,
Interest of territory, cares of state —
Which of you shall we say doth <u>love us most</u>? (*KL*, I, i)

Lear's question sets up a series of speeches by his daughters on the theme of love. Note how Shakespeare helps the actor by making the line which states the topic words monosyllabically emphatic.

For God's sake, let us sit upon the ground
And tell sad stories of the <u>death of kings</u>.
How some have been depos'd, some slain in war ... (*RII*, III, ii)

The next section of this speech is a litany of the "death of kings."

If it were done when 'tis done, then 'twere well
It were done quickly; if the <u>assassination</u>
Could trammel up the consequence... (*M*, I, vii)

The word "assassination" names the deed which Macbeth is soliloquizing about.

3. Emphasize *key words in rhetorical and figurative language.*

a. Persuasion: emphasizing *why*

What are the key words and phrases spoken in a debate or a proposal? What does your character set out to prove or disprove? What evidence is offered? What reasons are given? What distinctions are made? What conclusions are drawn?

You must judge which points are subordinate and which are most important; we should be able to hear in your voice the relative weight which your character gives to each element of their argument. You must be skilled in realizing many degrees of emphasis.

b. Metaphor

Emphasize the word which names the metaphor, and, secondarily, the main points of comparison.

Juliet is impatient as she waits for night to come, when she will consummate her secret marriage to Romeo:

> So tedious is this day
> As is the <u>night</u> before some <u>festival</u>
> To an impatient <u>child</u> that hath new<u> robes</u>
> <u>And may not wear them.</u> (III, ii)

Note how most of the words important to fleshing out the metaphor have been placed in endword positions.

Guildenstern has told Hamlet that he doesn't know how to play the recorder which Hamlet has insisted he should play:

> Why, look you now, how unworthy a thing you make of me. You would <u>play</u> upon me; you would seem to know my <u>stops</u>; you would pluck out the heart of my mystery; you would <u>sound</u> me from my lowest <u>note</u> to the top of my <u>compass</u>; and there is much <u>music</u>, excellent voice, in this little organ, yet cannot you make it speak. 'Sblood, do you think I am easier to be played on than a <u>pipe?</u> (*H*, III, ii)

c. Antithesis

An antithesis opposes or contrasts two ideas. e.g.:

- Give me <u>liberty</u> or give me <u>death</u>.
- I come to <u>bury</u> Caesar, not to <u>praise</u> him. (*JC*, III, ii)
- A <u>sickness</u> caught of me, and yet I <u>well</u>? (*WT*, I, ii)
- 'Tis <u>torture</u> and not <u>mercy</u>. (*R&J*, III, iii)

Antitheses are given vocal shape by voicing the contrasting words on different pitches: one word is markedly higher or lower in pitch than the other. Which word is higher or lower is a question of vocal shape; your choice will depend on the context.

Here are some double antitheses, a common figure involving two related sets of opposites:

- The <u>prodigal</u> robs his <u>heir</u>; the <u>miser</u> robs <u>himself</u>.
- <u>Excess</u> of <u>ceremony</u> shows <u>want</u> of <u>breeding</u>.
- *George Bernard Shaw*: Although my <u>trade</u> is that of a <u>playwright</u>, my <u>vocation</u> is that of a <u>prophet</u>.
- The grey-ey'd <u>morn</u> <u>smiles</u> on the <u>frowning</u> <u>night</u> (*R&J*, II, iii)

You might use the same pitches for each pair of opposites: high-low, high-low. Or you might vary the pattern: high-low, low-high. You might also use four different pitches for the four words. The third pitch, for example, might fall between the first and second; the fourth would be the lowest (or highest).

Antitheses may contrast not only single words but phrases, clauses, or sentences.

d. Oxymoron

Related to antithesis is another figure of speech involving opposites, the oxymoron, which combines two opposite ideas so that the seeming self-contradiction is understood to be true, at least in context. e.g.: *to make haste slowly, cruel kindness, thunderous silence*. The opposing terms of an oxymoron should both be emphasized.

411

Good night! Good night! Parting is such <u>sweet</u> <u>sorrow</u> ... (*R&J*, II, ii)
Both words should be emphasized.

4. *Antecedents of a pronoun which repeats* throughout a passage
   should be emphasized so that the audience is clear about who
   "she" is, what "it" is, etc.

> Came there <u>a certain lord</u>, neat and trimly dressed,
> Fresh as a bridegroom. He was perfumed
> (his ... He ... his ... his ... he ... He ... his ... etc.)
> (Speech 12, Appendix B)

That this anonymous lord never appears makes it even more
important that the Hotspur actor set the audience up clearly, lest they fail
to grasp who exasperated him.

In sum, assume that only endwords — of lines and of half-lines — are
emphasized, unless you are forced to think differently by:

- a trochee at the beginning of a line or the second half of a line;
- a spondee;
- a monosyllabic line or half-line;
- the need to emphasize both elements of an antithesis or oxymoron;
- the requirements of making sense.

A. Varieties of emphasis
After you have determined which words in your text require
emphasis, read through it, exploring different means of giving emphasis
to the words you have underlined. Among the ways in which you might
do this:

- pitch change (higher or lower);
- stress — the relative force with which a word is pronounced;
- giving a word expressive texture or color;
- increasing the sharpness of your articulation, especially by etching
  the consonants;
- taking a small pause before a word;

- rhythmic change (quicker or slower);
- dynamic change (louder or quieter);
- nonverbal means: gesture, movement, facial expression, an action with a prop, etc., scored in relationship to the word you wish to emphasize.

A change in pitch is by far the most common means of emphasizing words in English. Since it is the simplest, quickest mode of emphasis in briskly flowing verse, it is also the most useful.

These modes can be used in an endless variety of combinations and intensities.

B. Emphasizing what is especially important

Shakespeare's speeches are carefully constructed; you must pay attention to their "architecture" as you shape them (see Chapter 14).

Framing a key moment

Actions and words which are key moments in the development of a plot or a theme need to be given *extra* special emphasis — more than the spine, more even than what we have termed "important words." You need to develop skills which allow you to heighten particularly significant texts and moments.

Imagine a *Tempest* production in which Ariel has been suspended in the air in Peter Pan-fashion until given his freedom, at which point this spirit of the air is slowly lowered to the stage floor: the first steps he takes on earth are an event. Time, space and movement combine to frame the moment. Lighting and sound might also contribute to the effect.

To *frame* a moment is in the first place to take time with it. When a key moment is framed, the audience senses that what is happening or what is being said is especially significant. Framing also gives the audience time to experience what the moment signifies. It is as if theatrical time has been slowed; an action may even be played in something like slow motion. You may even freeze-frame a moment on stage — as lights fade, as the curtain falls, or simply until action is resumed.

Framing is not only a question of taking time, however. All of theater's resources may be used toward the end of heightening significant moments. The size of an action — making it larger — can make it more

413

important. Space may quite literally be used as a frame. You can also heighten a moment by using space in a novel, unexpected fashion. Costuming, lighting, props, sound, music — every element of theater — can play a role in framing moments.

Text may be shaped so that a particular line or word is framed. Actors and directors sometimes speak of putting a box around a crucial bit of text. Time (rhythm, pause, pace), varieties of emphasis, and staging may all play a role in accomplishing this. Modes of emphasis may be used in an especially emphatic way: for example, a big pitch change, heavy stress, slowing the rhythm and separating each word, or choreographing an arresting action or a striking bit of staging. You may also combine various modes of emphasis to frame a text.

You can mark texts that you mean to frame by putting a box around the words in question.

Arcing to a central text or action

You must make decisions about which parts of your text are especially important. Questions to ponder include:

- What are the key words in your text? What are the key ideas and the key events? What must you get across above all else? How can your voice and body make clear that *this* is especially important? How can you shape your speech so that everything leads up to and away from key moments?
- Where is the climax of this thought, this argument, this passion? How should you speak the text so that it arcs to that climax?
- Where is the central moment in your speech? This may be a conclusion, a moment of epiphany, a turning point, a decision, a confusion, the resolution of a character's inner conflict, etc. How do the component parts of your speech rise toward this moment? How should you shape the speech so that it aurally culminates at that point? How should you use emphasis to make clear that this moment is the upshot?
- What is the relative importance of other parts of the text? How do they contribute to making the main point? How may you use relative degrees of emphasis to give each part its due?

Everything leading to a key moment should be relatively less emphatic. Emphasis can have its effect only if secondary emphases are subordinated to what is most important. If your approach to the key moment is carefully modulated so that what you say becomes gradually more emphatic, the result is an arc, a curving ascent to what is most important.

Appendix D
Shopping for Speeches

Stores specializing in scripts and theater books

Applause Theatre & Cinema Bookstore
211 West 71st Street
New York, NY 10023
212-496-7511

The Drama Book Shop
250 W. 40th St. *(between 7th and 8th Avenues)*
New York, NY 10018
1-800-322-0595
Fax: 212-730-8739
www.dramabookshop.com

Samuel French, Inc.
45 West 25th St. — Dept. W
New York, NY 10010
212-206-8990
Fax: 212-206-1429
www.samuelfrench.com

Samuel French, Inc.
7623 Sunset Blvd. — Dept. W
Hollywood, CA 90046
323-876-0570
Fax: 323-876-6822
Samuel French also has stores in Toronto and London.

Act I Bookstore
2540 N. Lincoln
Chicago, IL 60614
1-800-55-PLAYS · 773-348-6757
Fax: 773-348-5561
www.act1books.com

Baker's Plays
1445 Hancock Street
Quincy, MA 02169-5235
617-745-0805
www.bakersplays.com

The Internet Theatre Bookshop
www.stageplays.com

Publishers of scripts

Baker's Plays
P.O. Box 699222
Quincy, MA 02269-9222
617-745-0805
Fax: 617-745-9891
www.bakersplays.com

Broadway Play Publishing, Inc.
56 E. 81st St.
New York, NY 10028-0202
212-772-8334
Fax: 212-772-8358
www.BroadwayPlayPubl.com

Contemporary Drama Service
PO Box 7710
Colorado Springs, CO 80933-7710
719-594-4422
Fax: 719-594-9916
www.contemporarydrama.com

Dramatists Play Service, Inc.
440 Park Avenue South
New York, NY 10016
212-683-8960
Fax: 212-213-1539
www.dramatists.com

Methuen Publishing
215 Vauxhall Bridge Road
London SW1V 1EJ UK
(+44) 20 7798 1600
Fax: (+44) 20 7828 2098
www.methuen.co.uk

Samuel French, Inc.
45 West 25th St.
New York, NY 10010
212-206-8990
Fax: 212-206-1429
www.samuelfrench.com

Publishers of anthologies of speeches and monologs
Apart from the anthologies issued by mainstream publishers, several companies specializing in theater books publish anthologies.

Applause Theatre & Cinema Books
151 W. 46th St., Fl 8
New York, NY 10036

Dramaline Publications
36-851 Palm View Road
Rancho Mirage, CA 92270
760-770-6076
Fax: 760-770-4507
www.dramaline.com
Dramaline's list includes collections of monologs from Shakespeare, Moliere, Chekhov, and Oscar Wilde.

Heinemann
88 Post Road West
P.O. Box 5007
Westport, CT 06881
1-800-793-2154
Fax: 800-847-0938
www.heinemann.com

Meriwether Publishing Ltd.
PO Box 7710
Colorado Springs, CO 80933-7710
719-594-4422
Fax: 719-594-9916
www.meriwether.com

Routledge (Theatre Arts Books)
7625 Empire Drive
Florence, KY 41042
1-800-634-7064
Fax: 800-248-4724
www.routledge-ny.com

Smith & Kraus Publishers
6 Lower Mill Road
North Stratford, NH 03590
603-669-7032
1-800-895-4331
Fax: 603-922-3348
www.smithkraus.com
An extensive list including period collections and annual contemporary collections.

Theatre Communications Group
355 Lexington Avenue
New York, NY 10017
212-697-5230
Fax: 212-983-4847
www.tcg.org

Collections of Monologs

Contemporary: Men

Contemporary American Monologues for Men, ed. Todd London, Theatre Communications Group, 1998.

The Contemporary Monologue: Men, ed. Michael Earley and Philippa Keil, Methuen Drama, 1993.

The Methuen Audition Book for Men, ed. Annika Bluhm, Methuen Drama, 1989.

The Modern Monologue: Men, ed. Michael Earley and Philippa Keil Theatre Arts Books / Routledge, 1993.

One Hundred Men's Stage Monologues from the 1980's, ed. Jocelyn A. Beard, Smith and Kraus, 1991.

One on One: The Best Men's Monologues for the Nineties, ed. Jack Temchin, Applause Theatre Books, 1992.

Solo! The Best Monologues of the 80s (Men), ed. Michael Early and Philippa Keil, Applause Theatre Book Publishers, 1987.

Contemporary: Women

Acting Scenes and Monologs for Young Women, Maya Levy, Meriwether Publishing Ltd., 1999.

Contemporary American Monologues for Women, ed. Todd London, Theatre Communications Group, 1998.

The Contemporary Monologue: Women, ed. Michael Earley and Philippa Keil, Methuen Drama, 1995.

The Methuen Audition Book for Women, ed. Annika Bluhm, Methuen Drama, 1989.

The Modern Monologue: Women, ed. Michael Earley and Philippa Keil, Theatre Arts Books / Routledge, 1993.

Monologues for Women, Beth Henley, Dramaline Publications, 1992.

Monologues for Women by Women, ed. Tori Haring-Smith, Heinemann, 1994.

More Monologues for Women by Women, ed. Tori Haring-Smith, Heinemann, 1996.

One Hundred Women's Stage Monologues from the 1980's, ed. Jocelyn A. Beard, Smith and Kraus, 1991.

One on One: The Best Women's Monologues for the Nineties, ed. Jack Temchin, Applause Theatre Books, 1993.

Solo! The Best Monologues of the 80s (Women), ed. Michael Early and Philippa Keil, Applause Theatre Book Publishers, 1990.

Contemporary: Men and Women

50 Great Monologs for Student Actors, Bill Majeski, Meriwether Publishing Ltd., 1987.

57 Original Auditions for Actors, Eddie Lawrence, Meriwether Publishing Ltd. 1983.

100 Monologues, ed. Laura Harrington, Mentor, 1989.

The Actor's Book of Contemporary Stage Monologues, ed. Nina Shengold, Penguin, 1987.

Another Perfect Piece, ed. Tony Hamill, Playwrights Canada Press, 1995.

Audition Monologs for Student Actors, ed. Roger Ellis, Meriwether Publishing Ltd., 1999.

Audition Monologs for Student Actors II, ed. Roger Ellis, Meriwether Publishing Ltd. 2001.

Encore! More Winning Monologs for Young Actors, Peg Kehret, Meriwether Publishing, Ltd., 1988.

The Flip Side, Heather Henderson, Meriwether Publishing Ltd. 1998.

Great Monologues for Young Actors, Vol. I, ed. Craig Slaight and Jack Sharrar, Smith and Kraus, 1992.

Great Monologues for Young Actors, Vol. II, ed. Craig Slaight and Jack Sharrar, Smith and Kraus, 1997.

Monologues for Young Actors, Lorraine Cohen, Avon Books, 1994.

Moving Parts: Monologues from Contemporary Plays, ed. Nina Shengold and Eric Lane, Penguin, 1992.

Outstanding Stage Monologs and Scenes from the '90s, ed. Steven H. Gale, Meriwether Publishing Ltd. 2000.

The Perfect Piece: Monologues from Canadian Plays, ed. Tony Hamill, Playwrights Canada Press, 1990.

Scenes and Monologs from the Best New Plays, ed. Roger Ellis, Meriwether Publishing Ltd., 1992.

Spotlight, Stephanie S. Fairbanks, Meriwether Publishing Ltd., 1996.

Teens Have Feelings, Too!, Debra Karczewski, Meriwether Publishing Ltd., 2000.

Tight Spots, Diana Howie, Meriwether Publishing Ltd., 1999.

Tough Acts to Follow, Shirley Ullom, Meriwether Publishing Ltd., 2000.

Two-Minute Monologs, Glenn Alterman, Meriwether Publishing Ltd., 1995.

The Ultimate Audition Book: 222 Monologues, 2 Minutes & Under, ed. Jocelyn A. Beard, Smith and Kraus, 1997.

The Way I See It, Kimberly A. McCormick, Meriwether Publishing Ltd., 2001.

Winning Monologs for Young Actors, Peg Kehret, Meriwether Publishing, Ltd.,1986.

For Actors of Color

Monologues for Actors of Color: Men, ed. Roberta Uno, Routledge, 2000.

Monologues for Actors of Color: Women, ed. Roberta Uno, Routledge, 2000.

Monologues on Black Life, Gus Edwards, Heinemann, 1990.

More Monologues on Black Life, Gus Edwards, Heinemann, 2000.

Voices of Color: Scenes and Monologues from the Black American Theatre, ed. Woodie King, Jr., Applause Books, 1994.

Classics: Men

Absolute Monologues: European Classics for Men, ed. Simon Reade, Theatre Communications, Group, Inc., 1994.

Alternative Shakespeare Auditions for Men, ed. Simon Dunmore, Theatre Arts Books / Routledge, 1997.

Classical Audition Speeches for Men, ed. Jean Marlowe, Heinemann, 1996.

The Classical Monologue: Men, ed. Michael Earley and Philippa Keil, Theatre Arts Books / Routledge, 1992.

Classical Monologues for Men: Monologues from 16th, 17th, and 18th Century Plays, ed. Kyle Donnelly, Heinemann, 1992.

Soliloquy! The Shakespeare Monologues: The Men, ed. Michael Earley and Philippa Keil, Applause Theatre Book Publishers, 1988.

Classics: Women

Alternative Shakespeare Auditions for Women, ed. Simon Dunmore, Theatre Arts Books / Routledge, 1997.

Classical Audition Speeches for Women, ed. Jean Marlowe, Heinemann, 1996.

The Classical Monologue: Women, ed. Michael Earley and Philippa Keil, Theatre Arts Books / Routledge, 1992.

Classical Monologues for Women, ed. Simon Reade, Theatre Communications Group, Inc., 1994.

Classical Monologues for Women: Monologues from 16th, 17th, and 18th Century Plays, ed. Kyle Donnelly, Heinemann, 1992.

Soliloquy! The Shakespeare Monologues: The Women, ed. Michael Earley and Philippa Keil, Applause Theatre Book Publishers, 1988.

Classics: Men and Women

The Actor's Book of Classical Monologues, ed. Stefan Rudnicki, Penguin, 1988.

Monologues from Classic Plays, 468 B.C. to 1960 A.D., Jocelyn Beard, Econo-Clad Books, 1999.

100 Great Monologues from the Neo-Classical Theatre, ed. Jocelyn A. Beard, Smith and Kraus, 1994.

100 Great Monologues from the 19th Century Romantic and Realistic Theatres, ed. Jocelyn A. Beard, Smith and Kraus, 1994.

100 Great Monologues from the Renaissance Theatre, ed. Jocelyn A. Beard, Smith and Kraus, 1994.

The Theatre Audition Book, ed. Gerald Lee Ratliff, Meriwether Publishing Ltd., 1998.

From Literature

The Actor's Book of Monologues for Women from Non-Dramatic Sources, ed. Stefan Rudnicki, Penguin, 1991.

Monologues from Contemporary Literature, ed. Eric Kraus, Smith and Kraus, 1992.

Monologues From Literature, ed. Marisa Smith and Kristin Graham, Fawcett Columbine / Ballantine Books, 1990.

Sudden Fiction International, ed. Robert Shapard and James Thomas, W.W. Norton & Company, 1989.

From Film

The Actor's Book of Movie Monologues, ed. Marisa Smith and Amy Schewel, Penguin Books, 1986.

Film Scenes for Actors, ed. Joshua Karton, Bantam Books, 1983.

Film Scenes for Actors, Volume II, ed. Joshua Karton, Bantam Books, 1987.

Appendix E
A Sample Syllabus for a
Course on Acting Narrative Speeches

A course focused on narrative speeches should be a core offering in every performance curriculum. The skills and sensibilities that can be taught in this context are as essential to the development of actors as those addressed in scene work. The substance of this book has been successfully taught to beginning and advanced students, majors and non-majors, professionals and amateurs.

The semester-long course outlined in the following syllabus guides students through the development of two speeches. By way of a final exam, students present a third speech and perform two of their three speeches in an audition showcase — to which the public (or guests) may be invited.

I have sketched twenty-eight classes, as if the course met twice a week for fourteen weeks. The syllabus may certainly be adapted to other time frames. In a shorter course, students might work topic by topic on one speech and perhaps shape a second on their own. Or work on narrative speeches might become one unit in a larger acting course.

I have noted which exercises might be done in class and made suggestions for performance assignments. Covering all of this material would require classes that meet for a substantial amount of time, but the number of exercises and assignments may be trimmed if classes are shorter.

With a few exceptions, this syllabus follows the book. An alternative order for topics would, after the first speeches have been introduced in class seven, proceed to onomatopoeia and rhythm, then return to story sense to cover gesture, movement and space.

[Suggestions and possibilities addressed to instructors appear in italicized brackets.]

1. Overview of course. The Actor's Art: Conjuring Another Time and Place.

[After a brief statement about the nature of narrative speeches, the class might play with possible choices for Nat's speech from I'm Not Rappaport *in Chapter 1. As time permits, students should get on their feet to explore moments in Juliet's speech about the tomb (e.g., 1.1-9) and Mercutio's Queen Mab speech: (e.g., 1.18-20). Approaches to acting that do not focus on telling the story are defined in exercises 1.26-29.]*

[You might assign other moments from the Juliet and Mercutio speeches for performance in the next class: e.g., 1.10-11, 1.13-14, 1.17; 1.21-25; 1.30-31, 1.33-34. Some moments might be assigned to several students, others to everyone.]

[When students are presenting assignments, keep everyone active by having them perform in multiple rounds — one or two moments in each round. If you do not view all of the performance assignments at the beginning of class, you can, after introducing the new topic, finish with a final round of moments.]

[Feedback should focus on the issue at hand. Encourage students to position themselves farther inside the story and to make more specific choices.]

Story Sense

2. DUE: Read Chapter 1: "The Other Time and Place"
     Moments from Chapter 1
     Read Appendix A: "Excerpts"
As you read through Appendix A, take note of the "other time and place" that the actor must create in each excerpt. Choose one sentence from an excerpt to perform in class, and work on making it clear that the character is in another time and place.

A moment from the excerpts in Appendix A

NEW TOPIC: WHERE TO LOOK FOR YOUR FIRST SPEECH — AVAILABLE RESOURCES

[A library of speeches and monologs is a convenient way to access a class to materials. To supplement published collections (see Appendix D), file folders of photocopied narrative speeches can be created for men and for women in categories such as American, British, European, Shakespeare, the Greeks, Restoration and Moliére, Nineteenth Century, from Literature, Oral History, Voices of Color, etc. While they are searching for materials, students should check out a book or a folder (or more, if resources allow) in each class. Returning items in the next class keeps the library circulating. Students should be encouraged to make photocopies of speeches in which they are seriously interested. From these they can select, in consultation with you, a first speech.]

[To encourage students to explore a diversity of periods and styles, you might require that one of the first two speeches has to be material that is either not American or pre-twentieth century.]

3. DUE: Read Appendix B: "Speeches"
Read Chapter 2: "Choosing a Narrative Speech"
Begin searching for your first speech

NEW TOPIC: SETTING THE SCENE

[The sequence of exercises exploring Speech 5 (3.1-14) can introduce students to work on setting the scene. Other exercises might be explored if time permits.]

["For Your Own Speech" at the end of Chapter 3 asks students to explore three moments of setting the scene with brief texts (a sentence or less) chosen from the excerpts in Appendix A. In addition, a couple of moments from Chapter 3 might be assigned to everyone — for example, 3.53 and 3.58. Or specific moments might be assigned to several students — for example, 3.17-18, 3.23-27, 3.31-32, 3.35-36, 3.49.]

4. DUE: Read Chapter 3: "Setting the scene"
Setting-the-scene moments

NEW TOPIC: IMPLICIT SCENES

[Exercises 4.1-4, 4.6, and 4.18 can introduce implicit scenes. 4.9 and 4.15 might be assigned to the whole class, plus two implicit scene moments developed with short texts from Appendix A or B.]

[Students should be told that the work outlined at the end of the chapter in "Beginning work on your own speech" will be assigned later. In a shorter course or workshop, work on the first speech might begin at this point, as it might for individuals who are using the book on their own.]

5. DUE: Read Chapter 4: "Implicit scenes"
Implicit scene moments

NEW TOPICS: CHARACTERIZATION AND INDIRECT QUOTES

Sign up for a twenty-minute conference on the choice of your first speech.

[To introduce characterization and indirect quotes, all might explore moments of setting the scene, characterization, and indirect quotes from Hotspur's speech (Speech 12): see 5.44-51.]

[Students might be asked to develop two moments of characterization and two of indirect quotes from the materials in the appendices, and each student might be assigned one of the ages of man in Jaques' speech (Speech 11) as an exercise in setting the scene, characterization, and indirect quote.]

CONFERENCE on the choice of your first speech
Bring at least five narrative speeches, ranked in order of preference

[It is best to avoid having two students work on the same speech. Students should be guided to choose material that is rich in narrative and that will allow them to explore inner conflict later in the process. If several speeches fit the bill, the choice can be left to the actor. One or more possibilities for a second or third speech may emerge in this conference. Occasionally it is necessary to ask a student to search again for more suitable or challenging material.]

6. DUE: Read Chapter 5: "Playing All the Parts ..."
   Characterizations
   Indirect quotes
   One of the Seven Ages of Man
   See the discussion of this material under "Practice in
characterization and indirect quote" in Chapter 5.

*[Guidelines for initial work on the first speeches appear at the end of
Chapter 4.]*

7. DUE: For your first speech:
   Photocopies for the class
   Three setting-the-scene moments
   One characterization
   One indirect quote

*[Students should assemble packets of the speeches. Each speech
should be read aloud to introduce its story. Two people might be asked to
point out a few story-sense possibilities by quoting a phrase or sentence
from the text and then naming an approach that might be applied: setting
the scene, implicit scene, characterization, or indirect quote. After reading
his or her speech, the actor might present two setting-the-scene moments.
Once all the speeches have been introduced, students can perform a third
moment of setting the scene, then a round of characterization moments
and finally a round of indirect quotes.]*

8. DUE: Read Chapter 6: "Gesture"
   One gesture moment from Appendix A or B
   Three gesture moments for your speech
   Dress to move!

NEW TOPIC: MOVEMENT

*[Exercises 7.1-12 will introduce students to a variety of ways of
thinking about movement. If time permits, scale can also be explored:
7.13-15.]*
[Students should be encouraged to use the spaces afforded by the

room in which you meet — corners, windows, pillars, levels, etc. The class can move or re-orient itself whenever a moment requires. When the time comes to perform whole speeches, they should be staged so that space helps the actor tell the story. For now, students can put together simple sets and bring in substitute props, as if they were in rehearsal for a full production.]

9. DUE: Read Chapter 7: "Movement"
Read Chapter 8: "Space"
One movement moment from Appendix A or B, two for your speech
One space moment from Appendix A or B, two for your speech

NEW TOPIC: SOUND SENSE

[By way of introducing sound sense, one or more poems from Chapter 9 might be considered in terms of onomatopoetic sound sense, or a speech might be explored — for example, Jaques (Speech 11) or Hotspur (Speech 12): see 5.43 and 5.52. For contemporary dramatic material, consider Excerpt 21: see 9.20-27.]

[A possible format for the onomatopoeia assignment: First speak the word or phrase on which you are focusing out of context. Give the word(s) expressive color and texture. Then put the word or phrase in its context, using as much text as you need to let us hear how you bleed into and out of the sound sense you have created.]

[If time permits, all might be assigned to prepare several moments from Hamlet: e.g., 9.61 and 9.65-66. These can be used as a quick warm-up at the beginning of next class.]

Sound Sense

10. DUE: Read Chapter 9: "Onomatopoeia"
Three onomatopoetic moments for your speech
Hamlet moments

NEW TOPICS: RHYTHMIC SOUND SENSE, ACCELERATION AND DECELERATION

[To introduce the new topics, you might guide the class through a close examination of Juliet's "The clock struck nine..." (Speech 14): 10.38-54.]

11. DUE: Read Chapter 10: "Rhythm"
   Develop contrasting rhythms for two different sections of your speech
Name each rhythm with language from your text. In class, you will read each section (about 3-6 lines for each).
Craft an acceleration and a deceleration.
These may be consecutive or they may occur in separate sections of your speech. You will read these in class just as you might perform them on your feet.

NEW TOPIC: FADES AND BUILDS

[You might do two rounds for accelerations and decelerations that stand alone, and then a round of accelerations linked to decelerations.]
[In class, exercises 11.1-10 can introduce the many uses of fading. The principles of building might be introduced by focusing on a couple of texts: e.g., 11.3 and 11.15. Exercises that explore pullbacks include 11.16-17, 11.18-19 and 11.23-24. Steps can be defined by way of exercises 11.27-28 and 11.30.]

Shape Sense

12. DUE: Read Chapter 11: "Fades and Builds"
   A fade to a climax, with the following pullback
   A fade from one energy to a very different energy

NEW TOPIC: FROM/TO

[The goal of shaping transitions that help to tell the story might be illustrated by exploring 12.1-2 and 12.3-4. "Knitting the seams" might be introduced by 12.15-20, and 12.25-27 can define transformational transitions.]
[See "For Your Own Speech" at the end of Chapter 12 for specifics about the from/to assignment, including the distinction between "from/to moments" and "transitions."]

431

13. **DUE: Two from/to moments**
    Two transitions
    Read 6-8 lines of your speech as an exercise in
        un-punctuation
    Choice of your second speech
Sign up for a conference to receive feedback on the first draft of your speech.

[Divide the class into A and B groups for the showing of the first speech in classes 15 and 16.]

CONFERENCE on your first speech
In preparation, read Chapter 13: "Putting together the first draft." This conference is a working rehearsal, but you will be graded for the thoroughness of your preparation. Your speech should be fully memorized and carefully developed in terms of story sense, sound sense, and shape sense. Before you perform the whole speech, you will show your first picture and final freeze frame, a take-in moment, and a moment of eye contact that helps to tell the story.

[During conferences, it is useful to make notes about possible opposites for each speech. These can be shared with students after they have presented an opposite draft of the speech in class 18.]

14. **DUE: For your second speech:**
    Photocopies for the class
    Five moments of your choice
Use a variety of approaches to creating story sense, sound sense, and shape sense.
    5-8 lines with a focus on from/to

15. **DUE: A group: first speech**
        B group: two moments of choice and one from/to
            moment for the second speech
[The B group can show its second-speech moments while the A group warms up.]

[Feedback to those performing speeches can include:
- *in the first place, pointing out choices which succeed in telling the story — and perhaps having the actor repeat one or two of these;*
- *working a few moments in front of the class;*
- *verbal notes about what might be explored before the speech is shown again.*

Feedback should take advantage of opportunities to reinforce principles and explore possibilities.]

16. DUE: B group: first speech
A group: two moments of choice and one from/to moment for the second speech

[An assignment for the second speech — for example, performing 6-8 new lines, with an emphasis on from/to — will keep students at work on its development.]

Opposites and Layering

17. DUE: Read "Chapter 15: Opposites"
Stop at "A new pair of opposites for your speech."
6-8 lines of your second speech with an emphasis on from/to

NEW TOPIC: OPPOSITES

[In class, explore opposites for Speech 2 (Joan of Arc): 15.1-11; and for Speech 1 (Clytemnestra): 15.12-18, 15.22. Emphasize that "not caring is not an option."]

18. DUE: Opposite draft of your first speech
Procedures are spelled out under "For Your Own Speech" in Chapter 15.

[After a student has performed an opposite draft, feedback can include your notes about possible opposites to explore. Watch your language!]

19. DUE: New opposites for your first speech
See "A new pair of opposites for your speech" in Chapter 15.
Sign up for a conference on your second speech.

[Students should not be expected to include opposites work as they prepare the initial draft of their second speech. Once the topic has been introduced, of course, students will be more aware of impulses that suggest opposites, and feedback in the second speech conferences can include a conversation about radically different energies that might be explored for the assignment on second speech opposites (see classes 26-27).]

20. DUE: Read "Chapter 16: Single images"
> **Perform a single image for both speeches, using about 1/4 to 1/3 of the text**
> **Internalize one of these images so that it energizes and shapes your text**

In class you will perform this internalized image in a sit-down version, in which you literally sit on your hands.

CONFERENCE on your second speech

21. DUE: Read "Chapter 17: Layering"

NEW TOPIC: LAYERING

[In class, layering exercises might include 17.2-6, 17.8-11, 17.14, 17.15-16, 17.17-18. Clarify when the layered first speech will be performed.]

22. DUE: B group: second speech
> **Read "Chapter 14: Architecture," and apply these issues to your second speech**

[For each speech, a couple of students should be assigned to draw on paper the shape of what they see and hear. After performing, the actor should hold up his or her own graph, so that it can be quickly compared

to what others have sketched. Those giving feedback might also do a brief show-and-tell about one moment of effective storytelling — a specific choice that helped them to experience what was happening in the other time and place.]

23. DUE: A group: second speech
> **Read Chapter 14: "Architecture," and apply these issues to your second speech**

24. DUE: B group: layered version of first speech
> **(A group: Begin work on your second speech opposites and on the third speech)**

[For each layered speech, two students might be assigned to give feedback by identifying the moments that define for them the actor's A and Z. They should do this by getting up and doing the two moments as fully and precisely as they can. They may have to paraphrase or ask for the text. The performer should then show the moments that s/he believes are quintessentially A and Z. This is good practice in the art of identifying acting issues in terms of what an actor is actually saying or doing.]

25. DUE: A group: layered version of first speech
> **(B group: Begin work on your second speech opposites and on the third speech)**

26. DUE: B group: Opposites for the second speech
For this exercise, you will perform half of your speech (any half) as pure A, and the same half as pure Z. You will then play a layered version of the whole speech.

You may choose between three approaches to presenting your A and Z. One approach would be to perform two single images with opposing energies. Another would be to create two very different sets of circumstances, as you did when you explored a new pair of opposites for your first speech. A third approach would be to play the basic blocking of your layered speech, while allowing the opposite on which you are focused to create differences not only of mood but also of action. Whatever approach you take, your focus should not be on playing emotions but on the circumstances, the actions, or the images you have proposed to yourself.

[Students assigned to give feedback in class should focus on clarifying the dynamic between A and Z.
- *Name the A and the Z with a word or phrase from the text or with an action from the performance, or both.*
- *Using these terms for A and Z, state the conflict of the character.*
- *Do a show-and-tell of how these opposites push and pull the character. How do the opposites interact? How does the character get from A to Z to A again?]*

27. DUE: A group: Opposites for the second speech

The Finals

28. Third Speech

[Student feedback for this part of the final should use the vocabulary of the class and focus on specifics.
- *What is working in the speech? Identify three moments that told the story, shaped the speech, or embodied the character's conflict.*
- *Was anything unclear? Did you have trouble hearing any words, reading actions, understanding transitions, etc.?*
- *What dimensions might be explored or further developed?*

None of the feedback should take the form of "you should have" or "it would be better if" — since such suggestions are based on what the person giving feedback might do if s/he were acting the material. Feedback should encourage actors to make their own choices and to find their own answers.]

[Some students will be interested in working with you on the third speech, whether or not they are considering it for the audition showcase. I offer an optional conference sign-up, which has no effect on grades.]

Audition Showcase: TBA

****

The following explains to students two events that might constitute the final exam for a course on acting narrative speeches.

The Finals

The third speech and the audition showcase are opportunities for you to demonstrate that you have learned how to use the approaches of this course. Both events are meant to be learning experiences as well.

The third speech

The third speech must be less than two minutes; it may, if you wish, be a bit shorter (between a minute and a minute and a half).

This narrative speech is to be developed on your own. Your work on this material should evidence your skills with respect to all the issues we have covered. Review the syllabus, the book, and your notes as guidelines for a comprehensive, self-directed rehearsal process that explores story sense, sound sense, shape sense, and layered opposites.

The choice of material does not have to be approved prior to performance. You may wish to try something refreshingly "different" in terms of character, mood, or style. This is another opportunity to consider adapting material from fiction or from oral history.

In general, search for material which stimulates, challenges, and stretches you; which allows you to show off your command of narrative acting skills; which will intrigue, surprise, or shake us up; which is worthy of your time and effort. Continue to exercise taste: avoid stand-up jokes or melodramatic emotions that are not really justified by the events.

Please bring an unmarked copy of the text of your third speech on the day you perform it. Include the author and title.

As with real audiences, many of us may be encountering the material for the first time (or for the first time in a while). Your work must tell us where we are, what happens, and who's who. Tell the story clearly, with a carefully shaped architecture that helps us to grasp the whole.

Pay special attention to making sure we hear key words:

• the statement of central themes, conclusions, and discoveries — with which you should also take more time;
• topic sentences and words that tell us what the next section is about

437

(e.g., "So we decided to have a *contest*" if the speech is about a contest);
- people's names when they're introduced;
- place names and where words;
- the antecedents of repeated pronouns — or we might not know who "she...she...she..." is;
- important transitional phrases that transport the audience ("Later that night...," "Inside the house, meanwhile...").

Articulate especially well:
- when speaking loudly or quietly or rapidly;
- when your mouth is hidden from sight;
- when making large moves;
- when you say anything unfamiliar or wholly unexpected.

Imagine that someone said to you, "I don't get what happens in your speech; show me clearly what happens and how." Imagine that you then got on your feet and performed your material so as to walk the other person through the events of the story. Your speech should be *that* clear — which doesn't mean that it can't be subtle or complex. You have to develop an audience eye for your own work: if you were seeing your third speech for the first time, would you get it?

The audition showcase
This event, which will be publicized and to which you can invite friends, is a chance to show your stuff — what you've learned, what you can do.

Each of you will perform two of your three speeches. Which two is your choice. The fact that this is part of your final and a public event doesn't necessarily mean you should pick your "two best." Exams and performances are part of the process of developing skills and materials. You may choose a speech because you still want to work on it, have some new ideas you wish to try out, etc.

The space for the audition showcase will be bare except for one chair, with another available to one side. An "auditioner" will be seated behind a table. When you know where this event will take place, you should carefully consider what spatial possibilities it offers and explore adjustments that might take advantage of them. Space matters, and ignoring it — failing to locate your speeches dynamically in their new setting — will limit your work.

The usual garb for professional auditions is dressy casual. What you wear should not be distracting nor wildly inappropriate for the characters you play. No T-shirts with writing, no shorts, no hats, no clunky shoes or sandals, no tight garments that restrict movement. A neutral approach is best when you are doing two very different pieces. It is sometimes possible to make a simple, quick adjustment between speeches: a fast hair change, a scarf rearranged, a jacket off, a tie pulled down, a button undone, a shirttail pulled out, etc. But this is not at all required.

We will meet for a half-hour before the showcase to warm up and to clarify procedures.

You will perform in several groups, with short breaks in-between.

You will enter, greet the audience with solid eye contact (which is not only connective but also relaxing), introduce yourself, and say something articulate and brief to identify the source for your two speeches. In the case of famous plays and roles, it isn't necessary to name both playwright and play. You might say, for example, that you are going to do a speech from Tina Howe's *Painting Churches* and another from *Miss Julie*, and not bother to identify Strindberg as the author of that famous play. Or you might announce that you will be doing a speech by Joan of Arc from Jean Anouilh's *The Lark* and Juliet's speech before she takes the potion.

Then you will set up for your first speech, moving the chair(s) as needed. Be exact about where you place yourself and the chair(s), so that your blocking is properly set up. In the rehearsal halls in which many auditions are held, you need to be careful not to place yourself too close to the auditioners; they want to see you as an audience might, not have you acting on top of them. As in class, you should place the person(s) to whom you are speaking out in the audience, perhaps playing directly to audience members; but since an actor does not usually play to the main auditioner, don't use the person behind the table as your scene partner.

Settle into your initial moment so as to ground yourself and begin. At the end of the first speech, hold the last picture for three beats, relax, move to the beginning moment of your second speech (will you need to move the chair?), ground yourself, do the speech, hold the last moment and slowly relax. Then look at us, say thank you in some form, and exit.

Index

Material used in exercises, by character

Betty 64, 100-101, 371
Billy the Kid vi, 37, 38, 49, 81, 109, 163, 381
Bootleg Emma 88, 109-110, 371
Briseis 124, 234-235, 380
Carol 133-134, 156, 178, 326-327, 376
Cavale 67, 82, 106-107, 297, 315, 354, 358, 374
Claudius 167, 195, 228, 338
Clytemnestra 1, 105, 136, 138, 263, 283, 285-290, 292-293, 295, 316, 339-341, 351, 354, 357, 377, 433
Dorothea 58, 81-82, 90-91, 104-105, 358
Dysart 312-314
Electra 73, 138-139, 288, 365, 372
Elizabeth 43-46, 68, 84, 92, 106, 127, 248, 372-373
Friar Laurence 12, 15, 162-163, 279-281, 399
Ghost (Hamlet) 79, 114, 165-167, 179-180, 240, 297, 391, 407
Halie 329, 382
Hamlet 1, 12, 79-81, 102, 161-162, 164-168, 179-180, 182, 184, 195, 228, 240, 250, 264, 297, 301, 314-315, 338, 341-342, 373, 404, 410, 430
Helena 196, 226-227
Henry V 224, 263, 291, 294, 322, 364
Hermia 196, 226-227
Hotspur 95-98, 103, 105, 210-212, 214, 343-344, 387, 398, 401, 412, 428, 430
Jacques 86
Joan of Arc 128, 241, 282, 284, 296, 309, 315, 354, 433, 439
John of Gaunt 195
Johnny 61-62, 109, 342-343
Juliet 11-19, 31, 48-49, 56, 72, 84-87, 93, 106, 112-114, 121, 130-131, 162-163, 165, 182-183, 191-195, 215, 279-281, 316, 373, 389, 391, 397, 399, 406-407, 410, 426, 431, 439
the Nurse 93, 112, 191, 193, 316, 389, 399
the tomb 12-18, 31, 49, 106, 121, 130, 215, 250, 280, 390, 426
King 7, 52, 76, 80, 95, 97, 104, 105, 151, 158, 168, 195, 197, 210, 211, 224, 228, 241, 260, 294, 297, 298, 338, 372, 378, 379

Laureen 92, 102-103, 137, 215, 218, 226, 291, 386
Lear 104, 151, 158-160, 298-299, 301, 400-402, 409
Macbeth 76, 87-88, 197, 338, 392, 404-406, 410
Malvolio 351, 354, 367
Mercutio 81, 104, 106, 112, 241, 391, 426
Nina 309-311, 314, 316
Ophelia 79-81, 102, 164, 195, 240, 250, 264, 297, 314-315, 341, 373
Patroklos 71, 235, 379
Puntila 41-43, 73-74, 88, 103, 105, 107, 109-110, 208, 248, 299, 371
Richard III 1, 297, 346-348, 353-354
Romeo 11-13, 15, 18-19, 21, 72, 84, 86-87, 93, 106, 112-114, 162-163, 165, 182, 191, 194, 250, 279, 281, 373, 389-391, 396-397, 399, 406-407, 410
Rosalind 111-112, 133, 291-292, 299, 357, 374
Rosie 46-48, 55, 63-64, 74-75, 238, 245, 372
Titania 7, 52-55, 81, 103, 164, 196, 215, 388
Val 112, 376
Wesley 21, 57-58, 82-83, 85, 92-93, 107, 112, 116, 118-120, 123-124, 132, 137, 185, 187-188, 190, 199, 206, 209, 213, 216, 225, 251, 307, 328, 374, 382
Weston 21, 23, 26-28, 65-66, 71, 91-93, 101-102, 107-108, 110, 123, 127, 129-132, 136-137, 185, 207-208, 219-220, 232-233, 242-244, 296, 299-300, 321, 328, 333, 353, 357, 375, 383-384

Topics and Terms

A

A and Z 334-339, 344-350, 352-360, 435-436
  fading 336, 340, 346, 356, 431
  simultaneous 338, 340-341
Acceleration and deceleration 186-191, 198-199, 206, 430
Acting on the line 239
Ambivalence 165, 167, 284, 338-339, 342, 359
Antithesis 163, 280, 404, 411-412
Architecture 78, 126, 134, 139-140, 185, 271-274, 366, 413, 434-435,
Audience eye contact 262-265, 267, 432, 439
Auditions 33, 258, 263, 420-421, 423, 439

B

Backing off 128, 189-190, 198, 207, 216-218, 229
  accelerations and decelerations 189-190
  builds 153
  fades 164, 188-190, 193-194, 203-207, 209, 211, 213, 215, 217, 219, 221, 223, 225-230, 236, 245-246, 254, 265
Bleeding 160-161, 169
Builds ix, 37, 41, 203, 205, 213-219, 221-230, 271, 272, 274, 328, 333, 336, 349, 366, 431
  control 218, 221, 286, 303-304, 310, 318, 320
  elements 214, 229, 358, 366, 412
  principles 189, 207, 215, 350, 361, 366, 400, 431, 433
  shape sense 201, 203, 214, 225, 255, 257, 269, 366, 431-432, 437
  steps 14-15, 205, 221, 226-229, 264, 287, 312, 334, 345, 413, 431

C

Caesura 394, 401-402, 404-405
Central moment 271-274, 409, 414
  arcing 414
Climax 2, 17, 55, 106, 110, 122, 129, 164, 171, 186, 195, 199, 203, 213-214, 217-220, 222-225, 227-229, 235, 265, 271-273, 326, 328, 337, 340, 342, 344, 407, 414, 431
  holding back 190, 211, 217-218, 229, 355

Conscious 12, 41, 49-51, 57, 78, 100, 112, 120, 173, 231-232, 278, 306, 349
Continuant consonants 151, 156, 159, 168, 172-173, 177, 183, 195
Converging 162
Cut 35, 41, 100, 110, 186, 192, 195, 200, 223, 226, 235, 237, 261, 318, 359, 365, 371, 385, 387
Cutback 222-226, 229, 271, 336

D
Decrescendo 219, 222-225, 229, 271

E
Editing 35, 186, 256
Emotions 1, 23-25, 30, 35, 41, 52, 98, 181, 186, 197, 205, 229, 261, 287, 304, 331, 342, 344, 363, 367, 436-437
  emoting 23-24, 35, 52, 304
  emotional substitution 14, 24-25
  labels 72, 117-118, 181, 197, 206, 215, 308
  physical reactions 261, 288
  translating emotion words 342
Emphasis 2, 76, 170, 197, 229, 252, 257, 270, 311, 393-394, 397-399, 401-402, 404-410, 412-415, 433
  important words 397, 403-404, 409, 413
  metrically emphasized 405, 407
  varieties 205, 412, 414
Endwords 404-406, 408, 412
Enjambed lines 177, 179, 185-186
Epiphany 11, 257-258, 272, 414
Explicit 61-64, 66-67, 70, 72, 75, 103, 130, 312, 327, 366
Eye contact 262-265

F
Fading 54, 161, 164, 173, 186, 198-199, 204-213, 216, 223, 226, 229-230, 235, 239, 244
  decrescendos 219, 222
  depth 2, 212
  dynamic fades 188
  fading into and out of the story 54
  importance 204
  onomatopoeia ix, 145, 152-155, 157, 160-165, 167, 169, 176, 183, 206
  rhythm 49, 206, 221, 249, 251, 253, 257
  varieties 31

Faust 281
Film 1, 10, 33, 80, 112, 134, 186, 327, 366, 391, 424
First picture 259-260, 265, 267, 318, 432
Footage 327
Framing 260, 270, 413-414

G
Gender 12
Geography 128-129, 137, 140

H
Hitching 252
Holding back 8
Hyphenated 344, 347

I
Idiosyncratic choices 46, 273
Images 16, 22, 43, 76, 87, 117, 119, 120, 133, 136, 137, 138, 139, 146, 155, 184, 191, 192, 195, 197, 216, 298, 311, 312, 324-325, 332, 342, 343, 358, 359, 399, 434, 435, 436
Implicit 61-66, 68-71, 75-76, 86, 105, 108-110, 125, 130, 139, 162, 196, 235-236, 239-242, 313, 329, 331, 333, 342-343, 357, 359, 364, 427-429
Inner conflict 3, 30, 217-218, 272, 274, 284-285, 290, 294, 302-303, 306, 311, 318, 320, 332, 339, 348-350, 352, 414, 428
Inside, getting 40-41
living a story 28
sound sense 171, 175-176, 183-184, 186-187, 195, 198, 219, 221, 231, 257
Internalizing 329, 362, 365-366

J
Journey 34, 88, 128, 194, 204-205, 230-231, 254, 262, 272, 277, 287, 336, 349-350, 360-362, 365, 389

K
Knitting the seams 245, 346-347, 431
opposites 190-191, 256

L
Language of the text 309-314

M
Malvolio 351, 354, 367
Mask 82, 294, 299, 302, 312-313
alternative self 302
Metaphor 50-51, 71-75, 86-87, 118, 120-121, 125, 156, 158, 209, 248, 254, 307-308, 324, 333, 366, 410

characterization 79, 81, 82, 83, 85, 86, 87, 88,89, 93-99, 191, 211-212, 428-429
implicit scenes ix, 61-78, 125, 342, 359, 427, 428
listening 9, 46, 48, 58, 116, 118, 187-188, 209, 246, 260-261, 323, 328, 363, 382, 385
movement ix, 18, 19, 38, 42, 43, 54, 57, 63, 73, 85, 86, 116-125, 132, 134, 136-139, 145, 147, 153, 167, 181, 187, 192, 193, 194, 197, 206, 208, 233, 253, 257, 259, 267, 270, 271, 284, 306, 328, 343, 348, 352, 355, 402, 413, 425, 429, 430, 439
scenes ix, 16, 19, 20, 21, 30, 31, 32, 119-120, 125, 126, 181, 214, 224, 256, 298, 308, 320, 321, 342,344, 359, 363-364, 420, 421, 422, 424, 427, 428
unpacking a metaphor 74
Metrical feet 145, 172, 182, 400
Monosyllables 113, 147, 174, 181-182, 185, 191, 193-195, 227-228, 250, 395, 400-401, 406
Moral dilemmas 338
Moving in space 125

N
Naming 180, 309, 314, 429
building 172, 220, 229, 271, 303, 325, 337, 353, 431
rhythms 269, 400, 402, 431
Narrative acting 13, 28-29, 361-367, 437

O
Objectives 1, 25-26, 278, 305-306, 311, 317, 338
opposites 3, 30, 366
stories 1, 7, 8, 10, 11, 21, 25, 26, 31, 32, 37, 44, 56, 291, 324, 362, 364, 367
Opposite moments 49-51, 314-316
Opposites and single images 358
Opposites as a starting point 279
Opposites of equal intensity 294
Oxymoron 281, 411-412

P
Pace 86, 168, 170, 177, 179, 183, 186-188, 190-191, 193, 197, 214, 216, 223, 227-229, 251-252, 269-270, 273, 337, 392, 398, 404, 414
Pauses 85, 175, 185, 237-239, 248, 250, 252, 346
Personalizing 362
Phonetic intensives 151
Playing against the grain 315

Point of view 9, 28, 39, 41, 56-58, 66, 77, 79, 81-88, 91, 96, 98-99, 102-103, 106, 123, 164, 174-175, 177, 204, 211-212, 241-242, 279, 282, 287, 291, 297, 311, 313, 317, 334

Polar opposites 300-301, 317, 319, 335

Proteus 43

Pulling back 219, 222-223

Punctuation 177, 179, 185, 248, 250-251, 253-254, 393, 402, 408, 432

R

Rate of change 189-190, 199, 211, 219, 222-223

acceleration or deceleration 186-190

fade 186, 188-190, 193-195, 198-199, 204-213, 216, 221-226, 228-229, 239-246, 248, 261-262, 266, 336-337

Reacting 47-48, 56, 79, 221, 260, 321, 336

S

Scale 75, 88, 121-122, 162, 169, 265, 273, 353, 429

onomatopoetic sound sense 163, 171, 198, 430

Scansion 183, 393-402

Sensuousness 146

sound sense 95, 98, 143, 145-148, 151-157, 159-169

Shakespeare 393-415

Shamans 18

Snapshots 46-47, 92, 133, 325-327

Sound sense 162-163, 183-184, 195-197, 257

Space ix, 14, 17, 18, 20, 27, 32, 44, 57, 78, 102, 106, 111, 116, 120, 121, 125, 126-141, 162, 165, 172, 232, 237, 242, 250, 253, 254, 257, 258, 259, 265, 270, 272, 285, 326, 382, 413-414, 425, 430, 439

auditions 111, 139-140

expressive tool 126, 132

your speech 33, 36, 37, 40, 59, 65, 76-78, 98-99, 114-115, 125, 128, 140-141, 169, 197-200, 229-230, 253-255, 265-268, 273-274, 317-323, 330-331, 358-360

Speed-throughs 269

Stanislavski 2-3, 25, 40, 179, 306

Steps 97, 100, 139

Stories 63, 70, 78, 81, 95, 103, 119, 127, 153, 171, 257-258, 264, 409

Storytelling 11, 28, 37, 49, 56, 70, 78, 81, 89, 100-101, 127, 265, 363, 435

Subordination 170, 269

T

Taking in 221, 246, 260-261

Transitions 203-205, 231-236, 239-242, 247, 254-255, 262, 344-346, 348-349, 355-356, 359, 402, 431-432, 436

Triggering a text 139

Trochaic firstwords 405-407

U

Unconscious 49-51, 61, 278, 306

V

Verbal actions 157-158, 168

W

Warming up 93, 266, 330

Watch your language 215, 308, 317, 321, 434

Work-throughs 332

About the Author

Tim McDonough began his acting career in Boston's small theaters, where he collaborated on the development of many new works. In 1980 he and Vincent Murphy co-founded Theater Works, for which he performed, directed and wrote. Regional theater appearances include the American Repertory Theater, Trinity Square Repertory, the Sacramento Theater Company and Shakespeare festivals in California and Idaho. In Atlanta he has acted at Theater Emory, the Alliance, Theater in the Square, Horizon Theater, Theater Gael and the Georgia Shakespeare Festival, where he is an Associate Artist. He is a member of the Theater Studies faculty at Emory University, where he teaches acting.

Order Form

Meriwether Publishing Ltd.
PO Box 7710
Colorado Springs CO 80933-7710
Phone: 800-937-5297 Fax: 719-594-9916
Website: www.meriwether.com

Please send me the following books:

_____ **Acting Narrative Speeches #BK-B255** $19.95
by Tim McDonough
The actor as storyteller

_____ **The Art of Storytelling #BK-B139** $14.95
by Marsh Cassady
Creative ideas for preparation and performance

_____ **Introduction to Readers Theatre #BK-B234** $16.95
by Gerald Lee Ratliff
A guide to classroom performance

_____ **The Director's Eye #BK-B246** $19.95
by John Ahart
A comprehensive textbook for directors and actors

_____ **The Stanislavsky Secret #BK-B254** $16.95
by Irina and Igor Levin
Not a system, not a method but a way of thinking

_____ **The Art of Acting #BK-B171** $16.95
by Carlton Colyer
The complete artist-actor training process

_____ **Theatre Alive #BK-B178** $39.95
by Dr. Norman A. Bert
An introductory anthology of world drama

These and other fine Meriwether Publishing books are available at your local bookstore or direct from the publisher. Prices subject to change without notice. Check our website or call for current prices.

Name: _____

Organization name: _____

Address: _____

City: _____ State: _____

Zip: _____ Phone: _____

❑ **Check enclosed**

❑ **Visa / MasterCard / Discover #** _____

Signature: _____ Expiration date: _____

(required for credit card orders)

Colorado residents: Please add 3% sales tax.
Shipping: Include $3.75 for the first book and 75¢ for each additional book ordered.

❑ *Please send me a copy of your complete catalog of books and plays.*